AF394425

THE MAN
WHO STOLE
THE GODS

THE MAN WHO STOLE THE GODS

A True Story of War, Obsession
and the World's Biggest Art Heist

MATTHEW CAMPBELL

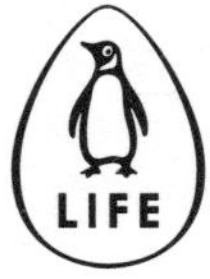

PENGUIN LIFE

AN IMPRINT OF

PENGUIN BOOKS

PENGUIN LIFE

UK | USA | Canada | Ireland | Australia
India | New Zealand | South Africa

Penguin Life is part of the Penguin Random House group of companies
whose addresses can be found at global.penguinrandomhouse.com

Penguin Random House UK,
One Embassy Gardens, 8 Viaduct Gardens, London SW11 7BW

penguin.co.uk

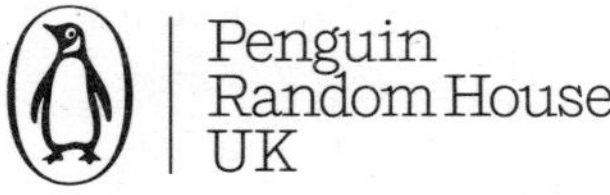

Penguin
Random House
UK

First published in the United States of America by Portfolio /
Penguin, an imprint of Penguin Random House LLC 2026
First published in Great Britain by Penguin Life 2026
001

Printed and bound in Great Britain by Clays Ltd, Elcograf S.p.A.

The authorized representative in the EEA is Penguin Random House Ireland,
Morrison Chambers, 32 Nassau Street, Dublin D02 YH68

A CIP catalogue record for this book is available from the British Library

HARDBACK ISBN: 978–0–241–82793–2
TRADE PAPERBACK ISBN: 978–0–241–67598–4

Penguin Random House is committed to a sustainable future
for our business, our readers and our planet. This book is made from
Forest Stewardship Council® certified paper.

CONTENTS

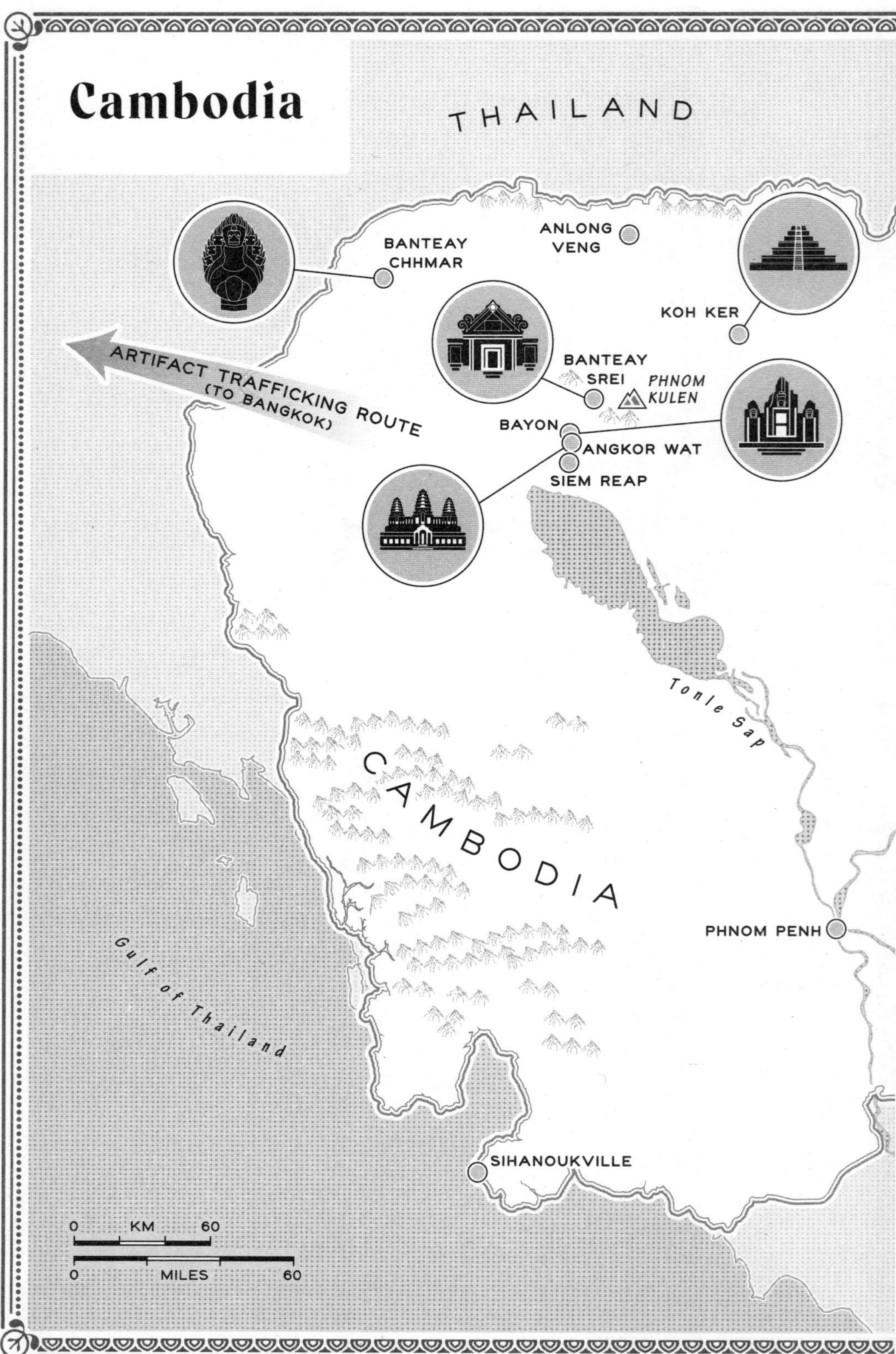
Cambodia
THAILAND
BANTEAY CHHMAR
ANLONG VENG
KOH KER
BANTEAY SREI
PHNOM KULEN
BAYON
ANGKOR WAT
SIEM REAP
ARTIFACT TRAFFICKING ROUTE
(TO BANGKOK)
CAMBODIA
Tonle Sap
Gulf of Thailand
PHNOM PENH
SIHANOUKVILLE
0   KM   60
0   MILES   60

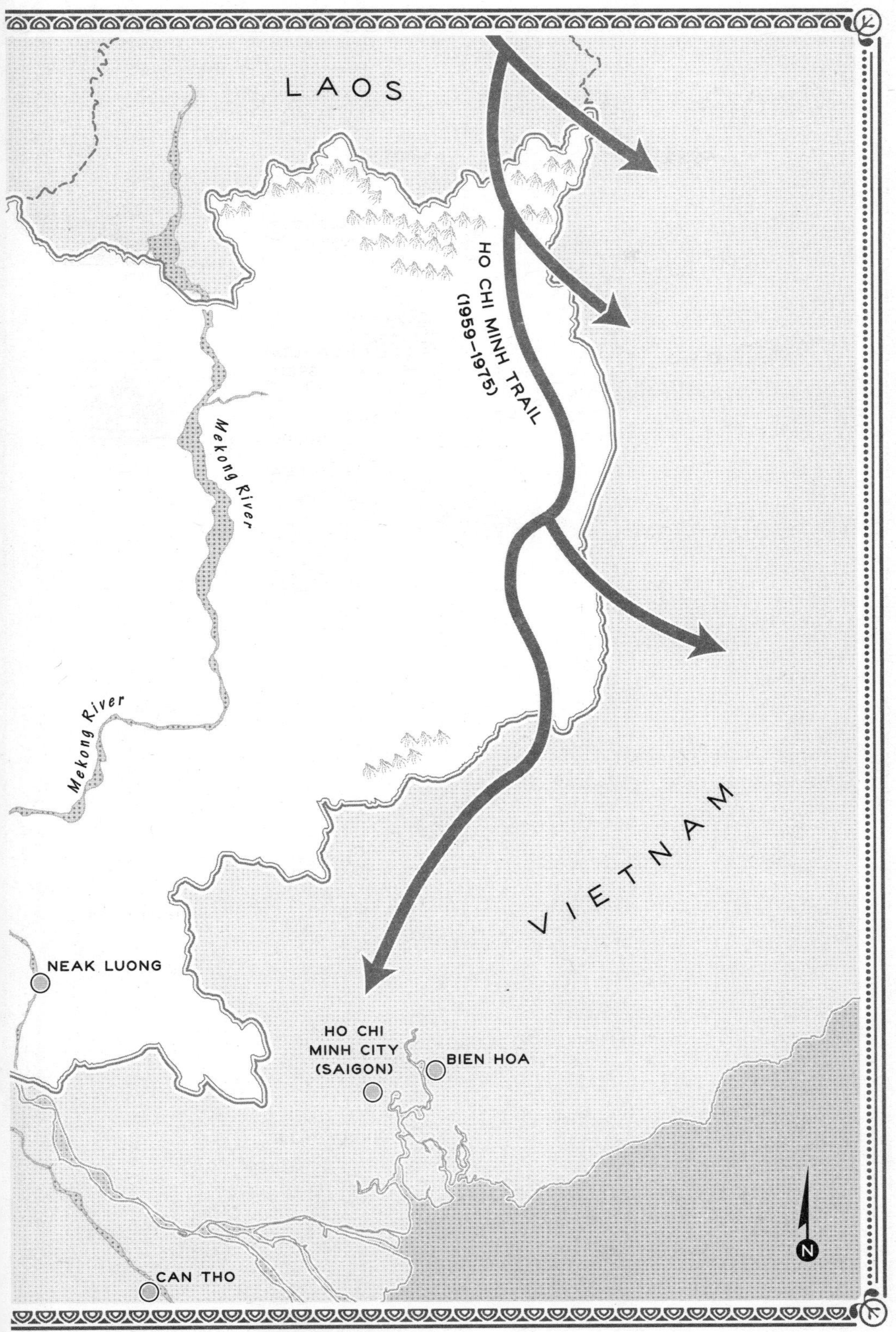

LAOS
HO CHI MINH TRAIL
(1959-1975)
Mekong River
Mekong River
VIETNAM
NEAK LUONG
HO CHI
MINH CITY
(SAIGON)
BIEN HOA
CAN THO
N

Foreword

Toek Tik's work was a kind best done by night.

As an adolescent in rural northwest Cambodia, he had been a foot soldier in a military force whose very name was a byword for terror: the Khmer Rouge, the radical communists whose rule had left perhaps two million people dead before they were driven from power. Now, twenty years later, hardened by the long internal conflict that followed, Toek Tik was a leader of men. The members of this group served no ideology, however. Their only purpose was to survive.

Toek Tik's mission for them, on this evening in 1997, was to reach the base of a towering square chamber deep inside the Cambodian jungle. Built from an iron-rich material called laterite, its rough-hewn blocks had shifted with age, time sanding down their edges. But the chamber remained solid, seemingly as robust as the day it had been built a millennium before, forming one of the central structures of a temple called Prasat Thom. The temple, in turn, sat at the center of a city called Koh Ker, about seventy miles from Cambodia's best-known archaeological site, Angkor Wat.

For a brief period in the tenth century AD, Koh Ker was the capital of the Khmer Empire, which would come to dominate all of Cambodia, as well as much of modern-day Thailand and Vietnam, making it one of the most powerful polities of the medieval world. Enriched by trade, agriculture, and slaves, its rulers were wealthy beyond imagining; a later chronicler would describe a Khmer king who wore "some three pounds of great pearls" around his neck and traveled on an elephant with tusks sheathed in gold. At Koh Ker, Angkor, and other temple-cities, they left buildings so imposing that European explorers speculated the edifices had been constructed by a wandering Jewish tribe, or perhaps by Alexander the Great—certainly not by the Cambodians, who, the visitors assumed with the prejudices of their era, never could have accomplished such a feat.

But by the time Toek Tik and his men approached Prasat Thom, carrying shovels and spools of rope, the dominance of the Khmer Empire was a distant memory. Their lives had been shaped, instead, by modern ideologies and the superpowers that espoused them, clashing in Cambodia to devastating effect. Every one of the men knew that in their battles for territory, the combatants of the civil war—the Chinese-backed Khmer Rouge and proxy forces supported by the United States and the Soviet Union—had littered the countryside with land mines. On another expedition, some had watched a wandering cow get blown up. So they walked carefully, measuring each step as they made their way to the center of the laterite chamber, which was surrounded by dense stands of trees. A thick trunk extended into its depths; undisturbed by humans, its roots had penetrated the walls, becoming one with the structure.

The treasures that Toek Tik sought were also underground, buried under layers of sediment. Soon the crew began digging down, attentive to the jolt of a shovel hitting stone instead of dirt. With each discarded clod of earth, they came closer to exposing the objects that would allow them to keep hunger and desperation at bay a while longer—works of otherworldly beauty, created by hands as skilled as any in human history. The artifacts were three nearly life-size stone statues, standing in a row on a rectangular pedestal. Two were divine female figures, with full lips and high breasts, carved with such vivid precision that it was possible to imagine them coming to life and embracing the right visitor. The third was a powerfully built male, likely a representation of Shiva, the Hindu god of destruction, which seemed to contain, in its muscular torso and taut, determined face, some spark of the power of that awesome deity.

Toek Tik and his band were the first to see the statues in centuries. Cambodians were raised to revere such objects, viewing them at once as embodiments of the souls of their ancestors, and as avatars of the gods. To stand before them was to gaze into the eternal, and in another context, the men might have kneeled to their bases and begun to pray, or left offerings of lotus flowers and incense. But the customers who sustained Toek Tik's livelihood in a war-shattered nation made no allowance for their spiritual role, and he had work to do. It took hours to excavate the statues, and then days to move them by oxcart and truck to Cambodia's border with Thailand. There, brokers were standing by to transport them to Bangkok, mainland Southeast Asia's portal to the world.

At this point, Toek Tik's role in the process was over. He and the others would receive a modest payment—enough to live on for a time, but a tiny fraction of the sums that the works were about to fetch on the international art market, where demand for pieces like them was booming. From the Thai capital, they went in three separate directions. The male figure would ultimately be purchased by an American billionaire to decorate his home in Palm Beach, Florida, a short distance from Donald Trump's Mar-a-Lago. One of the females would be sold by a London dealer called Spink & Son and then disappear into an anonymous private collection.

The other female statue took a more rarefied path. By 1998, it was in the possession of Doris Wiener, a prominent dealer with a gallery on New York's Upper East Side. Not long afterward, it made the short journey to one of the most prestigious addresses in Manhattan: 1000 Fifth Avenue. Barely five years after being ripped from its pedestal by a former child soldier of the Khmer Rouge, in the last days of one of the twentieth century's bloodiest conflicts, it had entered the collection of the Metropolitan Museum of Art. And it would be far from alone.

1

On a humid evening in 1957, a young businessman named Douglas Latchford saw the object that would change his life. It was a Khmer female figure, about two feet tall, carved in stone. Around him, men in linen suits and women in flowing dresses of Thai silk—guests at an elegant dinner party in Bangkok—clinked glasses and conversed in myriad languages. But Latchford could only stand among them in silence, staring at the statue: the cool gray of its torso, the fine curves of its waist and shoulders. Like most educated Britons of his generation, he was familiar with Greek and Roman sculpture. This was different, less detailed—no rippling muscles or individually sculpted strands of hair—but no less refined. The piece was like nothing Latchford had ever seen, and it stirred a desire he had never before experienced. He felt that he was looking at the human form reduced to its absolute essentials, somehow made more powerful in its simplicity.

New experiences had been a constant since Latchford had arrived in Bangkok the year prior. He was tall and robustly built, with a firm jaw and wavy auburn hair; in the right light, he had a passing resemblance to the actor Roger Moore. Just twenty-four years old, he had to get to know a city that could feel impossibly exotic to outsiders. The only country in Southeast Asia never to have been colonized by a Western power, Thailand—or Siam, as many still called it—was a world apart. Buddhist monks roamed barefoot from house to house, feeding themselves with alms from strangers. The streets teemed not with cars but with *samlors*, sturdy trishaws pedaled by laborers who dripped sweat in the tropical heat. Barely anyone outside the elite spoke English, and social norms bewildered the uninitiated. To touch a Thai's head, considered the most sacred part of the body, was a major faux pas, while a smile could indicate anger just as easily as it could signal happiness.

The host of the dinner party, a Belgian aesthete named François Duhau de Berenx, soon noticed that his guest was transfixed by the statue. Its effect was gravitational, magnetic. Latchford knew nothing about its origins, but he knew he needed to possess a figure of his own. "There's another one at the shop where I bought this," Duhau de Berenx told him. It was located in the Woeng Nakhon Kasem, or Thieves' Market, a bazaar in Bangkok's Chinatown where, as the name suggested, neither the merchants nor the customers were especially concerned about the provenance of goods. Latchford went there the next day, weaving between shirtless children and stores stuffed with so many wares—furniture, luggage, pots, and pans—that they spilled over the sidewalk onto the road. The twin to Duhau de Berenx's statue was priced at eighteen thousand Thai baht, or about $900—far more than Latchford could afford. He went to his bank, where he meekly explained why he needed a loan. Happily, the manager agreed. Latchford took the object home, where he could adore its form in private, and began reading whatever he could about the Khmer Empire, the civilization that had produced it.

He had virtually no prior exposure to the subject. Latchford had been born in 1931 in Bombay, during the dying days of the British Raj. His father was a banker, and Latchford had led a relatively privileged life. For an English education, his parents sent him to Brighton College, a well-regarded boarding school in Sussex, where he'd read works like *The Jungle Book*—reminders of the thrilling, verdant land he'd left behind. Compared with India, the United Kingdom of the late 1940s was a depressing place. For Latchford, its leaden skies and economic privation couldn't compete with the opportunities, and pleasures, on offer in Asia. He skipped university, instead working in Madras and Singapore before moving to Bangkok, where his older brother, Trevor, also chose to pursue a career.

In addition to the challenges of adjusting to the culture, the city had its inconveniences: drinking water had to be boiled, and it was advisable to carry a flashlight when walking at night, to spot the many species of venomous snakes. But for a young man looking for a little adventure, there was nowhere quite like it. Life was lived largely on the water, with hawkers selling melons and coconuts from narrow boats on the *khlongs*, or canals, that threaded through each neighborhood. On the main waterway, the Chao Phraya, ferries and fishing skiffs puttered past Wat Arun, the Temple of Dawn, its 270-foot spire decorated with snail shells and pieces of Chinese porcelain. Embassies placed their front doors facing the river, since guests of any distinction were likelier to arrive afloat.

Simply being an expatriate conferred some of that status. For perhaps $200 a month, a foreigner could rent a villa in the heart of the city. For not much more, he could populate it with a full household staff, including a driver, cook, maid, and gardener, plus a managerial "number one," ideally with a basic command of English, to keep them all in line. Because Bangkok had nothing like the professional competition in London or New York, the barriers to success were relatively low. Some among the expats joked that it was a first-rate place for second-rate people.

Since Thailand was too distant for many foreign companies to set up their own operations, they relied on "agencies"—local firms that imported goods and handled distribution on behalf of multinationals. Despite not having a university degree or much professional training, Latchford soon got a job as an assistant manager at one such firm: Eastern Agencies, which brought to Southeast Asia some of the consumer bounty of the 1950s. The business was relatively simple, and lucrative. Manufacturers had already done the hard work of developing their products. All that was left for an agency to do was to find retailers to stock them and figure out a marketing plan.

The number of people in Bangkok who could afford such goods would soon grow. Early in the Cold War, the US had identified Thailand as a potential bastion for the West. Viewed from Washington, such a fortress was essential. France had just suffered a humiliating defeat in Vietnam, where forces led by Ho Chi Minh had ejected their former colonial masters; to the south, Malayan Communists were aiming to do the same to Britain. Meanwhile, Mao Zedong's China appeared to have revolutionary designs on much of the continent, starting with the countries closest to its borders. In 1954, Thailand became a founding member of the Southeast Asian Treaty Organization, the American-led attempt to create a regional equivalent to NATO, and the alliance's headquarters were placed in Bangkok.

The US plowed tens of millions of aid dollars into Thailand each year, helping to build highways, airfields, and port facilities, and the economy grew briskly. Soon there were enough US businesses in Bangkok to form an American Chamber of Commerce; at the Oriental, a graceful riverside hotel preferred by every traveler who could afford it, a new, modern wing opened, complete with a French restaurant, Le Normandie, and the capital's first elevator. In less prestigious quarters, around industrial sites and railway tracks, an unceasing flow of rural migrants erected their own crude shelters—shanties of plywood and sheet metal, accessed by narrow footpaths.

As he settled in, Latchford learned the city's peculiar social geography. The pinnacle of Thai society was occupied by the royal family, a dynasty that traced its roots to the thirteenth-century Sukhothai Kingdom. For both Thais and foreigners, proximity to the royals was the ultimate currency. Though the country had become a constitutional monarchy in the 1930s, each king remained a powerful political force. Beyond the royals themselves were concentric circles of Thai aristocrats, many of whom were educated overseas. Latchford would eventually befriend some of them, bonding through vigorous games of squash.

But there was also an expatriate elite, centered on a blue-blooded American whom Latchford deeply admired. His name was Jim Thompson. Worldly, cultivated, and at ease in Asia, Thompson was exactly the sort of man Latchford wanted to become. He was also a spy. His route to Bangkok had begun in the Office of Strategic Services, the wartime forerunner to the Central Intelligence Agency. As a graduate of St. Paul's School and Princeton, Thompson fit right in; the OSS had a habit of recruiting operatives from wealthy East Coast families, prompting some wags to joke that its name really stood for "Oh So Social." He served heroically, helping prepare the ground for the Allied invasion of southern France. As the conflict in Europe wound down, he was sent to Thailand, tasked with helping to secure it as a postwar ally. Though Thompson had formally resigned from government service in 1947, he remained in Bangkok and continued to do unofficial intelligence work. As the Cold War heated up, the city became a hub for the CIA's increasingly violent efforts to contain the spread of Communism in Asia.

At the same time, Thompson built a profitable textile business, hiring traditional silk weavers and exporting their fabrics. He abhorred being without company in the evening and so threw constant dinner parties, sometimes with as many as one hundred guests. It seemed that every notable visitor to the city, from Eleanor Roosevelt to Truman Capote, made sure to attend. For many of them, his home was an attraction in itself. Rather than live in a European-style villa, Thompson had bought six traditional Thai houses, built from butter-smooth teak and topped with steeply gabled roofs, in different locations. He then had them floated into Bangkok by barge and assembled on the side of a khlong—an extraordinary homage to the country's vernacular architecture.

Once Thompson's guests had finished sipping cocktails on the veranda, boat traffic churning by, he would take his place at the dining table. There he would tell stories about his life in Thailand while his houseboy, Yee, darted about barefoot, keeping glasses refreshed. While the talk was often of politics—Thompson was growing openly disillusioned with US foreign policy, at one point prompting the FBI to investigate him for "un-American activities"—his other favorite topic was antiquities. Like Latchford, Thompson felt a powerful attraction to Khmer statuary, and by the late 1950s he had become a major collector. At one end of his dining room, he kept a stone carving of the four-armed Hindu god Vishnu; elsewhere in the house, Thompson and his guests mingled among bronze Buddhas and dancing *apsaras*, the heavenly nymphs of Hindu legend.

Thompson and Latchford were friendly at the time, and the younger man listened, rapt, as Thompson recounted his travels to source artifacts—conveying knowledge that Latchford would eventually put to use. Much of what Thompson obtained, he was willing to part with for the right price. In his early days selling statues and bronzes, relatively few outsiders had any experience of Southeast Asia, let alone the objects left by its ancient cultures. But that would begin to change as wealthy travelers took advantage of the shrinking distances of the Jet Age. One of the most enthusiastic was "the richest girl in the world": six-foot-tall socialite Doris Duke, the only child of tobacco magnate James Buchanan Duke. After a visit to Bangkok in 1957, she attempted to purchase a series of Thai houses for shipment to her home in Hawaii. John D. Rockefeller III was another prolific buyer, building a collection that he would eventually put on display in Manhattan.

In what was still an impoverished region, such works seemed like they were there for the taking. In 1959, Thompson became intrigued by rumors of a "lost temple" on the Cambodian border. One Friday in November, he and two friends set out from Bangkok to find it. Driving in a Land Rover, it took them until past midnight to reach Aranyaprathet, the last major town before the frontier. They snatched some brief sleep in a country hotel and set out at dawn into the forest. For much of the morning, they bumped along a track used by logging trucks, lucky to make ten miles an hour. Finally, they emerged into a clearing, where there stood a village of modest wooden houses, ringed with palm trees and rice paddies.

There, the group found some men who agreed to guide them to the place Thompson was looking for. They crossed a flat, grassy area, which Thompson identified as the remains of an ancient moat, pierced by an island of tall trees. Then, "in we went over a huge laterite wall," he wrote in a letter to his sister Elinor.

It was all cool and green with 150-ft. high trees—ferns of every description, air plants, shafts of sunlight—a great walled enclosure of sandstone and laterite—great towers 60 ft. high still partly standing—piles of gigantic stones carved with dancing Bodhisattvas, acanthus leaves, and other decorations—maidenhair ferns growing out of every crevice—strange birds calling in the trees— blue and orange butterflies flying through the shafts of sunlight.

While his companions snapped photos, Thompson took out a pencil and notepad and surveyed the ruins, producing a detailed sketch of their layout. Later, with a storm moving in, they returned to the village and installed themselves in the open-air hall of its Buddhist pagoda. The residents watched curiously as their visitors tucked into a dinner of canned baked beans and chicken breasts, accompanied by Ballantine's whisky. The next day, Thompson left with several artifacts, including a stone piece he dated to the seventh or eighth century. "Only known one in Siam is in the museum in Bangkok," he boasted to Elinor. "Very very rare."

Armed with Thompson's advice, Latchford had been trying to educate himself about the Khmer Empire. As a schoolboy in England, he had been captivated by the idea of forgotten temples deep inside trackless jungles. Now, though he excelled at his job importing foreign products to Bangkok, that interest was growing into an obsession, occupying more and more of his waking hours. In Thailand, the legacies of the Khmer civilization were plain to see. At their greatest extent, its dominions had extended nearly to Bangkok, and the country was dotted with ruins. The written form of the Thai language—a forty-four-consonant alphabet of gracefully looping forms—was derived from classical Cambodian script.

Following in Thompson's footsteps by visiting Khmer sites in Thailand was interesting enough. But Latchford had still never traveled to Cambodia itself. He needed to go to the source.

2

The sun climbed steadily up from the tropical horizon, bathing the sandstone below in a brilliant golden hue. In a pair of reflecting pools, five conical towers mirrored themselves precisely, gilded by the advancing dawn. The same light streamed through the pillars at the opening of a cool stone gallery, illuminating carved friezes of breathtaking intricacy—scenes from the Hindu epics that anchored the spiritual lives of their makers. Just beyond, in the jungle that extended almost to the perimeter of the structure, macaques and gibbons called out to one another across the foliage, indifferent to the presence of one of humanity's most impressive architectural achievements.

Latchford had vistas like this one largely to himself in Siem Reap, the Cambodian town abutting Angkor. It was 1961, several years into his fixation with Khmer culture. Though there had been some degree of tourism there for decades, Siem Reap remained far from anything resembling a beaten path. Away from the tiny town center, Cambodian peasants lived as they always had, in simple wooden houses open to the tropical breezes and raised on stilts to evade floodwaters.

Highways ran northwest to the Thai border, just under one hundred miles away, and southeast to the capital, Phnom Penh, but in most other directions, the roads devolved into dirt tracks that turned impassable with the monsoon. Almost all foreign visitors stayed at the same place: the Grand Hotel d'Angkor, built in an incongruous art deco style in the 1930s, where Latchford had booked in.

He rented a motorcycle to explore the area. As Latchford learned, its best-known site, Angkor Wat, was just one of hundreds of ancient Khmer structures within a short drive. At its height in the twelfth and thirteenth centuries, "greater Angkor" sprawled across an area of more than 1,150 square miles, with perhaps three-quarters of a million inhabitants. That made it one of the largest and most complex urban centers in premodern history. By comparison, in the same period, London was a city of about forty thousand people. Studying all of Angkor's ruins would take a lifetime. On a first trip, Latchford would have to focus on the highlights: Angkor Wat itself, with its central spires and 190-meter-wide moat; Angkor Thom, whose name literally means "great city," a walled complex accessed through one of five imposing stone gates; and, within its perimeter, the Bayon, an astonishing pyramidal structure ornamented with more than two hundred carved faces, possibly modeled on that of the king who ordered it built.

Even with this rich architectural legacy, a great deal about the Khmer Empire—or the Angkorian civilization, as some referred to it—remained a mystery. Its surviving structures were religious—either Hindu, the faith of most of its kings, or Buddhist, the latter reflecting a branch of the religion that would ultimately become dominant in Southeast Asia. No other buildings had been constructed with permanent materials, and by the time Latchford arrived in Cambodia, all had been lost to the jungle. The written record was also maddeningly sparse. The ancient Khmer wrote texts by inscribing them on palm leaves, but no such manuscripts had ever been found.

To piece together their story, researchers were forced to rely on just a few categories of sources. The most ubiquitous were about twelve hundred stone inscriptions, either on freestanding blocks or etched into the doorjambs of temples, that described the deeds of kings and the functioning of religious institutions. Then there were the works of art known as bas-reliefs: stone panels, particularly at Angkor Wat and the Bayon, carved with detailed tableaux of military campaigns and daily life. In one, an army marches into battle alongside war elephants—the tanks of their time—rendered with such precision that the folds in the animals' ears are captured in stone. Another depicts a scene pregnant with anticipation: the moment before the start of a cockfight, with men crowding shoulder to shoulder to get a glimpse of the roosters being released into combat.

Finally, historians could consult the account of Zhou Daguan, a Chinese traveler who resided in Angkor Thom for almost a year at the end of the thirteenth century. While it presented a detailed snapshot—Zhou recorded his impressions of everything from rice harvests to local sexual mores, which he found scandalously liberal—that source had its drawbacks. Only some of Zhou's writings survived, and he spoke little of the Khmer language. Much of what he learned was probably related to him secondhand by Chinese traders who lived in Angkor.

Historians had nonetheless assembled a basic narrative, which Latchford devoured. The start of the Khmer Empire was conventionally dated to the ninth century, when a centralized state supplanted the kingdoms that had previously existed in Cambodia. Its culture drew on Indian concepts, which had filtered into Southeast Asia through centuries of trade and migration. The majority of Angkorian inscriptions were written in Sanskrit, the sacred language of Hinduism, and for much of the history of the empire, that religion influenced aspects of statehood.

Part of the power of the Khmer monarchy was the belief that a given ruler had a privileged relationship with one of the principal Hindu gods: Shiva, the destroyer, or Vishnu, the preserver. While the idea of rule by divine right was familiar to anyone who'd studied, for example, the absolute monarchs of France, other aspects of Khmer politics were more unusual. There was neither hereditary nobility nor a caste system along Indian lines. No system of succession existed: Only eight of the twenty-six Angkorian kings were the sons or brothers of the rulers who preceded them. Not surprisingly, this encouraged conflict when a ruler died. It also stoked the ambitions of would-be usurpers, coveting perquisites of power that impressed even a traveler from imperial China. In Zhou's telling, the Khmer king's retinue included between three thousand and five thousand "concubines and palace girls." When it was time for him to travel, hundreds of young women, holding candles and wearing flowers in their hair, stood at the head of his procession. "The ministers and princes are mounted on elephants," Zhou recounted. "In front of them one can see from afar their red parasols, which are innumerable." They were followed by a further troop of wives and concubines. "After them is the sovereign, standing on an elephant."

———

Every summer in Cambodia, the monsoon rains swell the Mekong, the great river, murky with sediment, that courses from the Tibetan

Plateau all the way to the South China Sea. What follows is a hydrological event of rare force. The Mekong surges so intensely that it causes an intersecting river, the Tonle Sap, to flow in reverse, overfilling a lake of the same name. The resulting flood inundates a vast area, and when the waters recede later in the year, the silted shore is ideally fertilized for growing rice, the crop that gave the Khmer Empire its worldly power. With a surplus of food, increased through vast irrigation projects, Angkorian rulers could buy off rivals and raise armies, extending their territorial dominance.

The wealth of Khmer society also allowed for the accumulation of slaves, whom Zhou described as a ubiquitous presence. "Those who have many slaves possess more than a hundred," he wrote. "Those who have few possess ten to twenty; only the very poor have none at all." Though the term encompassed a range of legal statuses, the slaves Zhou observed enjoyed no civil rights; if they tried to escape, they might be punished with branding. Elaborate codes of etiquette governed their behavior. They were permitted to sit or lie down only underneath the homes of their master, not inside them. When entering, they were obliged to "kneel down, join their hands together, and prostrate themselves." Only then could they move forward.

Slave labor was crucial to realizing a Khmer king's ultimate aspiration: the construction of his own spiritual center, a "temple-mountain" that made tangible his union with the divine. For the tenth-century monarch Jayavarman IV, that was Koh Ker, an entirely new capital devoted to the worship of Shiva. (The god's potency was symbolized there, as at other sites consecrated to him, by a massive stone cylinder known as a linga.) In the twelfth century, a new king, Suryavarman II, began the construction of Angkor Wat as a monument to Vishnu. Later, it was the turn of Jayavarman VII, a Buddhist, who commissioned Angkor Thom and its architectural centerpiece, the Bayon.

These complexes were among the most ambitious construction projects ever undertaken. Angkor Wat alone encompasses an area of about four hundred acres, more than three times the size of the Vatican. Millions of tons of sandstone were quarried in nearby hills. The blocks were likely hauled by elephants and then loaded onto bamboo barges for transport; elephants took over again at the other end, possibly traveling up ramps to access each building site. In addition to slaves, much of the labor force would have been made up of peasants summoned for a period of mandatory service to their king. The precise number of workers involved is unknown, but it certainly would have been in the tens of thousands.

At the same time, Khmer artisans were creating the sculptures, in stone and bronze, that Latchford would find so captivating centuries later. Like the temples where they were installed, such works of art served a dual purpose. They were religious, depicting gods and other figures from Hindu tradition and, later, the Buddha and bodhisattvas, beings on their way to enlightenment. Some also probably bore a not-so-subtle resemblance to the kings who commissioned them, as well as to their heirs and consorts—yet another way to meld the ruler's temporal grandeur with the eternal. As with so much else Latchford learned, the story of the statues had huge gaps. Not a single one was signed by its creator: If there had been a Khmer equivalent to Michelangelo or Cellini, they'd left no record. Aside from the fact that stone pieces were generally carved from a single block, relatively little was known of the techniques or tools employed. And yet there they were, at every temple Latchford visited, dotted around like jewels.

The end of the Khmer Empire was nearly as mysterious as its beginning. In the traditional account, its proximate cause was the invasion of Angkor in 1431 by an army from present-day Thailand. But scholars have never agreed on how Angkor became weak enough to make such a sacking possible—if it even happened. (The archaeological evidence is minimal.)

Whatever the reasons, Angkor gradually ceased to be a major urban center, and Cambodia as a whole entered a period of isolation. This deepened at the beginning of the eighteenth century, when the Vietnamese took control of the Mekong Delta, where the river meets the South China Sea. Under the Khmer, the region's principal port had been known as Prey Nokor. Its new rulers called the city Saigon. At a time of intense international exchange, Cambodia was cut off. This had certain advantages, sparing the country some of the brutalities of colonization inflicted elsewhere in Asia. It also left the Cambodian state at the mercy of more powerful neighbors, which vied to dominate its politics.

In 1860, a French explorer, Henri Mouhot, disembarked from a small boat on a tributary of the Tonle Sap. Skilled in linguistics and the emerging art of photography, Mouhot was partway through a series of expeditions in the interior of Indochina. Once on shore, he followed a raised causeway and then a sandy path through the forest. Plump cicadas sang among the trees; kingfishers and cormorants darted overhead. Mouhot hiked for hours, eventually coming to a broad plaza flanked by sculpted lions. What he saw next, though ravaged by time and overgrown with vegetation, was unmistakably the temple-city of which he'd heard tales. "It is grander than anything left to us by Greece or Rome," he wrote of the place he called Ongcor. "Was this incomparable edifice the work of a single genius, who conceived the idea, and watched over the execution of it? One is tempted to think so; for no part of it is deficient, faulty, or inconsistent."

Of course, Mouhot hadn't discovered Angkor any more than Columbus had discovered the Americas. Nor was he the first European to reach the site: Incredibly, a Capuchin friar had somehow found his way there in the sixteenth century. But Mouhot's account was the first to reach a wide audience, through an illustrated book, *Travels in the Central Parts of Indo-China (Siam), Cambodia, and Laos*. Like other early Western visitors, Mouhot could not imagine that the poor, largely illiterate Cambodians he encountered were the same people who'd built the temples. Condescendingly, he speculated that they had been constructed by "ancient settlers, who introduced Buddhism and civilization" before being "succeeded by some barbarous race, who drove the original inhabitants far into the interior, and destroyed many of their buildings." He saw only one way to restore the nation's lost grandeur: "a wise government," which would ensure that "labour and agriculture were encouraged instead of despised."

Mouhot died in Laos in 1861 and would never see that wish fulfilled. But two years later, French officials concluded a deal with the reigning Cambodian monarch, King Norodom. France, which was in the process of gaining control of Vietnam, hoped to extend its reach in Indochina and gain access to Cambodia's resources of timber and gemstones. Norodom wanted an ally who would stop Thailand from meddling in his country. From that point forward, Cambodia would be, in effect, a protectorate of Paris, even though the monarchy remained in place. Gradually, it became something more like a full colony, with France taking over basic functions, such as tax collection, and installing a network of *résidents* throughout the provinces.

The French claimed to be guided by democratic values—*Liberté, Égalité, Fraternité.* The colonial authorities built a road network and opened schools where the children of the Cambodian elite could receive European educations. In addition to soldiers of the ordinary kind, France also dispatched a small army of archaeologists and architects, tasked with cataloging, studying, and, where possible, restoring the physical legacy of the Khmer Empire. Taking little interest in what their Cambodian subjects thought of the matter, they removed many of the statues and artifacts that they discovered and shipped them off to Paris, though more remained, either in situ at temples or on display at the National Museum they built in Phnom Penh.

But for most in Cambodia, little changed for the better. Spending on education and medical care was minimal outside the capital, and the electric and water grids were largely nonexistent. Poverty was the rule, exacerbated by stiff taxes that were levied to cover the salaries of French administrators, mustachioed men in starched white uniforms and pith helmets, who might only be glimpsed as they sped past in imported motorcars. Those Cambodians without enough money to pay risked being called up for ninety days of annual labor for the state, not unlike their forebears in the days of Angkor.

In 1941, following the death of Cambodia's then king, France threw its support behind his eighteen-year-old grandson, Norodom Sihanouk. He took the throne later that year. The French government—led by the collaborationists of Vichy—appeared to be betting that a teenager with no leadership experience would be weak and pliable. It was a fateful error. Soon after the end of World War II, Sihanouk began agitating for greater autonomy. Already fighting an insurgency in Vietnam, France was wary of becoming embroiled in another struggle with Southeast Asian nationalists, and by the end of 1953, Sihanouk had secured Cambodian independence. Two years later, he abdicated the throne to compete in electoral politics, which he came to dominate.

Baby-faced, thin-skinned, and sexually voracious—he had six wives and many concubines, with whom he would father at least fourteen children—Sihanouk was a protean figure, as likely to charm as to infuriate those he encountered. He spoke flawless French in an unmistakable high-pitched voice and liked to entertain visitors into the wee hours by playing saxophone and clarinet. On one occasion, he insisted that foreign diplomats in Phnom Penh roll up their sleeves to help build a new stretch of railway track—and then offered them Champagne and a pleasant luncheon. He became enraged when journalists described Cambodia as "tiny" or "minuscule," once issuing an official statement listing, in alphabetical order, forty-seven countries that were smaller in land area.

By the time of Latchford's visit to Angkor in 1961, Sihanouk led a nation that felt like an oasis from the turmoil spreading across Southeast Asia. The conflict between Communist North Vietnam and the American-backed South, divided since the French withdrawal, was growing bloodier. But Sihanouk remained neutral, determined to keep Cambodia from being drawn into the fighting, and the country was at peace. As one journalist wistfully recalled, Cambodia was "seemingly immune to the upheavals ravaging its neighbors." But that impression obscured seething passions just below the surface.

Sihanouk was a near-absolute ruler; tellingly, he didn't mind being compared to Jayavarman VII, the Khmer king responsible for building Angkor Thom. Open criticism was taboo, and dissidents disappeared without a trace. If they were unlucky enough to get caught, members of the Khmer Serei, an anti-monarchist guerrilla force, were executed by firing squad, with films of their deaths screened for the public. The growing number of Cambodian Communists, inspired by the same ideology as their Vietnamese counterparts, could expect similar treatment if captured. In such a repressive environment, some opponents of Sihanouk's rule concluded that the only way to survive was to flee into the jungle.

One opposition leader who did so was a young leftist, Saloth Sar. Raised in relative privilege, he had lived in Paris as a student in the early 1950s. There he was admitted to a group of Cambodians who called themselves the Cercle Marxiste. After returning to Phnom Penh, he'd worked as a schoolteacher—and had also become a senior official in the nascent Communist Party. Fearing execution if he showed his face, Saloth Sar would remain in the forest for years. When he finally emerged, he would be known by a different name.

Pol Pot.

3

Douglas Latchford took his position on a flimsy chair inside an arena in central Bangkok. He was surrounded by a tight crowd of Asian and Western men in shirtsleeves, looking down from the stands at a pair of Thai boxers who were naked apart from their shorts, their bodies glistening under harsh overhead lights. A referee hovered a few steps away, shadowing the fighters' movements around the ring. Each was looking for his moment, bobbing on the balls of bare feet. One lifted a knee, preparing to strike, then dropped it down again—a feint that caused his opponent to jerk backward. In a blink, he hurled his leg into a wide, powerful arc, landing his foot square in the center of the other combatant's torso. But the man remained upright, and they began grappling at each other's shoulders, moving as one across the floor, each seeking leverage for a bout-finishing blow.

In the stands, Latchford roared his approval with the rest. As after-hours diversions went, watching Muay Thai—the no-holds-barred combat sport beloved in Thailand—was hard to beat. Latchford didn't mind that the matches occasionally ended in chaos, with liberally refreshed spectators expressing their dissatisfaction over the outcome by hurling projectiles at the ring. When mayhem erupted at the end of this fight in 1963, he and his companion, a visiting colleague named Robbie Brothers, protected themselves by holding their chairs over their heads like shields. For Latchford, it was just another night in Bangkok, where he'd lived for the better part of ten years and felt entirely at home.

Latchford no longer worked at the agency for imported goods that had first employed him. Now he ran the local operations of a Hong Kong–based conglomerate, Wheelock Marden. His brother, Trevor, had similarly thrived, rising to become a senior executive at the English-language *Bangkok Post*. With a seventh-floor office in the capital's commercial heart, high above what remained a city of squat shophouses and migrant shanties, Latchford was close to the top of the local business world in every sense. Still, he hadn't entered the inner circle of the true expatriate elite, dominated by men with degrees from Oxford or Harvard and, in many cases, connections to agencies known by three-letter initialisms. Latchford had none of those credentials. Nor did he have the kind of clubby personality that might have opened doors without them; indeed, he had little talent for conversation, struggling to express much interest in what an interlocutor was saying unless it affected him directly.

Among its other business lines, Wheelock Marden distributed cosmetics and pharmaceuticals in Thailand. As Latchford sometimes boasted, it wasn't a terribly demanding gig, leaving him plenty of time and money to indulge in what had become his true vocation: the acquisition of Khmer artifacts, which he'd stepped up after making his first trip to Cambodia in 1961. Latchford wanted nothing more than to be surrounded by the objects he treasured, allowing him to adore the silky perfection of their figures.

When Brothers came to see him at his office, Latchford was excited to show off a sandstone statue he had recently procured. "I bought it for two thousand pounds," Latchford said. Brothers was astonished; he'd never heard of someone paying so much—the equivalent of more than $45,000 today—for a piece from Cambodia. But among Bangkok's collectors, such prices were growing more common. As a figure of aesthetic discernment, Latchford had some way to go before he could match Jim Thompson, the silk entrepreneur and intelligence agent whose dinner parties were still an important stop on the social circuit. But he'd begun to be seen as a man of taste, with the means to act upon it.

As he prospered, so did Bangkok, becoming a far more developed city than the isolated capital that Latchford had first gotten to know in the 1950s. There were still pedal-powered *samlors* on the streets, but they fought for space with growing numbers of imported cars. To make room for all those vehicles, many of the *khlongs* were paved over and new roads blasted through communities of waterside homes. Thailand was still a unique place, governed by a culture that beguiled and bewildered new arrivals. But it would never again stand so apart from the rest of the world. In fact, Southeast Asia was coming to occupy the center of global consciousness.

At the end of 1965, there were well over one hundred thousand American military personnel in Vietnam. Their numbers would more than double the following year. And for what would become the defining conflict of the decade, Thailand was an essential staging area. Its government had granted the US Air Force use of several bases in the country's East; meanwhile, American servicemen on R&R poured into Bangkok, invigorating commerce while encouraging the growth of a shadow economy made up of massage parlors and go-go bars.

The country fizzed with intrigue. From a clandestine facility in an outlying province, the CIA was organizing a massive effort to support anti-Communist militias in Laos, in a conflict that would eventually be known as the Secret War. Even in the course of selling makeup and prescription drugs, Latchford crossed paths with spies. At Wheelock Marden, he employed the services of an advertising agency located just a few minutes' walk from his office. The admen shared their building with an airline, Air America Inc., which operated under the slogan "Anything, Anywhere, Anytime, Professionally." A traveler looking to book a ticket was likely to be disappointed. Though nominally a commercial enterprise, Air America was a thinly veiled CIA front that flew unacknowledged missions in support of US-backed forces around the region. Occasionally, a taciturn American would appear in the hallways with a freshly bandaged hand or missing foot—the result, presumably, of an up-country operation that had gone sideways.

These mysterious operatives lived on the fringes of what had become a large expatriate community. With its inexpensive living and ample diversions, Bangkok attracted an increasing number of eccentric, mostly male Westerners who, like Latchford, felt they fit in better there than at home. One American resident kept a pet Malayan brown bear that he brought with him to bars. Evidently pleased to be included in the social scene, the animal would perch on a stool and drink highballs. Another expat held afternoon pot parties where the sauce for the satay skewers was spiked with marijuana, if not something stronger. Later, the group might land for the evening at a night-club called Sani Chateau. Its air-conditioning filters were rumored to be soaked in Chanel No. 5, and for about five dollars, an attendee could choose a female "companion" of his preferred nationality.

In early October 1965, a fifty-one-year-old American, Darrell Berrigan, was found dead in a Volkswagen sedan just a short walk from his Bangkok home. He had been shot through the back of his skull, apparently in the course of an intimate encounter—his pants and underwear were pulled down around his shins. Berrigan was the editor and publisher of the *Bangkok World*, the main rival to the *Post* among the city's English publications, and his murder was a major story. (A twenty-two-year-old Thai would confess to killing him in what was apparently a botched robbery.)

The crime also brought unprecedented public attention to Bangkok's permissive attitudes toward homosexuality, compared with even the most liberal precincts of the US and Europe. As one Thai paper said, "It was general knowledge that Berrigan loved young men the way other men love young women." But that hadn't stopped him from holding a prominent job, as it would have in many Western cities. A significant number of male expats kept Thai boyfriends, younger lovers who welcomed the attention of foreign paramours before later marrying and having children.

Nevertheless, gay men in Bangkok—Latchford among them—understood that a degree of discretion was advisable. Latchford kept up a pretense of being straight, avoiding any discussion of his romantic life with colleagues, but they and others around him were under no illusions, and generally speaking, they didn't care. The foreigners who chose to make their lives in Southeast Asia at the time were not often of the judging type. Those who traded and admired antiquities were even more tolerant; Thompson, for his part, was almost certainly bisexual. And in their arena, Latchford was growing into an important player. By the mid-1960s, he was no longer simply buying Khmer statues for his own enjoyment. He was also selling them, earning himself a place among the tiny number of people in Bangkok who could source the best pieces as soon as they were discovered in remote temples. In addition to Latchford, this included Thompson; a Thai Chinese entrepreneur known as Peng Seng; and one of Thompson's closest friends, a fellow former intelligence operative named Connie Mangskau.

The group's members could be competitive, each vying to prove that they were a more refined connoisseur. In one letter, Thompson boasted of getting his hands on a tenth-century stone head from the Cambodian temple-city of Koh Ker, with half of the face representing the Hindu god Shiva and the other half his wife, Parvati. "Connie + Douglas Latchford all turned down as they said it had been recarved," Thompson wrote. But he knew better: "Boisselier"—a French art historian who was among the world's foremost experts on the Khmer civilization—"says it should be in a museum."

For Latchford and the others, the business of selling artifacts was growing more lucrative. Several years earlier, the New York auction house Parke-Bernet had sold a painting by Rembrandt, *Aristotle with a Bust of Homer*, for $2.3 million. That was the highest price ever paid for a work of art at a public auction, and a milestone in an extended boom, with marquee pieces continuing to shatter records. Not surprisingly, those willing to pay the most were located in the US—the prime mover of the postwar economy. There, the titans of

Wall Street were hungry for trophies with which to decorate their Park Avenue co-ops; the same was true for the rising moguls of Los Angeles, where modernist mansions were marching ever higher into the Hollywood Hills. According to one estimate, the average price of Old Master drawings would rise more than twentyfold between 1951 and 1969; Impressionist works weren't far behind.

Khmer artifacts had nowhere near the same power to command top-dollar bids, but they were no longer an obscure corner of the market, coveted by only a few enthusiasts, as they had been in the 1950s. Instead, they were attracting growing interest from collectors who were fascinated by Asia, curious about Hinduism and Buddhism, or who simply thought they were beautiful. American museums, attentive to the preferences of their patrons, were also looking to expand holdings that remained dominated by works from Europe and the Mediterranean. Latchford soon grasped that these buyers were willing to snap up whatever new treasures he could provide.

Prasat Hin Khao Plai Bat II was a Khmer temple located on a forested rise in northeastern Thailand, a short distance from the Cambodian border. Small and overgrown, it had largely escaped notice by archaeologists; the site was better known to local rice and cattle farmers. After an unusually heavy rain in the summer of 1964, however, some of them noticed, at the edge of the temple structure, a chunk of stone that they hadn't seen before. Curious, they began probing the ground, eventually finding several large pieces of laterite lying in the soil. They moved the slabs away and exposed something extraordinary: a kind of hand-dug vault containing a row of bronze sculptures of the Buddha and four-armed bodhisattvas. Even more were buried nearby. The statues were of rare beauty, lithe figures that ranged in height from a few inches to more than four feet, with piercing eyes and gently smiling lips.

Word of the discovery reached Latchford in Bangkok. It was exactly the kind of opportunity that Thompson might jump at. But this time it was Latchford, a quarter-century younger and armed with the ambition of a man entering the prime of his career, who acted first—and instigated a frenzy. With a Thai associate, he quickly drove to the nearest town, where he inspected the finds and paid cash for those he wanted, overwhelming any qualms that the residents had about removing sacred objects. Some of them began sleeping on the temple grounds, their wives bringing food so they could spend more time hunting for artifacts. Latchford returned frequently to buy up more of their discoveries; his Thai collaborator set up a small office in a village house to keep an eye on the progress.

The pillaging continued for more than two years, until every part of Plai Bat II had been scoured over, leaving a cratered moonscape of empty pits. Because none of the excavation was formally documented, it was impossible to know how many objects were taken. The total may have been as high as three hundred. Nor did experts get the opportunity to try to understand the site before it was torn apart. The temple dated to the tenth century, but the sculptures were considerably older. Why they were brought there and hidden underground would remain a mystery.

What is clear is that when the works, which became known as the Prakhon Chai bronzes, began to filter onto the international market with Latchford's help, they proved extremely popular. Many were sold in London by Spink & Son, a storied firm of art dealers that had a showroom on tony King Street, just off St. James's Square. By the end of 1967, examples had been acquired by the Art Institute of Chicago and the Philadelphia Museum of Art, as well as by the Metropolitan Museum of Art in New York.

At the time that Latchford made his buying trips to eastern Thailand, Bangkok's expat A-list was still centered on Thompson and his immediate circle. But the guard was gradually changing as the American began his seventh decade. Thompson appeared exhausted, dogged by the effects of various tropical illnesses. He was also deeply angered by the war in Vietnam, which he criticized so bitterly that some in the CIA concluded he was a Communist.

Thompson, then, was a diminished figure by the time he and Mangskau went on holiday to Malaysia's Cameron Highlands in the spring of 1967. A mountainous region of tea plantations and dense forests, the Highlands are unlike almost anywhere else in Southeast Asia—cool and misty, with a climate so temperate that farmers can grow strawberries. Thompson and Mangskau were staying at Moonlight Cottage, a retreat owned by friends of Thompson's from Singapore. On Easter Sunday, the group attended a church service and had a picnic before returning to the house for afternoon naps. Around 3 p.m., one of Thompson's hosts heard him padding down the gravel driveway, apparently headed for a stroll in the surrounding woods.

Later, as they and Mangskau gathered for predinner cocktails, they realized that Thompson had never returned. They called the local police, who combed the area until dark, finding no sign of him. The next day, the authorities began what was probably the largest land search in Malaysian history, aided by soldiers, Boy Scouts, Aboriginal trackers, and local volunteers. Brigadier General Edwin F. Black, a close friend of Thompson's and the commander of American forces in Thailand's Northeast, flew in to assist in the hunt, which was attracting high-level attention from the US government. An American diplomat in the region cabled Washington, stating that Thompson was BELIEVED TO HAVE BEEN KIDNAP[P]ED, ALTHOUGH NO RANSOM DEMAND TO DATE.

None would ever come. Nor would any of the searchers locate the slightest trace of Thompson or his remains, despite several attempts in 1967 and over the years that followed. One of Asia's most unusual personalities had, it seemed, simply vanished from the face of the earth. In Bangkok, Thompson's disappearance represented the end of an era and, for Latchford, something of an opportunity. The city had just lost its leading expatriate aesthete, leaving a vacancy that he was ready to fill.

T homas Hoving was finishing his morning routine—orange juice, three medium-boiled eggs, coffee, extra sweet—when the phone trilled at his apartment on East Seventy-Third Street. A young art historian who'd recently taken an incongruous job running New York City's Parks Department, Hoving instantly recognized the voice on the other end of the line. It belonged to the executive assistant to James Rorimer, director of the Metropolitan Museum of Art and Hoving's professional mentor.

"Brace yourself, Tom," the assistant said gravely. "Jim died last night. They think it was a cerebral hemorrhage."

For Hoving, this was devastating news. He'd seen Rorimer just the night before at a meeting of the Met's Acquisitions Committee, where the director had convinced a group of wealthy trustees to spend almost half a million dollars on a twelfth-century wooden statue of the Virgin Mary cradling the infant Jesus. It was a victory for Hoving, who'd scouted out the piece in his previous role as head curator of the Cloisters, the Met annex devoted to medieval art at the northern tip of Manhattan. Afterward, Rorimer had apparently gone home and expired in his sleep.

It was May 1966. Rorimer's death was a seismic event in New York's cultural world, and its aftershocks would be felt all through the city and beyond. He had run its preeminent museum for more than a decade, a role that required Olympian levels of political and financial savvy, as well as world-class artistic knowledge. Before that, Rorimer had served as one of the famed Monuments Men—curators and art historians deployed after D-Day to locate works stolen by the Nazis. After cultivating a source in the French resistance, he helped recover the private collection of Reichsmarschall Hermann Göring, stuffed into trains at Berchtesgaden in the Bavarian Alps.

The Met's president tasked members of the board of trustees, a group of major donors representing some of the city's wealthiest families, with finding his replacement. It soon became clear that Hoving had an inside track. To lead an institution enmeshed with New York's social elite, he was almost absurdly well qualified. Tall and patrician, he'd spent his childhood on the Upper East Side, within a short walk of the Met. After his parents divorced, he made weekly visits to his father's sixteen-room apartment on Sutton Place. There, Hoving wrote, "my sister and I were expected to demonstrate that we could properly use the right silverware" and to "practice sweeping the doily deftly from underneath the finger bowl while lifting it aside just so." Hoving was also made to learn the science of small talk, "a formula no less rigid than an Oriental tea ceremony." He practiced it during summer lunches with the socialite—and Met trustee—Brooke Astor, who had a country home near the Hovings' in western Massachusetts. (She called him Tommy.)

Hoving maintained a rebellious streak—he had the distinction of being kicked out of two top private schools, Buckley and Exeter. But he eventually made it to Princeton, where he stumbled into a passion for art history and went on to the university's doctoral program. As he completed his PhD, he presented a paper that caught Rorimer's eye. Hoving was soon hired as Rorimer's "confidential assistant," permitted to sit in on even the most sensitive meetings, then became a curator in the Met's medieval department before Rorimer put him in charge of the Cloisters.

It was one of the museum world's most coveted jobs, but Hoving, ambitious and restless, found himself drawn to politics. In late 1965, John Lindsay, the newly elected mayor, whom Hoving had impressed as a volunteer on his campaign, made him a surprising offer. Would Hoving take charge of New York City's vast park system? Hoving said yes. It didn't hurt that as parks commissioner, he would be the effective landlord of the Met—which sits on city land in Central Park—and his privileges would include an ex officio board seat. He'd been exercising that prerogative at the meeting he attended right before Rorimer's death.

One might think that, given Hoving's background, his tenure at the Parks Department would have been characterized by stuffy continuity. Instead, he revealed himself to be an agent of dramatic change, a man eager to embrace the social convulsions beginning to shake the nation. Hoving hired a young staff who he set to work redesigning public spaces—and bringing New Yorkers into them through events that came to be known as Hoving's Happenings. There were jazz concerts, capture-the-flag events, meteor-shower parties, and—this being the mid-1960s—"a park contest for go-go girls," judged by Hoving himself. Key to the whole endeavor was press coverage, which he sought relentlessly. A joke at the time had it that his middle initials, P. F., stood for "Publicity Forever." (More revealing is that Hoving was said to have come up with the line.)

Thus, when it came time for the Met's board to choose a new director, Hoving offered a unique package: impeccable society credentials as well as city hall connections and a democratic sensibility, in tune with what even old-money trustees understood were changing times. He also had all the right allies, including Astor, who—in Hoving's telling, anyway—informed him on the day of Rorimer's memorial that he was her top choice. Though he'd been parks commissioner for barely a year, he readily accepted the trustees' offer. On March 17, 1967—just days before Jim Thompson disappeared in a Malaysian forest—Hoving arrived at the Met for his first day on the job. He was just thirty-six years old and would be responsible for the largest museum in the Western Hemisphere, with twenty acres of floor space and an operating budget of $5.5 million, equivalent to nearly ten times as much in today's dollars.

The Met's first director was an inveterate liar and looter named Luigi Palma di Cesnola. As a Piedmontese soldier of fortune, he fought with distinction for the Union in the Civil War and thenceforth referred to himself as "General," a promotion he claimed to have received directly from Abraham Lincoln in early 1865. The former president was not in a position to dispute his account.

The reward for Cesnola's service was an appointment as the US consul in Cyprus, where he passed the days by breaking into tombs around the island. He followed none of the practices embraced, even at that time, by professional archaeologists, such as cataloging the precise findspot and condition of each object. Nor was he bothered about obtaining government permission before exporting a piece. One of his signal finds, the so-called Treasure of Curium, was in fact a grab bag of artifacts from different parts of Cyprus that Cesnola had attempted to pass off as coming from a single temple, the better to raise its sale value. But this didn't trouble the trustees of the nascent Metropolitan Museum of Art, established in 1870 and initially housed in rented premises in Midtown, without a director on staff. Eventually, the group of well-off New Yorkers who founded the museum bought Cesnola's collection for about $60,000, and in 1879, they appointed him to run the Met, which he did for more than twenty years, dying in office in 1904.

The trustees' disinterest in what art professionals today call provenance—the story of how an artwork came to be on the market in the first place, and of all the transactions that followed—was hardly unusual. In creating the Met, they hoped to build an institution equal to the best museums of Europe, one that would embody the grandeur of its country and city by accumulating the objects of other nations. In Paris, the crowning glory of the Louvre was the spectacular Egyptian collection, built to a considerable extent with works removed during Napoleon's expedition at the end of the eighteenth century. In London, the British Museum had peerless holdings of Greek and Roman works—among them the Elgin Marbles, hacked off the Parthenon by a Scottish earl—as well as pieces taken from every corner of the Empire with out regard to the opinions of the "Natives." At these institutions, a visitor could feel the power of possession. For Britain or France, to own the works of a great past civilization was at once to become its heir, and to assert superiority over it.

To the Met's original benefactors, New York deserved no less, but theirs was a private institution, in a country that had no formal imperium. It would have to build its collections the American way—through the free market. In 1880, at a ceremony to mark the Met's move to its permanent location in Central Park, the lawyer and early museum supporter Joseph Hodges Choate delivered a speech aimed at the city's burgeoning upper classes. "Think of it, ye millionaires," he said, "what glory may yet be yours if you only listen to our advice, to convert pork into porcelain, grain and produce into priceless pottery, the rude ores of commerce into sculptured marble." Stocks and bonds would "perish without the using," Choate continued, and "in the next financial panic shall surely shrivel like parched scrolls." But the ambition of the Met was more eternal: to "convert your useless gold into things of living beauty that shall be a joy to a whole people for a thousand years."

As fundraising pitches go, Choate's was unusually eloquent, and it wouldn't take long to fulfill his vision of an institution growing in scale and esteem alongside the fortunes of the wealthiest New Yorkers. Just a few months after he gave his speech, Cornelius Vanderbilt II, the grandson and namesake of the archetypal tycoon of the Gilded Age, purchased nearly seven hundred Old Master drawings that he donated to the Met. Over the subsequent decades, the museum continued to absorb the largesse of the city's richest citizens—families with names like Morgan, Rockefeller, and Astor. It also proved adept at attracting the energies and generosity of those whose wealth was of more recent vintage.

Part of the appeal to donors was practical. After the passage of the War Revenue Act of 1917, US taxpayers could deduct charitable contributions—for example, of artworks whose dollar values could be determined by friendly appraisers—from their incomes, providing potentially enormous fiscal benefits. Other elements of the attraction were harder to quantify, but no less important. A degree of noblesse oblige certainly figured, but America lacked a nobility in the European sense. The boundaries of its elite were to some degree permeable, while the dynamism of its economy guaranteed a steady supply of families whose monetary resources outstripped their social cachet. This was an imbalance that close association with the museum might help correct.

After the end of World War II, as Rorimer and the other Monuments Men returned to their civilian lives, a different kind of imbalance became evident, especially once the US entered the boom years of the 1950s. To put it simply, America—the Met and its supporters above all—had the money, but Europe had the art. In France, Italy, Germany, Austria, and elsewhere, cash-strapped families were looking to off-load their collections, whether of Roman sculptures, Impressionist paintings, or Old Masters. Other sellers came into their wares by more dubious means, picking up some of the estimated six hundred thousand artworks stolen by the Nazis, far more than the Monuments Men could ever hope to track down. For US museums with less comprehensive collections than their European counterparts, it was a once-in-a-century opportunity. Soon, an industry of fleet-footed dealers—and a broader network of forgers, smugglers, and small-time crooks—had emerged to cater to the needs of the buyers flying in on Pan Am.

One of the most energetic among the travelers was the future Met director Thomas Hoving. As a medieval curator at the museum, and then in his role managing the Cloisters, he saw it as his core responsibility to build a pipeline of spectacular acquisitions—the kinds of pieces that would wow the public and impress his fellow art historians. Hoving made three or four buying trips to Europe each year, staying for weeks at a time. In a memoir that would cause considerable consternation at the Met when it was published after his time as director, he wrote, "My collecting style was pure piracy, and I got a reputation as a shark."

Hoving's triumphs included obtaining a vivid twelfth-century stone relief depicting the Annunciation. Like many of his conquests, this one required ratlike cunning and a willingness to look past inconvenient export laws. Hoving located the relief, originally from a church in Florence, in a garage outside Genoa. He later wrote that he magicked it out of Italy with the help of a dealer whose usual tactic was to hide an artifact under mattresses and then drive toward the border with a small child who would be furnished with a messy treat. By the time they arrived to be inspected by "the smartly dressed, white-gloved and harried customs officers, the child ha[d] smeared the gelato all over his face." Inevitably, the dealer would be waved through. The Florentine relief was soon in Geneva. "Two weeks after that," Hoving recounted, "it was in the storeroom of the Cloisters."

Later, once the norms of the cultural world had changed, figures like Hoving would say that in the 1960s and '70s, no one particularly cared whether works were looted. This was a convenient myth; in fact, myriad government officials, historians, and even just interested citizens in archaeologically rich nations cared very much indeed. That was why so many of them, from Peru to Italy to China and beyond, had passed laws that explicitly banned the unauthorized removal and export of artifacts.

For one thing, stealing statues and friezes deprived the people of those countries the opportunity to appreciate and take pride in their heritage. For a sense of how dispiriting this could feel, try to imagine a world where the Lincoln Memorial adorns the courtyard of a museum in Jakarta, or where Britain's crown jewels reside in the home of a wealthy family in Quito. Even worse, clandestine excavations, carried out by gangs of thieves using picks, shovels, and sometimes dynamite, routinely destroyed irreplaceable works. Even when objects were removed intact, there was no recovering the loss of their contexts: information about their origins and conditions that would allow archaeologists to make inferences about the civilizations that had produced them. With no record of its discovery, even the finest artwork was an orphan from the perspective of historical understanding.

Despite the laws on their books, the countries where American buyers operated had little ability to stop them. In the late 1960s, Italy set up the Tutela del Patrimonio Culturale, probably the first police unit in history devoted exclusively to interdicting stolen art. But given the breadth of Italian cultural patrimony and the resources of those trying to acquire it, the squad's officers faced a Herculean task. The situation was much worse in poorer nations. Some of the most severe looting of the mid-twentieth century was of Mayan and Aztec sites in Mexico. Under Mexican law, the journalist Karl E. Meyer wrote in 1973, there was "virtually no legal market in pre-Columbian antiquities. But because Mexico has thousands of archaeological sites, because much of the country is poor, and because prices for pre-Columbian art are high, the law is about as effective as the Prohibition Amendment."

Cambodia, where Khmer Empire sculptures were objects of worship, was in a similar situation. Virtually all the Khmer works that Douglas Latchford dealt in were, by any normal understanding of the terms, looted and smuggled: Cambodian law explicitly prohibited the unauthorized removal of artifacts and their shipment abroad. In a 1968 letter to the London art dealer Spink & Son, Prince Norodom Sihanouk complained that "Cambodia's historic heritage has been ruthlessly pillaged" and warned that "stern measures are now being taken" to halt the destruction. But fortunately for Latchford, Sihanouk's government had even less capacity than Mexico to enforce its laws, and the authorities in Western capitals weren't going to help.

It's sometimes said that looting is the second-oldest profession, and on one level, all of this was familiar. As long as there have been tombs, there have been tomb robbers. What had changed was the scale. The wealth accumulation of the postwar period created a far larger number of potential collectors than had ever existed before, while air travel gave them the ability to range more widely than connoisseurs of earlier eras could have imagined. Then there were the voracious American museums, some of them well established, like the Met, and others new, such as the Los Angeles County Museum of Art. The pace of acquisitions appeared to be pushing matters to a crisis point. As Meyer wrote, "The tempo of destruction is presently so great that by the end of the century most remaining important archaeological sites may well be plundered or paved over."

With something like that scenario in mind, governments in the developing world, led by Mexico and Peru, had begun pushing in 1960 for an international treaty to regulate the antiquities market. The forum they chose was UNESCO, the United Nations agency responsible for cultural heritage. Newly decolonized countries in Africa and Asia offered their support, and in 1970, the idea came to member states for final consideration. The result was a mouthful—the UNESCO Convention on the Means of Prohibiting the Illicit Import, Export and Transfer of Ownership of Cultural Property—

and a milestone. The core of the agreement was the establishment of an international process for recovering stolen artworks. Under that mechanism, a nation from which an item of "cultural property" had been illicitly removed could make a formal request for its return from the place where it had ended up. As long as the paperwork was in order, the government of the destination country was supposed to comply.

But there were important caveats, starting with the fact that the return mechanism was, by definition, retrospective: UNESCO had no power to stop looting in the first place. That would remain the responsibility of individual governments, whose track record did not inspire confidence. Repatriation would occur through diplomatic channels, ensuring that the process was gradual, prone to stalling, and likely to be employed only in rare circumstances. Most important, for the convention to have any power, governments would have to ratify it through national legislation. While some source countries were quick to do so—both Mexico and Cambodia completed ratification in 1972—nations on the buying side of the market were in no hurry. The US would wait until 1983. It would take France and the UK until 1997 and 2002, respectively.

Like all American museum directors, Hoving kept a close eye on the UNESCO proceedings. But as he began to put his mark on the Met, any broad restrictions on what he could obtain for the museum were in the future. In fact, it was still open season.

Hoving believed that everything about the institution he took over in 1967 needed to change. To him, the Met was hopelessly out of touch with the churning city around it. While the Woodstock era unfolded outside, the trustees still met over dinner in black tie. *The Village Voice* wrote witheringly, and not inaccurately, that the Met's board was "a crusty, patrician, elitist claque that looks at New York through the tinted glass of a Lincoln Continental."

With the same energy he brought to organizing "happenings" in parks, Hoving set about transforming the museum's physical space and its programming. The overhaul was so comprehensive, and so enduring, that much of what New Yorkers today associate with the Met—and, to some extent, with museums in general—began with him. Hoving came up with the idea of advertising exhibitions through huge banners on the Fifth Avenue facade, and he built the broad plaza that's still among the city's most animated public spaces. When the government of Egypt offered to donate the Temple of Dendur, a Roman structure threatened by the Aswan High Dam, to the United States, Hoving successfully lobbied the White House to have it placed in the Met, where it became a major attraction. The heavily marketed, corporate-sponsored blockbuster show was another Hoving innovation, reaching its apotheosis in *Treasures of Tutankhamun*, the largest Egyptian exhibition in American history.

The core of the Hoving ethos, however, remained unchanged: A great museum needed great objects, acquired and unveiled with a much fanfare as possible. As he wrote later, Hoving wanted "only the big, rare, fantastic pieces, the expensive ones, the ones that would cause a splash." One of the most significant reveals of his tenure was the Euphronios krater, a twenty-five-hundred-year-old vase illustrated with a radiant scene from the *Iliad*. Hoving was vague about the origins of the piece, which the Met had spent $1 million to acquire. Media reports appeared almost immediately suggesting it was looted, but Hoving told the public he'd been assured that "the krater was definitely not a hot pot." It would be more than thirty years be-fore the Met would officially acknowledge the truth, which Hoving had more or less known all along: that his prized acquisition had been stolen by tomb robbers working near Rome in 1971.

Still, even the most revered Greek and Roman pieces would take the Met only so far. Attuned to cultural shifts, Hoving wanted to ensure that the museum responded to the evolving interests of its patrons. Increasingly, these included a fascination with Asia. The year Hoving was named director, a Hindu guru founded the Hare Krishna movement—not in India but in Manhattan's Tompkins Square Park. Two years after that, in 1968, the Beatles traveled to the Himalayas to study meditation with Maharishi Mahesh Yogi, who followed their visit by going on tour with the Beach Boys. Their journeys and those of others would inspire thousands of young Americans to join what became known as the Hippie Trail, a chain of destinations that started in Afghanistan before ranging across India and into Thailand and beyond.

But as Hoving would lament in his eventual memoir, the Met had little to attract visitors who wanted to know more about South and Southeast Asian cultures. Its holdings were so scant that curators esti-mated it had fewer than sixty objects from the region that were wor-thy of display. To correct this deficiency, Hoving certainly needed works from the Hindu civilizations of India, along with pieces from the likes of Thailand and Nepal. He also needed art from the jungle temples of Cambodia, sites that held a mystical allure for growing numbers of people in the West, and whose treasures Latchford stood ready to provide.

5

The guerrillas began their assault at dawn on a January morning in 1968. Their leaders had been confident that they would surprise the government troops manning an army post in Bay Damram, a plain of sunbaked farm fields and one-road villages in northwest Cambodia. But an informant had tipped off the soldiers, who killed two of the attackers and sent the rest into retreat. All that the insurgents managed to do was steal some weapons and, in other areas, ambush and murder three police officers. But their actions were nonetheless the start of something much larger.

Since leaving Phnom Penh for the safety of the forest, the Communist leader Saloth Sar had grown more disciplined, and more radical. He'd lived for a time in a rugged camp on the Vietnamese border, under foliage so thick that sunlight barely filtered through. Later, he traveled on foot, over a route that would soon be known to the world as the Ho Chi Minh Trail, to consult with the North Vietnamese leadership in Hanoi. From there he flew to Beijing, where he learned about the societal transformations being advanced by Mao Zedong. He was still developing his own version of socialist ideology, which would eventually combine extreme nationalism with a determination to completely extinguish markets, private property, and even the family, leaving citizens with no loyalties other than to the state.

Saloth Sar's guerrillas conducted further raids in the following weeks, ambushing government forces and seizing more arms. Saloth Sar was intensely secretive—he wouldn't officially reveal himself as the leader of the Cambodian Communists until 1977—and claiming responsibility wasn't his style. But it was clear to the country's mercurial ruler, Prince Norodom Sihanouk, who was behind the provocations: the "Khmers Rouges," a term Sihanouk coined. He responded with ferocious violence. Sihanouk boasted of personally ordering the execution of rebels by firing squad. Others were decapitated, their heads put on public display. "I do not care if I am sent to hell," the prince declared with characteristic ardor. "I will submit the pertinent documents to the devil himself."

His reprisals failed to contain the growing insurgency, and none of them reached Saloth Sar, hiding deep inside the malarial jungle. Outwardly, at least, Cambodia had remained largely placid for most of the 1960s. Now the inferno next door was beginning to sweep across its borders, with consequences that no one in Phnom Penh, Bangkok, or Washington could yet imagine.

For Douglas Latchford, however, Cambodia remained a source of enchantment. Since his buying trips to Plai Bat II, the temple in eastern Thailand where villagers had unearthed a trove of extraordinary bronzes, he'd continued to broaden his obsessive collecting and dealing of Khmer antiquities. Though he still worked for the Hong Kong conglomerate Wheelock Marden, what had begun as an intense hobby was now a real business, requiring much of his attention. He would soon be making plans to open his own gallery, where he could welcome potential buyers in an atmosphere of hushed luxury, and show off the knowledge and discernment that he had worked so hard to cultivate.

Other Bangkok dealers relied on a supply chain that had evolved to meet the ever-expanding demand for artifacts, connecting looting crews in Cambodia to brokers and "runners" who carried them into Thailand. But Latchford wasn't content to sit in his office and wait for masterpieces to come to him. In the city's business community, he had built a reputation as a rare man who knew how to get things done in Cambodia, with contacts in small towns across the country. And during the tumultuous year of 1968, as Saloth Sar's guerrillas ranged farther into the countryside, he loaded up a car with four friends and set out for Angkor, where he could see—and, if possible, acquire—new pieces firsthand.

After crossing the border, the group passed through Sisophon, a crossroads town not far from the center of the insurgency, and drove on to Siem Reap. The temples just outside the city were considerably more popular with foreign tourists than they'd been when Latchford first visited, seven years earlier. Shortly before this trip, the most famous woman of the era, none other than Jackie Kennedy, had toured them at Sihanouk's invitation. Still, if he arrived at the right time of year, and the right time of day, and if he knew what he was looking for and where to leave the beaten track, it was possible for a visitor like Latchford to feel as though he had the run of the ancient sites.

Before he could get to the temples on this trip, though, Latchford had to sort out a problem. The hotel where he and his friends were supposed to stay had mixed up their reservation, and there were no rooms available. Nor could they get into the Grand Hotel, the most distinguished option in town. Latchford had only one alternative, which surely would have been out of reach for a traveler of lesser standing. Across the road from the Grand, on the bank of a languid river shaded by mango trees, Sihanouk had built a bungalow for his personal use. The visitors drove over and asked the sole visible staff member, a guard keeping watch over the house, if it was vacant and, if so, whether they could stay there. It was, and to their surprise, the guard permitted Latchford and his party to move in, giving them the use of three bedrooms and a swimming pool. Cambodia might have been on the verge of an all-out civil war, but Latchford was being treated like royalty.

On March 16, 1969, the president's assistant for national security affairs, Henry Kissinger, sent a memorandum concerning Cambodia to his boss, Richard Nixon. Historically, a poor Southeast Asian country of perhaps seven million citizens would not have merited the attention of the Oval Office. But in the weeks since Nixon's inauguration, Kissinger had made Cambodia a priority. The reason was the conflict in Vietnam, where there were now some five hundred thousand American troops. Nixon had campaigned on "an honorable end" to US involvement: a settlement that would allow GIs to withdraw without admitting defeat. To get such a deal, America needed to negotiate from a position of strength. And events in Cambodia were making that much harder.

Nixon and Kissinger had little interest in the Khmer Rouge, who at the time weren't widely understood to be a distinct force from the Vietnamese communists. Rather, US commanders had concluded that the North Vietnamese Army and Viet Cong guerrillas they were fighting relied on supply lines from Cambodia. Some were convinced that the Vietnamese even maintained a secret headquarters there—a "Bamboo Pentagon" whose destruction might turn the tide. The possible downside of striking Cambodia, as Kissinger saw it, was that the operation could prompt critics to "seize on this to renew attacks on war and pressure for quick US withdrawal." Congress had never authorized the Nixon administration to expand the deeply unpopular conflict into a new country, and no one could be sure how Sihanouk would react to incursions by a foreign military. Cambodia was neutral, and the prince had severed diplomatic relations with the US four years earlier.

To minimize the risks, Kissinger came up with a proposal, dubbed the "Breakfast Plan," that was extraordinary in its audacity: a major aerial offensive that the administration would neither announce nor acknowledge, not even to many of the personnel involved. In Kissinger's ideal scenario, American opponents of the war would have no idea, or only a vague one, that it was happening. The action could hardly be concealed from the Communist forces being bombed, who would also inform their Soviet allies. Kissinger's bet was that, having taken note of American resolve, they would choose not to escalate in turn.

The first missions, by B-52 bombers based in Guam, began two days later. Pilots were given one set of targets before taking off, then diverted in the air to their true objectives in Cambodia and instructed to make no mention of the change in their subsequent debriefings. Most of their mission records would therefore indicate that the planes had struck sites in Vietnam. The supervisor of the relevant American radar crews was ordered to collect the few documents that showed otherwise and incinerate them.

In the narrowest terms, the gamble succeeded. Sihanouk's protests were muted, and a few months afterward, he formally restored diplomatic ties with the US. Word of the Breakfast strikes and subsequent missions did leak to the American press, but in a pre-internet news environment, it "aroused no public interest," as the journalist William Shawcross later wrote. (The coverage nonetheless prompted a search for leaks in the Nixon administration, leading to the illegal wiretap by the FBI of a White House aide—an early example of the practices whose exposure would end Nixon's presidency.)

Before precision-targeted weapons, B-52s carried thirty-ton loads of unguided bombs. Each was assigned to hit a two-mile-long "box"— about the distance between the Lincoln Memorial and the Capitol in Washington, DC. None of the boxes contained the Communists' supposed rear headquarters, which never existed. Most, if not all, were home to at least some civilians, though the precise number of casualties has never been documented. The Vietnamese, meanwhile, responded by shifting their operations farther into the interior of Cambodia. This brought their estimated thirty thousand troops closer to populated areas, where they could destabilize Sihanouk's regime, and ultimately into more regular interaction with the Khmer Rouge. Saloth Sar's guerrillas had continued attacking government positions, and were winning support among peasants attracted, as in Vietnam and China, by the promise of a better life under communism.

As chaos and violence roiled his country, Sihanouk did what any leader confronted with a crisis might do: He presided over a film festival, held in Phnom Penh in November 1969. For the judges' consideration, he entered *Twilight*, a saccharine romance starring himself and his wife. He was also the director, producer, narrator, and screenwriter, and provided the musical score. The film won first prize: a solid-gold statue forged from the reserves of Cambodia's central bank.

The people around Sihanouk were growing impatient with his antics, and with the expanding Vietnamese presence. In January 1970, he left the country for an extended trip, "taking a cure" on the French Riviera. Sihanouk was thus unable to intervene when the general he'd appointed as his prime minister, Lon Nol, joined forces with a vehemently pro-American, anti-Communist member of a rival royal line. On March 18, they staged a coup. Within hours, the Cambodian National Assembly decreed that "Prince Sihanouk shall cease his function as Chief of State."

Officials in Washington quickly grasped that Cambodia's new rulers might be more useful to them. Just after they seized power, the Nixon administration effectively declared that it viewed Lon Nol as Sihanouk's legitimate successor. Within a few weeks, Nixon would tell Kissinger by phone to "get the CIA jerks working on Cambodia." The US, the president said, was "supporting the government in power"—the one led by Lon Nol. "If anyone disagrees," Nixon barked, "I want his resignation on my desk by noon." (It was just after 11:30 a.m.)

After dominating Cambodia for more than twenty years, Sihanouk might have taken his ouster as a chance to retire, probably to a well-appointed corner of France, and amuse himself with movies, music, and mistresses. Instead, he flew to a destination with fewer amenities: Mao's Beijing. There, in his unmistakable, high-pitched voice, Sihanouk delivered an address to the Cambodian people, broadcast into the country by radio.

Adopting the vocabulary of the rebels he'd previously promised to crush, he urged his compatriots to revolt against the "reactionary clique" in Phnom Penh, "and their masters, the American imperialists." He announced the formation of a National United Front devoted to taking back Cambodia through "guerrilla warfare in the jungle against our enemies." It would be supported by China and North Vietnam, who issued their own statements in support of Sihanouk. And soon, its principal fighting force would be the Khmer Rouge.

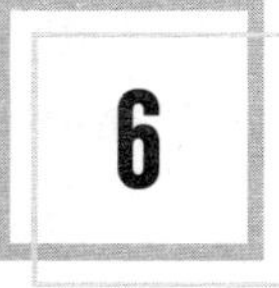

Douglas Latchford rang in the 1970s in style, at a packed New Year's Eve gala in Bangkok's Rama Hotel. At thirty-eight, he remained a powerful presence in his pinstripe suit, a head or more taller than most Thais. The evening was merry. A mix of expatriates and wealthy locals thronged the dance floor, some in goofy paper hats, others smiling from ear to ear as they toasted with coupes of Champagne. For friends who were still ambulatory the next day, Latchford was hosting a buffet lunch at his new house in central Bangkok. "If they happen to fall in the pool and hear heavenly music, they are not to worry," wrote the *Bangkok Post*'s social columnist. "It is merely Douglas' new underwater stereo set." The twenty-four-year-old who'd made his way to Thailand in 1956, with no formal credentials and little understanding of his new home, would perhaps not recognize the man he had become, a prosperous fixture on Bangkok's expat scene. But here Latchford was, and the new decade would bring even more dramatic changes in his life, starting with a surprising milestone: marriage.

His bride, Phuangpaka Tarmallpark, was more than fifteen years his junior and came from a Thai family that had grown wealthy during Bangkok's postwar boom by importing office equipment. The Tarmallparks had sent Phuangpaka to the UK, France, and Switzerland to be educated. When Latchford met her, she was working at the local office of an American baby-formula company. Why he chose to marry is a mystery. Living as a confirmed bachelor might attract nasty whispers in London, but in freewheeling Bangkok, it carried less stigma. Even so, it appeared that Latchford wanted to remain at least officially in the closet—with a homelife to match.

His sexuality might have been unconventional, but Latchford's idea of matrimony was not. He soon demanded that Phuangpaka leave her job to become a housewife. By early 1971, she was pregnant, and in September of that year, she gave birth to a daughter, Julia. With a young family and a thriving career, Latchford was outwardly the picture of respectability. Unusually for an expatriate, he'd become a naturalized Thai citizen and taken a Thai name, Pakpong Kriangsak, that he used in official settings. He would soon engineer a deal to buy out the local operations of Wheelock Marden, where he'd worked since 1963, a transaction that would deliver considerable financial benefits. And he hosted regular parties, though even as he gained wealth and status, guests could still be startled by Latchford's indifference to conversation that didn't directly pertain to him or his interests—principally, Cambodian antiquities, which enthralled him above all else.

Through study, travel, and incessant acquisitions, he had developed an encyclopedic knowledge of Khmer civilization. Some archaeologists and art historians in the field looked down at dealers, viewing them as dilettantes who'd never put in the effort required for true mastery. Latchford's view was almost the exact opposite. He may not have had formal training, but he'd been examining sculptures and exploring lost temple-cities in Thailand and Cambodia for more than a decade, seeing and touching them firsthand. To him, even a doctorate's worth of research couldn't compare to that real-world experience.

By 1974, he had realized another ambition by opening a high-end gallery, a place where he could display his best pieces to potential buyers and boast about how unique they were. The showroom was located on Bangkok's main commercial thoroughfare, Sukhumvit Road, and hosted a rotating selection of Khmer statues for sale at rich prices. Latchford had recently donated three objects to the British Museum, including a beautifully carved lintel, a stone block that would have been placed above the door of a temple. It depicted two figures—probably the Hindu god Shiva and his consort, Parvati—seated on a bull. Below them was a toothy, fearsome makara, a mythical sea creature frequently presented as a guardian of holy places. For a rising dealer, such donations served a dual purpose. They contributed to public awareness of Khmer history, a pursuit close to Latchford's heart. They also helped legitimize one's status as a connoisseur. If Latchford's pieces were fit for one of London's most prestigious cultural institutions, he obviously possessed a fine eye.

All the while, he was continuing to develop his relationships with buyers in Europe and the US, always with a focus on the top. One of the visitors to Latchford's Bangkok home was Sherman Lee, the director of the Cleveland Museum of Art. An eminent historian of Asian art, Lee was a hero in the field, already on his way to transforming the Midwestern institution into one of America's finest. For someone in Latchford's position, even to have a conversation with him counted as a sign of legitimacy. Latchford evidently felt it went well enough that two years later, he wrote to Lee in Ohio, asking for advice on pinning down the date and style of a twenty-eight-inch stone figure he had recently obtained. Lee responded graciously, prompting Latchford to write with further queries and some light flattery. "The amount of people that one can communicate with on the style, beauty, etc., is very limited, so please do forgive me if I bombard you with questions," he signed off.

Before Lee could reply again, Latchford sent a follow-up note—one that suggested he was eager to switch into salesman mode. This time, the subject was a trove of painted pottery recently excavated in northeast Thailand, not far from the Cambodian border—some of which Latchford had acquired. "I am enclosing a photograph of one that I have," he told the American. "If you are interested please do let me know."

By the spring of 1970, it was impossible to explore the temples of Angkor, as Latchford had so relished doing in earlier years. Since the coup against Norodom Sihanouk, Cambodia had exploded into civil war. On one side were the North Vietnamese and the Cambodian Communists—the Khmer Rouge—under the banner of the exiled prince's United Front. On the other was General Lon Nol's anti-Communist government, which was rapidly becoming a client of the Nixon administration.

At 9:00 p.m. on April 30, Nixon addressed the nation from the White House. Ten days before, he had announced plans to withdraw 150,000 US service members from Vietnam. "I was making that decision," Nixon said, "despite our concern over increased enemy activity" throughout the region. Since then, "North Vietnam has increased its military aggression in all these areas, and particularly in Cambodia."

He declared that US forces would enter Cambodia in pursuit of communist sanctuaries—this time with none of the subterfuge that surrounded the earlier B-52 strikes. To Nixon, events in a place that most Americans couldn't find on a map now presented a fundamental test of resolve: "If, when the chips are down, the world's most powerful nation . . . acts like a pitiful, helpless giant, the forces of totalitarianism and anarchy will threaten free nations and free institutions throughout the world."

In popular American memory, the invasion of Cambodia has been subsumed by the broader tragedy of the Vietnam War. At the time, however, it was understood as a discrete outrage. Within hours of Nixon's announcement, campuses across the country erupted in protest, with activists calling for a national student strike. On May 4, members of the Ohio National Guard opened fire on demonstrating students at Kent State University, killing four and providing a new locus of anger for the anti-war movement.

In the meantime, Nixon's Cambodian allies were losing control. By early summer, the front line ran directly through Siem Reap. Travel by road was prohibitively dangerous, leaving the city dependent on a daily resupply flight from Phnom Penh. The Grand Hotel was now a command post for Cambodia's army; more of Lon Nol's soldiers had set up artillery positions on an adjacent sports field. Just to the north, Communist forces were dug into the temples of the Angkor complex, where thick stone walls built by Khmer kings protected them from small-arms fire. American warplanes roared overhead; amid public disapproval and congressional opposition, Nixon would pull out US ground troops after two months of combat, although air support and huge shipments of supplies to the Lon Nol government continued.

Not for the first time, the White House had thrown its support behind a leader totally unsuited to the task of defeating a disciplined insurgency. Lon Nol was erratic even before being struck, in 1971, by a severe stroke. He had a long-standing interest in mysticism and encouraged Cambodian soldiers to adopt occult practices, such as the wearing of Buddhist amulets that would supposedly shield them from harm. His commanders included characters like Um Savuth, a hard-drinking officer who was partly paralyzed after an insane, William Tell–style stunt; depending on the source, it involved either a cat or a milk tin, which Um Savuth placed on his head and demanded that a subordinate shoot off. And corruption undermined the war effort at every level. In Phnom Penh, almost any category of US military aid was available for purchase, including rations, helmets, mosquito nets, and boots—while some Cambodian soldiers fought barefoot.

By mid-1972, the Khmer Rouge's military had ballooned to thirty-five thousand men, supplied from China via the Ho Chi Minh Trail. Steadily, they supplanted the North Vietnamese as the main Communist force in Cambodia, a development that their leader viewed as crucially important. The man born under the name Saloth Sar was now known as Pol Pot, an alias chosen for reasons he never publicly explained. Like many of his compatriots, he was suspicious of Cambodia's larger neighbor, even if the Khmer Rouge and the Hanoi government were nominally on the same side. Pol Pot was determined to ensure that the revolution he envisioned would be made real by Cambodians, not foreigners.

From nearly the start of the war, cultural leaders understood what such intense combat could mean for Cambodia's historical inheritance. As fighting reached the center of Angkor, the Met's director,

Thomas Hoving, joined a group of New York art figures in sending a telegram to Nixon, urging him to see to it that the temples weren't damaged by American strikes. They sent a similar plea to the North Vietnamese. In Siem Reap, French and Cambodian curators planned the evacuation of the Conservation d'Angkor, a large storehouse where they kept artifacts that were undergoing restoration. They gathered the pieces that they deemed most significant, excluding those too big or too fragile to be moved. Around one hundred sculptures, along with bronze works and ceramics, made the final list and were loaded into a convoy of fifteen heavy trucks, which were then driven under armed escort to the relative safety of Phnom Penh. More than four thousand sculptures were left behind at the conservancy, which the curators did their best to fortify with sandbags and reinforced concrete.

These measures succeeded, for the most part, in protecting Angkor and its artworks from stray bombs and artillery rounds. But they couldn't prevent a different kind of destruction that accompanied the fighting. In 1970, a young US Navy intelligence officer, H. Lawrence Serra, was stationed on the border between Cambodia and Vietnam. Serra had developed about half a dozen Cambodian sources, mostly traders and businessmen who crossed the frontier frequently. His primary mandate was to keep an eye on communist supply lines, and especially on the flow of Chinese weapons, then send his observations onward, by encrypted message, to the American headquarters in Saigon. But one day in June, Serra received a very different kind of intelligence. It was a dispatch from one of his assets in Cambodia, written on rice paper in elegant French script. The man reported that North Vietnamese soldiers in the Angkor area were hacking sculptures and bas-reliefs out of temples to sell them on the black market. Where the artifacts went after being stolen, he didn't say.

In 1973, less than two years after she gave birth to their daughter, Latchford's wife demanded a divorce. She could no longer ignore his true sexual orientation. In Phuangpaka's telling, Latchford reacted furiously, screaming and swearing at her, then kicking her out of the house along with their child, Julia. She responded by filing a lawsuit in a Thai court, claiming that Latchford's "defective penis" left him "unable to pleasure his wife, showing no interest in the opposite sex but being satisfied with the same sex." On the grounds of "severe mental distress," Phuangpaka asked the court to order a separation and a division of assets. A Western businessman accused of wronging a wealthy Thai woman, and in such salacious terms, was an irresistible story, and the suit was picked up by *Thairath*, a Bangkok tabloid. Amid the publicity, the split proceeded. Julia would remain with her mother throughout her childhood, seeing Latchford only as a visitor.

This embarrassment didn't prevent him from deepening a series of professional relationships that would serve him for decades. In particular, Latchford was fast becoming a trusted partner to Spink & Son in London. Spink's, as the company was known, had been founded in 1666 and boasted a pair of royal warrants—as "medallists" to both Queen Elizabeth II and the Duke of Edinburgh. It was also Britain's premier source for Asian antiquities, a category in which it rivaled the better-known Christie's and Sotheby's. And despite—or perhaps because of—the ongoing conflict in Southeast Asia, Spink's buyers suddenly wanted Khmer works, and were willing to pay unprecedented prices for them. "They were available, they were beautiful, and there were none in museums," a London dealer who was active in the early 1970s recalled. "They became a sort of aesthetic and cultural ideal." As interest rose, Latchford positioned himself as Spink's main Khmer supplier, becoming so dominant that he appeared to have a near monopoly on the artifacts that made it to the UK.

The business had changed in another important respect, too. Since long before Latchford began his career as a serious dealer, the trade in Khmer artifacts had been an illicit one: Cambodia had clear rules against looting and unauthorized exports. Before the civil war, getting around this was simply a matter of ignoring the laws of a small, poor country, one of many archaeologically rich nations without the resources for enforcement. Now, with intense fighting occurring at ancient sites, the situation was different. The conflict had sparked an explosion in looting, particularly of the largest, most impressive works—near-life-size statues whose theft might have attracted too much attention in peacetime. Some were removed by temple robbers who took advantage of the chaos, using the breakdown in security to stage more audacious raids. Others, as Serra's intelligence suggested, were almost certainly being stolen by the forces fighting for control. In either case, the dealers who handled and sold them were profiting directly from Cambodia's agony.

There's no evidence that this perturbed Latchford, and American and European buyers remained remarkably incurious about the origins of the pieces they acquired from him; indeed, it would be decades before concerns about provenance seriously affected the market. Nonetheless, they wanted certain assurances, if only to avoid the risk of future trouble—especially after the 1970 UNESCO convention, which provided a framework for source countries to reclaim artworks. To make major sales, Latchford needed to provide a minimally plausible origin story, whatever the truth really was. In May 1974, a Spink's executive wrote to him about an object from Funan, a Hinduized maritime kingdom that predated Angkor. A customer was interested and had been quoted a "special price" of £460,000, but was anxious about violating the UN rules. "Naturally, I have not mentioned where it was found, nor any further details," the Spink's man wrote. "I think it is very important to see that one story is maintained and I hope that you will see that there are no loose ends on which we can be caught."

Soon, Latchford and one of Spink's managers, an energetic former Royal Air Force pilot named Adrian Maynard, were closing in on an even bigger prize: a five-foot-tall stone statue that was one of the most remarkable either of them had ever encountered. Somehow, its sculptors had succeeded in capturing a kind of motion. The male figure had a powerful chest, large round eyes, and plump lips curled into a hint of a smile. It seemed to be almost bouncing on bent knees—an athlete or warrior, ready to spring into action. The effect was spellbinding.

Based on the style, Latchford could say with confidence that the statue dated to the tenth century and originated from Koh Ker, the remote temple-city that had briefly served as the Khmer capital in that period. Compared with the more stoic, angular figures seen in other Cambodian statuary, Koh Ker pieces were unmistakably expressive, almost sensual. Latchford found them more mesmerizing than anything else produced by the Khmer civilization. No one knew why one city, over a period of just a few decades, had developed such a unique artistic style, nor could anyone say why that style had disappeared after the center of the kingdom shifted back to Angkor. Events in the more recent past presented a significant problem, however.

The head and then the torso of the figure, as well as another of the same size that stood opposite, had been looted from Koh Ker and moved out of Cambodia in 1972. (The severed parts were later reattached.) As Latchford almost certainly knew, Koh Ker was, by that time, deep inside the combat zone of the civil war. To have any hope of selling the statue, which they referred to as a "guardian," the British pair would need a cover story. "I have a man who is interested in the big guardian but he wants a provenance for it, or an export licence," Maynard wrote to Latchford in late 1974, something that he conceded "sounds crazy." He asked Latchford to "put your thinking cap on and see whether you can find a way round it."

Shortly afterward, one of Maynard's colleagues, Isidor Kahane, visited Latchford in Bangkok. By the time he left, they had a plan. It involved Peng Seng, the Thai-Chinese merchant who'd been a prominent local dealer since the 1950s. Kahane wrote that he had "explored extensively with Peng Seng and Latchford how to get 'legitimate' papers for the large Koh Ker guardian." Specifically, he said, "Peng Seng will send us a letter written and signed by somebody in Bangkok. He will say that he [saw] this piece in Peng Seng's shop three years ago." This would serve as apparent evidence that it had been in Thailand since before Cambodia's ratification of the UNESCO treaty. Kahane explained that Spink's could specify precisely which boxes needed to be ticked: "Peng Seng would like us to give him the exact text that we want in this letter."

7

A little before dawn on August 6, 1973, an American B-52 passed over Neak Luong, a small town on the Mekong south of Phnom Penh. On the ground, Cambodian Army personnel activated a radio beacon to direct the eight-engine plane to its target. But as it neared the release point, a navigator on board made a mistake. He forgot to toggle a control called an offset bombing switch, which meant that the aircraft would not drop its payload over the intended location. Instead, it would home in on the beacon itself, which was mounted to a pole in the center of Neak Luong.

More than twenty tons of bombs fell on the town—an event that one US embassy official initially described as "no great disaster." Homes, shops, and much of the central market were flattened, along with perhaps a third of the local hospital. Entire families were killed as they slept, leaving ripped flesh and scraps of clothing strewn through the streets. Many of the other victims were Cambodian soldiers—the very troops that US raids were supposed to be supporting. In all, 137 people were left dead.

It was a particularly ugly episode in a brutal and counterproductive campaign. In 1973, airstrikes in Cambodia were being planned by American military staff in Phnom Penh. Their maps were printed at a scale of one to fifty thousand and were often out of date, failing to reflect the movements of refugees. Civilians died by the tens of thousands, though historians have never disentangled the number of these casualties from the overall toll of the civil war. A similarly unknowable number of Cambodians were driven by the deaths of their families into supporting the Khmer Rouge. None of this deterred Lon Nol and his generals from maintaining an almost supernatural faith in the efficacy of airpower. The Cambodian leader had a habit, after an enemy formation was ordered bombed, of simply erasing it from the map of the forces opposing him.

The truth was, of course, more complicated. Militarily, it's not clear that the strikes did anything more than slow the Khmer Rouge down. And just a week after the Neak Luong accident, Lon Nol lost the ability to call in the US Air Force at all. An increasingly hostile Congress had mandated a halt to all US-led air operations after August 15. American planes had hit Cambodia with around five hundred thousand tons of ordnance, half of it since the beginning of the year. By comparison, the volume of bombs dropped on Japan during the entirety of World War II was well under two hundred thousand tons.

Free of American attacks, the Khmer Rouge steadily expanded the territory under their control. In rural areas, they arrived in communities where Cambodians went about their lives much as they had for centuries, even since the time of the Angkorian kings: farming their paddies, celebrating Buddhist festivals, and trying to stay out of the way of predatory officials. At first, it was possible to take a sanguine view of Pol Pot's men. The guerrillas wore the same black pajama-style clothing as the peasantry, accented with a traditional checked scarf called a krama and sandals with soles cut from tire treads. They forsook bribes and behaved courteously, helping farmers plow their fields and compensating villagers for requisitioned property. Khmer Rouge members avoided even using the term *Communist*; officially, all belonged to an entity called Angka, the Organization, devoted to Cambodian self-reliance and the betterment of ordinary people. Those who didn't interfere were largely left alone.

None of this meant, however, that it was wise to defy Angka. To be deemed an opponent was to risk execution—perhaps, in the Khmer Rouge fashion, with a hoe to the back of the head. And as they consolidated their control over the countryside in 1973 and 1974, they began to implement a much more ambitious program. Lenin and Mao had set out to transform the societies they ruled. For Pol Pot, the goal was destruction: of urban life, of the family, of even the idea of the self. Only by starting from a blank slate, he believed, could Cambodians be marshaled to create a new kind of nation. In this twisted utopia, all vestiges of capitalism and individuality would be absent. Instead, citizens would work as one to grow rice, build irrigation canals, and manufacture tools, subordinating every personal need to the good of the collective. This governing philosophy was both radical and austere, enforced with pitiless discipline.

The most important step was the establishment of agricultural cooperatives, surrounded by no-man's-lands from which families were forcibly relocated. Those who protested might be taken away and never seen again. Others died during the journeys to their new homes, some of which were in remote jungles. Possessions and land were seized and then redistributed. The Khmer Rouge then set about rupturing the bonds between parents and children, taking young people away from their homes and indoctrinating them to respect the authority of Angka over that of their elders.

While this process continued, Pol Pot intensified his parallel campaign against the Lon Nol government. One by one, his fighters cut off the roads to Phnom Penh, leaving the airport, and the occasional convoy up the Mekong, as the only means of bringing in food and ammunition. Soon even those river journeys were too dangerous, as guerrillas raked freighters with machine-gun fire. Swollen by refugees, who arrived from their villages in ragged caravans of oxcarts, the city's population soared from a prewar total of about six hundred thousand to two million or more. Amid food shortages and hyperinflation, many were starving. Each day, weeping parents, surviving relatives, or total strangers carried listless children, already half dead, into a handful of clinics. Overwhelmed doctors had no choice but to turn many of them away.

Still, a fortunate, mostly foreign elite was able to maintain a not-unpleasant lifestyle. American supply flights were hopelessly inadequate to meet the nutritional needs of the Cambodian capital. But at the right price, such provisions as fresh lobster and good French wines were freely available, especially at the Hotel Le Royal, the city's best, and its outdoor restaurant, La Sirène. Journalists found the situation particularly commodious. There weren't many postings that offered such proximity to combat, and the prospect of regularly landing on the front page, with no loss of material comforts. As one correspondent recalled, it was possible for reporters to "ride out, catch an unpleasant whiff of cordite in their nostrils and be back at Le Royal for breakfast by the pool."

By the spring of 1975, the Khmer Rouge were preparing for their final assault on Phnom Penh. The war clearly lost, Lon Nol agreed at the start of April to step down. In a final transmission, the US ambassador informed Washington: "Embassy Phnom Penh is closing down its communication facilities." Protected by US Marines and carrying a folded Stars and Stripes, the American walked to a helicopter that was waiting on a nearby sports field to fly him out of the country. Khmer Rouge mortars streaked onto the landing zone as the last chopper took off.

No one could be sure what the future held. Cambodians with money or foreign connections got out on the final flights to Bangkok, rockets arcing over the tarmac. Of those left behind, some were guardedly optimistic, reasoning that life under the Khmer Rouge couldn't be worse than what they'd just endured. Elements of the remnant population of foreigners, a mix of reporters, doctors, and aid workers, engaged in one final bacchanal, emptying the wine cellars or, in the case of a young Frenchwoman, making love to two different partners in the pool of Le Royal—one at the deep end, the other at the shallow—while diners applauded from La Sirène.

Khmer Rouge forces entered Phnom Penh on April 17. The government radio station aired some valedictory bars of music, then went silent. Soldiers of the Cambodian Army, with no orders for what to do next, removed their rifles' magazines and awaited their fate. In simple black uniforms, laden with bandoliers and clutching AK-47s, the Khmer Rouge arrived on foot in disorganized groups. Many of the fighters were startlingly young—teenagers who'd just defeated an opponent furnished with all that the American military-industrial complex could provide. They appeared astonished by the infrastructure of a modern city, with its broad boulevards and multistory buildings. Abandoned cars were everywhere. Seeing an opportunity, the fighters began to remove the tires of the vehicles. Then they cut up the treads to make new soles for their sandals.

Eleven time zones away from Phnom Penh, Thomas Hoving was fully absorbed in his ambitious plan to overhaul New York's Metropolitan Museum of Art. The early 1970s had seen a steady expansion of interest in Asian cultures, some of it tied to the embrace, on both American coasts, of Eastern-inflected practices like transcendental meditation. When it came to Asian art, however, the Met had serious competition—from established institutions such as the Smithsonian, in Washington, DC, as well as upstarts like the tycoon Norton Simon, who'd just set up an eponymous museum in California. In March 1975, the Met opened a new exhibition, *Bronze Sculptures from Asia*, to show off some of the early fruits of Hoving's effort to assemble a world-class collection of South and Southeast Asian works. Organized by a young curator named Martin Lerner, it featured as its centerpiece a stunning eleventh-century sculpture of a "kneeling queen," clasping her hands above her head in a gesture of veneration.

Lerner devoted almost two pages of the exhibition catalog to the sculpture, which he said might be "the single most important and beautiful Khmer bronze outside of Cambodia." In his essay, Lerner was silent as to how it might have come to *be* outside Cambodia, although the statue's entry onto the market was undoubtedly recent. The Met had purchased it just three years earlier from a Manhattan dealer, Doris Wiener, and there's no evidence, such as previous publication in a catalog or display by another museum, that it had prior international owners. Even as *The New York Times* ran regular, above-the-fold stories about the advances of the Khmer Rouge, the paper's chief art critic was as unconcerned as the trustees of the Met with the provenance of the "magnificent bronze," which he credited with dominating the show. "This unpretentious exhibition," the critic wrote, "has an elegance and a profundity that many a more elaborate one strives for and fails to achieve." It was just the kind of coverage that Thomas "Publicity Forever" Hoving craved.

Although Douglas Latchford would eventually build an extensive business relationship with Wiener, it's not clear whether he sourced the Kneeling Queen for her. There is no doubt, however, that he and his partners at Spink's were benefiting from the art-world buzz that such museum acquisitions generated. Around the same time as the Met exhibition, Spink's executives successfully imported the five-foot standing Guardian, looted from Koh Ker during the chaos of the civil war, that Latchford had helped them determine how to transport to London without attracting unwanted scrutiny. They photographed the statue from all angles and featured it in the September 1975 issue of their in-house magazine, *Octagon*, above a reminder that "all illustrated items are for sale." It was now sitting in their showroom near St. James's Square, waiting for a buyer rich enough to afford it—and to accept Spink's assurances that it had been obtained legitimately.

By the end of the year, such a buyer had emerged: a Belgian businessman who'd made so much money running garages in Brussels that he was known as the city's "King Parking." A Spink's receipt recorded the description of the piece ("a highly important buff sandstone Guardian figure of heroic proportions") and the sale price (£105,000), equivalent today to about £800,000, or just over $1 million.

8

Within hours of taking control of Phnom Penh on April 17, 1975, young Khmer Rouge fighters fanned out through the capital, shouting a single order: Everyone had to begin marching out of the city immediately. The command even applied to hospitals, and soon families were pushing patients through the streets on their gurneys, still attached to IV drips, passing amputees who shuffled along the pavement. Some Khmer Rouge said that the evacuation was necessary because American bombing was imminent. Others mostly communicated by firing their rifles into the air. When they were asked how evacuees would be fed or housed, the fighters simply said that Angka, the mysterious Organization to which they belonged, would provide.

What occurred next was perhaps the fastest displacement of a large population in history: Some two million people walked out of Phnom Penh, clutching what possessions they could. April is the hottest month of the year in Southeast Asia, and many collapsed from exhaustion. Heedless, the columns kept moving, watched over by black-clad soldiers. In some places, they had set up loudspeakers to broadcast screeching propaganda slogans:

"Resolutely maintain high revolutionary vigilance to defend the Cambodian nation and people at all times!"

"Resolutely maintain the position of struggle to defend the country and people without hesitation!"

For a time, merchants set up roadside stalls selling food in exchange for riel, the currency of the defeated Lon Nol government. But before long, the pavement was dotted with discarded banknotes. Cambodians had grasped that the money no longer carried any value. The only way to buy food, or anything else, was through barter.

In pursuit of total self-reliance, the Khmer Rouge had sealed the country's borders and canceled virtually all international flights. They cut phone lines and terminated overseas mail service, ensuring that little news of what was occurring filtered into the outside world. The foreigners who remained in Phnom Penh were confined to the French embassy and eventually driven to the Thai border. They bore fragments of information, gleaned from what they'd been able to directly observe, as well as snatches of gossip from passersby. Cambodians who'd also managed to escape filled in some of the gaps for journalists, who did their best to make sense of the situation. But none could yet grasp the enormity of what Pol Pot intended: the erasure of an entire society, and its replacement with a system of complete totalitarian control.

Gradually, the Khmer Rouge herded the former residents of Phnom Penh and other urban centers toward their new homes—rural communes where they would be reeducated as ideal socialist citizens, willing to perform whatever tasks the revolution demanded of them without complaint. Almost no one would be permitted to remain in the cities, where commerce and education had provided paths to advancement. In the communes, professional skills were irrelevant.

Worse, in fact. Those who revealed that they had advanced educations or overseas contacts risked being tarred as class enemies, with potentially deadly consequences. Even the staff of the Conservation d'Angkor, who'd continued working to preserve artifacts while the civil war raged around them, were sent into the rice fields.

After days of marching into the interior, first on paved highways and then along a narrow dirt road, Khmer Rouge overseers guided a column of evacuees to Koh Ker. As they entered the tenth-century temple-city that so captivated Douglas Latchford, they passed fresh graves, dug for soldiers of the vanquished Cambodian army who had been killed amid the ruins. This was the exact same place where, three years earlier, the huge Guardian statue that Latchford had helped sell to a Belgian parking tycoon had been ripped from its pedestal.

Just beyond, there was a small village. "Cadres," as Khmer Rouge officials were known, informed its residents that they would now live communally with the arrivals from Phnom Penh. They were made to give up their personal belongings, which were gathered into a central storehouse. Like most Cambodians, the villagers were Buddhist. They nevertheless revered Koh Ker's Hindu temples, viewing their statues as avatars of the divine and vessels for the spirits of their ancestors. The community punctuated the passing of the seasons by holding festivals inside the ancient complex, the men playing music while women danced. But the Khmer Rouge had no tolerance for what they viewed as superstitious rituals, and Koh Ker was abandoned, left to the elephants and tigers who occasionally moved through. Looting largely ceased, which meant, for a time, that Latchford's supply had dried up.

Angka's authority over Koh Ker was now supreme. Hard labor was expected of everyone, even the youngest. Cadres organized "child units" to work the rice fields or look after livestock; schooling, if it happened at all, took place for perhaps an hour per day, between shifts. The experience of a boy named Lim Sotr was typical. Born in Koh Ker, he was barely a teenager in 1975. The Khmer Rouge took him from his parents and assigned him to a "mobile brigade" tasked with hauling loads of soil to build canals. Work began at dawn and continued without interruption until about midday, when he and the rest of his unit broke for the first of two daily meals of thin rice porridge. Then they worked until the light faded.

The rations were far too meager for such physical exertion, and Lim Sotr saw many of his fellow laborers succumb to starvation or disease. An uncountable number of people were dying in the same ways, their conditions exacerbated by a Khmer Rouge conviction that modern medicine was another capitalist luxury that Cambodia could do without. Care was sometimes provided by "child doctors" who barely knew how to read. By contrast, senior cadres lived well. In nearly empty Phnom Penh, Pol Pot's lieutenants were growing fat.

Soon, Lim Sotr could think of little other than his next bowl of porridge. He nevertheless lived in fear of a more acute peril than starvation. It was too easy to be accused of harboring incorrect ideas, or of the counterrevolutionary act of foraging for food, which betrayed a lack of faith in Angka's ability to meet the needs of the people. Most terrifying of all was to come under suspicion of being "CIA"—an allegation that flattered the agency, which had long since lost the ability to operate in Cambodia. In a vast proportion of cases, the penalty was imprisonment and torture, followed by execution.

Such a revolution could not long proceed without devouring its children, and Koh Ker was no exception. Some decided to take action before they were thrown into the Khmer Rouge penal system, beginning a process that could only have one outcome. Around 1977, a local commune leader was suspected of treachery. The loyalty of other senior cadres in the area had been called into similar doubt, and they had disappeared. This man was well liked by the villagers, but that was no defense. Before he could be taken away, he walked up to a rain tree in a nearby field and hanged himself.

During the initial phases of this destruction, Pol Pot was publicly silent, and largely unknown beyond Phnom Penh. The head of state of Democratic Kampuchea, as the Khmer Rouge called their new polity, was Prince Sihanouk, though they eventually discarded this pretense and placed Cambodia's former ruler under house arrest. Only gradually did they articulate the ideology that cadres were putting into practice in places like Koh Ker. In 1976, the Khmer Rouge published a short constitution. "There is absolutely no unemployment in Democratic Kampuchea," it declared in one article. Another stated, without addressing the inherent contradiction, that "every citizen of Kampuchea has the right to worship according to any religion," but "reactionary religions . . . are absolutely forbidden."

Around the same time, the government formally abolished money, making official what evacuees from Phnom Penh had come to understand on the roads out of the capital. Among the totalitarian governments of the twentieth century, this was unprecedented. In the summation of the biographer Philip Short, Pol Pot's regime amounted to a "slave state, the first in modern times." Even during the most extreme periods in China and the Soviet Union, Short wrote, workers received nominal wages that provided "some measure of choice, even if it amounted to no more than whether to buy a packet of cigarettes or a tablet of soap once a month." By contrast, Cambodians were "deprived of all control over their own destinies—unable to decide what to eat, when to sleep, where to live or even whom to marry."

It wasn't lost on some observers that aspects of this system mimicked the Khmer Empire, which had also relied on the labor of enslaved people. In addition to constructing temples like those at Angkor, those slaves' task was often to build dams and dig canals—also a central focus of Khmer Rouge economic doctrine. And when he finally chose to reveal himself to the world, through an extended speech in the autumn of 1977, Pol Pot made the parallels between the ancient and modern regimes explicit.

Much of his six-hour address repeated standard revolutionary language, promising that under his rule, Cambodia would become "an industrialized country by standing firmly on the principles of independence, initiative, and self-reliance." But Pol Pot also emphasized that the future he envisioned had a unique precedent: the power of the Khmer kings and of Angkor, whose spires were depicted at the center of his government's flag. (They also appeared on Khmer Rouge banknotes, which were printed but never used.) "We all know the Angkor of past times," Pol Pot declared. "If our people were capable of building Angkor, they can do anything."

Toek Tik was eleven years old when the Khmer Rouge arrived in his village during the early stages of the civil war—long before the assault on Phnom Penh, the forced marches out of the city, and Pol Pot's attempt to impose his vision of socialism onto the entire population. One of twenty-five children born to his father, Toek Tik lived in a thatched-roof hut close to the ruins of Koh Ker. Angka demanded the allegiance of everyone in the community, regardless of age, so he had little choice when he was told that he would serve as a messenger, carrying information between commanders in the field. While his assignment precluded formal education—Toek Tik would never learn to read or write beyond a rudimentary level—it spared him from involvement in the initial brutalities of the period, and it also meant that he could travel the countryside at a time when others were confined to their communes.

But he would not be permitted to remain a noncombatant for very long. As the conflict intensified, every able-bodied person was required on the front lines. Entering his teenage years, Toek Tik was no exception, and he became a soldier, joining the tens of thousands of guerrillas who helped bring the Khmer Rouge to power in 1975. The length of his service meant that after their victory, he belonged to the relatively privileged class of "old people" who had lived under the cadres already, as opposed to the "new people" they had just conquered. Supposedly less corrupted by foreign and capitalist influences, old people were more trusted and given accordingly greater autonomy.

For his part, Toek Tik had been given one of the most sacred duties of the revolution: the elimination of internal enemies. The people of every commune knew, and feared, those like him—stern, unforgiving figures in black, many of them little more than children, whose devotion to Angka appeared to outweigh any moral scruples. When a citizen was overheard making an ill-considered remark, or accused of failing to work hard enough, or suspected of some other act of disloyalty, it was they who appeared, uttering a chilling mantra: "To keep you is no benefit, to destroy you is no loss." It was they who oversaw the fetid Khmer Rouge prisons, structures of bamboo and corrugated metal where men and women alike, some of the latter pregnant, were chained to long blocks of wood and forced to lie in their own excrement as dysentery racked their bowels. And it was they, when Angka deemed the moment right, who marched those prisoners into a field at nightfall and administered the skull-shattering blows, before piling the bodies into shallow graves.

This was Toek Tik's lot for years, until he could no longer stomach such an existence. Not yet twenty, he had killed so many, so ruthlessly, that the act felt sickeningly meaningless. Nor could he be sure that the next grave he saw wouldn't be his own. Suspected of disloyalty, cadres he knew were disappearing, including his own commander. Despite spending his entire adolescence in the Khmer Rouge, he had concluded that he could trust no one.

For most in his position, attempting to leave the violence behind would have been impossible—and probably fatal. But Toek Tik was different. He was intimately familiar with the area around Koh Ker. A short distance away was Kulen Mountain, a long plateau covered in rugged jungle and shot through with caves—as well as ancient stone temples—where one might find refuge. What he had in mind was dangerous to the point of insanity, but he was determined to try it anyway. And so, as the Khmer Rouge continued to fertilize the killing fields with the corpses of his countrymen, Toek Tik slipped away and went on the run.

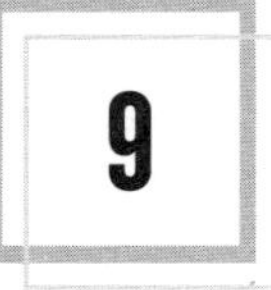

In fleeing from the Khmer Rouge, Toek Tik had made a lonely choice. There was virtually no one else on Kulen Mountain, the long plateau where he'd chosen to hide from the cadres, with their black uniforms, checkered scarves, and AK-47 rifles, who still governed the countryside. Over four hundred meters high, Kulen was enveloped in dense jungle, patrolled underfoot by huge Burmese pythons and overhead by silvered langurs, monkeys with shocks of fine gray hair framing their inquisitive faces. Clear streams meandered through the trees and plunged over waterfalls, descending to the plains below.

To survive, Toek Tik would have to evade both the Khmer Rouge and starvation. He studied the animals around him intently, sitting absolutely still as he observed how they had adapted to the landscape. Gradually, he learned to live off what the forest could provide: fruit, fish, and wild game. To shelter himself from the elements and passing predators—whether roaming cadres or hungry tigers—he slept in sandstone caves. He also took refuge in some of Kulen's many temples. In AD 802, the Khmer ruler Jayavarman II declared the independence of his kingdom from a city that stood on the plateau, a moment accepted by historians as the dawn of the Angkorian era.

Kulen was thenceforth treated as a sacred site, and artisans left behind a series of exquisite works there. These included the complex where Jayavarman II was said to have made his declaration, Prasat Rong Chen—the first of the Khmer civilization's pyramidal temple-mountains, an architectural form that would reach its apotheosis with Angkor Wat more than three centuries later. At another site, Kbal Spean, some one thousand lingas, representations of the power of the Hindu god Shiva, were carved into a riverbed alongside other images of deities.

As Toek Tik remained in hiding, cracks were beginning to emerge in the totalitarian state he'd risked his life to escape—a regime that had sought to associate itself directly with the power of the Angkorian kings. Unlike those monarchs, Pol Pot demanded a level of ideological commitment, and material deprivation, that was proving impossible to sustain. In early 1978, his government loosened a few of its more ferocious rules. Cooperative residents were now permitted to forage in the jungle for food, an act that was previously punishable by death, and to cook in their own homes. The pace of killing also slackened, as cadres were told to try to spare the lives of those who'd violated Khmer Rouge strictures. Instead, Pol Pot instructed them to ensure that offenders "mend their ways, achieve illumination and return to the bosom of the Party."

Cambodians still lived under some of the most brutal circumstances endured by any population in the twentieth century, and they remained too terrorized for organized opposition. The acute threats to Pol Pot came from abroad, where governments of diverse ideological orientations had concluded that his rule was unacceptable. As the international press uncovered more evidence of Khmer Rouge atrocities, President Jimmy Carter said that America had a "responsibility to speak out" against the regime, which he called "the worst violator of human rights in the world today." With the US still exhausted from its previous armed adventure in the region, there was little prospect of his words translating into action. Pol Pot's fellow Communists were less reluctant, although not out of concern for Cambodians' human rights.

As relations between the two socialist superpowers, China and the Soviet Union, deteriorated through the 1970s, Cambodia had aligned itself with Beijing. Vietnam, now united under the leadership of Hanoi, had thrown in its lot with Moscow. This was more than an ideological dispute. The Chinese and Soviets had already fought one border war, in 1969, and kept large military forces on their respective frontiers. Before 1975, Cambodian and North Vietnamese soldiers had fought side by side, but Hanoi now viewed the Khmer Rouge—fanatical, allied with China, and too geographically close for comfort—as a serious threat.

The end was swift. Fourteen divisions of Vietnamese troops invaded Cambodia on Christmas Day in 1978. Even if they hadn't been weakened by purges of supposed traitors, the Khmer Rouge were hopelessly outgunned. By early January, the Vietnamese were approaching Phnom Penh, moving so quickly that they were able to capture the bulk of the Cambodian air force, still on the tarmac. Pol Pot and his senior lieutenants fled, resolving to continue their fight as guerrillas. They left one last set of orders: At a former high school in central Phnom Penh known as S-21—where the regime interrogated, tortured, and then murdered its opponents—the remaining prisoners were put to death.

With the collapse of the Khmer Rouge, Cambodians who'd lived as slaves for nearly four years were suddenly free, emerging dazed and malnourished. Soon, great numbers were on the move. People dragged themselves onto the roads in halting processions, trying to return to their communities or simply looking for food—a desperate reversal of the march from Phnom Penh in April 1975. One of the signal cruelties of Pol Pot's regime had been its habit of separating families, taking children from parents, husbands from wives, brothers from sisters. With no means to locate their relatives, some of the refugees posted handwritten signs on trees along the way, leaving word of where they'd gone. In many cases, that was to the Thai border, prompting fears of a humanitarian crisis as they filled squalid refugee camps.

After taking control, Vietnam installed a puppet government. Many of its officials were Khmer Rouge defectors—cadres who'd decided to flee across the border before the invasion, rather than wait to see if they would be taken in the next purge. Though still committed Communists, they and their Vietnamese "advisers" were marginally more open to outsiders than Pol Pot, and in the summer of 1979, the world got its first glimpses of what had become of Cambodia. A small international delegation flew in, aiming to assess humanitarian needs.

Its members found that at one of Phnom Penh's main hospitals, just three doctors were attempting to treat more than eight hundred patients, without soap or sterilizing tools. The interpreters assigned to assist the group were prone to fainting, apparently from malnutrition. But what particularly disturbed these visitors, and others who followed, was the quiet that pervaded the country. In what had been a vibrant Asian capital, the streets were empty; outside the city, rice fields were untilled, villages abandoned. The Mekong, once thick with merchant vessels, flowed silently. One witness later compared the landscape to "the wake of a nuclear cataclysm which had spared only the buildings."

So extreme was their violence, and so complete their erasure of normal social structures, that the number of Cambodians killed by the Khmer Rouge is still unknown. Some estimates put the total between one and a half and two million, out of a prewar population of perhaps eight million. The oft-repeated claim that cadres marked for death anyone who wore eyeglasses is probably an exaggeration, but there's no question that educated people faced poor odds of survival. A startlingly low proportion of surviving refugees spoke French—an obvious marker of membership in the professional classes. There was almost no one left who had the training to operate a power plant or perform a surgery. Despite Pol Pot's professed admiration for the Khmer kings, the experts who understood their legacy had effectively been exterminated: In 1979, only three archaeologists were known to still be alive and in the country.

It was said, around this time, that the scale of the catastrophe could be understood through the way friends greeted one another after a long separation. Before 1975, the aphorism went, Cambodians would ask, "How many children do you have?" Under the Khmer Rouge, it became, "How much food do you get?" And afterward, in an encounter on the road or in one of the growing refugee settlements, the question was, "How many of your family are still alive?"

It was into this shattered society that Toek Tik emerged from his hiding place on Kulen Mountain. Living through the Khmer Rouge didn't mean he was safe. Hunger, disease, attacks by bandits—all were very real threats to his survival. But unlike many of his compatriots, who tried to improve their odds by setting out for Thailand, Toek Tik resolved to stay and rebuild his life in the region where he'd grown up. This required a considerable degree of enterprise. Toek Tik worked odd jobs, taking care of livestock and serving as a local policeman. He then began trading cattle, which were in desperately short supply amid the broader collapse of agriculture.

In the months after his departure from Kulen, Toek Tik happened to pick up an artifact—a Khmer Empire statue. He put it in his oxcart for one of his trading expeditions to the border, where much of the commerce of post–Khmer Rouge Cambodia took place. Then something happened that surprised him. When selling cows, Toek Tik was usually paid by barter; after the abolition of currency under Pol Pot, there was little money circulating. But for the statue he was carrying, he was offered cash—a relative pittance, but far better than nothing in a nation where many people still couldn't be sure how they would get their next meal.

Toek Tik gladly accepted the funds. He didn't know anything about the international art market or the evolving legal standards for the provenance of antiquities. He had never heard of the Met, nor, at that point, of a man named Douglas Latchford. But he did understand, better than most, that there was a great deal more where the artifact came from—in the huge monuments of Angkor, in the little-known temples on Kulen Mountain, and, above all, among the spectacular ruins of Koh Ker, near where he'd been raised. From that day on, Toek Tik was in the statue business.

10

When Jim Thompson was choosing a site for his home, which would serve as the center of expatriate social life in Bangkok, he selected a location on the banks of the Khlong Saen Saep, a brackish canal that runs through the heart of Thailand's capital. For Douglas Latchford, who had attempted to follow in Thompson's footsteps ever since coming to Asia as a young man, there was a certain poetry, then, in choosing a plot of land on the same watercourse, just a short distance away, to make his own mark on the city in the mid-1980s.

Whereas Thompson had built a graceful re-creation of a traditional Thai structure, Latchford had in mind something much more contemporary: one of Bangkok's first-ever high-rise condominium developments. It would tower over a very different landscape than the one that the American spy and art connoisseur knew. Since the rush of investment that had accompanied the US engagement in Vietnam, the metropolis had changed beyond recognition. Its population had more than doubled, exceeding five million in 1985. Wooden houses had given way to concrete office blocks, floating markets to air-conditioned department stores. Living there as a Westerner no longer required an adventurous spirit and a willingness to endure the privations of a developing country. Instead, Bangkok had become a place where the rich of many nations were betting that they could get richer, and where global corporations competed to dominate a fast-growing economy, developing everything from five-star hotels to electronics plants.

Thanks to Latchford's buyout of his former employer's Thai business, his resources had grown commensurately. He was now a wealthy man, and putting his money to work in the property market was an obvious opportunity. It helped that financing was cheap, with Thai and foreign banks eager to get in on the action. Latchford envisioned a building of unprecedented luxury, complete with a white marble swimming pool framed, at one end by a "Mughal pavilion" that housed a statue of a Hindu goddess. He intended to populate its thirty-one units exclusively with what he considered the right kinds of residents. In the main, this meant upmarket expatriates and moneyed, foreign-educated Thais, people of ample means and quiet sophistication. Anyone who might, for example, commit the faux pas of hanging their laundry on the balcony was not welcome.

Latchford hired a respected American architect, who designed a kind of postmodern ziggurat that would be clad, beautifully and expensively, in ocher-red terra-cotta tiles. Rising from its base, the tower would taper twice before terminating in a curved crown at its top story. In its stepped-back upward procession, the structure had a certain resemblance to the central pyramid at Koh Ker, a site that Latchford found endlessly interesting. Chidlom Place, as the project was named for an adjacent street, was completed in 1987. Latchford later moved in, relocating from his house nearby. His dalliance in real estate, however, was a sideline.

Latchford's true passion was still for antiquities, and he was reaching new heights as a dealer—even as conditions in Cambodia made it impossible to travel to Angkor or other ancient sites. Khmer Rouge guerrillas, led by Pol Pot, were engaged in a bloody insurgency against the Vietnamese-backed regime that had replaced them, and much of the country was extremely dangerous. And, in any case, it was very hard to get in. The government in Phnom Penh admitted few foreigners apart from citizens of allied socialist countries on official business. No Western expert had so much as seen Angkor, let alone more remote ruins like Koh Ker, since fighting overtook the complex in 1972.

But Latchford was now a player in the market of such importance that to source the best works for sale to museums and collectors, particularly in the US, he no longer had to go anywhere. The people who could move freely among the Khmer temples, and then transport the fruits of their work over the border and into Thailand, knew exactly where to find him.

With the end of their enslavement by the Khmer Rouge, villagers trickled back to the area around Koh Ker and set about rebuilding their devastated lives. Virtually everyone had lost a relative; some, many more than that. Those who had survived without physical injuries were traumatized psychologically, and it would be more than a generation before their community, and others throughout the Cambodian countryside, regained anything like a normal existence. The horrors they had endured between 1975 and 1979 would continue to haunt them, as would the horrors still to come.

Located a relatively short distance from Pol Pot's remaining jungle strongholds, Koh Ker was on the front line of the combat between the Khmer Rouge and forces aligned with the newly established Cambodian government. Vietnamese troops were dug into a base by the temple complex. Suspicious of the local population, they periodically accused villagers of aiding their enemies. Not long after they arrived, they alleged that a local rice farmer, a father of three young children, had been spying for the Khmer Rouge. The Vietnamese took him, along with others suspected of the same offense, to a prison in a nearby district. When rainstorms flooded the prison compound, the detainees drowned. As the brutalities continued, and as fighting in the area intensified, many decided to flee.

The resilience of the Khmer Rouge owed a great deal to a forgotten perversity of the Cold War, one that the passage of four decades has rendered no less astonishing. In short, they had the backing of a good portion of the international community. In 1982, the UN General Assembly voted to effectively recognize a trio of Cambodian groups opposed to Vietnam—of which the Khmer Rouge were by far the strongest—as the country's legitimate international representative. The flag of Pol Pot's ousted regime, with its yellow silhouette of the spires of Angkor Wat against a field of deep red, would keep flying outside the UN Building in New York. China, the traditional foreign sponsor of the Khmer Rouge, was among the countries in favor. It was joined, incredibly, by the United States and the United Kingdom, along with Canada, Italy, and West Germany.

No one in the White House or on Downing Street was under illusions about who they were endorsing with this position, which they would maintain throughout the 1980s. The recent history of Cambodia was common knowledge, especially after the 1984 release of *The Killing Fields*, a harrowing depiction of the Khmer Rouge takeover that won three Academy Awards. In the larger geopolitical chess game, it didn't matter. Vietnam was a client of the Soviet Union; to the US and its allies, anyone who was making Vietnamese troops bleed was, to some degree, on the right side. They wouldn't stand in the way as China provided Khmer Rouge guerrillas with weaponry and other military supplies, which were transported to the front with the assistance of Thailand, a key American partner.

Amid the fighting, some Cambodians sought out the temples as a means of survival—among them Toek Tik, who gradually parlayed his early, almost accidental sale of a single statue into a livelihood. Many of the men who came to loot the ruins of their ancient artifacts had been taught to revere them, but hunger had a way of shifting one's priorities. Looting crews were soon at work across the country, and there was plenty to steal. After the raids of the early 1970s, Cambodia's ancient sites were relatively undisturbed throughout the period of Khmer Rouge rule; in a country that had terminated all trade with the outside world, there were only limited opportunities to smuggle stolen works abroad. Nor was there much incentive to sell them for cash in a society that had abolished money.

But now, looters had easy access to temples that were unprotected and unpoliced, as well as a clear export route through market towns on the Thai border, then onward to Bangkok and international buyers. The looters struck in and around Angkor, which was the scene of intense fighting between Khmer Rouge and Vietnamese troops; at the vast twelfth-century city known as Banteay Chhmar, not far from the border; and, perhaps most profitably, at the temples of Koh Ker.

In 1986, a group of Cambodian men approached a site called Prasat Chen—the "Chinese Temple"—located within walking distance of Koh Ker's ziggurat-like pyramid. More than one thousand years earlier, its anonymous architects had laid it out as a walled square that enveloped three central towers. To enter, visitors would pass through entrance pavilions known as gopuras, one located on the west side of the temple and another on the east. The focus of this expedition was the western side, where the remains of ancient brick walls were visible in the reddish laterite soil. It was precisely the location where, fourteen years earlier, a different group had removed the life-size Guardian that eventually wound up in the hands of a Belgian businessman. As they approached Prasat Chen, the men had to walk carefully. Like much of rural Cambodia, the area was thick with land mines laid by troops on all sides of the civil war. It would be easy to trigger a pressure plate or snag a trip wire, blowing off a limb deep inside the jungle.

The group reached the western gopura and began to dig, straining in the tropical humidity. Gradually, the earth they removed gave way to smooth stone, and then to the contours of human features: eyebrows, noses, gently upturned lips. After more turns of their shovels, they revealed the forms of seven male figures arranged in two rows. Three of the statues were seated on their pedestals. The others were kneeling with their right arms crossed firmly over their chests, left hands cupping their opposite elbows—legible as a gesture of strength and vigilance even across ten centuries of history. One of the men digging thought that the figures looked like the Chinese warriors of myth. But neither he nor anyone else in Cambodia would be able to contemplate them for long. First, some of the statues were dismembered, their heads broken off with chisels and sent to Thailand with the help of the brokers who had taken over the cross-border antiquities trade. The heavier torsos would follow later; reattached, the works would fetch a much higher price abroad.

In the otherwise devastated Cambodian economy, such sales were becoming a significant business, one that could hardly escape the notice of the powerful. A number of Koh Ker's villagers were familiar with a Khmer Rouge commander, Ta Mok, who had fled to a mountainous stretch of the border not far from their community. He was sometimes known by an alias, Brother Number Five, that denoted his seniority in the movement, just a few rungs down from Brother Number One himself—Pol Pot. Even by the standards of his comrades, Ta Mok was a figure of uncommon brutality, a zealous enforcer of collectivization policies and the man charged with carrying out some of the regime's most indiscriminate purges.

In the 1980s, living in a jungle camp as he had before the Khmer Rouge took over the country, Ta Mok revealed another side of his character: a deep interest in antiquities. He visited Koh Ker on at least one occasion during the period, flanked by soldiers loyal to him. He ordered the cutting back of the vines and brush that had grown around the complex. Then he took pictures of a number of statues at Prasat Thom, a large temple adjacent to the city's pyramid. Soon, the works Ta Mok had photographed were gone.

To find success as a Manhattan curator during the 1980s—an era of black-tie benefit galas, sprawling museum expansions, and soaring prices for artworks of every kind—one needed both top-level expertise and a big checkbook. Martin Lerner, the chief curator of Indian and Southeast Asian art at the Met, possessed both. A native New Yorker, Lerner had gone from a bachelor's degree at Brooklyn College to postgraduate work at NYU's Institute of Fine Arts, arguably the most prestigious training ground for future art professionals. After working at the well-regarded Cleveland Museum of Art, he'd been recruited by the Met in 1972. Not yet forty, Lerner had been called to the Olympus of American cultural institutions, situated atop the nation's largest base of wealthy donors.

Under the Met's ambitious and publicity-hungry director, Thomas Hoving, Lerner's mission was clear: to use the museum's resources to buy up the very best Asian pieces he could—the stuff of blockbuster exhibitions and media adulation—before rivals in Washington, Los Angeles, and European cities could get their hands on them. Lerner worried at first that it was an impossible task, since so many of the top works were already spoken for. "In those institutions which did not pursue a vigorous acquisitions policy during the twenty-five years after World War II, it is unlikely that another major collecting opportunity will arise," he wrote in 1975. But encouraged by Hoving, and with a generous budget at his disposal, Lerner began to assemble a portfolio of significant new objects.

Hoving stepped down as director in 1977, ending a decade-long tenure in which he transformed virtually every aspect of how the Met related to its audience. His successor was more buttoned-up, and made no secret of his distaste for Hoving's showman-like tendencies. But the core of Hoving's philosophy—that New York's greatest museum needed to be constantly acquiring the world's greatest artworks—hadn't changed, and neither had Lerner's mandate. He scored a coup in 1982 by securing fifteen pieces from the Pan-Asian Collection, the personal trove of a recently deceased financier. The following year, Lerner's department bought a stunning Khmer statue of a bare-breasted woman, which he dated to the mid-eleventh century. As Lerner wrote in the Met's *Notable Acquisitions* bulletin, the thirty-inch stone figure was obviously meant to be a goddess, and it "represented [her youth] in a most sensual way," by "taut and tactile" flesh as well as "firm breasts and stomach."

The statue's only flaw was that it was incomplete. At some point, it had lost most of both arms and its feet. The latter had been broken off at the ankles, leaving a pair of uneven stumps. Since the figure could no longer stand on its own, it was placed on a subtle black base and held upright with vertical pins. For someone in Lerner's position, questions about the provenance of such an item were, if not an overriding concern, at least a topic of conversation, and he used one of the city's preeminent public forums to emphasize that he operated with the highest ethical standards. Lerner had felt compelled to weigh in following a *New York Times* story on the pending US ratification of the UNESCO convention on cultural property, which allowed source countries to demand the return of artworks that had been exported without their permission. BILL TO CURTAIL STOLEN-ART TRADE IS NEAR PASSAGE, the headline read.

In a letter to the editor that ran with his Met title, Lerner complained that many countries had banned artifact exports entirely, an "unenlightened policy" that "prompts the frustrated seller to bypass official channels"—a somewhat elliptical way to describe illegal smuggling. (He did not take the opportunity to say that he or the Met condemned this practice.) But that wasn't Lerner's main objection to the *Times* piece. What incensed him was the adjective used in the headline, which he felt elided "the distinction between stolen art and art which enters this country without the blessings of the country of origin." He continued: "No reputable dealer, collector or museum professional would go near a stolen object. The responsible segment of the art community abhors the trade in stolen objects, the desecration of monuments or the nocturnal activities of tomb robbers."

At almost exactly the same time, Lerner's strategy to keep finding and acquiring pieces from Cambodia involved working closely with Latchford. The dealer seemed to have an unparalleled ability to source the tiny minority of objects that curators would deem worthy of display in New York. Even when Latchford wasn't the direct supplier, he was often just a step or two removed. For example, the Met bought its statue of a standing Khmer goddess, the one praised by Lerner for its sensuality, from Spink's in London, and Spink's had purchased it from Latchford in 1982. There's no public record of it being outside Cambodia before that year. (If such a record exists privately, the museum has never released it.) Just months later, Latchford donated the head of a tenth-century stone Buddha to the Met, also without any published history of sale or display. Like Latchford's earlier gifts to the British Museum, this one put a work associated with him into the collection of a top cultural institution—an endorsement of his connoisseurship, and a powerful calling card when pitching buyers in the US and beyond.

In late July 1986, Latchford sent a letter from Bangkok to one of those buyers. Nathan L. Halpern was the founder of Theatre Network Television, a pioneering broadcaster of live events like concerts and political conventions. A pillar of Manhattan society, he had a seat on the Board of Trustees of the Central Park Conservancy and an apartment at 993 Fifth Avenue, directly opposite the Met. Halpern also had a growing collection of Asian art, and Latchford wanted him to know about one of his latest offerings. Latchford noted that earlier in the year, he'd received "a large Kor Ker [*sic*] male head," which had been "sent to Spinks, and sold almost immediately" to another US collector. "I was contacted earlier this week by the suppliers who found the head," Latchford continued. They had discovered a second, matching head "in one of the temples deep in the jungle in the vicinity of Kor Ker," the same spot where the first had been removed. "They were able to bring the second head through," he explained, and it would be available for viewing in London by the end of the summer.

Latchford said he was asking $76,000 for the "fantastic" object. And if Halpern wanted a more complete statue, he might be able to help. His suppliers had "indicated it may be possible to get the two torsos."

11

The who's who of London's Asian art world had packed into the gallery on Jermyn Street, a haven of genteel, upmarket businesses a short walk from Piccadilly Circus. They drank cocktails, ate finger sandwiches, and admired the bronzes assembled for a new show. Suddenly, amid the discussions about the booming market and debates about the latest policies from Prime Minister Margaret Thatcher, then at the peak of her power, many of them stopped talking and turned their heads toward the door.

Douglas Latchford had just entered. Tall and fit from his daily squash games, even as he neared sixty, the dealer would have been hard to miss. And he was, by the standards of this small community, a celebrity. No one else in the field had such a close relationship with the American collectors who were buying the top Southeast Asian pieces, and with the aggressively acquisitive Metropolitan Museum of Art. Nor could anyone in the room, or elsewhere, match his personal collection of Khmer antiquities, which he showcased at his main home in Bangkok and in the London apartment he had also purchased, just a few blocks away in Mayfair. "It was like Jesus Christ walking in," one partygoer recalled.

That didn't mean everyone wanted to talk to him; indeed, some of the people there, who knew Latchford from other gallery openings and auction-house functions, sought to spend as little time with him as possible. They found him intolerably self-centered and prone to grandiose boasting after a few rounds of his drink of choice, a White Russian. If Latchford expressed interest in what another person was saying, they thought, it was probably because he saw some advantage in it—intelligence on the latest works to hit the market, who was looking to buy, and how they might be convinced that he had just the thing they wanted.

Spink's remained his main pipeline to global buyers, and in correspondence with the firm from around this time, Latchford laid out some of his strategy. In the summer of 1989, one of his targets was the New York developer Sheldon Solow—the man responsible for the fifty-story Solow Building on West Fifty-Seventh Street, known to generations of pedestrians for the lipstick-red sculpture of a number nine on the sidewalk outside. "As Solow seems 'Hot' at the moment, it might be advisable to strike now," Latchford wrote, urging a Spink's man to call him to talk prices.

He enclosed a draft of a letter to Solow, offering him a four-foot-high "monumental sculpture," which Latchford explained had come from "an undiscovered temple ruin in the jungle, a short distance from Kor Ker [*sic*]." He highlighted some of the destinations of his other Koh Ker pieces: "Two went to the Metropolitan Museum in New York," he noted. There were more, including "a guardian which came from me, and is now in the Norton Simon Art Foundation, Los Angeles, a second (from me) Kneeling figure of Hanuman"—a warrior monkey prominent in Hindu tradition—"now in the Cleveland Museum."

As he put together his pitch, Latchford knew that men like Solow, who would eventually amass a collection worth an estimated $500 million, had never before been willing to spend so much on art. Indeed, it's probable that apart from luxury homes, no asset class absorbed a larger share of the fortunes being made in the greed-is-good '80s. In November 1989 alone, 160 paintings sold for at least $1 million apiece in New York and London, among them Picasso's *Au Lapin Agile*, bought by the media mogul Walter Annenberg for more than $40 million at auction. Though some warned that the run-up in prices was unsustainable, the record bids continued, with a Van Gogh portrait selling in 1990 for $82.5 million. Not surprisingly, American museums were eager to get their own share of this largesse, none more so than the Met. The institution had long been associated with New York's old-money elite—and had served as the ultimate proving ground for new money that aspired to join it. Now the museum embraced a flashier style, in keeping with the spirit of the times.

Part of its strategy was to build closer ties to auction houses like Sotheby's, which, like so many of the world's most desirable artworks, was now in American hands. A Michigan shopping-mall developer, A. Alfred Taubman, had acquired it from its British owners in 1983. The following year, Taubman threw a benefit for the Met at Sotheby's New York, blurring the lines between museum and market in a manner that was jarring to traditionalists. He also began talks for a major donation that would have put his name on a new Met wing for European sculpture and decorative arts. When those discussions broke down, the honor went to the rising private-equity titan Henry Kravis in exchange for a $10 million gift. Kravis was one among a number of donors whose generosity also bought the right to hold parties inside the Met—a previously unheard-of expression of financial power and social cachet. A member of the board of trustees joked that the Temple of Dendur, one of the museum's crown jewels, was hosting enough evening events that it was now the Temple of Din-Din.

In such a febrile environment, there were only so many top-drawer modern paintings to go around, and demand for trophy pieces spilled over into ancient works from Asia. In 1988, Sotheby's began holding regular, dedicated sales of South and Southeast Asian art; previously, works from these regions had been grouped under the category of general antiquities. Though Latchford's partners at Spink's remained important, Sotheby's would become a major player, capable of commanding impressive prices.

In one of its first dedicated sales, the auction house put a highly unusual Khmer artifact on the block in London. Believed to have come from Pre Rup, a tenth-century temple in the Angkor complex, it was a large sandstone bust of the five faces of Shiva, the Hindu god of destruction. Four of the faces were arranged like a compass, pointing away from one another at right angles, while a fifth sat atop them; each represented a different aspect of the deity's being, from the ferocious to the benign. Described by Sotheby's as "the property of a private collector," the bust sold to Annenberg's sister for £319,000—about $558,000 at the time, a record for a Khmer artifact. In the same sale, a monumental statue of the four-armed god Vishnu went to an unnamed buyer for £209,000.

Both unprecedented in value and executed in public, the transactions brought considerable attention to Sotheby's, and not all of it was favorable. At the Musée Guimet, France's leading museum of

Southeast Asian cultures, a researcher reviewed the auction brochure and recognized the Vishnu. It had been photographed in the 1930s at its original location, a temple situated between Angkor and Koh Ker, and again at the Conservation d'Angkor, the compound in Siem Reap where French and later Cambodian archaeologists brought statues for restoration and safekeeping. At some point after that, it had been moved to a government building in Phnom Penh. As far as anyone knew, it was still there when the Khmer Rouge took over in 1975, which meant that it only could have been removed from Cambodia through theft, during what anyone who had a passing familiarity with the headlines understood was a time of brutal conflict.

Alarmed, the director of the Guimet contacted Cambodia's government-in-exile, which lodged a protest with the British Foreign Office. After the auction went ahead anyway, the matter landed in the London papers. Sotheby's said that "had we received such information before the sale, we would of course have made every effort to investigate." But the company didn't expect such an inquiry into the works would have yielded anything alarming: "We do not doubt that our client, the vendor in the sale, was the rightful owner, having acquired them in good faith from a very reputable London dealer." According to reporters for *The Observer*, that dealer was Spink's, where the Vishnu and a companion piece, also stored at the Conservation d'Angkor, had ended up after apparently being "smuggled out through Thailand."

Martin Lerner, the Met's curator of South and Southeast Asian art, watched these developments carefully. With Latchford's assistance, he had built the museum's Khmer holdings into a respectable collection—and one on its way to being among the finest in the world. But unlike the parts of the Met that benefited from sleek new construction, Lerner's department had to make do with what a critic called "drab hallway vitrines." There was no reason to be satisfied with this state of affairs while so much money was flowing into cultural organizations from Wall Street and the other arenas of American financial achievement. So Lerner began planning a new wing of his own. It would give Southeast Asian civilizations a prominent place at the Met for the first time. Almost axiomatically, given the institution's importance, it would also be the premier venue for displaying Khmer artifacts in the United States, and Latchford was determined to be part of it.

Two heads from Koh Ker statues he had handled were already in the Met—one that he'd donated himself and another contributed by a Californian couple who'd bought it from Spink's. As preparations advanced for the new galleries, Latchford decided to give both of the matching torsos to the museum, "in honor of Martin Lerner." Experts reattached the dismembered pieces, revealing a pair of vigilant, kneeling figures with their arms crossed over their chests. Restored, they looked much the same as they had before the mid-1980s, when a team of looters, alert to hidden mines and the predations of the armed men who roamed the jungles, had hauled them out of Prasat Chen, the "Chinese Temple" near the center of Koh Ker.

Cambodia's civil war continued through the decade, with Khmer Rouge guerrillas harassing Vietnamese forces and then retreating to redoubts on the Thai border. Hundreds of thousands of displaced people took shelter on the frontier. In the largest settlement, Site 2, some 160,000 Cambodians lived, in the summation of a Western volunteer, in "a city of one-legged husbands and fathers." To discourage the notion that Site 2 and other camps could ever be long-term homes, the Thai authorities forbade them from building permanent structures. But they also imposed sweeping restrictions on emigration, fearing that if Cambodians were allowed to leave for resettlement through Thailand, many more would rush west. Conditions inside Cambodia were no better. Under pressure from the US and China, the United Nations refused to recognize the Vietnamese-backed government in Phnom Penh, which meant that many international aid groups couldn't operate there.

As the Cold War drew to its end, events far from Cambodia created an opportunity for change. The Soviet Union no longer had the resources to sponsor foreign adventures undertaken by its client states, and Vietnamese troops pulled out of Cambodia in September 1989. The withdrawal intensified criticism, in the media and in Congress, of America's stance toward the country. Officially, US support for Cambodia's government-in-exile consisted of diplomatic recognition, as well as aid to its non-Communist elements. But there was no way of knowing whether American funds were ultimately landing with the Khmer Rouge. In terms of optics, it hardly mattered, since extending assistance of any kind to an entity that looked a lot like the pre-1979 Pol Pot regime, complete with the same flag and foreign minister, was awkward, to put it mildly.

In mid-1990, Secretary of State James Baker announced that the US was terminating its sponsorship, telling reporters that "we want to do everything we can to prevent a return of the Khmer Rouge." China, which had generously supported the Khmer Rouge with weapons and cash, also agreed to stop its military aid. Meanwhile,

France, the former colonial power, made plans for peace talks in Paris. The Khmer Rouge continued fighting, aiming to maximize their leverage going into the talks. It was nonetheless clear, fifteen years after Pol Pot sealed his country off from the world, that Cambodia was opening back up. And few would benefit more than Douglas Latchford.

12

Even during Cambodia's long isolation, enough information trickled out that, by 1990, the dismal circumstances of its people were well documented. More than a decade after the Khmer Rouge were driven from power, per capita GDP stood at less than $200. Malaria and HIV were rampant. Every month, hundreds of patients arrived at hospitals missing limbs or bearing other grievous injuries from the mines that the Khmer Rouge continued to lay in rice paddies and along jungle paths. The injured could expect very little treatment, and not only because of dire shortages of medical supplies. As a result of Pol Pot's targeting of the educated, Cambodia remained a nation almost entirely without doctors.

Finally permitted to operate inside the country, the United Nations and various relief agencies made plans for a surge of aid. At the same time, a more specialized corps of international experts was also preparing to enter Cambodia, with no idea of what they would find. Virtually no Westerners had been able to visit Angkor since the early 1970s, when fighting first overtook the ancient complex and the adjacent city of Siem Reap. More remote sites, such as Koh Ker, where combat between Khmer Rouge and Vietnamese forces continued throughout the 1980s, were all but impossible to reach. In faculty lounges and pubs, archaeologists traded dark rumors: that the Angkor monuments, some of the largest and most culturally significant structures ever built by humans, were in a state of structural collapse, or had been pounded by artillery, or had been used by Khmer Rouge cadres for target practice.

Soon, small groups of specialists—mainly archaeologists, but also architects and historians—made their way to Siem Reap to survey the damage, working under the aegis of UNESCO, the UN cultural-heritage agency. Many of them were in their twenties and thirties, and new to the subject of the Khmer Empire. The last generation of academics with on-the-ground experience in Cambodia had long since retired, died, or moved on to other things; during the intervening years, few students were interested in devoting themselves to a country they couldn't visit. The new teams encountered a strange, devastated landscape—peopled by shoeless children with distended bellies and haunted eyes, merchants selling pieces of abandoned houses for firewood, and farmers unwilling to enter their own fields for fear of explosives. As in 1979, it was the stillness that some found most unsettling. Even the monkeys and birds seemed to have gone quiet. At night in Siem Reap, the only sounds louder than a ceiling fan were bursts of gunfire in the middle distance—a reminder that Khmer Rouge troops were still fighting nearby.

As they examined the sprawling Angkor complex, the surveyors walked the temple sites in single file, having been warned that a step off a well-trodden path might be the last they ever took with one or both of their legs. To remain outside Siem Reap after dark was wildly perilous, and members of the first missions were required to be back in their guesthouses by 5:00 p.m. Occasionally, danger found them anyway. At UNESCO's local office one morning, employees were eating breakfast when a group of Khmer Rouge fighters burst in, leveling their rifles and making clear that they were now in charge. The fear of the moment soon gave way to a more complex set of emotions, as the UNESCO workers saw that they were not being terrorized by battle-hardened veterans. The attackers were boys, perhaps thirteen or fourteen years old, and unsure what they were supposed to do with the foreigners whom they were suddenly holding at gunpoint. Fear was practically tattooed on their faces, as was hunger.

Noticing them staring at the food, one UNESCO staffer gestured toward it and said, "Eat." After a moment of hesitation, the young guerrillas lunged at the bread and jam on the table. It was a surreal sort of hostage situation, which ended when a radio in the office crackled with an update. Soldiers from the Phnom Penh government, nominally in control of the country, were on the move nearby. Alarmed, the fighters took the keys to a pair of UN jeeps—vehicles that they must have known wouldn't get them far, considering the state of the road network—and drove off. Later, the UNESCO team found the jeeps abandoned and two of the child soldiers dead in a ditch.

Despite the risks of operating in the area, international experts saw enough of Angkor to establish that the worst fears about its condition were unfounded. Remarkably, more than twenty years of war had produced "very limited damage to the structures, mostly the results of solitary submachine gun bursts," according to an early UNESCO report. The temples needed urgent restoration work—before the conflict, conservators had been trying to shore up the most vulnerable structures and repair damage from water that had seeped in over the centuries—but they were still standing and largely intact.

The surveyors were much more alarmed by evidence of recent looting, which was obvious even within the core of the Angkor complex. "More damage was apparent from wanton destruction of the temple fabrics in efforts to decapitate or separate a bas-relief from its stone backing than that caused by warfare," they wrote. "Some of these priceless works of art are in safekeeping with the Conservation d'Angkor while others have found their way into private collections." The group could only hope that things were no worse in the more remote temples.

Cambodia's international partners, to say nothing of its citizens, had good reason to be optimistic that such violence, against historical sites and human beings alike, was finally subsiding. In October 1991, the main opposition factions—the Khmer Rouge plus two non-Communist groups—signed a deal with the Phnom Penh regime, formerly backed by Vietnam. The agreement established a provisional government with representation from all sides, which would lead the country in collaboration with a UN body, the United Nations Transitional Authority in Cambodia. The following year, UNTAC began deploying a force of about sixteen thousand soldiers.

The troops, from dozens of countries, were tasked with keeping order until elections could be held. They would also be responsible for ensuring that the warring parties disarmed in accordance with the peace accord, a notion that turned out to be extremely ambitious. The Khmer Rouge still controlled territory and enjoyed the allegiance of a small but unignorable part of the population. Some supporters were motivated by genuine political sympathy, some by fear. Others simply may have seen Pol Pot as no worse than the alternatives, particularly since his party no longer enforced the most extreme elements of its ideology, such as banning private property, in the communities it governed.

Meanwhile, the Khmer Rouge hadn't been defeated on the battle-field. In fact, in the run-up to the treaty, their military position remained strong. They soon reneged on their commitments, refusing to lay down their arms or to submit to international supervision. Bound by restrictive rules of engagement, the peacekeeping force could do nothing to make them comply, and the war went on. An incident in May 1992 epitomized what critics believed to be the futility of the UN mission. The coheads of UNTAC were traveling in a convoy in western Cambodia when they encountered what was described by the press as a Khmer Rouge "roadblock": a single bamboo pole manned by teenage guerrillas. Despite having thousands of well-armed, well-trained foreign troops to call upon, the UN convoy turned back. Such an impotent force could hardly guarantee security—not for Cambodians, who were still being killed and maimed in large numbers, and certainly not for their ancient heritage. All of the country's factions needed cash to keep fighting, and ordinary people needed it to survive. Stealing artifacts was one of the few viable industries.

Just after 1:00 a.m. one night in February 1993, a squad of forty to fifty armed men approached the center of Siem Reap. Their loyalties were unclear; they would later be described as wearing a mix of different uniforms, belonging to "commando units of unknown origin." Once inside the city, they opened fire with assault rifles and B40 rocket-propelled grenade launchers, rugged Soviet weapons designed to take out tanks. First they bombarded the local UNTAC headquarters. Then they made their way to the Conservation d'Angkor. Firing in long bursts, they shot a guard in the stomach and barreled through the main gate, then proceeded through the compound and blasted open a security door with an RPG, exposing the trove of artifacts inside. The gunmen removed at least eleven statues, pieces that a UN spokesman said might fetch as much as $500,000 on the international market; in the process, three civilians were killed and eight wounded. Just two months later, a band of looters again invaded the conservancy, clambering over its outer walls. This time, they held a group of guards at gunpoint, demanding that the hostages lead the way to the highest-quality artifacts. That crew left with another nine works.

UN officials tried to stabilize the situation, paying for more guards at the Conservation d'Angkor and giving them flashlights and walkie-talkies—not of much use against opponents with heavy weapons. International donors provided funds to create a police force that would patrol Angkor. Even the provisional government, still unable to provide basic public services, deemed these efforts a priority. One of its first acts had been to adopt a temporary criminal code, listing just thirty-five offenses. Among them: "Any person who steals or attempts to steal cultural property . . . which is part of the Cambodian national heritage, shall be liable to a term of imprisonment." But the dangerous conditions in rural areas meant that security could be ensured only at the most accessible sites, within a few kilometers of Siem Reap. Cambodia's other temple-cities, which included some of the most significant remnants of the Khmer Empire, were beyond the zone of protection.

One such site was the vast complex of Banteay Chhmar, which was perilously close to Khmer Rouge strongholds. It had been commissioned in the twelfth century by Jayavarman VII, the most prolific builder among the Khmer kings, in what would have been the farther reaches of his realm. There his subjects constructed a temple more than 750 meters across—a scale matched by only the most spectacular Angkorian structures. Artisans decorated its walls with vivid bas-reliefs depicting battles between spear-armed Khmer warriors and their enemies from Champa, in present-day Vietnam. Above, sculptors constructed "face-towers," stone spires carved with three-dimensional eyes, noses, cheeks, and lips. It remains a mystery whom these hybrids of portraiture and architecture were meant to depict, but they rank among the most unique artistic achievements of the medieval world.

In the early months of the UNTAC mission, an opposition leader named Son Soubert traveled to Banteay Chhmar with a French archaeologist, Christophe Pottier. The Khmer Rouge were active nearby, but Son Soubert's affiliation with the Khmer People's National Liberation Front, the strongest non-Communist armed group, afforded a degree of safety. Inside the temple, Pottier reported, they found that theft was being carried out on "an almost industrial scale." Just a few days before they arrived, a dozen looters had been crushed to death when the chamber they were excavating collapsed. Other, luckier groups had dismantled sanctuaries with crowbars, ripped out sculpted lions, and broken the heads off *apsaras*, female celestial dancers often depicted in Hindu iconography. "We can only be surprised that the bas-reliefs," some of the most beautiful in Cambodia, "have not yet been dismantled," Pottier wrote.

To those fighting the losing battle against these thefts, there was no question as to where looted objects were going: to Thailand and then to collectors and museums in major Western markets, especially the US. And all understood that, like the trade in any illicit commodity, this one would thrive for as long as demand remained strong. The incentives were simply too great, whether for armed groups looking to fund their operations or for individual Cambodians struggling to feed their families. Around the same time that Pottier and Son Soubert were documenting damage at Banteay Chhmar, a UN official working on anti-looting programs walked into a gallery in Bangkok. Playing dumb, the official feigned interest in some of the statues on display, objects that were clearly of Khmer origin. He made some good-natured inquiries, enough to pass as a prospective customer. Then the dealer he was talking to expanded his pitch: "We have other pieces like this."

The gallerist retreated to the back and pulled out a binder full of photographs of sculptures and bas-reliefs, undisturbed inside their Cambodian temples. "You can buy these," he explained. To the UN man, the implication was clear: If he paid enough, they would be looted to order and delivered to him.

As UN troops tried to bring security to Cambodia, the curator Martin Lerner was working furiously on a project that would transform his portion of the Metropolitan Museum of Art. After seven years of preparation, the Met was putting the last touches on its brand-new South and Southeast Asian wing: eighteen galleries, spanning the length of two blocks on Fifth Avenue, that would display some thirteen hundred high-quality works of art. They'd been made possible by a $10 million donation from Herbert Irving, the founder of food-distribution giant Sysco, and his wife, Florence, who now joined the tiny club of donors with parts of New York's cultural institutions named after them—perhaps the ultimate honor among the city's status-obsessed superrich.

For Lerner, it was a moment of professional triumph. When he'd arrived at the Met twenty years before, it had hardly any display-worthy pieces in his area of specialty. Now it was running full-page newspaper ads to promote his new galleries, billing the gathering of works from Cambodia, India, and Nepal as "one of the finest collections ever assembled." Chest-beating claims like this reflected the philosophy that the man who'd hired Lerner, former director Thomas Hoving, had tried to instill in everyone at the Met: They should pursue "only the big, rare, fantastic pieces, the expensive ones, the ones that would cause a splash," and then promote them relentlessly. That securing those pieces might require the services of temple robbers or the violation of export laws was, to Hoving, of no great concern.

The Irving galleries opened in April 1994 to rapturous reviews. A leading critic hailed the expansion as "a watershed event—for Asian culture in this city, for a museum whose claim to be encyclopedic takes a giant step closer to reality, and for art lovers." He reserved special praise for the "glorious conclusion" of the Khmer pieces, which exhibited a "silk-smooth grace." No doubt aware of recent news from Cambodia, the critic added a caveat: "It is here in particular that one is prompted to speculate on exactly how art objects are extracted from their impoverished, often strife-torn, homes of origin to land in the lap of a rich American museum." But he and the other journalists who covered the opening took that line of inquiry no further. The Met, for its part, blandly noted that it complied with UNESCO's rules for acquiring artifacts.

Back in Bangkok, Douglas Latchford also had reason to celebrate. The two kneeling Koh Ker statues, looted in the mid-1980s, that he'd given in Lerner's honor stood sentinel at the entrance of the new wing, along with information cards bearing his name. Other pieces that he'd either sold or donated were among the jewels of the Met's enlarged Khmer collection. It was a milestone of huge significance. As a young man, Latchford had become obsessed with the legacy of ancient Cambodia; now he was among the world's foremost experts, having educated himself from scratch. Though he had no academic training, Latchford believed that he knew as much or more than anyone about the field he loved, and he'd worked for decades to be regarded as an authority. What could be a better endorsement of his taste and discernment and historical knowledge than to play such an important part in the growth of New York's greatest museum? What was a PhD next to the golden glow of the Met's trust?

Of course, the esteem of his peers wasn't Latchford's only concern. He also had a business to run, one that was increasingly focused on American buyers who were willing to spend huge sums on art. The Met's decision to shower Southeast Asian works with such attention would bring them new prestige, and almost certainly raise their prices. But its new wing also benefited Latchford in a practical way. As often as not, the collectors he targeted resided within a short distance of the museum, in the townhouses and co-ops of the Upper East Side. To see unassailable proof of his bona fides, they now needed only to walk over and take a look. The Met had just become Latchford's most powerful marketing tool.

13

Toek Tik had worked hard to make a life for himself in the wreckage of the civil war. After descending from Kulen, the forested plateau where he'd taken refuge from the Khmer Rouge, the former child soldier began stealing statues, at first with little idea of what to take or how to sell it. The country had thousands of ancient sites, and in the 1980s, Toek Tik was just one of many people trying to feed themselves by harvesting their contents. In some of his first sales, he'd certainly been swindled, persuaded to part with valuable objects for the equivalent of only a few dollars.

It was a poor return on work that entailed considerable risk. Cambodia was awash in cheap weapons, and even informal looting bands were armed. When rival groups coveted the same temple, the dispute might be resolved by Kalashnikov. Then there were the land mines, themselves artifacts of a kind. Virtually everyone in rural areas had a sickening familiarity with the Soviet-made OZMs, metal cylinders that fired themselves out of the ground and detonated at knee level; or the American Claymores, strung in trees or hidden in bushes, that burst open with a rain of ball bearings; or a dozen other models, all potentially lethal and still in place, their wires waiting to be tripped, long after the men who'd laid them had moved on, or been killed themselves.

Still, Toek Tik was better suited to this dangerous career than most. Wild boars, deer, and other game roamed the region where he lived, and he was known as a talented hunter. He seemed to have an uncanny ability to melt into the jungle, honed during his months in hiding. Alone, he could range through the trees at speeds that would leave others breathless, all while barely making a sound. Looting statues was, in a way, a similar endeavor, demanding patience, intimacy with the landscape, and a facility with firearms—but in pursuit of a quarry that could be far more valuable. Toek Tik was determined to become equally accomplished in his new trade, and he threw himself into building his skills.

One of Toek Tik's uncles had been part of looting crews at Koh Ker during his younger days, and he provided his nephew with some advice. Though Toek Tik struggled with reading, he took it upon himself to study an illustrated book of Khmer artworks. Over time, he learned to recognize the style of an object, and the period in which it was created, with remarkable accuracy. Yet there was only so much that he could accomplish as a lone operator. To find, remove, and then transport the most important statues—the kind coveted by American museums and collectors—he needed help. So Toek Tik began to assemble a team.

He pulled together a small crew of subordinates, skilled looters with whom he collaborated full-time. To provide the muscle necessary for major raids, he hired casual laborers, villagers who put in a few days at nearby temples in exchange for modest payment. When he couldn't find enough willing helpers, Toek Tik sometimes gave people no choice. As a man with experience enforcing the pitiless codes of the Khmer Rouge, he tended to get his way.

These untutored workers tried to remove objects without damaging them, but the collision of modern tools with thousand-year-old stone and bronze meant that they sometimes broke off arms, legs, or feet, or destroyed a work entirely while trying to blast it loose with dynamite. Still, by the end of the 1980s, Toek Tik was running an organized and successful operation. Near the border, a good-quality statue might bring in ten thousand Thai baht, or a little under $400—a tiny fraction of its likely price on the international market, but a meaningful amount of money in Cambodia. Unlike many who lived in the countryside, Toek Tik and his family—he would eventually have eight children—were no longer at risk of starvation. Then, in the mid-1990s, circumstances allowed him to expand on a scale that was unimaginable when he sold his first artifacts.

UNTAC, the largely impotent UN force, wound itself down in late 1993. In addition to facilitating the return of displaced people, its main accomplishment had been the organization of national elections, which were held in May of that year. Pol Pot had been invited to participate, in hopes that he would give up guerrilla attacks and compete in the political arena. Instead, he and the rest of the Khmer Rouge boycotted the vote. When neither of the other main parties won a majority, the result was an awkward power-sharing arrangement. Norodom Ranariddh, the son of longtime ruler Prince Sihanouk, became "first prime minister." Hun Sen, a former Khmer Rouge commander who'd defected to Vietnam before returning to lead the Hanoi-backed government of the 1980s, was "second prime minister."

The new administration was riven by infighting and operatically corrupt. It nonetheless succeeded in throttling the Khmer Rouge, who no longer enjoyed the Chinese arms supplies and American diplomatic support that had previously sustained them. At the time of the election, they controlled about 20 percent of the country; by 1996, when one of Pol Pot's deputies defected to the government with his troops, they could no longer pose a serious military threat. While life in much of Cambodia remained dangerous, conditions were calmer than they'd been in decades. Khmer Rouge ambushes were less of a threat on rural roads, and international teams were making gradual progress in removing mines and unexploded ordnance, opening up areas of the countryside that had been impassable. Pol Pot was still at large, protected by a retinue of armed followers, and the war wasn't yet over. But it was possible to imagine a future where Cambodia would be secure and at peace. Before it arrived, there was money to be made.

The decrease in violence allowed Toek Tik to expand his looting into something resembling an industrial operation, with multiple teams in the field at a given time. They coordinated by radio, using code words to foil eavesdroppers: "bricks" for bronze artifacts, "red objects" for gold, and "going dancing" for an attack on a temple. His men became more specialized, with some focused on scouting new sites and others on excavation and transport. The enterprise grew so large that his crews sometimes collided. On one occasion, two groups targeting the same site began shooting at each other with the assault rifles they carried for protection. Word of the battle reached Toek Tik, who barked at them through his walkie-talkie to cease fire; unbeknownst to their members, both teams worked for him.

The government had little ability to stop such raids: In what remained a desperately poor country, heritage-protection efforts were so underfunded that one of the officials responsible was keeping recovered artifacts in a cookie jar. Just as important, a significant number of police and military commanders had no interest in restraining looting, since they benefited from it themselves—either because they were being bribed to look the other way or because they were involved more directly. The prices paid at the Thai border were rising into the thousands of US dollars, and one way or another, the powerful expected to receive a cut.

Toek Tik's understanding of the larger trade in stolen artworks was, by necessity, limited. His teams brought works to the border, usually by oxcart, and sold them to a broker. After that, the pieces were out of his hands. The broker's role was to move them over the frontier and ensure that they reached buyers in Bangkok—the dealers who interfaced with the global market. At each step in this process, the price of a sculpture went up, culminating in sales to museums and collectors that, by the late 1990s, would be on their way to crossing the million-dollar mark. Toek Tik and those who worked for him understood that the overseas transactions were worth far more than they got paid for their part in the supply chain, though they had only a vague sense of the specific amounts. And even if they did know the numbers, to barely educated men in rural Cambodia, $1 million was an amount so large as to be inconceivable.

Toek Tik often worked with one particular broker, a man near the border town of Sisophon who had Khmer Rouge ties and a fearsome reputation. He knew that this broker had developed a profitable relationship with a buyer in Bangkok, who was so voracious that it seemed he alone was creating much of the demand that sent looting crews into the temples. The buyer handled a huge proportion of the works that Toek Tik stole. He also passed instructions over the border, specifying what he wanted next. At one point, Toek Tik was told that the buyer was seeking bronzes in the style of Prakhon Chai, a hoard of Khmer works looted in Thailand in the mid-1960s and quickly snapped up by international museums. On another occasion, he wanted bas-reliefs bearing images of the god Vishnu reclining on his back—an important Hindu motif. These were highly specific directives, which Toek Tik did his best to follow.

Toek Tik never met the person who was guiding his work. But he picked up fragments of information from his broker partner and from others in the looting supply chain. Toek Tik knew, for example, that the buyer was a Westerner who lived in Bangkok, and referred to him with a Thai honorific, *sia*, which roughly means "lord" or "don." Through the broken telephone of the border, and through layers of translation between English, Thai, and Khmer, the buyer's name had come to Toek Tik as Sia Ford—Lord Ford.

Toek Tik had been supplying Douglas Latchford.

Simon Warrack was skeptical of the instructions he'd been given: "Come to the military airport. You should be able to get on the flight."

Was it really possible to just hitch a ride on a Cambodian Army helicopter, heading on a mission to a part of the country that was largely off-limits to foreigners? But sure enough, after arriving at the airfield in Siem Reap one day in early 1999, Warrack heard the thud of rotors in the distance—a battered Russian-built chopper, inbound from Phnom Penh. The pilot touched down, and the soldiers inside beckoned Warrack aboard. A few moments later, he was cruising west, over the plains and jungles where the Khmer kings had built monuments to their gods—and where Pol Pot, their would-be heir, had buried so many Cambodians in pursuit of his own grandiose aspirations.

Warrack soon disembarked at his destination: the remote temple-city of Banteay Chhmar, near Cambodia's border with Thailand. A barrel-chested Londoner with skin ruddied by the tropical sun, Warrack had seen a great deal since first coming to the country five years earlier. After growing fascinated with historic architecture during a university term in Venice, he declined the conventional paths available to him and became a stonemason, trained in cutting and carving rock to human designs. Members of this ancient profession, to which the sculptors of Angkor also belonged, were in demand in Cambodia as conservation projects resumed in the 1990s. Warrack had been hired to work on Preah Ko, a ninth-century monument near Siem Reap, and then on Angkor Wat itself.

He had witnessed the devastation of looting firsthand as he traveled among temple sites. Warrack also had direct experience of the violence that, in much of the countryside, still loomed just one wrong turn away. Not long after arriving in Cambodia in 1994, he was on a road near Siem Reap when the minibus he was riding in convulsed with the force of an explosion. Khmer Rouge guerrillas had fired a rocket-propelled grenade and barely missed. Then they opened up with machine-gun fire that ripped through the vehicle. Warrack curled up into a ball, trying to make himself as small a target as possible. He and the other passengers shouted at the driver to accelerate as the fusillade continued, but the Cambodian man kept his speed low. Later, Warrack realized why: He was wisely checking for trip-wires laid across the highway.

None of this, however, prepared Warrack for what he was about to witness at Banteay Chhmar. After the helicopter touched down in a clearing, he tramped into the Banteay Chhmar complex, mindful, as always in Cambodia, that there could be mines just off the trail. Entering the massive site, he turned in all directions, surveying the damage with astonishment. Huge portions of the temple's bas-reliefs—carved walls of staggering detail, depicting scenes of twelfth-century battles and daily life—were simply gone. One of the missing sections was over thirty feet long and eight feet high; another was twenty-three feet by six feet. In total, more than five hundred square feet of carved surfaces had been removed. Whereas the rest of the temple was overgrown with eight centuries of moss and creeping vines, these walls were now fresh, bare stone, pocked with the telltale punches of pneumatic drills.

In some areas, looting crews had destroyed the reliefs they were trying to take, which lay in ragged chunks on the ground. In others, they had operated with remarkable precision, cleanly slicing the outermost segment of the wall into pieces and then pulling them free. Warrack, who handled stone for a living, figured the job would have required a large, skilled group of workers and weeks of undisturbed time. For good measure, they had also smashed the heads off pediments and lintels, which were also missing.

Warrack and the other international experts who soon arrived at Banteay Chhmar were months too late. The temple was so remote that news of its looting had reached the outside world only by chance, when a French historian happened to walk into an antiquities gallery in Bangkok. The shop was offering a four-foot stone fragment, inscribed with the unmistakable script of Old Khmer, for $8,000. The historian recognized it immediately. He'd helped translate the text, which was part of a larger inscription known as K.227, describing the protection of a Khmer prince by his companions; as far as the historian knew, it was still in situ at Banteay Chhmar. He immediately contacted the Thai police, who impounded the stone block, and alerted colleagues around the world. UNESCO, the UN's heritage agency, began to investigate how such an ambitious theft could have been carried out.

The Khmer Rouge, or remnants thereof, were among the suspects. Banteay Chhmar was located near their heartland, and elements of the party had certainly engaged in looting to supplement their finances after being driven from power. But by the mid-1990s, they were weaker than at any time in the past three decades. Relentless pressure from government forces had reduced them to a tiny rump of territory. In 1997, isolated and in poor health, Pol Pot ordered the execution of a longtime deputy whom he suspected of betraying him. The man was shot, along with his wife, children, and grandchildren. Even in an organization that frequently purged its own, this signaled a new level of savagery. If someone who had fought at Pol Pot's side for decades could be treated so cruelly, then so could anyone else. Soon, another member of the Khmer Rouge's inner circle—Ta Mok, "Brother Number Five," who had grown fascinated by antiquities while living in the jungle—turned on its leader.

Pol Pot, so weak that he had to be carried in a hammock by his guards, tried to flee, but was quickly captured in the jungle along the Thai border. Ta Mok's men subjected him to a show trial—not for the murders of millions of innocent Cambodians but for the killings of the deputy and his family. Still, it was a moment of modest justice. Just before dying out for good, the flames of the revolution were consuming its creator. The proceeding was marked by the same sort of ritual denunciations to which Pol Pot had subjected so many Cambodians, with a crowd repeating the slogan "Crush, crush, crush Pol Pot and his clique!" He sat in silence, an exhausted figure with hunched shoulders and a deeply lined face. The trial ended, of course, with a conviction, and Pol Pot was sentenced to lifelong house arrest. All but bedridden, he professed to have no regrets. "Look at me, am I a savage person? My conscience is clear," he told an American interviewer. The most he would concede was that the Khmer Rouge had "made mistakes, like every other movement in the world." Pol Pot died in April 1998 at age seventy-three. Barely anyone came to watch his body be cremated, with car tires and an old mattress used as fuel.

Though it would take until the following year for the last members of the Khmer Rouge to surrender, they likely lacked the resources to have pulled off the massive raid of Banteay Chhmar. Through interviews with local residents, investigators and journalists eventually pieced together what really happened, and who was responsible. One day in late 1998, a large group of government soldiers had appeared at the temple at dawn, carrying AK-47s and heavy construction equipment. They told the people of the adjacent village, only three hundred meters distant, that entering the ruins was now forbidden. Then they got to work, marking with red paint the sections of wall slated for removal. As Warrack suspected, the demolition had taken weeks, and it appeared to have benefited from the advice of skilled Cambodian stonecutters. After the troops had sheared off the bas-reliefs with drills and jackhammers, they loaded the carvings, weighing an estimated thirty tons, into six trucks, which set out for Thailand.

The direct involvement of military units—hundreds of personnel, by some accounts—revealed a level of official complicity that was difficult for UNESCO, an agency staffed by diplomats and scrupulously respectful of national sovereignty, to discuss in public. Clearly, local commanders had been involved in the looting. Their superiors, in turn, probably would have expected a share of the proceeds: In corrupt political systems, money flows upward. But how high did it go? The Cambodian Army now answered to the erstwhile second prime minister, Hun Sen, who had seized control of the government in a swift, violent coup in the summer of 1997, and then ratified his rule with an election that his opponents denounced as fraudulent.

He was, to many outsiders, an extremely distasteful character. Opposition figures began turning up dead in the weeks after the coup—with bullets in their brains and wearing nothing but blindfolds and handcuffs. In Washington, DC, some had taken to denouncing "Saddam Hun Sen." A former Khmer Rouge officer himself, he was distinctly reluctant to discuss holding large-scale trials for those responsible for the genocide, or to impose some alternative form of accountability on Pol Pot's surviving collaborators. Such a process might have raised uncomfortable questions about his own actions or those of other senior officials in the 1970s. And yet, as ever, there was realpolitik to consider. Hun Sen was no democrat, but with the Khmer Rouge defeated, Cambodia appeared to have a real chance at stability for the first time in a generation. Gradually, foreign governments made their peace with its leader.

The near destruction of Banteay Chhmar was swept under the rug. The only direct action by law enforcement came in January 1999, when Thai police stopped a ten-wheeled cattle truck near the border— their suspicions triggered, apparently, by the fact that it wasn't carrying any cattle. Inside, in eighty-five sacks, officers found bas-reliefs that corresponded to more than thirty feet of Banteay Chhmar's destroyed walls. They arrested the two drivers, one of whom said he'd been hired only a day earlier for $300 and had no idea what he was transporting. The men were ultimately given eighteen-month prison sentences. No one else was ever charged, in Thailand or Cambodia. And apart from a few recovered pieces, like the inscribed stone that was identified in a Bangkok gallery, the contents of the other five trucks disappeared.

Toek Tik wasn't involved in the assault on Banteay Chhmar. It was a larger operation than even he and his crews could have put together. He was, however, in the middle of a major score around the same time, one that would make him more useful than ever to Latchford. The area around Koh Ker, which was close to the front lines of the civil war, remained depopulated for much of the 1990s. Latchford had long been enthralled with Koh Ker and its sculptural style, which was marked by expressive, almost emotional figures, sometimes depicted as if they were moving. For a looter as experienced as Toek Tik, the deserted complex presented an irresistible target.

Like Angkor, Koh Ker wasn't a single location. At its apogee in the tenth century, it was a thriving city, and about forty of its major temples had survived, spread across an area of almost three thousand acres. The worst looting of the 1970s and '80s had focused on just one: Prasat Chen. It was the source of both the Guardian that Latchford had helped sell to a Belgian businessman and the kneeling figures he'd donated to the Metropolitan Museum of Art. With that site cleaned out, Toek Tik and his teams shifted their focus to treasures that might be hidden elsewhere. They found some at a temple known as Prasat Thom, next to Koh Ker's seven-tiered central pyramid.

There, in a towering chamber built from rough-hewn blocks of later-ite, they discovered three nearly life-size figures standing in a row. After Toek Tik pulled the trio out, one of them, a stone goddess with full lips and high breasts, would be acquired by the Met. The others would be sold to private collectors.

But the most significant prizes, for both Toek Tik and Latchford, lay at a smaller temple called Prasat Krachap, some distance from the center of Koh Ker. The sun was low in the sky when Toek Tik and his men approached it in the autumn of 1997. They passed a gate topped with a soaring lintel of filigreed stone, and four outer sanctuaries, some of their walls so worn by time that they resembled low, angular mounds rising from the earth. On surviving pillars, inscriptions in Old Khmer fixed the date of the temple's foundation, AD 928, and the names of some of the hundreds of laborers pledged to its service. Carrying shovels and chisels, the group descended into the central shrine, a rectangular enclosure half buried by soil, its bricks threaded and displaced by arm-thick roots. They began to dig, gradually re-vealing a pair of objects unlike anything Toek Tik—or, for that mat-ter, any archaeologist—had seen before.

One of them, about three and a half feet tall, depicted the Hindu god Shiva, his hands drawn together in prayer, sitting cross-legged in front of his son Skanda, who was rendered as a small boy gazing up at him. The child's hands were extended to clasp those of his father—a gesture of devotion, certainly, but also of love, crafted with vivid po-tency. Like many ancient Khmer works, this one carried a double meaning. The Shiva figure's prominent nose and square chin may have lent him a resemblance to Jayavarman IV, the king who built and ruled from Koh Ker. Its sculptors probably intended to associate their monarch with Shiva's power—and, in the same way, to link his son and heir, Harshavarman II, to Skanda, who serves in Hindu tradition as the defender of the gods.

As they dug, Toek Tik and his crew also came upon another sculpture of Skanda, roughly equivalent in height to the father-son tableau. This one depicted him as an adult, sitting astride a powerfully built peacock: Paravani, the mount on which Skanda was said to ride into war. The figure was carved into a muscular posture, clearly girding for combat. There was also an undeniable grace to the depiction. Above Skanda's plump lips, it was possible to make out a delicate mustache, its ends curving gently upward. Behind him, the peacock's fan was at once solid and richly detailed, dense with striations that gave it a three-dimensional texture. Viewed straight on, it could have been a throne made from stone feathers.

The team worked all night to remove the soil around the two sculptures. Straining under the weight of the stone, the men heaved the statues up, inch by inch, using pieces of wood as levers. Finally on flat ground, the figures were hoisted onto oxcarts for the first stage of their journey away from Koh Ker. After handing the works off, the members of the crew were each paid about fifteen thousand Thai baht, around $400 at the time.

Toek Tik knew enough about his country's artistic heritage to understand that he'd just made a unique discovery. So did Latchford, who also understood its value on the burgeoning market for Khmer artifacts. The two sculptures, which would be dubbed Skanda on a Peacock and Shiva and Skanda, soon made their way to him in Bangkok. He sold the first to a collector for $1.5 million. The second, he kept for himself.

14

By the early 2000s, Latchford's life at Chidlom Place, the condominium tower that he'd built in the center of Bangkok, had settled into a comfortable routine. He would emerge around 10 a.m. from the sprawling ninth-floor apartment he shared with his brother, Trevor. Downstairs, Latchford would take up a position by the swimming pool, where he sometimes received visitors. One of his household staff—he employed two maids, two cooks, and two drivers—would bring down snacks on request.

Once the heat began to build in the early afternoon, Latchford would retire to his home office, pausing on the way to log whether any aspect of the building was falling short of his standards. If he noticed an unswept floor in the lobby, or unkempt plants in the garden, or, worst of all, a resident hanging laundry on the balcony in the style of the city's lower-class quarters, the management office could expect to hear from him. The building's employees dreaded the moment when the switchboard light for 9A, Latchford's unit, flashed on. What came next was sure to be an angry reprimand and a set of instructions, which Latchford would unerringly follow up on.

His days were largely divided between managing his antiquities business and pursuing another activity that had come to absorb much of his energy. It was the only endeavor that inspired in Latchford, who was now entering his seventies, an ardor comparable to the one he felt for the study and acquisition of Khmer artworks. In short, he had become obsessed with bodybuilders.

Over the years, he had used his growing wealth to become the principal financial supporter of bodybuilding in Thailand, paying for training and travel to competitions, where judges assessed athletes on the size, conditioning, and symmetry of their musculature. Oiled up to perform, they bore an unmistakable resemblance to the statues that Latchford so loved, and it wasn't hard to perceive parallels between the two pursuits. In both, he sought to surround himself with the finest physical specimens. Those in stone and bronze, he could own; over those made of flesh and blood, he exerted considerable financial power.

Latchford staged a regular competition in Bangkok, the Latchford Classic, which was a highlight of the local bodybuilding calendar. The tournament's namesake watched from offstage as the entrants, some of them fifty years his junior and wearing nothing except tiny briefs and winning expressions, flexed their glistening bodies. So great was his involvement that Latchford served as the president of the Thailand Bodybuilding Association, the national federation for the sport. He took credit for significantly elevating its competitive standard, turning a group that was previously "just pushing weights," in the words of one associate, into a serious operation.

Latchford's fellow condo residents got used to seeing him in the company of extremely muscular young men, who performed odd jobs or simply kept him company as he conducted his business poolside.

Even in Bangkok, a city dense with expatriate eccentrics, all of this caused some snickering, particularly since Latchford was still not openly gay. In the 1990s, he'd frequently been accompanied to social events by a much younger Thai who looked like he could bench-press a Volkswagen. Latchford described the man as his "business partner" and took offense when anyone suggested that they had a more intimate relationship.

Even so, it all seemed harmless enough, and the bodybuilders, for whom he sometimes threw all-male pool parties at Chidlom Place, appeared delighted by Latchford's interest. In any given period, he tended to focus most intensely on just one of their number—typically, a talented young man entering the prime of his career. In the 2000s, this was Sitthi Charoenrith, whose spiky black hair, rippling abs, and warm, dimpled smile won the attention of his older benefactor. He was a frequent visitor to Latchford's apartment and over time, neighbors watched as Charoenrith's muscles grew in tandem with his spending power.

Almost no one in Latchford's usual social circle thought of him as considerate, let alone generous; even his friends found him alarmingly self-centered. But Charoenrith appeared to awaken a different instinct. At one edition of the Classic, Latchford presented him with a check for one million baht—almost $30,000—to "show his appreciation" for the hard work that had achieved, by Latchford's assessment, such impressive results. At the start of his alliance with Latchford, Charoenrith usually arrived for his visits on foot. Soon he upgraded to a motorbike, then to a new pickup.

Then, when Charoenrith excelled in a competition overseas, Latchford made an extravagant gesture. As they walked into Chidlom Place together, Latchford guided his favorite into the parking garage.

A moment later, Charoenrith stopped in his tracks and took in the sight before him: a gleaming silver Land Rover, topped with a giant bow.

In the early months of 2002, Latchford and Charoenrith stepped off a helicopter under a pounding tropical sun, and into a landscape that the older man had been thinking about for decades. They'd touched down in a field at the edge of Koh Ker, which had become accessible, at least in theory, when the Cambodian civil war came to an end three years earlier. Under the strongman rule of Hun Sen, the country was relatively stable, and eager to welcome visitors. Still, a site like Koh Ker remained very difficult to reach—hence the helicopter, which Latchford had chartered from Siem Reap—and not without its risks. Among the first things that Latchford noticed upon landing were the bright-red warning signs, in both Khmer and English, with a skull and crossbones in the middle: "Danger!! Mines!!" A group of villagers had filed out into the clearing, suspiciously eyeing Latchford, Charoenrith, and the other friends with whom they were traveling. A substantial number of local residents had stayed loyal to the Khmer Rouge until 1999, the bitter end of their guerrilla war, and they remained wary of strangers.

Wearing a garish pink T-shirt and light blue shorts and clutching his camera, Latchford began walking the complex, guided by maps that French explorers had sketched in the nineteenth century. With months to go until the summer monsoon season, the ground was bone-dry, and Latchford's footfalls crunched along the narrow path, lined with more warning signs, from the landing zone to the temples. As the outfit suggested, he was unaccustomed to conditions in the jungle: His natural habitat was his Bangkok condominium, and by nighttime he would be back at a hotel in Siem Reap. Nonetheless, he was one of the very first outsiders to lay eyes on Koh Ker since the late 1960s, when fighting first broke out in the region.

There was a great deal for Latchford to see in a single day. The obvious highlight was the seven-tiered central pyramid, which erupted almost 120 feet from the scrubby jungle. With no one to tend it, foliage had grown upward through the structure, leaving the six lower levels dense with plant life that swayed in the wind. Latchford declined to scale the rickety bamboo ladders leading to the top, which, at the time of the pyramid's construction in the tenth century, would have featured a giant linga.

Nearby, Latchford picked his way through the jagged, displaced bricks of the adjacent temple, Prasat Thom. The site held special significance for him. Just a few years earlier, Toek Tik had pulled off one of his most significant raids there, removing two female figures, one of which would be donated to the Metropolitan Museum of Art by a New York dealer with whom Latchford worked closely. Then Latchford moved on to a place even closer to his heart, the compact temple of Prasat Krachap. He paused to take a photo of its overgrown central sanctuary—the source of Skanda on a Peacock and Shiva and Skanda, which Toek Tik had also stolen in 1997. Latchford knew both sculptures and their origin extremely well. He'd sold the former for $1.5 million, and the latter was the pride of his own collection.

It was hard for Latchford not to be moved by finally seeing Koh Ker in person, especially since he'd made it there before most academic experts. He and one of his companions on the visit, an American art historian named Emma Bunker, wrote in the magazine *Arts of Asia* that they were "elated that we had been among the first in modern times to revisit a site that still exudes a rare exoticism. Having seen its jungle-covered ruins *in situ*, we were now in some sense forever part of its history." For obvious reasons, they didn't mention the other sense in which Latchford was part of its history. In fact, they lamented the "large-scale looting for marketable artifacts" at Koh Ker, adding that "the architecture and sculpture remaining . . . must be protected in the future."

How Latchford, whose hunger for artifacts had driven so much of the looting, reconciled this contradiction in his own mind is a mystery. Such dissonance would be a theme of his ongoing relationship with Bunker, in whom he'd found an eager professional collaborator and a kindred spirit. Unlike Latchford, who'd had to build his network from scratch, Bunker had benefited from social connections her entire life. Formerly Emma Cadwalader, she was a member of an old-money Philadelphia clan whose original patriarch advised George Washington on military strategy. She'd married as well as she was born: her husband, John Bunker, was heir to a sugar fortune. (He also happened to be the son of Ellsworth Bunker, the wartime US ambassador to South Vietnam.)

Yet like Latchford, Bunker wasn't part of the academic elite in her chosen field. She'd given up her doctoral work at NYU to raise her five children, and never earned a PhD. She had few ties to the Met or other top American cultural institutions. Rather, her main relationship was with the Denver Art Museum, in the city where John had built his career at the family sugar company. It's not clear when Latchford met Bunker, but by the time of the Koh Ker trip, she was developing what would become an intense devotion to him. They were working together closely, especially on an endeavor intended to prove, once and for all, that Latchford was the world's foremost authority on Khmer art. It was a thick book on the topic, with stunning images of almost two hundred works, many of them never before published or seen publicly. Latchford assembled the pieces, some of which he owned. Others he had sold to private collectors around the world. Bunker contributed detailed descriptions and historical essays, giving the project a gloss of academic respectability.

Latchford and Bunker published the 520-page doorstopper, which they titled *Adoration and Glory: The Golden Age of Khmer Art*, in 2004. Shiva and Skanda, with its powerful depiction of the god reaching out to join hands with his young son, was on the cover. The authors provided no information about its provenance, and they identified it only as belonging to a "private collection." The same went for dozens of other works they presented, including Skanda on a Peacock and one of the female statues that Toek Tik had stolen seven years earlier from Prasat Thom, which they called Uma. They tried to justify this absence of information in the preface, writing that "there are many reasons for lack of provenance, and to ignore pieces without provenance denies the world the information they can provide."

Latchford also sought to emphasize in the book that he was respected in Cambodia, which had barely begun to investigate past looting. His annual sales probably amounted to more than the entire budget of the nation's Ministry of Culture, and he'd recently made some modest donations to the National Museum in Phnom Penh. The institution lacked such basic resources as modern display cases and an accurate inventory of its collection, so Latchford's small contributions made a difference. The grateful deputy director, Hab Touch, contributed a foreword to *Adoration and Glory*. Of Latchford and

Bunker, he declared, "I was very impressed by their knowledge and passion for Khmer culture"—a comment that Latchford must have found gratifying. But another line hinted, perhaps, at a degree of concern. "The first time I saw the photographs of Khmer sculptures collected by Emma and Douglas for this book," Hab Touch wrote, "I realized that while I work with Khmer art every day I had only been familiar with a small proportion of what exists."

International scholars of Cambodian history had a similar reaction, and unlike Hab Touch, they didn't depend on Latchford for donations. So many of the pieces in *Adoration and Glory* were new to them and, in some cases, radically different from documented examples. It's almost unheard of, in a well-studied field of art history, for a mass of unknown works to suddenly appear in public with no prior hint of their existence. Some academics concluded that they could only be modern fakes, which Latchford was trying to legitimize through publication. In an article on the controversy, *The Cambodia Daily* quoted a French expert who called *Adoration and Glory* "dangerous," adding a withering suggestion: that the book's "possible mistakes are due to the excessive optimism that sometimes characterizes our American friends."

Latchford was furious. He threatened to sue the paper—and not only because he'd been mistaken for an American. Serious scholars were treating *Adoration and Glory* and its authors as almost radioactive; one recalled citing it in the draft of an article, then being sternly told to remove the reference. Latchford's attempt to ratify his status as a giant of his field had backfired. As it happened, however, the academics were wrong. Works such as Shiva and Skanda and Skanda on a Peacock weren't new because they were fake; they were new because they'd been stolen by Toek Tik only a few years before. Latchford, who'd received them when they were still fresh from the temples across the border, knew this better than anyone. But he could hardly confront his critics with that evidence.

As angry as Latchford was, he took comfort in the fact that the controversy didn't seem to be harming his standing in the art market. His association with the Met had helped make him a trusted figure among American buyers, who appeared confident that in Latchford they were dealing with the best. One customer, in particular, was coming to rely on him heavily, and he had deeper pockets than almost anyone.

Jim Clark had founded a company called Mosaic Communications with a fellow software engineer, Marc Andreessen. They took it public in 1995 under a new name, Netscape, arguably doing more than anyone else to inflate the dot-com bubble. Clark had more or less invented the persona of the irreverent, restless tech billionaire, subsequently adopted by the likes of Elon Musk and Sam Bankman-Fried. He had immense amounts of cash and immense amounts of real estate to decorate. In particular, he had a brand-new forty-first-floor penthouse at the Setai Hotel in Miami, which he'd purchased in 2004 for $9 million. Somewhat incongruously for a home high above the art deco streets of South Beach, Clark's decorator was going for an Asian theme. Latchford stood ready to assist, though getting new works out of Cambodia and into the United States was trickier than it had previously been.

After the mass looting in 1998 of the temple complex of Banteay Chhmar, the Cambodian government had asked the US to impose an "emergency embargo" on imports of stone artifacts. (As the country opened up to foreign investment, senior Cambodian officials, who investigators thought could have been involved in the 1998 operation and other thefts, had plenty of other ways to make money.) The Clinton administration had granted the embargo, which covered all works exported from Cambodia after the date it went into force. In 2003, the ban was made semipermanent and expanded to include bronzes.

In the meantime, Toek Tik, the source of many of Latchford's best items, had left the game. On one of his expeditions in the Cambodian countryside, he'd discovered a statue that spoke to him like none he'd seen before: a half-male, half-female figure of rare perfection. Previously, Toek Tik would have had no qualms about hauling such an object to the border and selling it for whatever he could. But this time was different. It might have been a function of age, a slackening of the drive that had sent him into the temples for almost two decades. Or it might have been the result of something deeper, a belated reckoning with the damage he had caused. But either way, as he considered the beauty of the statue, Toek Tik decided that if pieces like it were going to be taken, he would no longer be the one to do it. His looting days were over.

Nonetheless, Latchford still had a steady supply of freshly stolen objects and several methods for getting around legal obstacles. He sold his first pieces to Clark in late 2003: a depiction of the Buddhist deity Avalokiteshvara, almost five feet tall, and another, smaller statue of the Buddha seated on a coiled serpent. Latchford provided a letter from a British businessman in Hong Kong, stating that he'd bought the first sculpture in Vietnam in the mid-1960s, thereby predating the US embargo by decades. The businessman in question, one Ian Donaldson, had died in 2001, making it impossible for Clark to confirm the story had he wanted to. In any case, he didn't, and Latchford realized that he had a whale on his hands. Soon he was offering Clark even more looted pieces, including a seated bronze Buddha and a giant statue of the Hindu elephant god, Ganesha.

This last work, which Latchford had featured prominently in *Adoration and Glory*, presented certain complications. Unlike many in the book, it had previous documentation. A French team had discovered it at Koh Ker in the 1930s, broken into pieces. They'd reassembled it and, crucially, took a photograph of it in situ, which was published by the École Française d'Extrême-Orient, a government-funded research institution in Paris. This record created two distinct problems. The first was the discomfort that could result from knowing too precisely where a piece originated. It was a bit like understanding that the cow responsible for your steak had a name and personality, and it might inspire unpleasant imaginings about the steps that brought it to you. The second, more important issue was that a conservator at Cambodia's National Museum had publicly said that the Ganesha was almost certainly looted amid the turmoil of the civil war. The piece weighed more than four thousand pounds, and it was hard to imagine it being removed before the first modern road was built to Koh Ker in the late 1960s. (Later evidence suggests that it was probably stolen around 1996.)

Latchford's solution was to tell Clark that it wasn't the same object. He had Bunker prepare a presentation for the billionaire, in which she claimed that "the famous published one has disappeared. Whether it was blown up by the Khmer Rouge is unclear." Bunker urged Clark to act, writing that such a piece "will never be available again, and is fabulous. There is nothing like it outside of Cambodia." There was no real basis for Bunker's assertion that the statue was a twin, and other experts considered the chance that there could be two identical objects of such enormous size to be remote. But Clark was sold. He bought the Ganesha in 2006, one of multiple items he acquired from Latchford around the same time. To sidestep the import ban, Latchford listed their countries of origin as the UK and Thailand, correctly betting that no one in law enforcement was going to check. In April of that year, Clark transferred Latchford a payment of $11 million. And he was just getting started.

15

For practically the entire modern history of the art market, poor countries have fought against the removal of their cultural treasures for display in much wealthier societies. The best-known case is that of the Elgin Marbles, a series of sculptures from the Parthenon that constitute one of the most important holdings of the British Museum. The Greek government, which prefers to call them the Parthenon Marbles, began asking for their return in 1835, to no avail. In the second half of the twentieth century, such archaeologically rich nations as Italy, Turkey, and Peru made similar demands of institutions including the Met and the Louvre. In the vast majority of cases, they were dismissed or simply ignored, and there was little they could do to force the matter.

But in the early 2000s, American law-enforcement agencies began to listen. In large part, this was the result of revelations about just how much art, including modern masterpieces by the likes of Picasso and Klimt, had been stolen from Jewish families by the Nazis. In 1998, the Clinton administration convened a major conference on the matter, which resulted in the Washington Principles on

Nazi-Confiscated Art, a forty-four-nation pact that called for "a just and fair solution" when such pieces were identified. In the US, this was generally taken to mean the return of stolen works to their original owners, or those owners' heirs. Prosecutors in New York, the hub of the global art market, were eager to enlist themselves in the effort.

The same year that the Washington Principles were adopted, Manhattan District Attorney Robert Morgenthau sought to block the Museum of Modern Art from returning two paintings it had on loan from the Leopold Foundation in Austria. Each of the works, by the expressionist painter Egon Schiele, was claimed by a different family. MoMA ultimately convinced a court to reject Morgenthau's attempt to keep the paintings in place while their status was adjudicated. Just hours later, his federal counterparts at the US Attorney's Office for the Southern District of New York stepped in with a seizure warrant for one of them, *Portrait of Wally*.

It had been owned until 1939 by a Jewish dealer in Vienna, who'd been forced to sell it to a Nazi collector after her gallery was "Aryanized." Taking the view that the dealer's heirs were the rightful owners, federal prosecutors began a process known as a civil forfeiture action, which allows the government to seize property allegedly connected with criminal activity, even if no one is ever charged with, or convicted of, a related crime. The litigation, which would take a decade to finally resolve, was a watershed—signaling that the Department of Justice was willing to act when major artworks were alleged to be stolen.

Looted antiquities, however, posed more complex problems than modern paintings. For one, they usually came with much less documentation; some even originated from cultures with no written language at all. It was also all but impossible for, say, Incan ceramics to be claimed by the descendants of an individual owner. Such works were generally stolen not from private collections but from religious or royal sites. The aggrieved party was therefore likelier to be a government than a family, and the owners, collectively, were the citizens whom that government represented. But the legal principle was similar.

With *Portrait of Wally*, prosecutors had relied on a piece of legislation called the National Stolen Property Act. First passed in 1934, the law was a response to interstate crime sprees enabled by the newly ubiquitous technology of the automobile. (Bonnie and Clyde's violent journey through the South and the Midwest ended in a hail of bullets that same year.) In its broadest terms, the NSPA made it a crime to knowingly transport, receive, or possess stolen goods. That was simple enough to understand when the good in question was a hot Ford V-8, but more complicated when it was a thousand-year-old statue.

Beginning in the 1970s, federal courts grappled with the question of what rendered an antiquity "stolen," eventually settling on three criteria. First, the source country needed to have asserted ownership, by passing a law stipulating that artifacts were the property of the state. Second, the object had to have originated within that country's modern borders; Turkey, for instance, wouldn't have any right to an item found in what was once an outlying Ottoman province. Third, the work had to have been taken out of the country after the relevant national ownership law came into effect. The second and third tests could be extremely difficult to pass, requiring detailed knowledge of where and when an artifact had been removed from its original location.

Nonetheless, in the early years of the twenty-first century, prosecutors began to use the NSPA more aggressively to target stolen antiquities. They also drew on another recent precedent, established by a federal court in New York: that the widespread practice of falsely describing an artifact to US Customs (for example, by lying about where it came from) could also be grounds for forfeiture. Most of the cases were brought as attempts to seize stolen works, which could then be repatriated to their countries of origin. But a few were criminal prosecutions against individuals whose actions investigators viewed as particularly egregious. One of the most prominent defendants was Frederick Schultz, a Manhattan dealer who was charged with violating the NSPA by conspiring to receive stolen items from Egypt. Schultz was convicted in 2002 and sentenced to thirty-three months in federal prison, with the presiding judge calling him "an ordinary thief in every conventional sense of that word." The conviction held up on appeal, and Schultz did his time.

With real legal consequences now a possibility, American collectors, dealers, and especially museums no longer had the luxury of dismissing foreign countries' complaints. The same year that Schultz was found guilty, the head of Italy's cultural-protection unit declared that he planned to "systematically scour" US collections for looted pieces. (If the actions of the DOJ weren't enough to put fear into the hearts of art-world figures in New York, Italy also launched its own criminal cases against Americans involved in the trade.) Not surprisingly, much of the scouring focused on the Met, with its huge assembly of artifacts from the Mediterranean basin. It didn't help that Thomas Hoving, the museum's former director, had grown inconveniently loquacious in retirement. "If you were a collecting curator back in the sixties, of course you knew where it came from," he told one interviewer. "This stuff is not found in Malibu."

Under pressure from Italy, the Met would soon be forced to give up one of its crown jewels: the Euphronios krater, a twenty-five-hundred-year-old vase, painted with a scene from the *Iliad*, that Hoving had acquired for $1 million in 1972. As Hoving knew but strenuously denied at the time, the krater had been stolen from an archaeological site outside Rome, and the Italian government had been demanding its return for decades. His successor, the aristocratic, French-born Philippe de Montebello, finally admitted defeat in 2006, agreeing to repatriate the krater and several other looted objects, albeit with a face-saving compromise that allowed the Met to keep the vessel on display temporarily. Aside from a vague mention of "past improprieties in the acquisitions process," the museum's official statement on the matter managed to avoid any admission of wrongdoing, or specific reference to why it was giving the pieces up.

The governments and advocates pushing for such repatriations, who'd come to include many professional archaeologists, emphasized that they didn't want to see American galleries emptied of their contents. (For one thing, the display of Italian artworks abroad was probably the country's best tourism lure after pizza.) Instead, they sought a future in which museums cooperated with foreign partners to obtain their treasures, whether through aboveboard sales, long-term loans, or traveling exhibitions. Rather than being left with only those pieces that the curators and collectors of New York and Los Angeles didn't want, source countries would have a role in deciding what went on display and where—and at what price. For his part, de Montebello, who'd led the Met since the late 1970s, made clear that if such a future were coming, his institution would enter it kicking and screaming.

Just after the announcement of the Italian agreement, he delivered a defensive speech at the National Press Club in Washington. Standing before a crowd of reporters in a light-gray suit, de Montebello declared in his clipped accent that "art-rich nations have always fed the merely rich nations," and complained that journalists were "captive to the thoughts and repeated quotes of a small group of radical archaeologists." He acknowledged the "ubiquitous and, frankly, understandable desire on the part of many nations to establish a sense of identity and of roots and to hold on to them." But, he continued, "the universal museum, on the other hand, is the cultural family tree where all people can find their roots."

After delivering his prepared remarks, de Montebello fielded a question specifically about Cambodia, a country whose impoverished citizens, still recovering from genocide and civil war, were unlikely to make it to the Upper East Side to find their roots anytime soon. The Met had acquired the vast majority of its finest Khmer pieces during de Montebello's long tenure—many of them, either directly or indirectly, from Douglas Latchford.

"Can you comment on the thefts of pieces of Angkor Wat?" the moderator asked. "Was this justified [by] making Angkor familiar to Westerners?"

"Well," de Montebello said, pausing, "that's a nasty question."

Some in the audience let out a surprised laugh.

"The dismemberment of actual monuments," he explained, "is a very different thing from finding pieces of the Dead Sea Scrolls," which had been recovered from desert caves in the 1940s and '50s. "Yes, there has been the corollary effect that by being able to see

Khmer art of Cambodia in the Musée Guimet of Paris, at the Met, and a great many museums around the world, that has obviously encouraged people to go to the site." De Montebello stressed, however, that he "would never, never condone the destruction of any monument."

Cambodia, with a per capita income of around $600 at the time of de Montebello's speech, had nothing like the financial resources or diplomatic influence of Italy. It was still led by the same strongman prime minister, Hun Sen, who'd used violence and legal harassment to ensure that no one could seriously challenge his rule. In the first decade of the twenty-first century, however, Hun Sen was also presiding over an economic boom. The country's GDP expanded by 10 percent in 2007, powered by tourism and rising foreign investment. Hun Sen and other senior officials were the biggest winners: Many would parlay their political connections into huge fortunes over the next several years. But ordinary citizens also benefited, with significant reductions in extreme poverty and the emergence of an urban middle class in Phnom Penh.

For a government with so many basic economic-development tasks still to complete, recovering looted artifacts was not a high priority. Cambodia had enough trouble protecting the works that remained within its borders, either in situ at temples or in institutions like its cash-strapped National Museum, from thieves looking to cash in on the global hunger for antiquities. And Hun Sen remained unenthusiastic about looking back into the painful history of the civil war. His government had dragged its feet on setting up a Nuremberg-style court to try those responsible for the genocide, pressuring international partners to keep the prosecutions as limited as possible. The court would ultimately convict just three people out of thousands of perpetrators, and even that would take more than fifteen years. In the 1990s, summing up his philosophy on the traumas endured by his compatriots, Hun Sen had urged Cambodians to "dig a hole and bury the past."

In this environment, it fell to a small band of international activists to do what they could to document thefts and, they hoped, lay the groundwork for returns in the future. Some set up a hotline for anonymous tips; others began to create inventories of international sales of Khmer works, aiming to track their locations. Different groups devoted themselves to conservation efforts at Angkor and more remote temple complexes. None of these foreigners were necessarily fans of Hun Sen, but they reasoned that the complexion of Cambodia's government didn't make its treasures any less stolen. Moreover, after the murder of so many professionals by the Khmer Rouge, the country was making rapid progress in developing a corps of archaeologists and art historians—guardians of a heritage that belonged to all Cambodians, not to the state. In turn, these newly trained experts were beginning to view reclaiming their history as a crucial part of the broader recovery from the genocide.

These efforts, however, were in their infancy, and for Latchford, who continued to spend his days trading sculptures and courting young bodybuilders, the alarm bells were faint, if audible at all. Despite rising concerns about the provenance of artifacts, his business was doing better than ever. As in the 1980s, a financial boom—this time driven by the US housing market—was pushing prices for all kinds of artworks ever higher. To tap the new wealth being created on Wall Street and beyond, Latchford had built a relationship with a

New York dealer, Nancy Wiener, whose gallery was now one of the prime sources of ancient objects for American collectors.

Meanwhile, his sales to the tech mogul Jim Clark were growing bigger and bigger. Soon, Latchford-sourced objects would adorn every part of Clark's Miami penthouse, which he shared with his fourth wife, a former model more than three decades his junior. While most trophy homes in the city were characterized by a sleek, white-on-white modernism, Clark's decorator had installed dark wooden wall panels, woven ceilings reminiscent of rattan, and furniture with cushions in saffron and burnt orange. It was a colonial fantasy that might have sprung straight from the pages of Kipling or Forster, transported forty floors up into the Florida sky.

Latchford's Khmer statues, works that many Cambodians would consider almost living avatars of the divine, were the perfect way to complete the look that Clark had invested millions in making a reality. In one of the bedrooms, Clark kept a bronze goddess, likely taken from the tenth-century temple of Pre Rup. In the airy kitchen, he'd placed a two-and-a-half-foot linga dating to the sixth or seventh century—a symbol that would have been a focal point for worship in the temple where it originated. In the dining room, a stone Buddha seated on a naga, or serpent, kept watch over Clark's dinner guests. And under the twenty-foot ceilings of the living room, another stone Buddha marked the separation between two seating areas, framed by a commanding vista of South Beach.

All told, between 2003 and 2007, Clark would spend about $35 million on more than thirty pieces from Latchford. But even as he became the dealer's most lucrative customer, Clark began to have misgivings. He'd first become interested in Khmer sculpture after a trip to Angkor. It was impossible, during such a visit, not to appreciate the violence of Cambodia's recent history, or to remain entirely ignorant of the scale of looting. No fool, Clark understood that the objects he was buying had to have come from *somewhere*, and in 2007, as Latchford pitched him a spectacular new piece, he had some questions. It was a twelfth-century bronze boat prow of uncommonly ornate detail, depicting Garuda, the eagle-like mount of the god Vishnu. As Latchford knew but Clark didn't, it had been looted near Siem Reap about three years earlier.

While he considered whether to buy it, Clark asked Latchford by email whether the prow had been recently found and if it qualified as a "national treasure." Latchford told his client that he had nothing to worry about. "It was found sometime [*sic*] ago, and would not be considered a national treasure," he replied. "It is clean, no problem, you have my assurance." Clark decided to go ahead. The prow was soon mounted on a tall pedestal in Clark's home office, its delicate traceries catching the morning light from the Atlantic.

Latchford had chosen a special piece for Sitthi Charoenrith, his favorite among the Thai bodybuilders whom he sponsored. It was an antique necklace with a thick chain made of tiny loops of gold. The chain's two ends met over Charoenrith's bare chest, where one, shaped like a serpent's curved tail, passed through the ring of the other and descended between his bulging pectoral muscles. Apart from a sarong knotted around his narrow waist, Charoenrith wore nothing else.

It was December 2007, and Latchford had asked Charoenrith to serve as the centerpiece of an important event: a party in Bangkok to celebrate the launch of a new book, again cowritten with the American art historian Emma Bunker. *Adoration and Glory* had been a comprehensive survey of the art of ancient Cambodia. This one, *Khmer Gold: Gifts for the Gods*, was more specialized, focusing on jewelry and other regalia. The ancient Khmer were believed to have adorned some of their statues with precious objects, and Latchford was using Charoenrith and another young athlete, similarly attired, as stand-ins. Behind them, he'd set up a series of display cases containing further treasures: bangles, rings, and, most impressive of all, a tall, filigreed crown with inlaid slots that once would have held jewels.

It was an unusually vivid pairing of Latchford's twin obsessions: young Thai flesh and ancient Cambodian stone. Thanks to his financial support, he remained the central figure in Thai bodybuilding, surrounded by a shifting cast of beautifully toned young men; he even employed one as his personal chef. And Latchford had since repaired any damage to his reputation from the controversy that followed the publication of *Adoration and Glory*.

Less than a year after the Bangkok party, he was the subject of a profile in *Apollo*, a prestigious British magazine of the visual arts. Though Latchford had told its author that he wanted a six-page feature, rather than the four that eventually appeared, the final product still contained the kind of adulation in which he delighted. "To visit Mr. Latchford," the writer gushed of the "tall and majestic" dealer's second home in Mayfair, was to experience "one of the most remarkable rooms in London." The accompanying photos showed a darkened apartment stuffed with Khmer works, arranged so densely that some resembled nothing so much as bowling pins. The pieces included Shiva and Skanda, which Toek Tik had stolen from Koh Ker in 1997. Some scholars had been skeptical about its authenticity, and in his Apollo interview, Latchford boasted that after examining it, the doubters "wrote and apologised."

The supposed incompetence of those who questioned his connoisseurship was one of Latchford's favorite subjects, and he took the opportunity to expound further. "The problem with scholars," he said, "is they learn from books, not out in the field. They haven't seen and touched. I've been looking at things for 50 years." He continued: "I would drive out two to three hours from Bangkok on bumpy roads through dry landscape and past villages, in a little Jeep, and just look and look at things. . . . I walked around, studied, learnt. It was an open-air encyclopedia."

Still, there was one scholar—his collaborator Emma Bunker— whose opinions Latchford deeply respected. In fact, she had come to be a crucial partner. Though Bunker had no PhD and hardly any academic publications to her name, her reputation carried enough weight that she could be relied on to help convince a potential buyer, like the Netscape billionaire Jim Clark, that whatever Latchford was selling was unique, fabulous, never to be seen again. All of these descriptors could help push up the price. Born into one wealthy family and married into another, Bunker had no need for a share of Latchford's proceeds. Instead, she seemed to be gaining something even more valuable from the partnership.

Her husband of nearly fifty years had died in 2005. Bunker was now in her seventies, her children long since grown, and Latchford soon became the focal point of her life. Some of her friends described it as an infatuation—one that she knew would never be reciprocated, at least not romantically, given Latchford's own preferences. The pair spoke nearly every day, and nothing appeared to excite Bunker more than traveling to meet the man she called "Puppy" in some location far more exotic than her hometown of Denver. Latchford would usually bring a gift: a scarf or shawl, perhaps, or some small item of jewelry. For an aging widow who'd given up some of her own aspirations in order to raise a family, it must have been a thrill to spend time with a man of such a radically different background, one with whom she nonetheless shared an artistic passion.

Like Latchford, Bunker had also come to relish the chance to prove doubters wrong—and to demonstrate the superiority of her own knowledge. Around the time of the *Khmer Gold* event, Latchford emailed her to complain about an executive at Sotheby's whom he said had mistakenly described the style of a piece. "Oh dear," Latchford wrote. "I fear [she] may have shot herself in the foot, [or] in the head. What she is referring to is a **Cham bronze from Vietnam, not** a Khmer pre-Angkorian female figure, I fear she does not understand this. . . . I wonder how much more damage she will do, out of ignorance?"

Bunker replied with her own, considerably harsher take. "I KNOW WE HAVE SAID IT AGAIN AND AGAIN," she wrote. "THESE PIECE[S] ARE SO RARE ETC. THAT THEY CAN NOT BE EVALUATED BY SOME LITTLE AUCTION CHICKIEPOO WHO GOT PROMOTED FROM CLERK RECENTLY." (In fact, the Sotheby's employee in question had been in the field for more than a decade.) Bunker proposed that she and Latchford intervene to "educate her, program her mind and make her our own creature, then she can be controlled." Then Bunker added a reminder of why, in her opinion, she was such a good partner for Latchford: "Lucky for you I'm smart, good company, never boring, seldom screw up, and always do as I'm told, with a few minor exceptions. TeeHee."

Latchford appeared to genuinely enjoy spending time with Bunker, and the pair were soon working on a third book, this one a catalog of Khmer works in bronze. (She was uninvolved in his other literary project, a coffee-table tome of racy bodybuilder portraits called *Adoration: The Siamese Male Physique*.) Given Bunker's background, the most obvious role for her, when it came to Latchford's pitches to buyers, was as a source of art-history expertise, albeit with evaluations that she was happy to tweak in order to help make a sale. But unlike many of his clients, she couldn't claim to be naive about how and when his works came to be available for purchase. Bunker knew too much about Cambodia, and about how Latchford operated. She also understood that as US prosecutors pursued more antiquities cases, buyers wanted firmer assurances about provenance—if only to protect themselves against the possibility that their trophy acquisitions would one day be repossessed by the Department of Justice.

The gold standard was evidence, such as a record of international publication or display, that a work had been exported before 1970. The cutoff corresponded to the start of the most intense phase of Cambodia's civil war, and it was also the year that saw the signing of the UNESCO treaty that regulated the international trade in antiquities. Meeting this standard didn't mean that an item wasn't looted, but the legal risks of buying it were generally understood to be minimal. Yet Latchford was dealing in pieces that had been ripped from temples in the 1990s and even the 2000s. There was no way to claim they'd been part of a museum show decades before; museums publish catalogs of their exhibitions, which can be checked. He might, however, be able to provide documentation that placed an object in a private collection or gallery during the right time frame. Who could say that such a provenance was wrong? That's what he'd done in Clark's case, with a letter from a British businessman who said he'd bought a statue of the Buddhist deity Avalokiteshvara in the 1960s.

In this, Bunker believed she could help her friend, and she was prepared to cross significant ethical lines to do it. She and her late husband were major art buyers and had corresponded with a wide range of dealers over the decades. "Went through all the old files in the Denver apartment," she wrote to Latchford in June 2009, "and found all sorts of letterhead"—from London's Spink & Son, as well as defunct commercial galleries in New York and Los Angeles, market players that plausibly might have sold any work while they were in business. Bunker reported that she also had a signed letter from a prominent, deceased Spink's executive, "so we have his signature too." She hardly needed to explain to Latchford how such paperwork could be useful: "I think we could be in business for quite a while and sell anything you want at auction."

What Bunker was proposing probably amounted to fraud, but the grandmother from Denver appeared to view it as a thrilling diversion. "What a giant hoot," she signed off. "Giggles and more giggles, e."

When visiting temple complexes in Cambodia, Simon Warrack had a habit of looking down. In part, it was a survival tactic. The burly British stonemason, who'd been nearly killed during a Khmer Rouge ambush in his early days in the country, knew how easy it was to snag a trip wire. It was also a matter of professional interest. Khmer Empire sites tended to be full of interesting fragments—bricks from a long-destroyed sanctuary, perhaps, or the eroded remains of a roof pediment. For a man who'd devoted his life to stone, it was fascinating stuff.

In May 2007, Warrack was examining the ruins of Koh Ker, which he'd never before managed to see. Though it was now a relatively easy drive from the tourist hub of Siem Reap, the onetime Khmer capital remained largely untrammeled and unknown, even to scholars. The vast majority of people in the adjacent village were poor and illiterate. Nine years after the death of Pol Pot, the former Khmer Rouge soldiers among them remained cautious toward outsiders. As a result, Warrack was one of the first experts since the end of the civil war to get a close look at Koh Ker. He was particularly interested in Prasat Chen, the "Chinese temple" near the heart of the complex. A few of its structural elements were still standing, monumental confections of mossy laterite that teetered over the landscape like Jenga towers. Other parts of its buildings had collapsed, disintegrating into uneven piles of stone. Demining crews had removed unexploded ordnance from the site and cut back overgrowth, so it was safe for Warrack to wander, so long as he didn't stray too far.

While he walked, keeping his head down as usual, he noticed something intriguing in a patch of ocher-red dirt. It was a pair of stone feet, facing outward, that had been sheared off cleanly at the ankles. Based on their dimensions, Warrack figured they had once formed the base of a large statue, perhaps even a life-size one, that was obviously long gone. This was notable, if sadly unsurprising, and Warrack leaned over with his camera, snapping a few close-ups of the feet. Then, with so much else to absorb, he largely forgot about them.

Warrack was unfamiliar with Koh Ker sculpture, and when he returned to Siem Reap, he visited the local branch of the École Française d'Extrême-Orient to learn more. There wasn't much of a reading list, but he soon found himself flipping through a copy of *Adoration and Glory*, published four years earlier. About a third of the way through the book, he paused over a photo of a large statue that was listed as belonging to the Norton Simon Museum in Pasadena, California. The five-foot-tall male figure, known as the Temple Wrestler, was clearly an extremely significant work. Like other Koh Ker statues, it was powerful and athletic, rendered as though it were in motion, with a robust chest and thick, muscular thighs that seemed to be almost bouncing on bent knees. It was also missing its feet. Instead, its ankles terminated in jagged stumps.

Looking at the photo, Warrack suddenly remembered what he'd seen on the ground at Koh Ker. The idea forming in his mind was nothing more than a hunch, though it was one he thought worth investigating. First, he took a picture of the page from *Adoration and Glory* and uploaded it to his laptop. Then, using Photoshop, he dragged one of his images from Prasat Chen to the bottom of the Norton Simon figure. Warrack let out a gasp. Both ankles fit perfectly. So did the statue's stone garment, which lined up precisely with a scalloped fragment between the two severed feet. It was like puzzle pieces snapping together, and as he stared at the composite image, Warrack realized that what he'd discovered among the ruins was a crime scene: the precise spot where one of the most impressive Khmer statues in any foreign collection had been stolen.

During his years in Cambodia, Warrack had seen extensive damage from looting. In 1999, he'd flown by helicopter into Banteay Chhmar after the industrial-scale theft of its bas-reliefs, most of which had vanished. But he'd never been able to make such a direct connection between destruction on the ground and treasures held overseas. He decided to produce a short report summarizing his findings for UNESCO and the Cambodian government. Conceding that his analysis was "a first impression," Warrack emphasized that "the match is still extremely good and would warrant [more] accurate examination." To do that, the Norton Simon would need to "supply further information and technical data concerning the piece."

Warrack's memo circulated in Cambodia and beyond. No one was quite sure what to do with it. The Norton Simon had acquired its Temple Wrestler in 1976 from a New York dealer. There was no public information on where it had been before that year or how it had left Koh Ker. The visual match, while a powerful piece of evidence, was unlikely to convince a deep-pocketed, well-lawyered museum to part with a prized part of its collection. And there was little precedent for making such a claim. At the time, only a few looted works had ever been returned to Cambodia—mostly small items that featured on a kind of most-wanted list published by UNESCO in the 1990s. While one of them, a tenth-century Shiva head, was eventually given up by the Metropolitan Museum of Art, the country had never conducted a high-profile campaign along the lines of what Italy had inflicted on various cultural institutions, and it didn't seem like it was about to start. Gradually, Warrack came to believe that his discovery was going nowhere.

As it happened, however, another expert would soon be looking into that same set of feet, as well as another pair, situated a short distance away. Éric Bourdonneau, a French archaeologist with sharp features and long, delicate fingers, had the deliberate manner of a man accustomed to presenting at academic conferences. But like Warrack, he had spent much of his career juddering down muddy roads to remote historical sites. And after getting his PhD, Bourdonneau had decided to focus his research on Koh Ker. He was developing a complex theory about its statues, particularly those at Prasat Chen. Rather than serving as static representations of deities, they had been designed, he believed, to tell stories—not unlike baroque artworks such as Bernini's famed sculpture of Apollo pursuing the nymph Daphne. Beyond their huge size and expressive physicality, this would make the Koh Ker pieces unique. Nowhere else had Khmer statues been used to express narratives in the way that Bourdonneau proposed. It was a breathtaking idea: that a thousand years earlier, the city's artisans had devoted their lives not just to depicting their gods but to rendering in smooth stone some of the foundational texts of their society.

Bourdonneau's hypothesis was rooted in the iconography of another tenth-century temple, Banteay Srei. There, a roof pediment was carved with scenes from the Ramayana and Mahabharata, epic Sanskrit poems that are among the central texts of Hinduism. On the eastern side of the pediment, the carvings illustrated one of the key moments of the Ramayana: a duel between two monkey brothers named Valin and Sugriva. In the poem, their battle ends with an intervention from the deity Rama, who shoots an arrow at Valin, mortally wounding him. Rama was also faithfully rendered in the carving, drawing his bow. The western side of the pediment, in turn, depicted the combat between the warriors Bhima and Duryodhana, whose families vie for power throughout the Mahabharata. The climax of their contest comes as Duryodhana leaps at his opponent. Before he can strike, Bhima swings his mace, breaking Duryodhana's thigh. That was precisely the tableau rendered by the creators of Banteay Srei: one warrior flying through the air as the other prepares to deal him a devastating blow.

Bourdonneau thought that Banteay Srei and Koh Ker were connected—so connected, in fact, that it was impossible to understand one without understanding the other. In the 1950s, French archaeologists had discovered a statue of Valin and Sugriva in the eastern entrance pavilion of Prasat Chen and had moved it to Phnom Penh. They hadn't conducted further excavations, so Bourdonneau had no way of knowing what other works had been inside the pavilion before looters got to them. But the monkey figures suggested that the site's sculptors were trying to illustrate the same scene from the Ramayana that appeared at Banteay Srei.

If the eastern side of Prasat Chen told the same story as the eastern side of Banteay Srei, then it stood to reason that the relationship also held on the western side. This meant that Prasat Chen once would have contained large statues of Bhima and Duryodhana doing battle. The two sets of dismembered feet left behind in the soil matched Bourdonneau's thesis perfectly. He was convinced that the athletic piece, known as the Temple Wrestler, featured in *Adoration and Glory* was in fact the missing Bhima. That left a mystery: If the Bhima was on display at the Norton Simon Museum in California, where was the Duryodhana? Did anyone alive have any idea where it had gone? Bourdonneau certainly didn't. But Latchford knew all about it. And that knowledge would soon make him a target of the US government.

Nothing like it had ever come through the doors of Sotheby's.

The five-foot-tall statue had been brought to the auction house, as major artworks sometimes were, by a European aristocrat looking to turn a family treasure into cash. The seller was a woman named Decia Ruspoli di Poggio Suasa, who had previously been married to a Belgian businessman. After he died in 1984, Ruspoli inherited the Koh Ker sculpture, which her late husband had purchased nine years earlier. It dated to the tenth century, a muscular male figure standing with its legs splayed outward and partially bent, while its head, decorated with stone earrings and an ornately carved diadem, turned slightly to the right. When Ruspoli decided she no longer wanted the statue, she consigned it to Sotheby's for sale in New York. Weighing over five hundred pounds, it arrived at John F. Kennedy International Airport in April 2010.

At Sotheby's headquarters on York Avenue, the Asian art team was abuzz. Pieces of such size and quality were extremely rare, and an executive deemed this one "a stunner" that would likely sell for millions at auction. In style, dimensions and physicality, it was a near twin to one of the finest Khmer works in any foreign collection: the Norton Simon Museum's Temple Wrestler. In addition to the prospect of hundreds of thousands of dollars in commission, landing it was also a coup in Sotheby's never-ending contest with its crosstown nemesis, Christie's. Operating out of sumptuous premises at Rockefeller Center, the rival house was considered the global leader in antiquities. This was the kind of item that proved Sotheby's was in the game.

In the spring of 2010, Anuradha Ghosh-Mazumdar, an assistant vice president for Indian and Southeast Asian art at Sotheby's, began developing a marketing plan for the new statue, which she and her colleagues were calling the Guardian. One of their key tasks was to gather information on its provenance. Up to this point, Sotheby's hadn't been especially concerned about the origins of Southeast Asian objects. According to a study published a year after this consignment, the auction house had offered more than four hundred Khmer artifacts for sale in New York since 1988, over two-thirds of them with no listed provenance whatsoever. Even more alarming, the number of such items for sale had tended to spike shortly after periods of turmoil in Cambodia's civil war—possible evidence of a direct connection between violence on the ground and the availability of artifacts on the auction block.

This lack of information, and the high probability that many of those pieces were freshly looted by players in the conflict, had not posed great problems before. The Cambodian government had never really tried to reclaim artifacts from the US, and the cases being pursued by American law enforcement tended to focus on the Mediterranean and occasionally Latin America. This situation was different. Something as important as the Guardian would surely attract attention—from both the arts press and mainstream journalists—when it went on sale. And anyone willing to spend the kind of money that Sotheby's intended to charge would want robust assurances about its origins. Selling the statue only to have the buyer end up in litigation with the Department of Justice would be a reputational mess and a legal liability—a nightmare scenario to be avoided. With that in mind, Ghosh-Mazumdar reviewed the available material.

Ruspoli's late husband was Charly De Pauw, the Belgian executive known as "King Parking" for his dominance of the Brussels garage business. He had purchased the Guardian in 1975 from the London dealer Spink & Son. Prior to that transaction, everyone at Sotheby's understood it to have been in the possession of Douglas Latchford, who was well known to the team for his past sales—and for his tirades about the supposed incompetence of Asian art experts. The question was when Latchford had first obtained the Guardian. In May 2010, Ghosh-Mazumdar met with an art adviser whose client was interested in the piece, but only if it had been outside Cambodia before the bulk of the civil war and the signing of the UNESCO treaty on antiquities, putting it beyond the risk of government seizure. "**<u>The most important question is the provenance.</u>** Can Mr. Latchford tell us if he acquired this sculpture before <u>1970</u>?" Ghosh-Mazumdar asked in an internal email. "It's what [the] client wants."

A colleague reached out to Latchford in Bangkok. He replied promptly: "I had the sculpture in London in 1970, and finally gave it to Spinks to sell in 1975." This was extremely helpful, especially if, as another Sotheby's executive suggested, Latchford could be asked "to sign to say he had it in [the] 60s." His business and writing partner, Emma Bunker, also claimed to have seen the piece in the UK in the late 1960s. But they were either misremembering or lying. In fact, the

Guardian had been taken out of Cambodia—its decapitated head first, followed by its body—in 1972. Latchford had then collaborated with Spink's on a plan to put together false provenance documents to help sell it. Sotheby's had no way of knowing any of this. Spink's had subsequently been acquired by Christie's, which was hardly going to disclose records to its archrival.

Another aspect of marketing a major work was convincing buyers of its artistic importance, and while she tried to pin down the provenance, Ghosh-Mazumdar also asked Bunker for a different kind of help. Sotheby's wanted her to give a presentation in New York on the Guardian and write a companion essay. Her commentary would, of course, be expected to emphasize its significance, hopefully inspiring buyers to make generous bids. Bunker agreed and began to research the statue. Seeking to understand its unusual pose, with its legs spread outward and bent at the knees, she contacted another scholar, who replied with a worrying attachment: the 2007 report from Simon Warrack, the British stonemason, that matched the Norton Simon's Temple Wrestler to the severed feet he had observed at Koh Ker. Though Warrack had investigated the connection mainly out of curiosity, and had long since returned to his day job of preserving monuments, the document had made the rounds among archaeologists and other experts.

Bunker, though, had never seen it. Given the resemblance between the Guardian and the Temple Wrestler, the implications were clear to her (and to Latchford, who'd also been the original seller of the latter). It was almost certain that they had once stood together. Even worse, there was a *second* pair of severed feet opposite those documented by Warrack; in all likelihood, they belonged to the statue that Sotheby's intended to sell. Both were stolen objects, and the

Cambodian government had high-resolution photos of the crime scene. "I think things could all get sticky," Bunker warned Latchford after sending him the document. "I wish you had not told Zara"—a Sotheby's staffer—"that these figures had originally come from you. Best change your tune if asked further, and simply say you considered them."

Latchford received Bunker's email before dawn in Bangkok—eleven hours ahead of New York. Later in the morning, he emailed Sotheby's. His story had changed. "I have re-checked my records and notice that I had the Guardian figure on reserve from Spinks in 1970 [but] never actually bought it," Latchford said. "I believe Spinks bought it locally from a dealer in BKK." An hour after that, Bunker sent Sotheby's the Warrack report, adding her own update on the Guardian: "The Cambodians in Phnom Penh now have clear evidence that it was definitely stolen from Prasat Chen at Koh Ker, as the feet are still *in situ*." Bunker advised against putting it up for auction, which risked prompting Cambodia to "block the sale and ask for the piece back. . . . I don't think Sotheby's wants this kind of potential problem." Then she forwarded her message to Latchford, with a stunningly frank comment about how the pair should do business going forward: "We all need to stick to Marble Ganeshas that don't leave their feet behind and gold jewelry that isn't traceable."

A public fight with the government of Cambodia over an obviously looted artifact was, indeed, a problem that Sotheby's didn't want. So it appeared, for a time, that the Guardian might be headed back to Belgium or into a New York storage facility. Then, a few weeks after reading Bunker's assessment, Ghosh-Mazumdar received some good news. Bunker had just visited Phnom Penh and caught up with what she called her "culture spies"—Cambodians and foreigners affiliated with the National Museum and the Ministry of Culture. She reported to Sotheby's that "there are no plans at all" to pursue artworks already in foreign collections. Instead, officials were focused on putting a stop to current thefts, which continued to be a problem at more remote temple sites.

Bunker didn't contest the notion that the Guardian was looted. Considering the evidence, that would have been ludicrous. Her view was nonetheless that "legally and ethically you can happily sell the piece," with the caveat that it would be "perhaps not good to show or mention the feet still *in situ*." Advertising a direct link to a ransacked temple might make buyers uncomfortable—or give authorities in the US or Cambodia a reason to pursue an investigation they might otherwise forgo. Bunker also urged Ghosh-Mazumdar not to send her essay about the Guardian to the Cambodian government ahead of time, which would be "like waving a red flag in front of a bull." But after consulting with Sotheby's lawyers, Ghosh-Mazumdar decided to send a cold email to a senior official at Cambodia's Ministry of Culture. "We wanted you to be amongst the first to know about the upcoming sale of this highly important Koh Ker sculpture," she wrote in November 2010, inviting him to contact Sotheby's if he wanted more information.

The official didn't reply, which Sotheby's took to mean that Cambodia had no objections. One of the biggest sales of a Khmer statue in history was on. By the beginning of March, Ghosh-Mazumdar was putting the finishing touches on her plans for the Guardian. She and her team placed it on the cover of the catalog for Sotheby's upcoming auction of Southeast Asian art, which would be a highlight of Asia Week—a regular festival of gallery exhibitions and sale events around New York. Bunker wrote the accompanying essay, with an elevated version of the sales patter she often deployed on behalf of Latchford. "The raw power expressed by the posture of this huge figure is heightened by the tense back muscles and bulging arms," she raved. "He must have been a major participant in a sacred mythological struggle, as yet unidentified, that would have been easily recognizable to the Khmer elite of his day." In sum, Bunker wrote, "If one could choose only one sculpture to represent the glory of Khmer art, this figure could fulfill such a challenge."

To promote the sale, Sotheby's PR team put a condensed version of Bunker's commentary into a press release, along with a photo of the Guardian and its estimated price: $2 to $3 million.

18

The moment he saw the press release from Sotheby's, topped with a photo of the statue headlining its upcoming auction of Southeast Asian art, Éric Bourdonneau knew exactly what he was looking at. In his research on Koh Ker, the French archaeologist had hypothesized that some of its large works were meant to illustrate narratives from Hindu tradition. He was certain that the piece known as the Temple Wrestler, held by the Norton Simon Museum, was really a representation of Bhima, the mace-wielding warrior of the epic Mahabharata. Now, Sotheby's was selling a figure that could only be the second half of the same tableau: Bhima's opponent, Duryodhana. It was an object that Bourdonneau was sure existed, but almost no one alive had ever seen it.

He was shocked—and livid. Everyone who worked on Cambodia's ancient sites was familiar with the toll of looting: pedestals shattered, statues beheaded, bas-reliefs sheared from massive walls. Bourdonneau couldn't really blame the Cambodians involved. He knew that most had just been trying to survive at a time when starvation was an ever-present risk. It was the actions of foreigners that he found most outrageous: comfortable professionals in Bangkok, Paris, London, and New York who'd taken advantage of a poor country in crisis—and, in some cases, made a great deal of money through pillaging its history.

By the time Bourdonneau saw the Sotheby's announcement, in March 2011, it was broadly understood that the great majority of Khmer artifacts in global circulation were products of looting, either before or after the legal cutoff of 1970. And yet, except for a small community of activists, almost no one spoke of it, much less tried to take action against those responsible. Here was one of the world's most important auction houses, focused on keeping the business humming and the money flowing—and with a work that ranked among Cambodia's finest masterpieces. Once sold, it might well disappear into a private collection for decades.

Someone had to do something, Bourdonneau reasoned, and attempt to reclaim the Duryodhana for its rightful owners: the people of Cambodia. Bourdonneau received the Sotheby's press release on Thursday, March 17, just one week before the sculpture was scheduled to go on the block. He contacted Anne Lemaistre, a Frenchwoman who'd recently been appointed as head of the UNESCO office in Phnom Penh. In her new role, she'd been attempting to lay the groundwork for the repatriation of some of the works stolen during the civil war, but she hadn't found much success.

This was clearly an opportunity, even if Bourdonneau wasn't quite sure how to seize it. As the clock ticked and he and Lemaistre debated various approaches, he landed on an idea. It was logical to assume that the Sotheby's Duryodhana corresponded to the second pair of severed stone feet at Koh Ker, which stood opposite the set that had already been matched to the Norton Simon's Bhima. But no one had proved it yet. "You know, we could make a kind of montage," Bourdonneau suggested—superimposing the Sotheby's image onto the feet, and making a clear case that the Duryodhana had indeed been stolen from that site.

He worked through the weekend to put together a preliminary ten-page report. Part of his argument was circumstantial, a summing up of his research and working theory: that there were close parallels between Prasat Chen, the "Chinese Temple" at Koh Ker, and the scenes depicted at the temple of Banteay Srei, about forty miles away. Bourdonneau also had hard evidence from the leftover feet, which he had already studied. Their size and orientation matched the broken ankles of the Sotheby's piece. There was even a faint mark where the bottom of a stone scarf, suspended between the statue's legs, had once been attached to its base. Of course, Bourdonneau would have preferred to take the figure's detailed measurements, rather than working from a photo alone, but he was still confident enough to conclude that "the ensemble of characteristics . . . shows without any doubt that we are dealing with the statue of Duryodhana, erected at Prasat Chen in front of the image of Bhima."

By late Sunday, Bourdonneau thought he had enough evidence to confront Sotheby's. However, he had no standing to advocate on behalf of the Cambodian government, which had never pursued artifacts overseas in such a high-profile way. Nor did Lemaistre. She decided to phone Cambodia's deputy prime minister, Sok An, to talk him through Bourdonneau's findings.

"It's one hundred percent sure it's a stolen object," Lemaistre said.

"Do you have any proof?" Sok An asked. "Was it in a collection, or in an inventory?"

The politician had zeroed in on a weakness that Sotheby's might try to exploit. The sole published record of the Duryodhana was an old catalog from Spink & Son. The statue's origin had never been logged, nor had it been moved into a storehouse like the Conservation d'Angkor, where many Khmer works had resided, at least temporarily. Given Koh Ker's remoteness and the very limited research undertaken at the site before the 1970s, this lack of thorough documentation was understandable. But it was a problem.

"I'm sorry to say it, but no," Lemaistre replied. "It was never in a collection. It was illegally looted and removed."

"I need to think about it," Sok An told her.

There was very little time for thinking: the sale in New York was barely four days away. Lemaistre drafted a letter that could be sent to Sotheby's in the Cambodian government's name. All it needed was a signature. Yet as the hours sped by, she still had no word. The decision might have been caught in the gears of a slow-moving bureaucracy, or maybe, Lemaistre suspected, Sok An was worried that by taking on Sotheby's, he might somehow offend the Obama administration, with which Cambodia was trying to maintain cordial ties.

While she and Bourdonneau waited, there was one other thing they could do: get word to Interpol. The global policing organization had a unit devoted to art-related investigations. Contrary to popular belief, it is not an enforcement agency and has no power to bring cases on its own. It does, however, play a vital role in circulating information between national police forces. On March 21—now less than three days before the scheduled auction—its art-crimes team sent out an all-caps bulletin to a liaison office in Washington, headed VERY URGENT:

ACCORDING TO INFORMATION RECEIVED FROM EXPERTS, A STOLEN KHMER STATUE IS BEING OFFERED

FOR SALE AT SOTHEBY'S AUCTION ON INDIAN & SOUTHEAST ASIAN WORKS OF ART. . . . PLEASE EXAMINE THE POSSIBILITY TO SAFEGUARD THE SCULPTURE WITHIN THE FRAME OF YOUR LEGAL POSSIBILITIES.

What happened next would depend on whether anyone in the US government cared enough to act.

The Interpol alert landed at the Department of Homeland Security, specifically on the desk of Special Agent Brenton Easter. Created after the 9/11 attacks to integrate a wide range of law-enforcement functions, DHS had a vast mandate, ranging from counterterrorism to combating human trafficking to enforcing customs laws. Easter, a blunt-speaking New Englander with a square jaw and a widow's peak, had been assigned to its cultural property division—a squad that worked cases involving antiquities. Compared with tracking jihadist militants and disrupting human-trafficking rings, such investigations were never going to be a top priority. DHS was nonetheless putting more resources behind them, as terrorist groups, including al-Qaeda and later the Islamic State, were believed to be obtaining some of their funding by selling looted artifacts from the Middle East. As assets with murky valuations that changed hands in opaque international markets, antiquities also provided an obvious opportunity for laundering the proceeds of crime.

An allegedly stolen statue being sold for millions in New York was a clear target, and Easter contacted Sotheby's general counsel to ask for information about the Duryodhana's provenance. On March 22, the lawyer told him by email that "there is no need for you to run around hunting" for evidence. She attached a 1975 Spink's invoice for the statue. As for its whereabouts before that, she said, "We have identified two individuals who presently have no financial interest in the property and who personally saw the piece in London in the late 1960s." She was referring to Douglas Latchford and Emma Bunker.

DHS wasn't going to take Sotheby's word for it, and Easter began trying to gather the documentation that would be required to seize the Duryodhana through a forfeiture action. Almost immediately, he ran headfirst into the realities of Cambodia's twentieth-century history. Under the federal courts' interpretation of the National Stolen Property Act, the US government would need to show where and when the statue was looted, and to demonstrate that Cambodian law had made such an act illegal at the time. If it failed to meet any of those tests, the seizure wouldn't hold up. Thanks to Bourdonneau's report, the *where* was clear enough. But in the absence of further evidence, the *when* could have been any point in time prior to the Spink's sale in 1975. With no available photos of the Duryodhana in situ at Koh Ker, nor any archaeological records establishing its presence there, it was impossible to narrow down the date.

Even more frustrating, no one, including in Cambodia, appeared to have a clear sense of the legal framework. Over the previous century, the country had been governed under at least eight different political systems, ranging from French colonial rule to the totalitarian nihilism of Pol Pot. Almost every single Cambodian who might have remembered what cultural-heritage laws existed before he took power was dead, likely murdered in the Khmer Rouge purge of the professional classes. The survivors had more pressing priorities than the study of archived legislation, if those records even still existed.

The NSPA, however, didn't make allowances for the legacies of genocide. "I am unable to do anything," Easter told Interpol officials in an email sent two days before the auction, unless Cambodia provided a date of theft and confirmed the laws in force. If those pieces of information weren't available, he warned, "we are stuck."

Then, events far from New York created an opening. After deliberating over Bourdonneau's report, the one that matched the Duryodhana to its broken-off feet, the Cambodian government had finally decided to send a formal letter to Sotheby's. "In view of the tremendous historical and archaeological value of the Duryodhana," it read, "the Royal Government of Cambodia would like to take this opportunity to request Sotheby's to pull the object from sale and to facilitate its return." As such requests go, it wasn't especially forceful. The letter said only that Cambodia believed "this statue was illegally removed from the site" at Koh Ker—not when the removal had occurred, nor which laws had been violated. A Sotheby's lawyer might look at it and conclude that the company was in the clear, so long as it was willing to weather some negative publicity.

In Asia, it was already March 24. The Duryodhana auction was set for 10:00 a.m. Eastern time, the same day, and the time difference meant that Sotheby's would receive Cambodia's objections just before it began. As darkness fell in Phnom Penh, UNESCO's Lemaistre sat at her computer with a browser window open to the sale listing. There had been no immediate response to the Cambodian letter, and the statue was still there, available to be bid upon by anyone with a few million dollars to spare. At that very moment, wealthy collectors were making their way to the Sotheby's saleroom on the Upper East Side, getting ready to reveal their offers for a looted artwork of extraordinary cultural import. And as soon as someone purchased it, any recovery would become significantly more complicated, even for the US government.

Almost shaking with nerves, Lemaistre hit "Refresh." The listing remained as it was. She clicked it again, and again. The spectacular statue remained on her screen. She kept clicking, more out of anxiety than hope. Then, suddenly, the page changed. Lemaistre scanned up and down, left and right, making sure that what her eyes were telling her was really true: The Duryodhana was gone. Sotheby's had pulled it.

About a week later, the auction house explained its actions in a letter to UNESCO. Despite deciding at the last minute to take the statue off the block, Sotheby's hadn't concluded that it would be wrong to go ahead with the sale, which had merely been postponed "in the spirit of international cooperation and good faith." Its general counsel wrote that, after reviewing documentation compiled by the agency, "we do not believe the Cambodian government has a valid legal claim to ownership." She added that Sotheby's was relying on two people—Latchford and Bunker—who said they'd seen the Duryodhana in London before 1970, putting it outside Cambodia "prior to the date of all relevant laws." In other words, whether it was looted was immaterial. What mattered was that no one could prove the looting would have been illegal when it occurred.

Sotheby's offered a few options, none of which involved backing down. If a private buyer purchased the Duryodhana at auction, the company might donate some of the proceeds to conservation efforts at Koh Ker. It would also be happy to sell the work to "an appropriate museum or cultural institution," which could then lend it to Cambodia. Alternatively, the Cambodian government was welcome to buy the Duryodhana and bring it home, or to find a benefactor to do so on the nation's behalf. The letter emphasized that Sotheby's didn't want to set any precedents that could interfere with its business: "We fear that last-minute claims that disrupt public auctions will serve only to frighten owners away from the public auction market and drive important cultural pieces underground."

At DHS, however, Easter thought there could be another way forward—one that didn't involve forcing an impoverished country to buy back its stolen heritage. He'd been digging deeper into the case and was growing suspicious of Sotheby's claims about the Duryodhana's provenance. He also believed that he could document the progression of anti-looting legislation in Cambodia, which would make a seizure under the NSPA a possibility. The day after Sotheby's told UNESCO that it had no intention of giving up the statue, Easter emailed its general counsel with a warning: "We now have probable cause that the item was stolen after Cambodian cultural patrimony laws were enacted. I would like to respectfully request that you do not move the piece as it is now being considered stolen property."

Sotheby's consented to keeping the Duryodhana in New York, at least for the time being. Meanwhile, Easter began trying to piece together more of its history. That meant, above all, confirming when it had been taken out of Cambodia and by whom. One of the crucial witnesses, in the version of the story offered by Sotheby's, was Latchford. Up to this point, virtually no one in American law enforcement had any clear idea of who he was, nor any reason to look into his past. But if Sotheby's was going to rely on Latchford's claims, then his credibility—and, more broadly, exactly how he'd operated since the early 1970s—were obvious matters for investigation.

19

To carry a forfeiture case forward, Brenton Easter needed prosecutors who were willing to take Sotheby's to court. He found them at 1 Saint Andrew's Plaza, a squat, brutalist downtown block that houses the US Attorney's Office for the Southern District of New York.

SDNY, as it's known, has a long history of taking on complex, high-profile civil and criminal cases. In part, this is a function of its responsibility for enforcing federal law in Manhattan: Almost any major investigation of organized crime or international terrorism or financial fraud has some nexus with its jurisdiction. And since that jurisdiction is a magnet for hypereducated professionals, SDNY tends to attract the most ambitious young lawyers in the entire Department of Justice—men and women willing to put up with extreme hours on government pay for the chance to be part of legal history. Few stay longer than five to ten years before moving into private practice, incentivizing them to work furiously to make an impact in a short time.

When Easter approached SDNY in 2011, its ongoing investigations involved some of the hardest targets in New York City, including Citigroup, JPMorgan Chase, and the hedge fund Galleon Group, along with the Gambino crime family. No one working there was afraid of going toe to toe with the world's best-known auction house, and on April 4, 2012, the office filed a complaint in Manhattan, asking a judge to seize the Duryodhana from Sotheby's. "There is probable cause to believe," the document read, that the statue was "stolen property introduced into the United States contrary to law." Moreover, it was "of extraordinary value as a piece of the cultural heritage of the Cambodian people," to whom the US government ultimately wanted it to return.

Since beginning their work on the case, SDNY prosecutors had reviewed emails and other records from Sotheby's, giving them a view of the deliberations over the Duryodhana's provenance—including Douglas Latchford's and Emma Bunker's claims that they'd seen the piece in London in the late 1960s. The prosecutors had also drawn on work by an American lawyer, Tess Davis, who had been researching the history of cultural-heritage legislation in Cambodia. The country's government was fully supportive of the US investigation, but its officials lacked the expertise to support complex American litigation, leaving them reliant on outside help.

Davis went to the National Archives in Phnom Penh, trying to find papers that she feared might have been burned or discarded as the Khmer Rouge sought to remake society. Luckily, much of what she was hoping to find had survived; Pol Pot and his men had spent far more time destroying people than documents. Davis was able to pull records of laws that criminalized looting as early as 1900, when Cambodia was still under French control. She also found moldering files from what was, in its day, a major legal drama: the 1924 prosecution of André Malraux, a young intellectual who would go on to become France's minister of culture, for stealing some six hundred kilograms of carvings from the temple of Banteay Srei. Malraux had been convicted by a colonial court and sentenced to three years in jail—proof that the authorities of the time considered looting to be a criminal act. Davis was confident that this had continued to be true throughout the twentieth century.

There were still huge gaps in what the government team had assembled. Seizing an artifact under the National Stolen Property Act required clear evidence that it was looted from its home country at a time when that looting was prohibited. SDNY had no firm idea when the Duryodhana had been stolen from Koh Ker, and thus which Cambodian laws were in force. In their initial complaint, the best prosecutors could do was offer a mix of assumptions and circumstantial evidence. French archaeologists had published a description of Koh Ker in 1939 and made no reference to seeing signs of looting; nor, unfortunately, had they mentioned an artwork resembling the Duryodhana. Similarly, photos taken in the 1950s and '60s showed that the site had "generally remained intact"—but did not include any images of the statue that SDNY was chasing, making it impossible to confirm whether it was still there at that point. It seemed most likely that the Duryodhana had been taken sometime after 1965, when a new road made Koh Ker more accessible to the rest of the country. (The statue had to have left Cambodia before late 1975, when it was sold in London.)

Given what was known about the ransacking of archaeological sites during the Khmer Rouge insurgency, which began in earnest in 1970, this time frame made sense. Still, having to guess at the date was a major weakness in the government's case, and Sotheby's knew it.

Faced with a federal forfeiture action, many organizations in its position would have opted to settle, losing the artwork but avoiding the expense and potential embarrassment of litigation. The leaders of Sotheby's, no doubt conscious of the threats that a precedent-setting surrender might pose to their business model, thought they could win. The company said in a statement that "we have researched this sculpture extensively and have never seen nor been presented with any evidence that specifies when the sculpture left Cambodia over the last 1,000 years, nor is there any such evidence in this complaint."

The first hearing in *United States of America v. A 10th Century Cambodian Sandstone Sculpture* began on April 11. (Confusingly, the "defendant" in a federal forfeiture action is the object or asset in question rather than whoever possesses it.) SDNY had dispatched a pair of prosecutors from its Money Laundering and Asset Forfeiture Unit; Sotheby's, acting for itself and the European aristocrat who'd consigned the Duryodhana, had appointed the white-shoe firm WilmerHale. It was an odd spectacle: two teams of American lawyers with little prior knowledge of Southeast Asia, convening in a Lower Manhattan courtroom to debate Cambodian jurisprudence and the traumas of the Khmer Rouge. The first matter for the judge, George B. Daniels, was whether to sign a warrant of arrest for the statue, which would allow the government to take possession of it while the broader case was decided. SDNY's senior attorney rose to lay out her argument.

"Your Honor," she began, "there is no provenance for this statue prior to 1975. It was looted, as Sotheby's suggests, somewhere in the last thousand years. Where has it been? There is no record of anybody owning it up until 1975. . . . It is a giant red flag that should put somebody on notice." The prosecutor had read Bunker's emails to Sotheby's, cautioning that the Cambodian government had proof the Duryodhana was stolen from Koh Ker. And yet, she said, the company had continued "to market it and to attempt to sell it, all of which are in violation of numerous forfeiture statutes and make this property forfeitable to the United States, so it can be returned to its true owner, the Kingdom of Cambodia, and the Cambodian people."

Sotheby's lead lawyer, a former SDNY prosecutor himself, argued that the government had presented no evidence that the auction house knew when the Duryodhana had been taken, nor about the relevant Cambodian laws. And as he pointed out, Bunker had withdrawn her warning after meeting with officials in Phnom Penh and concluding that they weren't seeking the statue's return. "Sotheby's intends to vigorously dispute this," the attorney said. "Sotheby's view is that it acted in complete good faith here, and that it expects to be able to demonstrate that." After hearing from both sides, Judge Daniels declined to grant the arrest warrant, though thanks to an earlier restraining order, the Duryodhana wasn't going to leave New York without his permission. He instructed the lawyers to prepare for him to adjudicate the merits of the case, beginning later in 2012.

Over the spring and summer, lawyers at SDNY tried to gather information that would strengthen their argument for a forfeiture. Much of the work fell to a relatively junior prosecutor, Alexander Wilson. A lifelong New Yorker with sandy-blond hair and a deep, booming voice, Wilson was a rising star in the office. He'd shown a formidable talent for leading judges and juries through complex arguments, speaking quickly but clearly as he laid out his positions. In this, he was following in the footsteps of his father, who'd been a distinguished attorney at SDNY; trying cases there was the only legal job Wilson had ever wanted. Now he was faced with an especially tricky one, involving problems of history far removed from his usual work.

While extremely helpful, the documents that the government had obtained from Sotheby's filled in only part of the landscape. The company had nothing to do with the Duryodhana until the late 2000s, decades after it had first appeared on the international art market. It was like trying to look through the wrong end of a telescope. What Wilson and his team really needed to get ahold of were records from the 1970s, specifically from Spink's, the London art dealer that had sold the statue. But how? Few corporations kept documents for that long, and in the intervening years, Spink's had been acquired by Christie's and partially shut down, with other elements of the business spun off. The chances that its papers had been preserved—and if they had, that anyone knew where to find them—appeared slim.

The Department of Homeland Security approached Christie's, whose in-house lawyers had been following the Duryodhana case closely, to inquire about what Spink's records it might hold. The company's general counsel was willing to help if she could. So she and her colleagues did what many executives do when faced with an open-ended task that might come to nothing: They asked an intern. The young employee began rummaging through old storage boxes, looking for anything that could be relevant. In August 2012, she reported back with a surprise. Not only had the Spink's archive made it through the mergers and demergers of the preceding decades, but it had somehow been brought to New York. And it included several neatly typed letters between Spink's and Douglas Latchford on the subject of the Duryodhana.

Soon the file was with Wilson and his team. The lawyer was astonished by what he was reading. As Sotheby's had prepared to put the Duryodhana up for auction, Latchford had told the company—in emails that were now in SDNY's possession—that he'd never owned it, nor been involved in its 1975 sale to a Belgian businessman. He did say, however, that he'd first seen it in London in the late 1960s. Every part of this, Wilson could now see, was false. He was looking at a tidy internal memo from Spink's, dated November 1974, in which one manager told another that he'd "explored extensively" with Latchford "how to get 'legitimate' papers for the large Koh Ker guardian"—almost certainly the Duryodhana.

Then, after it was sold, Spink's had written to Latchford to tell him he would be "pleased to hear" that the piece had been taken. And in a later letter to an American collector, a copy of which he'd sent to Spink's in London, Latchford boasted of receiving two large Koh Ker heads in 1972, followed eight months later by the corresponding torsos. He stated explicitly that one of the figures had gone "to a private collection in Brussels," the other to the Norton Simon Museum in California. This was obviously the Duryodhana's near twin, now known as the Bhima, which had also been matched to a pair of severed feet at Koh Ker.

Sotheby's arguments against a federal seizure rested, in large part, on the fact that the government couldn't prove when the Duryodhana had come out of Cambodia. Based on the Latchford correspondence, it certainly looked like the year had been 1972—well into the civil war and, crucially, after the 1970 signing of the UNESCO treaty on antiquities, to which the US was a party. The letters also got Wilson thinking about the broader implications. If Latchford had sold one looted statue and then lied about it, he'd surely done the same with others; at eighty, he was still the world's foremost dealer of Khmer artifacts. He had enjoyed a particularly productive relationship with the Metropolitan Museum of Art, supplying some of the most important objects in its Southeast Asian collection and drawing on the resulting prestige in his sales to private collectors. It wasn't hard to imagine how some of those transactions, and Latchford's representations to buyers, banks, and other counterparties, could have violated federal laws—the kinds of offenses that can lead to prosecution and prison terms.

But without much more evidence, especially relating to more recent sales, Wilson didn't know if a criminal case against Latchford would ever be feasible. Trying to put one together would require a great deal of work, to which he couldn't yet commit—not least because his immediate priority remained taking on Sotheby's. The auction house was fighting tooth and nail to stop SDNY from seizing its prized statue, asking the court to dismiss the forfeiture complaint before litigation went any further. At a hearing in September 2012, Judge Daniels made clear that if the government was going to convince him to act, it would need more evidence. Knowing when the Duryodhana had come to Latchford in Bangkok wasn't going to be enough. "I am not sure you can tell me the last time anybody said they saw these statues in place where the feet are," he said to one of Wilson's colleagues. "Can you even represent that you're confident that they were there standing in the twentieth century?"

"We can represent we are confident," the prosecutor responded. "I think that is right."

Sensing the uncertainty, Judge Daniels pressed from the bench: "You don't have any basis to say that. Start there. Isn't that a correct statement?"

"It's not something we allege in our complaint, which is where we are, but as we continue with the case, we think we will be able to present that evidence."

The judge appeared skeptical, even as he conceded that the "total chaos" of the civil war would have created ideal conditions for attacks on temples: "Maybe somebody looted it in 1900 and kept it in their own private collection until they died and then the grandchildren decided to sell it." He continued, "Quite frankly, I think the government has significant hurdles to overcome and is maybe looking for a smoking gun in order to prove this case."

Judge Daniels was right. SDNY didn't have enough, even after gathering all the information that was reasonably available in New York. The whole truth—about the Duryodhana and about Latchford—could only be found in Cambodia.

Since identifying the statues at Sotheby's and the Norton Simon as the Duryodhana and the Bhima, Éric Bourdonneau had deepened his own investigation. If the archaeologist was correct in his analysis of Prasat Chen, the temple at Koh Ker where they'd originated, then the two male figures would not have stood alone. At the temple of Banteay Srei, the same characters were depicted on a roof pediment surrounded by fellow-warriors—also players in the epic of the Mahabharata—who had gathered to witness their duel. But at Prasat Chen, all that was visible on the surface were the four previously discovered stone feet. If there was evidence that the site had once held more sculptures, it was beneath those remnants, buried under compacted soil.

In July 2012, a Cambodian team excavated the area around the feet. They dug down by hand, gradually exposing the walls of a perfectly square chamber of brick and stone that measured four meters across. This was Prasat Chen's western gopura, or entrance pavilion, which worshippers would have passed through on their way to the center of the temple. As they descended farther, carefully photographing and cataloging each fragment they encountered, the team found seven previously unknown stone blocks: four on the south side of the chamber and three on the north. The blocks were empty pedestals. While their sides were intact, the tops of all seven were jagged with damage. Whatever works they had been designed to support had been violently removed.

The photographs went immediately to Bourdonneau in Paris. *OK, we have the full group*, he thought as he looked through them. His hypothesis had been proved right. The western gopura had originally contained nine statues, not two. All had been stolen in what could only have been a highly organized crime spree. And Bourdonneau had some idea of where the seven additional works might have gone. He'd been scouring records of Koh Ker–style pieces held around the world. Some were easy to find, since they were in the collections of major museums and well known to experts. Others were much more obscure, their only public appearances being single entries in auction catalogs. After that, they'd presumably entered the homes of private collectors and disappeared from view. In another case, all Bourdonneau had were a couple of small black-and-white pictures that he'd discovered after hours digging around online.

Bourdonneau began trying to map the objects in his database onto the newly discovered pedestals. The pattern of damage to the pedestals' stone indicated that four of the sculptures had been of seated figures, while three had been kneeling. (The left-behind toes, pressed flat and pointed forward, provided a strong hint.) That helped narrow it down, as did the pedestals' dimensions. Bourdonneau was looking for very large sculptures, probably life-size or nearly so. Soon he had a list. None of the works had appeared on the market before the mid-1980s, well after the Bhima and Duryodhana, suggesting the outer group had been looted in that decade. One had been placed in storage at the Conservation d'Angkor, in Siem Reap, in 1994. Another, a seated figure that Bourdonneau identified as representing the mythical warrior Dhrishtadyumna, had been sold the same year by the Chinese Porcelain Company, a gallery on New York's Park Avenue. Two others had been sold in the 1990s by Spink's; one of those had popped up again in 2009, in an auction at Christie's. From Bourdonneau's perspective, however, none of these were the most immediately significant.

Like any scholar of ancient Cambodia, he was familiar with the glories of the Khmer collection at the Met, and he knew that since 1994, a pair of Koh Ker figures had stood sentinel at the entrance to its Southeast Asian galleries. Known as the Kneeling Attendants, they were among the most impressive of the museum's holdings. Bourdonneau was now certain that they belonged to two of the empty pedestals at Prasat Chen.

Indeed, some of the evidence came from the Met's own longtime curator of South and Southeast Asian art, Martin Lerner, who'd retired in 2003. Lerner had once written a description of the statue that had been sold by the Chinese Porcelain Company, and in it he suggested that the Kneeling Attendants might "have been attendants to this very sculpture"—in other words, that they were part of the same grouping, just as Bourdonneau had concluded. At the time that Lerner offered this conjecture, Bourdonneau wrote in a subsequent report, it was an "adventurous" idea for which there was no basis in publicly available research. The archaeologist couldn't help but wonder if Lerner knew more about events at Prasat Chen than the Met had let on.

As a gesture of transparency, the museum published basic provenance information for items in its collection. Bourdonneau could see that the Kneeling Attendants had been donated, as disjoined heads and torsos that were later reattached, between 1987 and 1992. There was no prior record of their whereabouts. The donor of both torsos, and of one head, was listed as Latchford—who'd been seeking to burnish his credentials with high-profile gifts, some of them in Lerner's honor. The other head, meanwhile, had at least a possible connection to him: Its donor had bought it from Spink's, which counted Latchford as one of its principal suppliers.

After its initial reluctance to confront Sotheby's, by mid-2012, the Cambodian government had grown much more assertive in its attitude toward looted works. Thanks to SDNY, officials in Phnom Penh now understood that it was possible to challenge major American institutions in court, and that doing so wouldn't rupture their relations with Washington. In fact, the Department of Justice was eager to help. And with new evidence in hand, the Met was at the top of their list. Cambodia wanted the Kneeling Attendants back, a demand that soon made *The New York Times*. "The government is very serious about moving this forward, and we are getting much legal advice," a representative explained.

The *Times* contacted Latchford to ask how he had come to be in possession of the objects he'd donated. Uncharacteristically for a connoisseur who prided himself on obsessive research, and rarely missed an opportunity to show off the depth of his knowledge, he professed ignorance of their origins. According to his version of events, the Kneeling Attendants had been attributed to him almost accidentally. He said they had been sitting unsold at Spink's, and when the London dealer failed to find a buyer, its managers had asked him to "provide financial aid to donate them" to the Met. "That's what I did and why they are in my name," he declared. As for where Spink's had gotten them, Latchford said he had no idea.

What Latchford couldn't know, however, was that at 1 Saint Andrew's Plaza, Alexander Wilson was looking at documents that told a very different story.

20

American and European galleries, auction houses, and museums are allegedly full of Cambodian plunder. Many of these artifacts were allegedly stolen during the country's long conflict, making them 'blood antiquities,' little different than 'blood diamonds' from Sierra Leone."

In June 2012, after reading these words in an op-ed that appeared on the website of news network CNN, an attorney named Bradley Gordon felt moved to do something. Gordon wasn't involved in the international artifact trade and had no connection to the ongoing Duryodhana case. But he lived and worked in Phnom Penh, where he employed a team of young Cambodians at his law firm. He decided to send a cold email to one of the piece's coauthors, to see if there was any way he might be of assistance. As it happened, there was.

SDNY prosecutors had strong evidence that the statue they were trying to seize from Sotheby's had been stolen from Koh Ker around 1972. All their information, however, was from documents gathered in New York. They had no direct witnesses who could confirm the date, or anything else about the theft. And few lawyers at SDNY knew the first thing about Cambodia; before getting involved with the case, some might have struggled to find it on a map. To move forward, they needed someone with real knowledge of the country, as well as the folkways of the American legal system. In other words, someone like Gordon.

After a few calls, the prosecutors agreed to hire him as a consultant, tasked with finding out what he could about the looting of the Duryodhana. It was an assignment that would change the course of his life. Originally from Connecticut, Gordon had gone to college at Brown and then graduated from Harvard Law School. He landed at Linklaters, an elite British firm, where he advised on capital-markets deals and worked between Singapore, Bangkok, Hong Kong, and Tokyo. Unusually, though, he'd been interested in Cambodia since the late 1980s, when he took a year off college to teach English to refugees who'd fled from the civil war. He kept in touch with some of them as the country rebuilt, and when a friend told Gordon in 2007 that he was setting up a Cambodia-focused investment fund, looking for opportunities in its rapidly growing economy, Gordon jumped at the chance. He soon moved to Phnom Penh.

The fund didn't work out, and neither did another that Gordon cofounded; the global financial crisis had begun soon after his arrival, and most investors no longer wanted exposure to volatile emerging markets. So Gordon returned to his former career and set up a law practice. As one among a tiny cohort of US-trained lawyers in Cambodia, he got referrals from international firms to advise the overseas companies that were still interested in the country. He also became a confidant to senior businessmen and politicians; as in many developing nations, they were often the same people, or at least related to each other. Warm and courteous, with salt-and-pepper hair and an easy smile, Gordon wasn't hard for them to like, and he enjoyed being at the center of the commercial action.

Cambodia was still an extremely challenging place to work. In addition to murdering millions of their compatriots, the Khmer Rouge had destroyed the most basic foundations of the economy, even abolishing the currency. Then, nearly two decades of further conflict had ensured that almost none of these fundamentals could be restored. When peace finally arrived, Cambodia had to create a modern financial system from zero. In some respects, it had gone well. There was a successful textile industry that provided hundreds of thousands of jobs, particularly for women. Tourism was thriving, with foreign visitors piling into Phnom Penh and Siem Reap. But there were also massive obstacles. When a stock exchange opened in the capital in 2011, officials found that next to no companies had sufficiently clean accounting to go public. Corruption was pervasive, and the rule of law subordinate to the interests of the powerful.

Gordon had nonetheless come to love Cambodia. It was hard to imagine how people who had endured such agonies could go on. Anyone over forty, whether they were a corporate executive or a taxi driver, had, in all likelihood, been through unspeakable horrors. And yet go on they had, rebuilding a peaceful, if troubled, society. Younger Cambodians, like the junior lawyers who worked under Gordon, were particularly impressive. Educated, curious, and enthusiastic, they seemed remarkably free of the traumas that haunted their parents. And despite its recent history, they were proud of their country—and particularly of the legacy of Angkor, which remained on the national flag. Gordon had, of course, visited the ancient capital, as well as lesser-known sites, coming away awed by the artistic and architectural achievements of the ancient Khmer. When asked why he stayed in Cambodia, he said that he had no choice: The country had him under a magic spell.

At first, Gordon thought his Duryodhana assignment from SDNY would be simple, since there was no doubt that the statue had come from Koh Ker, and specifically from the site known as Prasat Chen. Presumably, it was just a matter of interviewing people in nearby communities about what they remembered from the 1960s and early '70s, then sending the findings to New York. Gordon dispatched an employee by motorcycle to do some reconnaissance. The staffer climbed to the top of Koh Ker's central pyramid to get a sense of the landscape. "This will be easy," he reported; with so few settlements nearby, "it'll only take us 24 hours." But when Gordon visited himself, he found that his early optimism had been misplaced.

The residents of the adjacent village were largely illiterate—rice farmers who worked their fields by day and illegally cut down trees by night. Many were former Khmer Rouge members. They were, by turns, suspicious of Gordon's intentions and amused by the presence of a friendly, sweat-drenched American asking them through a translator about events four decades in the past. When he pressed them about looting, the villagers gave only vague answers, saying that there had once been many statues in the Koh Ker temples, which were now gone. That much, Gordon already knew. The trip had been all but useless, and he returned frustrated to Phnom Penh. He needed to come up with a different strategy.

The Duryodhana almost certainly would have left Koh Ker by road, hauled first to Siem Reap and then toward the Thai border. Gordon went along the highway with his translator, carrying printed-out pictures of the statue. Buddhist pagodas were a good place to start looking for witnesses, since they tended to attract older people,

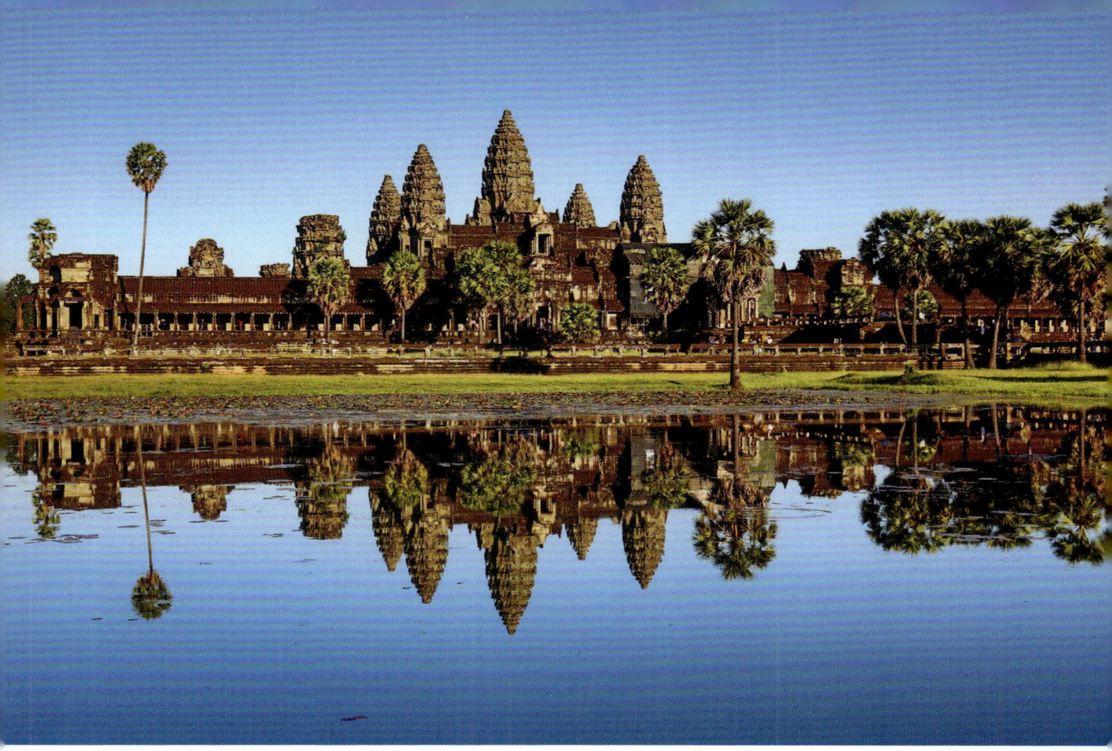

Angkor Wat, the world's largest
religious structure.

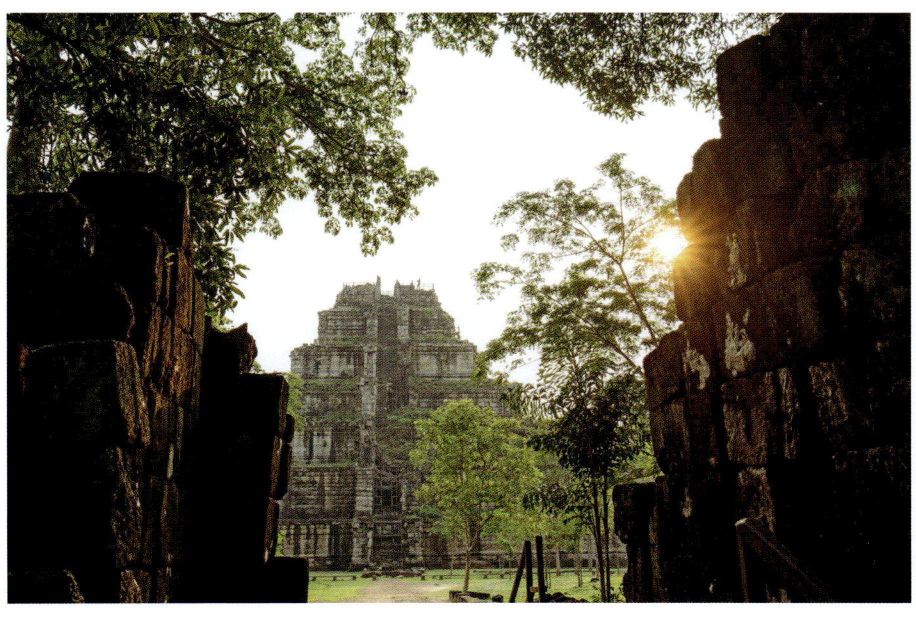

Koh Ker, which served as the Khmer
capital in the tenth century.

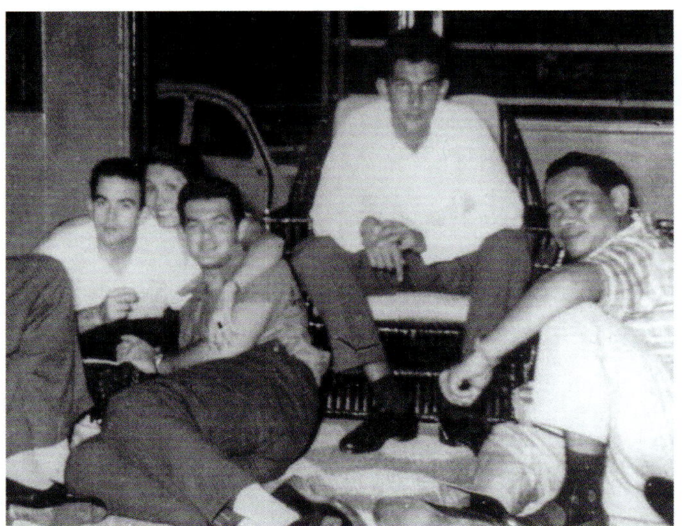

Latchford, third from right, as a young man.

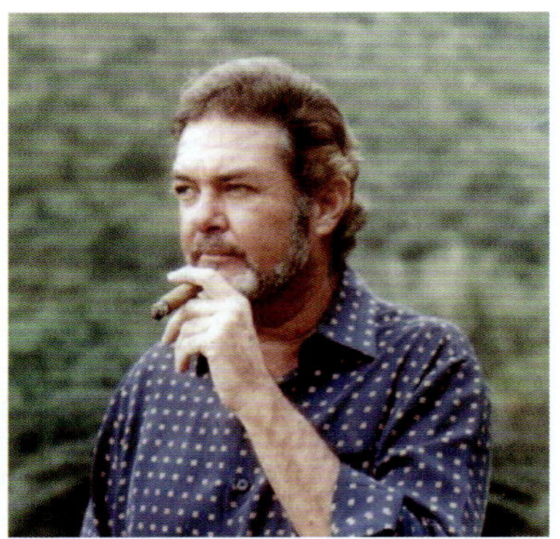

Latchford in the 1980s.

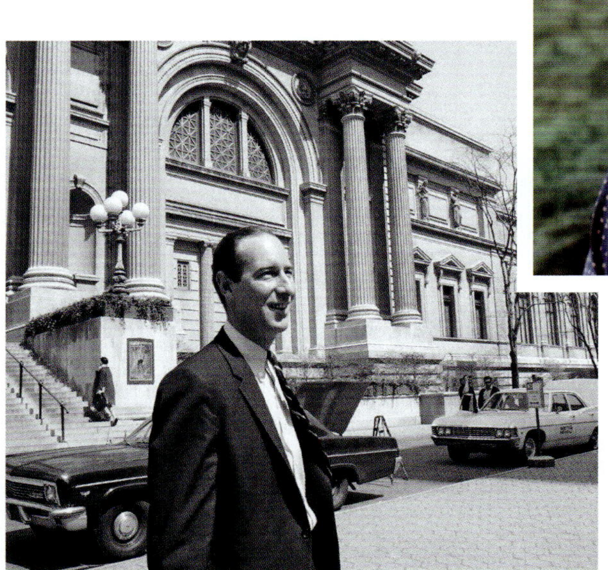

Thomas Hoving, the director of the
Metropolitan Museum, in 1967.

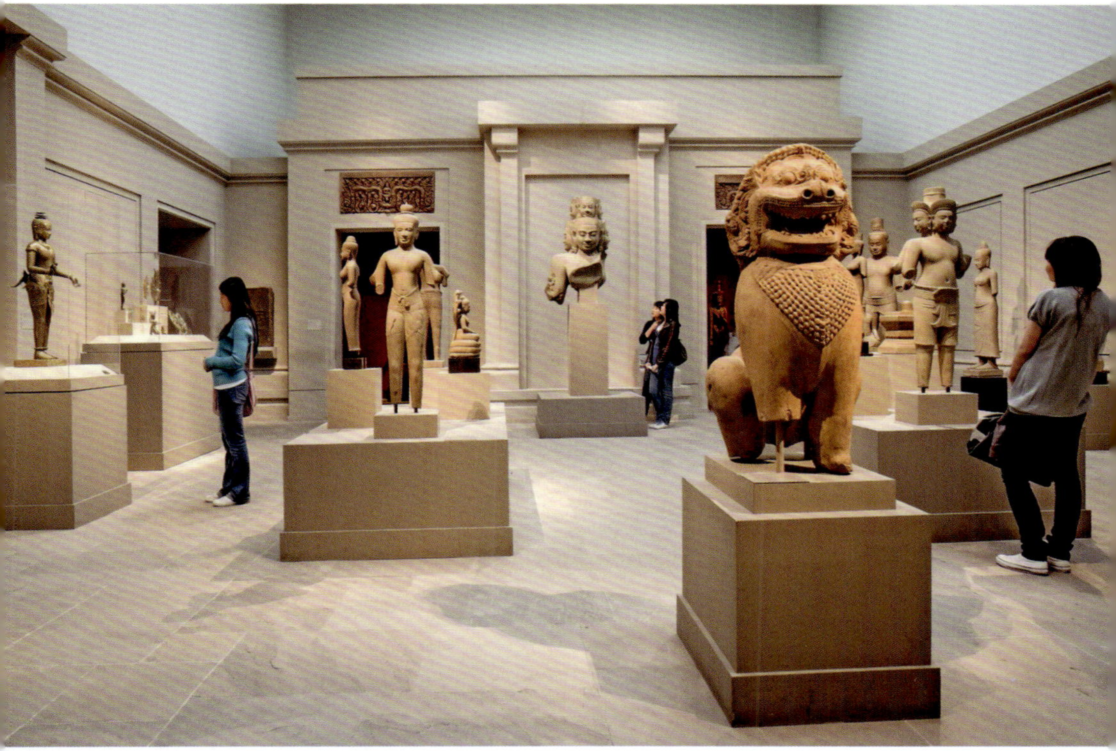

Part of the Khmer collection at the Met.

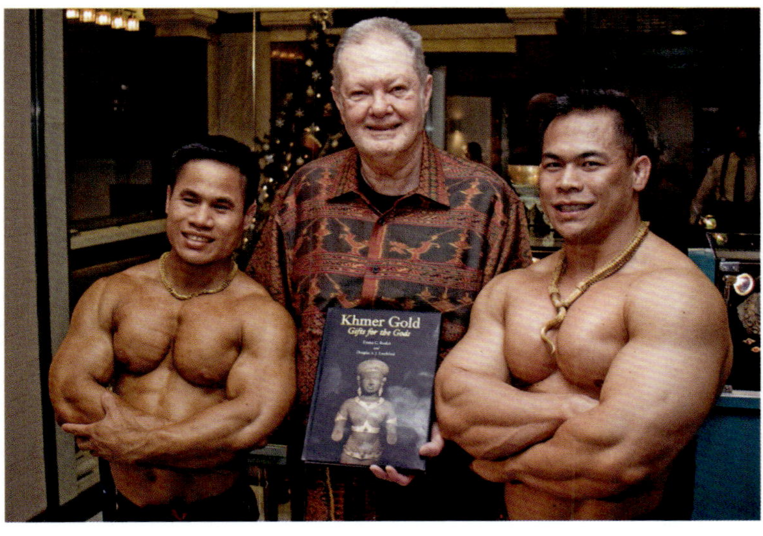

Latchford with bodybuilders in 2007. Sitthi Charoenrith is on the right.

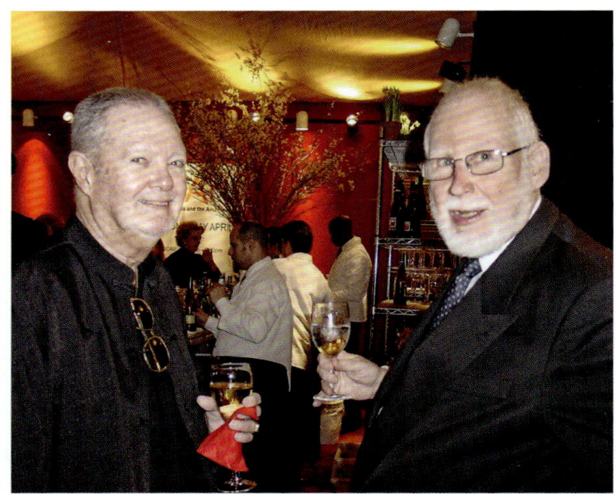

Latchford with the former Met curator Martin Lerner.

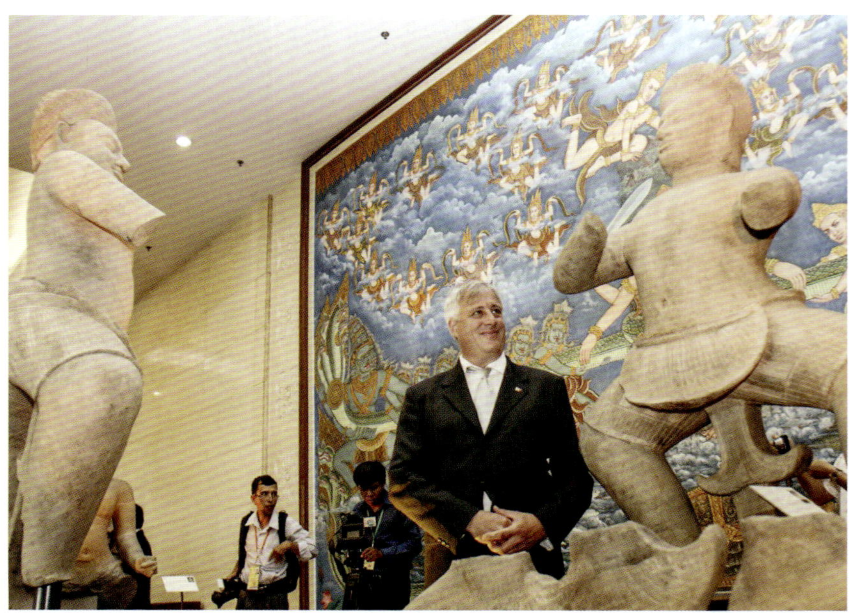

Simon Warrack with the Bhima and Duryodhana in Phnom Penh.

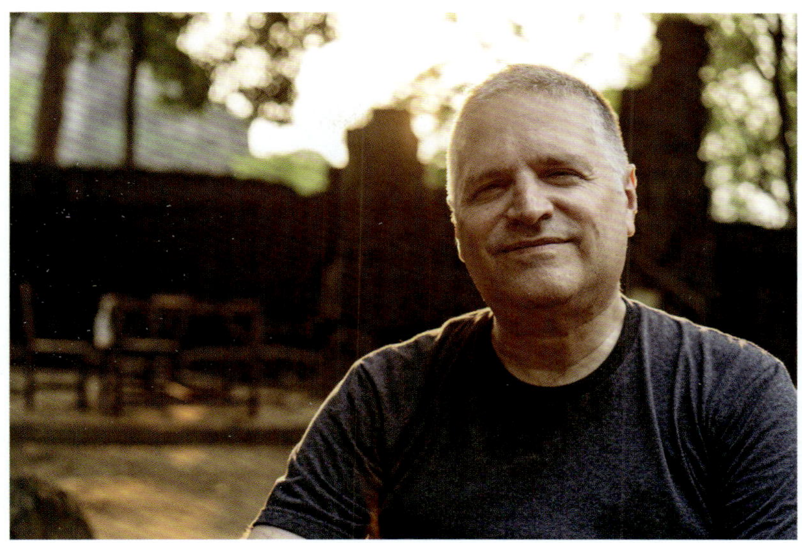

Bradley Gordon at Koh Ker.

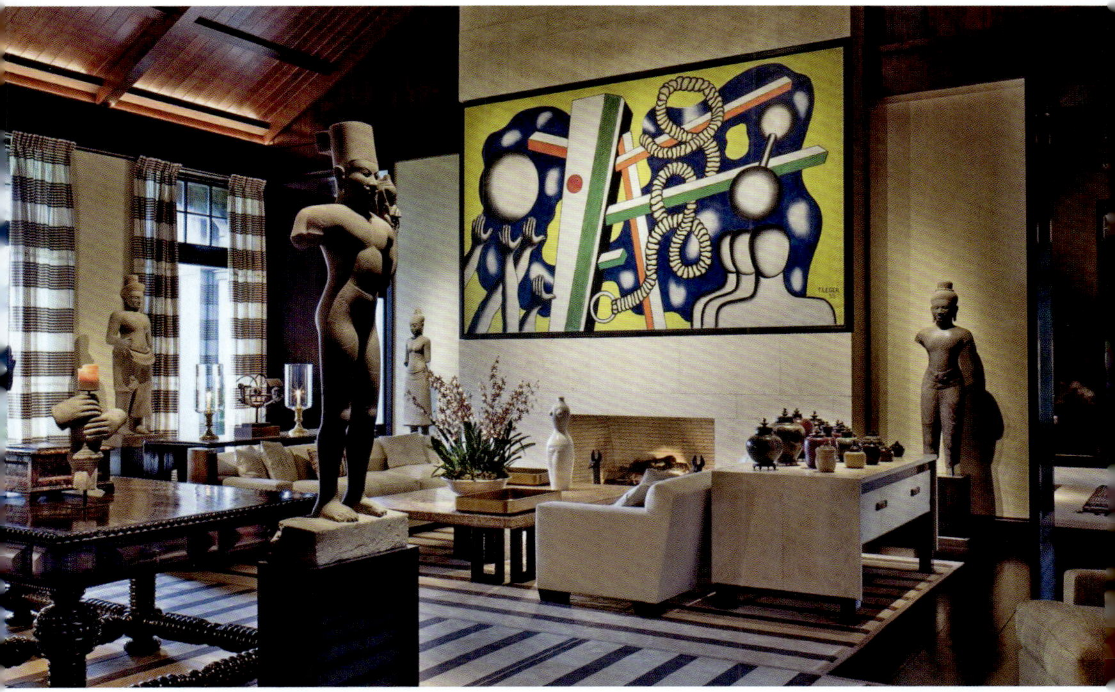

The Palm Beach home of billionaire
art collector George Lindemann.

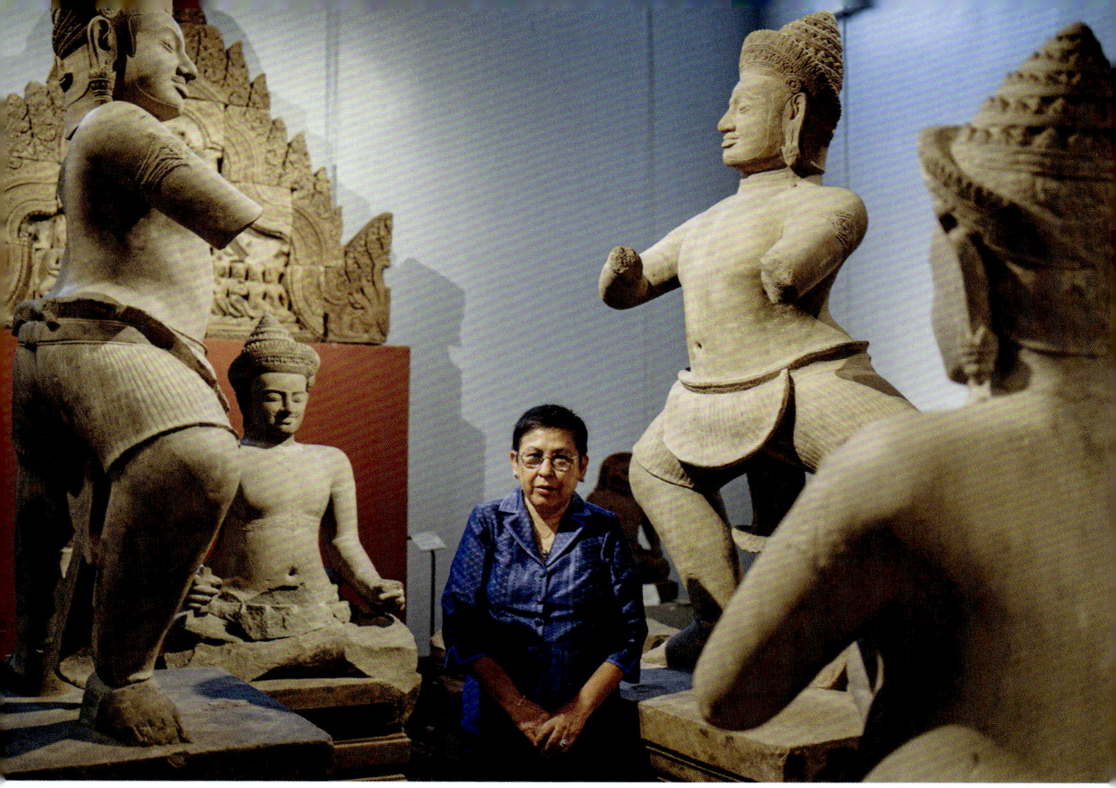

Phoeurng Sackona, Cambodia's
Minister of Culture and Fine Arts.

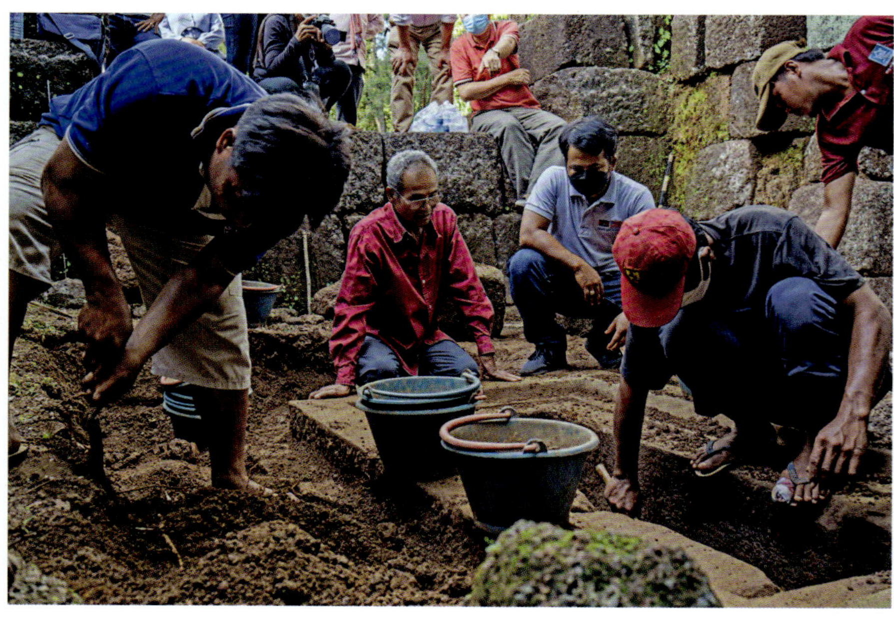

Lion, in red shirt, guiding an archaeological team at Koh Ker.

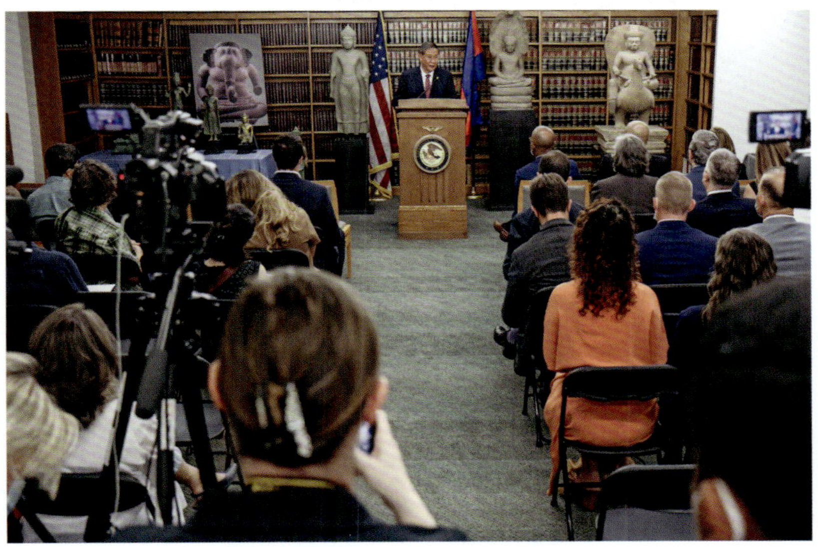

A ceremony in New York to mark the
repatriation of looted Khmer artifacts.

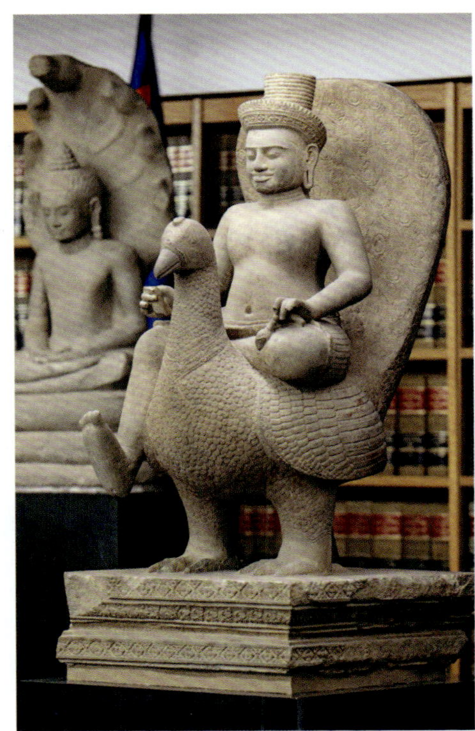

Skanda on a Peacock,
on display in New York.

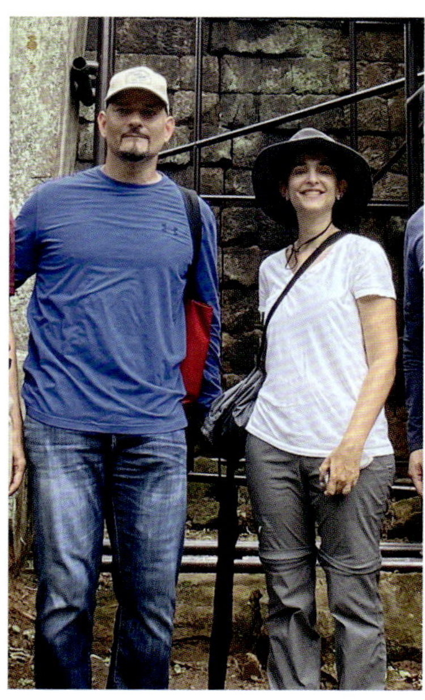

J. P. Labbat and Jessica Feinstein
in Cambodia.

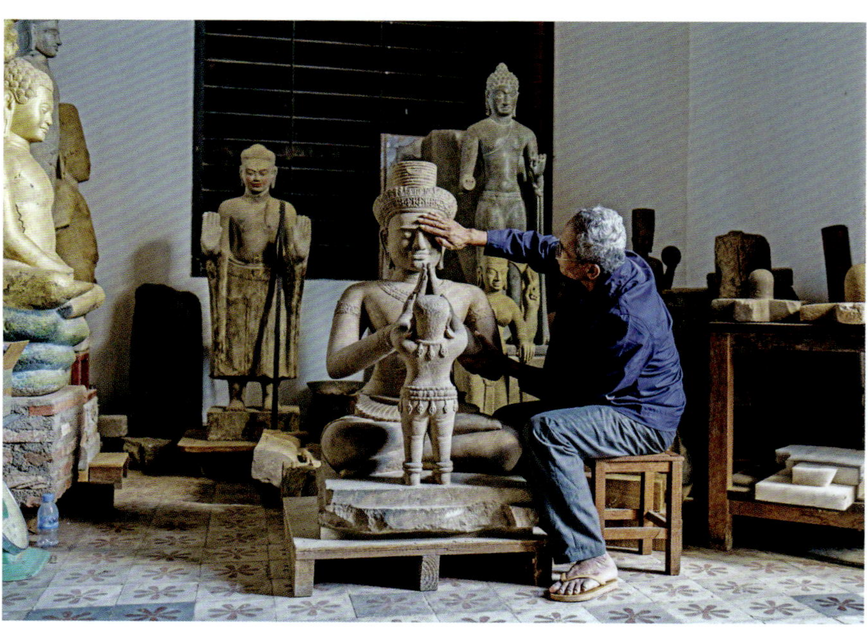

Lion with Shiva and Skanda in Phnom Penh.

especially during religious festivals. As he conducted more interviews, Gordon began to figure out how to get more accurate information. Asking a sixty- or seventy-year-old villager whether something had happened in a particular year was pointless. It was much better, he learned, to try to situate their memories around major events in Cambodian history, like the March 1970 coup that deposed Prince Sihanouk, or the final victory of the Khmer Rouge five years later. Within those bounds, the people he spoke to could be much more specific. And many had vivid memories of looting—just not of the Duryodhana.

Gordon had been hired to investigate the theft of only that single work, but as he continued his interviews, he began to grasp the astonishing scale of what had been done to Cambodia's historic sites— and found that he couldn't stop thinking about it. While significant, the Sotheby's statue was just one among thousands of pieces that had been systematically stolen during the country's deepest agonies—for which America, with its bombing campaign and, later, tacit support of the Khmer Rouge, bore no small responsibility. Entire ancient cities had been ransacked, to the benefit of wealthy collectors and expansion-minded museum curators. They had adored and profited off those works while the nation that had produced them starved. Collectively, Gordon concluded, it amounted to perhaps the most outrageous art theft in history. And beyond looking into a few high-profile pieces, no one was investigating the full breadth of the heist.

Gordon did eventually find one of the witnesses he'd been seeking, a man who worked as the caretaker of a Buddhist temple, not far from Koh Ker. He said he had a clear recollection of a statue that matched the Duryodhana's description being moved out on an oxcart. Surprisingly, he said he was sure that it was in 1972. A teenager at the time, he'd fallen in love with a girl from a village near the site. His memory of the statue was particularly vivid, he said, because it coincided with the last time he'd seen the girl before she was killed by the Khmer Rouge. Talking to him stirred something in Gordon. Unearthing deeply buried evidence was a thrill, one that he would go to obsessive lengths to experience again and again. The mysteries of the Duryodhana were close to being revealed, but Gordon was now driven by the knowledge that he'd assembled only the smallest corner of a vast historical puzzle—and that the missing pieces were out there, waiting to be discovered.

In November 2012, Alexander Wilson and his team at SDNY asked for permission to submit an amended complaint in the Duryodhana case, one far more detailed than their original filing. Thanks to Gordon's interviews in Cambodia, as well as the Spink's correspondence with Latchford that they'd obtained, the prosecutors were now confident of the year the statue had been looted: 1972. This specificity allowed SDNY to argue that the theft had been illegal at the time it took place, a basic condition for seizing an antiquity under the National Stolen Property Act.

But the draft complaint went further, saying that after the Duryodhana was taken—along with its near twin, the Bhima—the works were delivered to a Thai dealer and then "obtained by a well-known collector of Khmer antiquities" who "knew that the statues had been looted from Koh Ker." According to the document, this unidentified collector had consigned the Duryodhana for sale at Spink's, which also knew of its origins, and conspired "to fraudulently obtain" the necessary export licenses. It also claimed that as Sotheby's prepared to resell the statue decades later, the auction house had "knowingly omitted" the same individual's involvement from sale materials, as well as "communications with potential buyers, the Kingdom of Cambodia, and United States law enforcement."

These were explosive allegations, which Sotheby's didn't yet have to answer. The judge, George B. Daniels, hadn't given his permission for the amendments to be filed, and the updated complaint would have no legal force until he did. It was nonetheless attached to an SDNY motion, putting it in the public domain. To anyone who'd been following the litigation, the identity of the "well-known collector" was easy enough to figure out. Latchford wasn't being charged with a crime, yet just a few months after the revelations about the Metropolitan Museum's Kneeling Attendants, he was being directly accused of dealing in looted statues—and not by archaeologists or activists but by the US government.

At eighty-one, Latchford believed the crisis was manageable. Over the previous few years, he had reached new heights of esteem among the people whose opinions he cared about most: his fellow dealers and the buyers they served. In particular, he'd been working closely with Nancy Wiener, a prominent New York dealer with a gallery on East Seventy-Fourth Street, to make blockbuster sales. In the same Sotheby's auction from which the Duryodhana had been pulled, they'd jointly sold an eleventh-century Shiva figure for almost $600,000. Wiener had also provided Latchford with an appraisal of a bronze statue of the deity Krishna, valuing it at an impressive $3.5 million, and had paid him $500,000 for a sculpture of the Buddha seated on a serpent, which she would offer to clients for triple the price. The first two pieces were products of recent looting, so fresh they needed to be cleaned of dirt and debris. For the third, Latchford had provided a pair of provenance statements that contradicted each other—strongly suggesting that at least one was false, if not both.

None of this much troubled Wiener, and there was no sign that Latchford's private clients were starting to worry about the origins of their purchases from him. Museums were somewhat harder to satisfy; after embarrassments like the Met's repatriations to Italy, curators had grown more cautious. Latchford was managing to make sales all the same. In 2011, the National Gallery of Australia, one of that country's most prestigious cultural institutions, paid him $1.5 million for a trio of ninth-century bronzes, which it billed as "perhaps the most extraordinary work acquired this year." Latchford had provided the NGA with a provenance almost identical to what he'd given Netscape cofounder Jim Clark: a letter from a long-dead Hong Kong businessman, Ian Donaldson, stating that he'd acquired the pieces in Vietnam in the 1960s. It was accepted with few questions.

One reason why organizations like the NGA were happy to deal with Latchford was because he appeared to have an excellent relationship with Cambodia. He'd recently published a third book with Emma Bunker, *Khmer Bronzes: New Interpretations of the Past*. After a launch party in Bangkok, with some of the featured works carried in by shirtless Thai bodybuilders, he'd traveled with an entourage to Phnom Penh, booking out a large portion of the five-star Hotel Le Royal. There, in a ceremony at the National Museum, he donated a bronze boat prow dating to the eleventh or twelfth century, boasting that it was the only one of its kind ever found. He'd also assembled a group of foreign donors, including Bunker and Wiener, to contribute a total of about $190,000 to improving the museum's colonial-era lighting and electrical systems. Compared with the scale of his business, these were trifling gifts. They were nonetheless appreciated by

Cambodia's cash-strapped cultural professionals, and in mid-2011, the government awarded Latchford—for the third time—one of its highest civilian honors.

Amid all these successes, he was feeling confident when, in late 2012, a reporter who'd been covering the Duryodhana case came to interview him about SDNY's findings. Latchford conceded that he was the unidentified "collector" described in legal documents. But he denied any connection to the Duryodhana, saying that he'd been erroneously listed as the statue's owner in records at Spink's—a statement similar to his earlier claim that the Met's Kneeling Attendants had been attributed to him virtually by accident. Prosecutors, Latchford said, were "weaving together suppositions," animated by an "imagination working overtime." He also delivered a broad defense of his life's work.

Latchford was clearly incensed by the idea that his accumulation of Khmer art, which he'd studied, cataloged, and preserved since the 1950s, could make him some kind of villain. Indeed, he argued, the pieces were better off with him and his buyers than they would be in Cambodia. "Who is going to pay for repatriation?" he asked. "Where will it wind up? Rotting in some storage house? Who will pay for the conservation?" Latchford added an additional justification—another sense in which he believed that the objects he dealt in were exactly where they were supposed to be. Buddhist priests, he said, had informed him that "in a previous life I had been Khmer, and that what I collect had once belonged to me."

Meanwhile, in Cambodia, Gordon had been going beyond his brief—and spending much more time away from his usual corporate assignments than he'd expected. Rather than narrowly focusing on the theft of the Duryodhana, he wanted to know everything: how the looting networks operated in the countryside, how the Khmer Rouge and other players in the civil war used them to fund their operations, and what happened to artifacts when they entered Thailand on their way to the international market. On one expedition, driving over the border along the route that looted objects might have taken, Gordon interviewed relatives of Ta Mok, the Khmer Rouge commander known for both his brutality and his interest in antiquities: When he was finally captured by government forces in 1999, there were no fewer than sixty-one sculptures in his house.

Gordon tracked down other senior figures from Pol Pot's movement, living in comfortable circumstances and chillingly serene about their pasts. During a meeting in Anlong Veng, the final stronghold of the insurgency, his translator stood up and walked out, disgusted. After these journeys, Gordon felt that he knew enough to have an intelligent conversation with the father of one of his staffers, who'd also been an important player in the Khmer Rouge. The man was no expert on antiquities, but he told Gordon about someone who was: a looter so accomplished that he was considered the best of the best. To really understand the business, he said, "you need to find this guy."

Gordon couldn't get an exact address for this mysterious statue thief, only a general location, about a fifteen-minute drive from the entrance to Koh Ker. He went out to the area and began going from house to house. His translator had prepared a white lie to explain his presence—that Gordon was an investor looking to buy land and also happened to be interested in the local temples. At perhaps the fifth or sixth residence, a modest wooden house on a busy road, a woman answered the door and confirmed that the person Gordon was looking for was there. Warily, she invited him to enter. There was a middle-aged man inside, slightly overweight but with a proud, confident bearing—like a retired general, Gordon thought.

His name was Toek Tik.

Gordon had been traveling around the country with a copy of *Adoration and Glory*, Latchford and Bunker's first book. At 520 pages, it wasn't exactly easy to toss into a backpack. Yet he'd come to see it as an important tool for mapping looting networks, since in Gordon's estimation, nearly every piece it cataloged had been stolen. It was just a question of when, where, and by whom. His interviewees had generally never seen the book before, and it sometimes helped spark conversation. Gordon sat down on the floor, where he, Toek Tik, and the translator could all look at it together. After some small talk, he pulled the book from his bag, trying his best to seem unthreatening to a man who, like many Cambodians of his generation, had good reasons to be mistrustful of strangers. Suddenly, Toek Tik's face lit up.

"I know this, I know this!" he exclaimed in Khmer, tapping on the stunning cover photo of Shiva and Skanda, one of the most important works in Latchford's personal collection. Toek Tik appeared to be almost vibrating with excitement, calling his wife over to watch him flip the pages. He could read only with difficulty in his own language, let alone English, but as he turned through the glossy photographs, he seemed to recognize them. "I know, I know," he said again and again. Toek Tik was cagey about how he had come to be so familiar with ancient Khmer statuary, but Gordon almost didn't need to ask. He had a head-spinning list of other questions to consider. Was it really possible that Toek Tik had personally stolen the artworks in Latchford's book? How could anyone prove it if he had? Would he be willing to testify? And if so, what kind of guarantees would he need? Looting was a criminal offense in Cambodia, and the concept of immunity in exchange for providing evidence didn't really exist in the country's legal system.

All that would have to wait. Gordon was wary of overstaying his welcome, or of spooking Toek Tik by getting too specific about what he hoped to achieve. After some more guarded conversation, Gordon departed with his translator, promising to keep in touch about the works in *Adoration and Glory*. Back in Phnom Penh, he tried to make sense of how to proceed. For a lawyer who'd spent most of his career working on capital-markets deals, this was treacherous new territory. If Toek Tik was willing to share what he knew, he had to somehow be protected, and not just from the Cambodian authorities. The men who'd worked with him to steal statues might not like the idea of their past activities being revealed, and there was a good chance that some, if not most, had killed before. Gordon decided to refer to Toek Tik only by a code name. He chose "Lion," an animal sometimes rendered in stone by the artisans of the Khmer Empire. For now, at least, Lion's existence would be a closely held secret.

Gordon soon returned for another visit, then another, aiming to build trust and, above all, to listen. He sat, riveted, as Lion gradually revealed more of his story: how as a child he'd been forced to serve as a messenger, and then as a soldier, for the Khmer Rouge; how he'd escaped to the rugged Kulen plateau, living on what the jungle could provide; how, in the turmoil of the 1980s and '90s, he'd learned to survive and eventually thrive by looting ancient sites, Koh Ker in particular. Gordon gradually understood why he was willing to be so open with a relative stranger. The answer, it appeared, was a kind of remorse. Lion didn't regret his actions in the usual sense of the word; he'd done what he needed to do to stay alive, and to support his family and those of the men who worked for him. It seemed to Gordon, nonetheless, that he recognized the damage his actions had caused, and wanted to make amends.

In early 2013, after Gordon had been in contact with Lion for several months, Wilson came to Cambodia with his boss. With the Duryodhana case ongoing in New York, the pair's visit was partly diplomatic, beginning with a banquet in Phnom Penh where government representatives toasted US-Cambodian cooperation. Then they set off for Koh Ker, where they could get a firsthand look at the site where the Duryodhana had originated and speak to local residents. Gordon had spent enough time searching for witnesses in the countryside to understand that, from an investigative standpoint, this was pointless. The Cambodian government had decided to escort the prosecutors to Koh Ker in a convoy of SUVs, accompanied by soldiers and a camera crew. It was the opposite of how Gordon preferred to operate—unobtrusively, with the smallest possible entourage and immense reserves of patience. After rumbling into the village by the Koh Ker complex, officials pulled a few people aside to ask them, for the American delegation's benefit, what they recalled about the removal of artifacts in the area. Unsurprisingly, they said they knew nothing.

Gordon had an idea for making the visit more productive—and, just maybe, for getting the weight of US law enforcement behind a broader investigation of looting. Lion was too young to have been involved in the theft of the Duryodhana, the only matter that SDNY was actively litigating. Still, Gordon told Wilson, "This guy has the goods." In Gordon's opinion, talking to him was essential. While Wilson and his superior agreed, the proposal presented a problem. The Cambodian authorities still didn't know that Lion existed, and turning up at his home in an official motorcade would have instantly ended Gordon's relationship with him. So the three Americans arranged to give their hosts the slip. They borrowed a vehicle from the US embassy and disappeared from the Koh Ker convoy. As they drove off, Gordon silently hoped that no one would notice they were gone.

A short time later, they pulled up outside Lion's house, and he invited the group inside. The windows were closed, and Wilson, unaccustomed to the climate of Southeast Asia, felt a thick curtain of heat descend as they sat down. The prosecutors had brought their own copy of *Adoration and Glory*, and Lion, using the book as a kind of visual aid, began to tell them his story. "That's mine," he said as he pointed to the cover image of Shiva and Skanda. Then he continued, saying the same about dozens of other works pictured in the book's pages. Even though none of them was the Duryodhana, as he listened to Lion, Wilson was coming to the same understanding that Gordon had. The Sotheby's statue he'd spent so much time trying to recover was only a tiny part of a much bigger story. There had been a decades-long conspiracy to loot Cambodia's ancient treasures, then traffic them onto the international art market, and Latchford had been its principal organizer. Now, Wilson realized, his job was to find a way to prove it—and bring Latchford to justice.

21

Dressed in suits and clutching binders of documents, the SDNY team filed into a law office on the edge of downtown Denver just after 9:00 a.m. on June 6, 2013. Alexander Wilson and his colleagues had come to Colorado to interview the art historian Emma Bunker, a key witness in their ongoing Sotheby's litigation—and, potentially, in any criminal case against Douglas Latchford.

Bunker, who was about to celebrate her eighty-third birthday, hadn't yet been asked to provide a sworn deposition, and the discussion was to be relatively informal, at least by DOJ standards. Nonetheless, it had the potential to be a crucial moment. Just a few months earlier, while meeting with Lion in Cambodia, Wilson had been told that almost every item in *Adoration and Glory* was likely stolen. He suspected that Bunker knew a great deal that might be useful. Although one of the prosecutors opened the meeting by saying that she was "not a target of a criminal investigation" and would merely be helping SDNY collect background material, her lawyers were understandably on guard. The group from New York had come with a

Department of Homeland Security agent, who mostly scribbled notes in silence.

The bulk of the questions would be handled by an SDNY attorney named Sarah Paul. After some preliminaries, Paul opened a folder containing printouts of emails between Bunker and Sotheby's. She would allow Bunker to see only one email at a time; when Bunker's lawyers asked for a copy of the correspondence, the SDNY team refused. Paul soon flipped to a message that Bunker had sent in June 2010, warning a Sotheby's executive that the Cambodian government had "clear evidence" that the Duryodhana "was definitely stolen from Prasat Chen at Koh Ker, as the feet are still *in situ*."

"Why use the word 'stolen'?" Paul asked. The term, after all, had a meaning in US law—and surely not one with which a wealthy Denver widow would want be associated.

Bunker tried to retroactively soften her statement. Clearly, the statue had been removed without permission from Koh Ker. But, she said, "no one knows when, where, or how. Perhaps 'stolen' was too strong a word."

Paul then turned to an email from four weeks later, in which Bunker had reversed herself after a visit to Phnom Penh, reporting that Cambodia had no plans to seek the return of artifacts already abroad. "Legally and ethically you can happily sell the piece," she had told Sotheby's.

Once again, Bunker backtracked. "I don't remember writing this email," she said, explaining that she'd been jet-lagged at the time. In any case, Bunker conceded, she was not a lawyer, and certainly not an expert on anti-looting laws; indeed, in her telling, she didn't know that Cambodia had any. She said that Sotheby's had assured her that the consignor of the Duryodhana was its legal owner, which was good enough from her perspective.

Paul continued, shifting her focus to Bunker's relationship with Latchford. Why had she copied him on her correspondence with Sotheby's about the piece? Back in New York, SDNY had a trove of 1970s-era communications between Latchford and the London dealer Spink's, showing that he'd been deeply involved in its original sale. Bunker knew this well; she'd been the one to urge her partner to distance himself from the Duryodhana after its origin was revealed. But in the room with a team of sharp-eyed prosecutors, she decided to hedge. Bunker had kept Latchford in the loop simply because "I value his scholarship," she said. She nonetheless claimed not to recall speaking with him much about the statue.

Her other answers were similar, with Bunker professing a degree of ignorance, or amnesia, that was hard for Wilson to credit. It was a frustrating experience. If he was going to get the truth out of Bunker, more pressure would surely be required. But that decision was for later. In the shorter term, Wilson was feeling increasingly confident about his chances of defeating Sotheby's in a Manhattan courtroom. Two months earlier, Judge George B. Daniels had granted SDNY permission to file a vastly expanded complaint. The auction house would now have to answer a barrage of allegations from the government about the Duryodhana—including that it had knowingly concealed Latchford's part in the statue's history.

There had also been a major breakthrough involving another set of statues from Koh Ker. Over the previous year, the archaeologist Éric Bourdonneau had continued his efforts to map works in foreign collections onto the broken pedestals discovered at the site, and he had prepared a report that specifically looked at five pieces held by the Metropolitan Museum of Art. Among them were the Kneeling Attendants, the two Koh Ker figures donated by Latchford that guarded the entrance to the Met's Southeast Asian galleries. In size and style, as well as the pattern of damage on their naked bases, they were irrefutably a match, with all available evidence indicating that they'd been looted in the mid-1980s.

To its critics, the Met seemed to have an unwritten playbook for dealing with complaints about looted objects in its collection: first deny, then delay, giving in only when legal or public pressure became overwhelming. In this fashion, it had managed to hang on to the famed Euphronios krater for more than three decades after its theft was first documented. But this was an egregious case, involving works stolen during a bloody period in Cambodia's civil war, and it was backed by evidence that was hard even for the Met to dispute. So, uncharacteristically, the museum decided to cut its losses. In May 2013, it announced that in light of "new documentary research," it would be repatriating the Kneeling Attendants to Cambodia. The Met was careful to emphasize that the return was likely a onetime deal, with an executive telling a Cambodian newspaper that it "establishes no precedent." In separate comments, the same Met representative said there was no broader inquiry underway into other Latchford-connected pieces at the museum, which numbered at least a dozen.

Strictly speaking, the Met's concession had no bearing on the Sotheby's case, but it still gave SDNY a sense of momentum. The Kneeling Attendants' empty pedestals were just a few feet from the spot where the Duryodhana had once stood. If America's most powerful museum had declined to fight, surely the decision-makers at Sotheby's would soon come to a similar conclusion. Or would they?

On September 12, 2013, Wilson rose from his seat in a Lower Manhattan courtroom to address Judge Daniels. With his SDNY career on a fast track, the prosecutor had a busy docket, and the Duryodhana was just one of many cases that he was involved in. Yet over the past year, he'd become obsessed by it, and by the broader topic of looted Khmer works. It wasn't often that a lawyer got to spend their time learning the history of a lost civilization and then applying that knowledge to alleged wrongdoing in the present day. Nor did one get many chances, even at SDNY, to unravel what Wilson now thought of as a long-term criminal conspiracy that spanned from Cambodia's killing fields to the Upper East Side.

In the days before the September hearing, the battle with Sotheby's had grown nasty. Lawyers for the auction house had claimed in a written argument that Brenton Easter, the DHS agent who'd brought the Duryodhana case to SDNY, "had no probable cause" to believe it was stolen property, despite telling Sotheby's the opposite in writing. Moreover, they wrote, the understanding of Cambodian law that the prosecutors were relying on "was apparently unknown to anyone," including the government of Cambodia, "until the State Department invented it." The lawyers argued that as a backup, SDNY had developed a risible "inherent right of kings theory," whereby "because an ancient king built Koh Ker a thousand years ago, the modern Cambodian state owns it today."

In his response, Wilson made a series of claims that were much more serious, accusing Sotheby's of attempting to block his investigation. His opponents, he said, had "sought at every turn to prevent the government from unearthing the facts about the theft and sale of the

Duryodhana." His letter included a direct allegation against Sotheby's general counsel, who Wilson said had "provided false and misleading provenance information to the government while discouraging the government from obtaining the documents that ultimately showed that asserted provenance to be false." Wilson viewed this as fair play; by going after Easter, Sotheby's had been the first to make things personal. In the normally well-mannered world of the federal courts, it was a grave accusation, which lawyers for the auction house contested vigorously.

Now Wilson had to convince Judge Daniels to deny a Sotheby's motion to halt the discovery process, in which the two sides would be required to exchange correspondence and other documents relevant to establishing the facts. The move was "just improper and an effort to delay this proceeding," Wilson argued. Animated by his enthusiasm for the case, and a chance to win a precedent-setting victory, Wilson laid out plans for an extremely intensive information-gathering campaign. SDNY wanted to depose Latchford and Bunker, as well as another Bangkok dealer, a pair of stone conservators, and more than half a dozen current and former Sotheby's employees—as many as twenty people in all. Wilson was also contemplating whether he could get a formal statement from Lion; even though he hadn't been involved in the theft of the Duryodhana, the Cambodian professed an intimate knowledge of how looting networks operated, which would provide critical context. Judge Daniels was convinced. "The motion to stay discovery is denied," he declared from the bench. The litigation between SDNY and Sotheby's would move ahead.

Wilson returned to his office at Saint Andrew's Plaza to work on his next steps. Some eighty blocks uptown, Sotheby's had a critical choice to make. Its lawyers' attempts at procedural maneuvering had failed. Wilson intended to excavate every aspect of the Duryodhana's removal from Koh Ker, as well as all subsequent art-market transactions. That process could allow the government to spell out, in excruciating detail, exactly how a work looted in the preamble to a genocide had ended up in a Manhattan showroom—and what Sotheby's knew about it and when. It might also unearth uncomfortable facts about the company's broader dealings with Asian antiquities, and with Latchford in particular. Even if Sotheby's lawyers could eke out a win by asserting that the Duryodhana wasn't protected by Cambodian law, the headlines promised to be appalling.

As the warmth of New York's late summer began to fade into an autumn chill, it appeared to Wilson that Sotheby's was still determined to contest the forfeiture. Then he got an unexpected message from the auction house's attorneys. Before going further in trial preparations, they wanted to talk. Wilson wasn't sure why they were suddenly open to negotiating; later he would wonder whether his claims about the conduct of Sotheby's general counsel had been serious enough to change their calculus. Whatever the impetus, they told Wilson that they were willing to consider a settlement of the Duryodhana case under certain conditions, terms that would allow their client to shoulder as little blame as possible.

After Wilson's earlier statements, the DOJ would have to make clear that it was not accusing Sotheby's or "any of its lawyers, executives, officers or employees" of knowingly providing false information. The auction house, in turn, would deny ever knowing that the Cambodian government had a valid ownership claim. And, as far as Sotheby's and the European aristocrat who'd sent the Duryodhana for sale in New York were concerned, a settlement would have to put an end to the matter, with SDNY promising not to pursue any further civil actions.

In mid-December, Wilson submitted a letter to Judge Daniels, attaching a document that he and Sotheby's lead lawyer had signed the day before. It characterized their eighteen-month dispute as a "good faith disagreement" for which further litigation would be an unnecessary burden. Sotheby's and its consignor had come to a painful decision on how to resolve it. "In the interests of promoting cooperation and collaboration," the accord read, they had decided to return the statue to its country of origin. Contrary to Sotheby's earlier assertion that if the Cambodian state wanted the piece, it would have to make an offer, no payment would be required. The logistics would be put into motion immediately. Forty years after being ripped away from Koh Ker, the Duryodhana was going home.

Other auction houses and cultural institutions had been watching the case closely, and the settlement helped push some of them to reconsider their attitudes toward Khmer works—those from Koh Ker in particular. If Sotheby's had concluded that it wasn't worth trying to stop a seizure under the National Stolen Property Act, they seemed to reason, their chances were likely not much better. In May 2014, Christie's said it would repatriate a seated figure that, according to Bourdonneau's research, had been stolen from a pedestal opposite the Met's Kneeling Attendants. At almost the same time, the Norton Simon Museum announced a voluntary return of the Bhima, the warrior figure that had once stood across from the Duryodhana, although its attorney insisted to the *Los Angeles Times* that "there are extremely strong legal arguments for why we could defeat a claim."

The Cambodian government organized a welcoming ceremony for the three statues in Phnom Penh. In a spacious meeting hall, the Bhima and the Duryodhana were arranged much as they would have been in the tenth century: facing each other in combat, both preparing to strike. Reunited, they had a potency that was impossible to understand when each was alone, separated by thousands of miles. Just as Bourdonneau had hypothesized, they were obviously intended to be in dialogue, depicting a foundational Hindu narrative. As a crowd of dignitaries looked on, dancers in traditional gowns called *sampots* showered them with jasmine flowers; afterward, some of the attendees fell to their knees and prayed to the figures. They would soon be mounted atop their broken pedestals and put on display at the National Museum, where other Cambodians could express the same reverence.

From the beginning, Wilson's assignment had been to get the Duryodhana back to the society from which it had been stolen, and on one level, he was delighted. Still, such a restitution wasn't true justice. The treasures of Koh Ker hadn't transported themselves by magic to the US; they'd been taken and trafficked by people, none of whom had been held accountable. Ever since his trip to Cambodia, Wilson had been convinced that Latchford, more than anyone else involved, deserved to be charged criminally. The evidence indicated that he'd played a central role in the emptying of Koh Ker, selling both the Bhima and the Duryodhana in the 1970s, and later donating the Kneeling Attendants to the Met. Shiva and Skanda, a work so loved by Latchford that he'd put it on the cover of *Adoration and Glory*, was also from the complex, and Lion had admitted to taking it. Then there were the dozens, if not hundreds, of other Khmer artifacts that he'd sold to museums and collectors. If Lion was right, virtually all of them had been looted too.

The problem was that Wilson still didn't know if charging Latchford was possible. Only a tiny number of dealers had ever been successfully prosecuted for their connections to looting. And from Wilson's perspective, too much of Latchford's story was still a mystery. The Spink's correspondence that he'd obtained for the Duryodhana case was decades old, and it mostly related to sales outside the US. It wasn't clear whether Latchford had even done business in the American market since the early 2000s, and the bulk of his records were presumably in Thailand, where obtaining them through the cumbersome processes of law-enforcement diplomacy could take years. Even worse, SDNY was racing against the clock: Latchford had just turned eighty-two. The older he was, the harder it would be for Wilson to convince Thai authorities to extradite him. To have any hope of putting him in a courtroom, let alone federal prison, Wilson needed a breakthrough.

With Latchford's name all over the press coverage of the Duryodhana dispute, old contacts in the Cambodian government had cut ties with him—an abrupt end to relationships that he'd cultivated over decades. The DOJ hadn't approached him to ask for an interview, nor given any formal indication that Latchford could be a target for prosecution, but the jeopardy was real. He would, of course, fight any such case to the hilt, starting by making it as difficult as possible to extradite him from Bangkok. But even in the best-case scenario, an indictment in the US would upend his life—and probably be fatal for the business he had worked so assiduously to build. Not even the boldest collectors would want to buy from a man trailing American criminal charges.

As part of his effort to protect himself, Latchford wanted to convince his erstwhile Cambodian allies to vouch for his innocence, and to make clear that they viewed him as a friend of their country, not some kind of archaeological pirate. And he had a new argument for why he should be embraced. "Admittedly these things were moonlighted out of Cambodia and wound up somewhere else," he told an interviewer in 2013—a relatively candid statement, though one delivered in the passive voice. "But had they not been, they would likely have been shot up for target practice by the Khmer Rouge." (This was almost certainly untrue. For all their crimes, there's little evidence that Pol Pot's men intentionally damaged Angkorian artworks.)

Around this time, Latchford invited a senior Cambodian cultural official, Kong Vireak, for a meeting to clear the air. The official and one of his colleagues traveled to Bangkok and fought the traffic into the heart of the metropolis, soon arriving at Chidlom Place. As the pair exited the elevator on the ninth floor, they took in the statues and bronzes, artfully lit from above, that were arrayed throughout Latchford's apartment. Latchford began their discussion by complaining about his portrayal in the media and emphasizing his love for Cambodian culture. To drive home the point, he repeated his earlier line about having been told that he was Khmer in a past life. Then he made a proposal. To repair his relationship with Cambodia, Latchford said he was willing to donate a few pieces from his personal collection to the National Museum. There was a catch: In return, the government would have to make a public statement that he had never been involved in looting.

Sitting across from Latchford, Kong Vireak was incensed. An archaeologist in his early forties, he had intimate experience of his country's traumas. As a child, he'd been forced to live in a Khmer Rouge commune, where school consisted of an occasional outdoor lesson between shifts working. He'd been lucky, with his parents and siblings surviving the genocide. But an aunt and uncle had disappeared into the killing fields, along with much of his extended family. Kong Vireak wasn't going to accept a token offering from a man who had profited handsomely from the cataclysm. "No," he said. "You have to return everything." Only if Latchford forfeited his entire collection would the government be willing to talk about what it might do in exchange.

Latchford viewed this demand as absurd, and his visitors soon departed. A deal with Cambodia would have to wait. And in the meantime, he was still, remarkably, making sales. Though transactions with museums were now out of the question, Latchford had retained a group of loyal clients who were willing to ignore the headlines and pay heady prices for the finest works. In 2014, he would gross at least $9.8 million from sales of Khmer objects. To avoid unwelcome attention, they were described in paperwork as coming from Thailand, not Cambodia. Meanwhile, Latchford was also trying to rekindle his relationship with an especially important customer.

"Hi Jim," he wrote in an October 2014 email. "I have not written for sometime [*sic*] as I have been waiting for the Sotheby disaster to die down." Jim Clark, the Netscape co-founder, had made the last of his $35 million in purchases from Latchford over five years before. Clark had since sold his Miami penthouse, which he'd decorated from top to bottom with Khmer pieces, and many of them were now in storage. Latchford nonetheless wanted to gauge Clark's interest in a female figure that he described as "possibly the most important and finest Asian bronze known." The object, he wrote, was "not from Cambodia, so the past problem does not therefore involve her."

In his reply, Clark expressed no concerns about the provenance of the bronze. But he said that he was no longer in the market, because he had come to think of his prior purchases as a bad investment. "I recently did a financial statement for myself, and I had to mark the pieces I got from you as at best worth what I paid for them," Clark explained. "All of my other art work [*sic*] has gone up in value at the rate of about 7% per year."

Latchford assured his client that he had nothing to worry about: "There may be a lull in the market at present—due to Sotheby's bad handling and dishonesty in the recent saga, but in the long run it will pick up again. It's just like trading in anything—there are ups, and downs."

22

Asia Week, held every March, is one of the highlights of the antiquities market calendar. It's a rare moment when the most important dealers and buyers are all in the same place: a roughly triangular patch of Manhattan with its vertices defined by the headquarters of Christie's, at Rockefeller Center; Sotheby's, on York Avenue; and the imposing stone bulk of the Metropolitan Museum of Art, on the edge of Central Park. Within those boundaries, dozens of commercial galleries hold their most promising exhibitions during the event, hoping to make sales that can carry them through the year.

Special Agent Brenton Easter knew that the raid he had planned for March 17, 2016—partway through Asia Week—would attract plenty of attention from players in the artifacts business. In fact, he was counting on it. Over the past several years, Easter and his colleagues in the Department of Homeland Security's cultural property squad had been growing more ambitious, chasing down smuggled reliefs from Iraq, a finely painted sarcophagus from ancient Egypt, and even a pair of skeletons belonging to a Cretaceous predator called *Tyrannosaurus bataar*, which had been imported illegally from Mongolia. They wanted it known that they were continuing to investigate transactions involving illicit objects, and that they weren't afraid to act aggressively.

Their present target was the Nancy Wiener Gallery, which occupied part of a handsome brick townhouse on East Seventy-Fourth Street. Its eponymous owner was among the city's top dealers of Asian works—a status she'd inherited from her late mother, Doris, who'd counted among her clients Jackie Kennedy and John D. Rockefeller III. The younger Wiener, who was in her early sixties, was sitting in her office when Easter and his team of agents strode in, armed with a search warrant. This wasn't the kind of operation that required banging down doors, and they informed Wiener that they would go through the premises and seize three allegedly looted pieces: a pair of stone carvings from India and a Khmer bronze Buddha. Though the raid was a surprise, she didn't protest, and the agents fanned out through the gallery, gathering documents and, most important of all, taking Wiener's computer, which contained her correspondence with customers and suppliers.

The search had nothing to do with Douglas Latchford, who remained at liberty in Bangkok. Federal prosecutors at SDNY had yet to find sufficient evidence to charge him with a crime, and Alexander Wilson, now a senior figure in the office's Money Laundering and Asset Forfeiture Unit, feared it would never happen. As far as Wilson knew, Latchford's transactions in the US were simply too far in the past and his connections to more recent cases too tangential. It was as though he had vanished from the American market. With the Latchford file going nowhere, Easter, too, had moved on to other things, and his investigation of Wiener centered on her ties to a prolific dealer of Indian artifacts who had already been arrested in Germany.

At DHS, technicians copied Wiener's hard drive, extracting its contents into a searchable directory. Easter began going through her emails, searching for evidence on the Indian case. He quickly realized that he was looking at material very different from what he had expected. Latchford hadn't stayed clear of the US at all. He'd simply been doing much of his business through a proxy. Easter could see that Latchford had pitched Khmer works to Wiener again and again into the 2010s, some of which she bought or agreed to jointly sell. And they were, beyond any doubt, the products of recent looting. In 2005, the piece on offer was a seated bronze Buddha. "When it was found they took off most of the mud, or as it was, a sandy soil," Latchford had written, attaching photos of the artifact covered in dirt. He boasted that it had been unearthed "right in the Angkor Complex"—that is, inside Cambodia's most important archaeological site.

The following year, under the heading PRIVATE AND CONFIDENTIAL F Y E ONLY, Latchford told Wiener about a twelfth-century Shiva figure, "fresh out of the ground" at the vast temple of Angkor Thom, for which he wanted $175,000. After that, he offered her a bronze head, "recently found around the site of the Angkor Borei group. . . . They are looking for the body, no luck so far, all they have found last week were two land mines!! What price would you be interested in buying it at? Let me know as I will have to bargain for it." Then, a "56 cm Angkor Borei Buddha, just excavated, which looks fantastic." The messages continued, a mix of blustery sales patter and surprisingly candid context about how—and where—Latchford sourced his objects.

Even more intriguing, the emails showed Latchford appearing to assist Wiener with filling in the provenance for art that she wanted to move. In 2007, she'd been in discussions to sell a stone Buddha to the National Gallery of Australia for more than $1 million. Museums often asked for more information than private buyers, and to close the deal, Wiener needed paperwork indicating that the Buddha had been on the international market before the all-important cutoff of 1970. She asked Latchford if he could assist. "Is this OK?" he replied, providing an unsigned letter bearing the name of a British businessman, Ian Donaldson. "I herewith declare," it read, that the piece "was purchased by me in Hong Kong where I was posted from 1964–1966 and has been in my collection since then." Wiener then sent a signed version of the letter to the NGA. Donaldson, however, had died in 2001 and was presumably unavailable to provide his signature. Nonetheless, when it came to another piece, one sold to a museum in Singapore, Latchford provided Wiener with a similar statement from Donaldson—this time stating that he'd been "posted" in Vietnam, not Hong Kong, during the same two-year period.

The nearly dormant Latchford investigation was suddenly very much alive. It was clear from Latchford's own words that he was selling freshly looted pieces—and much more recently than it had been possible to confirm before. On top of that, there were strong indications that he had been forging provenance documents, not only on Wiener's behalf but likely for his own sales too. It was behavior that could easily violate several federal laws. Unfortunately, Easter couldn't just put a copy of Wiener's computer onto a flash drive and drop it off at SDNY. Her case resided with state-level prosecutors at the Manhattan District Attorney's Office, and sharing evidence with their federal counterparts required jumping through some legal hoops. Still, one way or another, Wilson needed to see Wiener's emails.

By 2016, Bradley Gordon's work on the Duryodhana case for SDNY was long complete. Though he'd kept in touch with Lion, the former looter he'd cultivated as a source, and worked with his local team to collect archival materials on Koh Ker, Gordon had largely resumed his previous life as a corporate lawyer. In nearly a decade of living in Cambodia, he'd witnessed remarkable change. Not long before his arrival, Phnom Penh had been a city with hardly any buildings taller than a few stories. Its nightlife had revolved around a seedy bar called Heart of Darkness, haunted by hard-bitten Asia hands, some of Vietnam War vintage, who'd found they could never go home again. Now it was coming to resemble a modern Asian capital, with shopping malls, upscale restaurants, and even a few skyscrapers. The number of annual visitors to Angkor and its environs had climbed past two million, making it one of the most popular historic sites in the world, and a huge economic asset. In this newly dynamic economy, Gordon, with his American training and international connections, was in demand. But he couldn't get statues out of his head.

After the Sotheby's settlement, several other American institutions had agreed to return items looted from Koh Ker. The most recent was the Denver Art Museum, which had repatriated a stone torso of the god Rama that it purchased from Wiener's mother, Doris, in 1986—likely only a few years after it was hacked out of the complex. Yet Gordon knew that thousands of stolen works remained overseas, including many of the finest examples of Khmer artistry. A few years before, he'd escorted a group of Cambodian lawyers on a trip to learn about the American justice system. In New York, Gordon had taken them to the Met, where they were shocked by the breadth of the Khmer collection. His companions hadn't known that artifacts of such obvious significance even existed, let alone that they were kept almost nine thousand miles away.

Between client meetings and business trips, Gordon found himself wondering about how his adopted country might one day retrieve those objects, along with the many others scattered around the world. So much of what had been taken from Cambodia in the twentieth century was impossible to restore. But these artworks, the physical legacy of an era when its people were united, confident, and prosperous, in which they still took rightful pride—they were different. They could be brought back. And while that would never compensate for the toll of the Khmer Rouge's genocide, or the American bombs of the early 1970s, or the starvation and warfare of the 1980s, or the violent chaos of the 1990s, it was something.

A global repatriation campaign was extremely ambitious. There were simply too many pieces, divided among too many institutions and buyers, any number of whom could put up a ferocious fight. Worse, many of the latter were essentially anonymous, with their purchases kept hidden from public notice. Just finding them could take years. Instead, Gordon was beginning to sketch the outlines of a different, more focused strategy. Latchford's personal collection, which he'd shown off in magazine profiles and invited curators to review, was known to be one of the most extensive in the world. Indeed, it rivaled the Khmer holdings of all but the largest museums. And Latchford was under pressure, his reputation—at least in Cambodia and among scholars, if not artifact buyers—shredded in recent years by his links to looted works. What if he could be convinced, or compelled, to give it all back? Beyond the importance of Latchford's pieces themselves, such a return would send a powerful message to other collectors, and perhaps influence them to make similar deci-sions.

In 2013, two Cambodian officials had attempted to get Latchford to do just that, and they'd returned empty-handed to Phnom Penh, but Gordon wanted to make another, more concerted attempt. Though it would be an effort on behalf of the Cambodian people, not just the state, he knew that a major repatriation was a matter with which the government had to be closely involved. And as passionate as he was, he was still an outsider. Gordon needed a sponsor, someone with a line to the top of the Cambodian power structure. He'd grown friendly with a man named Peter Sok, the American-educated son of Cambo-dia's longtime deputy prime minister. Sok was deeply embedded in the elite: His wife was one of Hun Sen's daughters, making the strong-man leader his father-in-law. Almost no one in the country was bet-ter connected.

Gordon told Sok about his work on the Duryodhana and what he'd learned of Latchford's activities. "Look, there's one man who seems to be so much of the market," he explained. Sok found the story fascinating. Like many Cambodians, he was loath to dwell on the past, and he couldn't really bring himself to blame the looters themselves. "Naturally, people want to do good," he reasoned. "But in desperate situations, they do something they don't want to do." Confronting Latchford, by contrast, sounded to Sok like a path to-ward some kind of justice.

Gordon presented Sok with two options: "We can either litigate, or we can go talk to him," he said. Latchford would soon celebrate his eighty-fifth birthday, and Gordon wasn't sure who stood to re-ceive his collection after he died. It was possible that Latchford's pieces would be dispersed across the world—and go to people who might reject any attempts at negotiation. The only way to avoid that outcome was to race toward a deal while the works were still in Latchford's hands.

In fact, the situation was worse than Gordon knew. Latchford was struggling with a number of illnesses, chief among them Parkinson's disease, and the Thai bodybuilders who were his constant companions now functioned as informal nursing aides. As he spent more and more time within the confines of his apartment, his circle of confidants nearer his own age, never large to begin with, dwindled further. His brother, Trevor, was dead, having met his end with an apparent heart attack in the Chidlom Place swimming pool. Friends had tapered off contact after losing patience with Latchford's disinterest in affairs beyond his own; as one member of his circle put it, Latchford "didn't do empathy." That associate also lost trust in him over an especially hurtful betrayal: Latchford had sold the man a series of minor Khmer artifacts that turned out to be fake.

Yet despite his worsening health, Latchford's obsession with the objects he'd pursued since the 1960s was undiminished—along with his zeal for selling them. Among his most important clients was a German-born tycoon, Harald Link, whose family company was one of Thailand's foremost industrial conglomerates. Link had enormous wealth, along with a long-standing interest in Khmer artifacts, and from late 2015, Latchford pitched him relentlessly. "I have this problem developing and I would like my collection here in BKK, or part of it, to go to a home where it is appreciated," he wrote to Link just before Christmas, attaching images of a "magnificent bronze." Not long after that correspondence, Latchford invited Link for dinner to "discuss quietly if any of the sculptures interest you."

The pitches continued, month after month, in emails that seldom mentioned the items' provenance; instead, Latchford focused on aesthetics, sometimes in terms that verged on the creepy. Of one stone statue, a bare-breasted woman, he wrote: "Just look at that mouth, but not before just going to bed, you will dream of her all night!!!" Link politely brushed off some of the proposals. Others he found more interesting, and with Latchford's help, he soon expanded the ensemble of artifacts that decorated his own home in central Bangkok. In May 2016, Link bought three pieces from Latchford—two stone figures and a bronze, which the dealer described on the invoice as "an exquisite example"—for a total of more than $500,000. Later in the year, Latchford offered to broker the sale of a spectacular sculpture of a kneeling woman, thought to be a representation of a twelfth-century Khmer queen, which he called "the finest example that exists." Latchford would later record that Link had purchased it for over $900,000. (Link said later that he was unaware of the allegations against Latchford at the time.)

These were private transactions, and Gordon wouldn't learn of them until long afterward. Nor could he know about Latchford's broader strategy for determining where the works he'd spent a lifetime accumulating should go. If he had to choose between giving them back to Cambodia or selling them to paying clients, his strong preference was to make the sales. Neither the passage of time nor his approaching mortality had made Latchford any less furious with the Cambodian government for its refusal to declare him innocent of the looting allegations that emerged from the Duryodhana case. As they near the ends of their lives, many older people try to mend broken relationships and let go of grudges; Latchford's response, by contrast, was to double down. Around the same time that he was pitching Link, Latchford received an email from Emma Bunker, his longtime collaborator, urging him to make a peace offering to Cambodia. "Try to give [them] something uncomplex and let's get the letter resolving the whole Sotheby's issue," she said, mentioning a particular bronze. "Then you can talk later about giving more, if this works well."

Latchford replied: "They will be lucky to get this or anything else, they don't deserve it as their performance has been a disgrace."

On the morning of December 21, 2016, Nancy Wiener reported as instructed to the Manhattan Criminal Courthouse at 100 Centre Street. It was almost Christmas, and on the uneven sidewalks of lower Broadway, retailers had set out fake conifers and strings of tinsel that glimmered in the flat winter light. In a few weeks' time, protesters would gather at nearby Foley Square to register their anger over Donald Trump's first presidential inauguration; for now, the triangular plaza was quiet, bare trees outnumbering the few pedestrians.

Wiener entered the building and crossed into a world very different from the one she normally inhabited. It was a place of terrified defendants and seen-it-all cops, of overworked judges and underpaid clerks, doing their best to manage the tide of humanity that entered their jurisdiction each day. The hallways and holding cells of the MCC and its adjoining jail, known for generations as the Tombs, were thick with accused drug dealers, armed robbers, fraudsters, rapists—people from every walk of non-law-abiding life, calling out for their lawyers or silently awaiting the next step in their journey through the system. Now, nine months after the DHS raid on her gallery, Wiener was among them.

She'd agreed to surrender herself voluntarily rather than risk the humiliation of being arrested elsewhere. Special Agent Brenton Easter met her inside the MCC and began the formalities, which would be handled by an investigator for the district attorney's office. Under harsh fluorescent lights, Wiener was handcuffed, fingerprinted, and told to look into a camera for a mug shot. Then she was led to a holding cell to wait her turn. When the judge was ready, Wiener entered a courtroom to be arraigned. She was charged with three state felonies: two counts of criminal possession of stolen property and one count of conspiracy. The judge set her bail at $25,000; after that, she was allowed to return to her home on the Upper West Side. Her time in custody had been mercifully brief. Whether she would have to return to it depended, in large part, on what she did next.

Around this time, SDNY's Wilson got a call from the prosecutor handling Wiener's case. The state was charging a gallery owner who had crucial knowledge about Douglas Latchford, he explained, and the defendant wanted to talk.

Nancy Wiener's legal jeopardy extended beyond her state-level charges. With SDNY targeting Douglas Latchford, she also faced the prospect of a federal indictment arising from her collaboration with him. She wanted to make a deal. Wiener was willing to provide testimony about her relationship with Latchford, their transactions together, and the fact that he had provided her with false provenance documents. In exchange, she wanted a commitment that she wouldn't be prosecuted by the federal government.

By mid-2017, Wilson had been investigating Cambodian antiquities for almost five years, and he found it impossible to let go of the topic. The history was fascinating, and the crimes, in his opinion, were abundantly clear. He'd long since concluded that Latchford had broken US law by selling looted works, but he'd never felt that he had enough evidence to move forward with a prosecution. Though other avenues of investigation were possible, with a busy schedule—Wilson was now a manager, supervising a team of prosecutors responsible for a bewildering array of cases—it was hard to carve out the time. Finding a way to indict Latchford was perpetually second or third on his list of priorities, a position that left him unable to make much progress. Suddenly, Wiener had changed all that. *OK, this is real*, Wilson thought. *Let's get it done.*

Wiener agreed to a meeting, to be held at SDNY's offices at Saint Andrew's Plaza. The discussion would be focused exclusively on Latchford; her dealings with other suppliers were being handled by the state. Legally, it would be deemed a "proffer session," a kind of temporary zone of immunity that the government can offer to criminal suspects. As long as she told the truth, nothing that Wiener said in the room could be used to prosecute her. And at the end of the process, Wilson and his colleagues would decide if she'd provided enough to earn a permanent break. Still, it wasn't simply a matter of taking a statement and putting what Wiener said into a criminal indictment.

Wilson needed her to guide prosecutors through her correspondence with Latchford in detail, telling them exactly what she understood about the origins of the artifacts he was trying to sell. This would bolster the evidentiary value of the emails, which SDNY had now obtained, helping to remove any doubt that Latchford was offering freshly looted pieces. She would also need to explain what she knew about the provenance letters that Latchford had given her, ostensibly signed by the late Ian Donaldson—specifically, that they were fake. Wilson had come to see this as the core of any potential prosecution of Latchford, since it avoided the obscurities inherent in trying to prove that an antiquity was stolen under the definition of the National Stolen Property Act. The details of outdated Cambodian heritage legislation could easily confuse a jury. By contrast, it wasn't hard to understand that forging a document to enable a seven-figure transaction constituted fraud.

Wiener had to relate all of this information without whitewashing or minimizing her own conduct. For Wilson, this was nonnegotiable. SDNY's policy was to grant immunity only to cooperating witnesses whom it was satisfied had been completely honest about their actions. Partly, this was a matter of trust. If prosecutors were going to rely on the statements of a witness to make a criminal case, they needed to be confident that they were getting the whole truth. It also reflected the risks of the courtroom. Anyone whose testimony was critical to an indictment would probably have to take the stand at an eventual trial. And if such a person lied in a proffer session, it was impossible to be sure that they wouldn't do the same in front of jurors. A good defense lawyer would zero in on any fabrications, with potentially devastating consequences for the credibility of the witness—and thus the government's case.

Soon, Wilson was sitting across from Wiener in one of SDNY's conference rooms—dingy spaces with peeling wallpaper, harsh lighting, and mismatched, sometimes broken furniture. She had been briefed by her lawyers, who were sitting next to her, and knew what was expected. Still, not long after he began the proceedings, Wilson saw that getting Wiener to where he needed her to go was going to be a challenge. Again and again, in her first interview with prosecutors and others that followed, the problem was the same. Wiener was extremely reluctant to admit what Wilson found obvious: that by selling pieces from Latchford, she was dealing in what she must have known were stolen goods.

To grasp that this was true didn't require great leaps of logic; indeed, Latchford had all but confirmed it. In multiple messages to Wiener, the dealer had described statues using phrases such as "just excavated," "fresh out of the ground," and "recently found." In some cases, he'd attached photographs showing the works just after their discovery, noting that a restorer had been hired to clean them up. Still, Wiener wouldn't say the words.

"You know what museum-quality looks like versus something fresh," a member of the government's team recalled saying to Wiener. "You must have been aware these pieces were bad."

"What do you mean by bad?"

"Well, you know what I mean. That the pieces were not legal."

"I'm not sure I could say that I knew that."

"This one's covered in dirt. Where did you think it came from?"

"I don't know where it came from. Well, I knew it was obviously taken from a temple at some point, but that doesn't mean it was stolen."

Wiener kept giving similar answers, however Wilson and his colleagues framed their questions. On their side of the table, the meetings felt endless; it might have taken more than an hour to get a few minutes of what they considered usable material. It was hard for the prosecutors to tell whether Wiener was being willfully obtuse or if she had somehow cordoned off everything Latchford had told her into a corner of her mind and never again considered it. A participant who sat in would later describe the interviews as the most maddening they'd ever experienced during decades in law enforcement.

Wilson was similarly frustrated. He couldn't join every session, and as they continued, he delegated them to a more junior prosecutor who had no better luck pushing Wiener toward what Wilson called a "come-to-Jesus" moment. She was by far the best witness Wilson had, and under the constraints of SDNY practice—and his own instincts as a lawyer—he didn't feel that he could move forward if she kept downplaying her role. Wiener had to come clean. And until she did, no charges could be brought against Latchford.

———

Bradley Gordon had no role in the SDNY investigation, and aside from a general sense that US legal action was a possibility, he knew none of the details of the case. Instead, Gordon was scrambling to figure out if Latchford was willing to make a deal. In early 2018, he made contact with one of Latchford's few remaining friends, who agreed to serve as an emissary and flew to Phnom Penh for an initial meeting. More extensive discussions followed. Gordon was beginning to sketch out the contours of an agreement that might be acceptable to all sides. It would start with Latchford repatriating his entire collection, with the possible exception of a few pieces that he deemed to have particular sentimental value—those could wait until after his death. In exchange, the Cambodian government would make a formal request to Washington, asking for leniency in light of Latchford's cooperation. Latchford wanted the same treatment for Emma Bunker, whom he feared might also be facing charges.

The final call on both would be made, of course, by American prosecutors, though Gordon figured that the opinion of the Cambodian state, representing the dealer's ostensible victims, would be meaningful. Pushing to get Latchford off the hook offended Gordon's sense of justice, but the upsides were undeniable. Never before had there been such an opportunity to reclaim so many stolen Khmer works all at once. Surely the best outcome for Cambodia would be to bring them home, rather than risk having them disappear once Latchford was gone. The man was entering his late eighties. He had plenty of cash, and if he were charged he would undoubtedly hire the finest lawyers in Bangkok to fight an extradition request. Getting him into a US courtroom was a faint hope.

Still, the talks didn't proceed smoothly. Late in life, Latchford had grown closer to his daughter, Julia—the product of his brief, unhappy marriage to a Thai woman in the early 1970s. She split her time between the UK and Abu Dhabi, with frequent visits to Bangkok to care for her father. Meanwhile, Julia's husband, Simon Copleston, was now playing a role in his decision-making. Copleston served as the general counsel for a Middle Eastern bank, and he advised Latchford with the instincts of a zealous attorney, insisting that Cambodia agree to a series of stringent conditions. Notably, Copleston wanted a declaration from the Cambodian state that Latchford had done nothing wrong in his dealings in Khmer artifacts, as well as guarantees that it would make no further claims against him or his family. Gordon viewed the first demand, in particular, as absurd. Though it would take some time for him to realize it, Gordon thought, Latchford didn't have that kind of leverage.

While these debates continued, Gordon was coming to understand another problem: that securing the return of the works in Latchford's possession would be only a partial victory. The Latchford friend with whom Gordon had made initial contact soon clashed with Copleston and was cut out of the negotiations. As a parting shot, he sent Gordon an astounding email in February 2018. It contained photographs, obviously scanned from a magazine article, of a sprawling, luxurious house decorated in a hazily Southeast Asian fashion, with walls of dark hardwood and an outdoor dining pavilion that could be enclosed with bamboo shades. Practically every corner was stuffed with Khmer statues, including some in the distinctive, dynamic style of Koh Ker. The message provided no further information, not even the home's location or the name of the magazine.

Gordon was developing obsessive tendencies in his antiquities work, and this couldn't have been better crafted to send them into overdrive. Soon he was driving himself half crazy trying to solve the mystery. Gordon bought subscriptions to various architecture and interior-design magazines, then spent hours scrolling through their archives. Finally, he found the article: a 2008 spread in *Architectural Digest* under the headline STRIKING A NEW NOTE IN PALM BEACH. The search wasn't over, however. The story didn't name the owners, describing them only as "a low-key couple based in New York." As for their enormous collection of artworks from Cambodia, the writer of the piece said that they "felt there was a karmic justice to installing their ancient stone warriors and divinities in an environment that recalled their birthplace."

Hunched over his laptop, Gordon tried to think of ways to divine who they were. Above their fireplace, the couple had a striking blue-and-yellow painting by the French cubist Fernand Léger. Gordon reached out to a friend with connections in the auction business to see if he could track down its ownership; unlike thousand-year-old Khmer statues, significant modern paintings tend to have well-documented provenances. Searching the local press was another option. The *Architectural Digest* piece implied that the house was located on or near Palm Beach's South Ocean Boulevard, and that it was close to Donald Trump's Mar-a-Lago Club. With those parameters, surely Gordon could find an item in one of the South Florida papers from when the home had last changed hands.

But it was a task that would take up a great deal of his time, and the challenge made it abundantly clear to Gordon that Cambodia needed more from Latchford than physical objects. The dealer had sold hundreds or even thousands of pieces in addition to those he'd kept for himself, and it was just as important that he hand over information: invoices, photographs, notes, and inventory files, which would help trace their whereabouts. (It would also be useful if he revealed which ones were fake, as experts suspected that some were.) In this way, a deal with Latchford wouldn't be the culmination of Cambodia's efforts to reclaim its lost heritage. It could instead be the beginning of a comprehensive global campaign targeting museums and private collections, which could proceed far more efficiently with the benefit of his records.

And Gordon, who had never been so passionate about a project in his life, wanted to be its manager—a role he would somehow have to balance with his other full-time job. Virtually every aspect of it inspired in him an intense focus, even when that focus had to be applied to mind-numbing trawls through old design magazines. Having the role occupied by a foreigner, albeit one who employed a team of Cambodians, might raise some eyebrows. But it was probably the only way. Anyone in the hierarchical Cambodian political system was beholden to its processes, which made it hard to move aggressively. As an outsider, Gordon had more freedom to operate, as well as an innate understanding of the culture and legal frameworks of the US, where so many of the looted pieces resided.

Through one of his contacts in the Phnom Penh elite, Gordon connected with Phoeurng Sackona, Cambodia's minister of culture and fine arts. A diminutive woman in her late fifties, with close-cropped hair and a face that often broke into a hearty laugh, the politician quickly understood the significance of what Gordon was proposing. She had been a teenager in 1975, when the Khmer Rouge took control of Cambodia. They killed her entire immediate family, leaving her an orphan. After their ouster, she'd thrown herself into school—the only way she could see to escape poverty—and won a scholarship to study engineering in the Soviet Union, after which she completed a doctorate in France. Along the way, she'd become fluent in the languages of both countries, as well as English.

Nothing in Phoeurng Sackona's genial manner hinted at what she'd been made to endure, yet she knew, better than most, what repatriations could mean—for her living compatriots as well as the memory of those who were murdered. When Cambodians saw statues of the kind that Latchford kept in his apartment, and that the still-unidentified Palm Beach couple had in their mansion, they often bowed down and prayed, out of respect for their heritage and love for their ancestors. Phoeurng Sackona viewed that connection as having an entirely different quality than the aesthetic appreciation of even the most dedicated collector, and it had been ruptured during the darkest period of her country's history. As angry as this made her, she wasn't particularly interested in punishing those involved. As a Buddhist, she said, she believed that they would be held accountable through karma, whether in this life or another to come.

Phoeurng Sackona was happy for the curiously enthusiastic lawyer now sitting in her office to go ahead, and with relatively little oversight. (It didn't hurt that Gordon was willing to work pro bono, at least initially.) In May 2018, she made it official with a letter to Gordon and his legal partner, a fellow American named Steve Heimberg. "The Kingdom of Cambodia has been in active discussions with numerous parties around the world in efforts to obtain Khmer antiquities," it read. "You have been officially appointed to assist the Kingdom of Cambodia in retrieving these objects. You are requested and authorized to speak to, and negotiate as necessary with, any and all persons and entities to this end." Then she signed and stamped it with her official seal: a bright-red circle surrounding the silhouette of Angkor Wat.

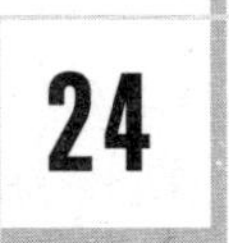

By the time Bradley Gordon received his official appointment from the Cambodian state, Douglas Latchford was warming up to the idea of making a deal. He feared that prosecutors in the US were taking a greater interest in him, and he was spooked. "I have been giving it some serious thought," he wrote in a May 2018 email to his son-in-law, Simon Copleston. Latchford said he was open to meeting directly with Gordon, "to sound them out as to what they want, and how they would go about curtailing the American harassment." Bunker, with whom Latchford spoke almost daily, was also urging him to find a solution. In an email, she warned him that "this is never going to go away, and will haunt everyone until it is resolved. This is a tragedy for you and your legacy." She signed off: "Please think about what I have written, as I care for you and your family."

Latchford had various conditions for an agreement with Cambodia, only one of which Gordon saw as truly nonnegotiable: In exchange for giving up his collection and documents, he needed assurances that neither he nor Bunker would be prosecuted in the US. Gordon's clients in the Cambodian government were willing to support this.

They were more interested in bringing stolen artifacts home than in seeing Latchford tried in court on the other side of the world. If he held up his end of the bargain, they would ask for Latchford to be treated with leniency. Still, that could be nothing more than a request, and Gordon had to get the proposal to Washington. He soon briefed the American ambassador in Phnom Penh, William A. Heidt, and prepared a memo that Heidt could circulate within the State Department and beyond. "A rare and perhaps singular opportunity now presents itself to obtain one of the largest known collections" of looted Khmer antiquities, it began.

> Two issues are central to Mr. Latchford's newfound cooperation: 1) Mr. Latchford is now 87 years old and seems to believe his death is on the near horizon, if not imminent; 2) Mr. Latchford and his family are fearful of information that the Government of the United States of America may possess about Mr. Latchford and his long-time collaborator, Ms. Emma C. Bunker (also in her 80s and residing in the United States), and of potential criminal charges that accordingly could be brought.

Gordon included the text of a formal letter from Cambodia asking that the US "play a role to alleviate Mr. Latchford's concerns and create positive results and not to use his admissions of taking the statues in any future criminal actions." If an agreement was reached, the memo said, "we will follow up with museums, auction houses and private collectors named by Mr. Latchford." It would be the beginning of the international repatriation campaign that Gordon so wanted to lead.

Heidt, the ambassador, was only vaguely familiar with Latchford, and asked subordinates to look into whether he really was being targeted for prosecution. The request landed with a Department of Homeland Security staffer, who wrote back: "I ran the name Douglas Latchford through our case management system and it hits for an ongoing case." Latchford wasn't wanted for arrest, suggesting that the investigation had some way to go before charges were laid. A career Foreign Service officer on his second tour in Cambodia, Heidt was under no illusions about his power to influence decisions at DHS and the DOJ. He was nonetheless willing to pass on Gordon's memo with his endorsement. His first posting in Phnom Penh had coincided with some of the worst looting of the 1990s, and Heidt had seen the resulting damage at Angkor and more remote complexes like Koh Ker. After returning as ambassador, he had helped facilitate the repatriation of stolen Khmer objects from institutions like the Denver Art Museum, and he had seen how meaningful they were to his Cambodian counterparts.

In addition to doing the right thing, there was also the possibility of a diplomatic win. Western aid, from the US above all, had stabilized Cambodia after the carnage of the civil war. In the years since, the country had steadily drifted closer to China, which was indifferent to Prime Minister Hun Sen's woeful human-rights record and eager to invest. Chinese money had poured into property and infrastructure projects, and one Cambodian city, Sihanoukville, was so dominated by mainland migrants that it had come to resemble a Chinese colony. In the meantime, Hun Sen had become a reliably pro-Beijing voice in forums of Southeast Asian leaders, and Pentagon officials worried that he might one day allow the People's Liberation Army to establish a local base. As it sought to keep Cambodia from being pulled further into China's orbit, the US couldn't match those inducements. But it could build goodwill by retrieving stolen artworks.

Soon after receiving Gordon's memo, Heidt sent a cable to Washington, under the heading CAMBODIA SEEKS GLOBAL SOLUTION TO DOUGLAS LATCHFORD ANTIQUITIES SMUGGLING RING. He summarized the proposal and asked that representatives from DHS come to Asia to "facilitate conversations with the Cambodian government, and potentially to meet Mr. Latchford in Bangkok. The Embassy views the return of a reportedly large amount of looted Khmer antiquities as in the U.S. government's interest."

After being forwarded around for a few days, the cable reached a group that was tangentially involved with the investigation into Latchford: the Manhattan District Attorney's Office, the state body that had charged the art dealer Nancy Wiener with three felony counts. Latchford himself wasn't under its purview, since his case belonged to the federal attorneys at SDNY. The lead state prosecutor still felt that he needed to weigh in. "It is inappropriate to have mediating third parties—no matter how well-meaning—acting as liaisons between a law-enforcement agency and defendants and their co-conspirators," he replied. "Make no mistake about this request: they are asking to buy Latchford's immunity. In this case, it is not a cash payment, but far more insidious: the return of looted antiquities." He asked that no one in government engage with the matter.

Gordon's proposal hadn't even reached SDNY, the office that actually was trying to charge Latchford, albeit with great difficulty. After the state prosecutor's intervention, there was nothing he could do to affect the decisions of American law enforcement. But Gordon didn't know that yet, and neither did the man he was negotiating with.

Before going further with Latchford, Gordon wanted to arm himself with more information. In particular, he wanted to compile specific evidence about the origins of Latchford's stolen statues, of a kind that the dealer would struggle to dispute. Toek Tik, the man he called Lion, was the one person who could tell Gordon what he needed to know. Since wrapping up his work for SDNY on the Duryodhana case, Gordon had spoken to his old source periodically, mostly out of his own fascination, and with no real agenda other than to keep their relationship going.

Now it was time to get more serious—by collecting comprehensive, formal testimony. He'd previously kept the Cambodian government in the dark about Lion, worried that any contact with officials would scare him off. Yet if Gordon was going to use him to pressure Latchford, his clients had to be made aware of it. He also wanted to be confident that Lion wouldn't face retribution for disclosing what he knew. Warily, Gordon revealed his secret to Phoeurng Sackona, the minister of culture and fine arts.

She said she was willing to forgive Lion, and she agreed that obtaining information was more important than punishment. Though it was only a verbal pledge, it was enough for Gordon, and for Lion, who didn't seem to fear the government at all. After what he'd experienced over the course of his life, it appeared that very few things scared him. And he had his own reasons for sharing more of what he remembered. As a teenage soldier, responsible for enforcing the merciless doctrines of the Khmer Rouge. "I was so sickened by what I was doing," Lion told Gordon. "I didn't want to be involved in killing anymore." Looting had provided a path to survival, but only through actions that he knew were destructive. Now he was being offered a chance to take part in a kind of repair, for his country and for himself.

Gordon began interviewing Lion much more systematically, aided by translators and staff from his law office. They went through Latchford's books page by page, with Gordon asking Lion whether he recognized each piece. Lion claimed to recall where and when he'd removed dozens of them. In his telling, many of his most audacious thefts had occurred at Koh Ker. In other raids, he or his crews had ranged much more widely, as far as Cambodia's frontier with Vietnam.

Lion had no role in what happened to the works after he hauled them to the Thai border and passed them to brokers, who arranged for their onward transport. But he did know that many of the pieces went to a particular buyer in Bangkok, a Westerner he referred to as Sia Ford. Gordon, who spoke Thai, quickly recognized the word *sia*, the Thai honorific that loosely translates to "lord" or "don." After that, it took him only a moment to realize what he was hearing. The man Lion was describing had to have been Latchford. It was an astounding revelation. The dealer had evidently been so active in the market for looted works that his name, or something like it, was known all along the supply chain.

The more he learned from his interviews with Lion, the bigger Gordon began to think. Even in the cases where Lion said he hadn't personally stolen an artifact, he often indicated that he knew who had—and he was willing to make introductions to men who were now in their fifties and sixties, and long out of the business. If Gordon could also convince them to talk, he might be able to map the history of not just dozens of looted works, but hundreds, maybe even thousands. The testimony would, of course, have to be corroborated. To a nonexpert eye, many Khmer pieces could look similar, particularly after decades had passed, and Lion or other ex-looters might misre-member which objects they had taken. The obvious solution was to excavate the temples. After digging at Koh Ker's Prasat Chen, archae-ologists had been able to conclusively match statues held by the Met-ropolitan Museum of Art, among other institutions, to the stone on their shattered pedestals. The same could be done elsewhere, with firsthand accounts helping crews determine where to start digging.

What Gordon was contemplating would take years, and his more urgent challenge was to reach a deal with Latchford before he died. Since the start of the negotiations in early 2018, the group surround-ing the dealer had changed. In addition to Copleston, it now included a man named Charles Webb, who was apparently a "consultant," though of a most unusual kind. Officially, Webb—who had a cut-glass English accent, bushy facial hair, and an uncanny knack for making an interlocutor feel like they were being allowed into his confidence—had worked for a security firm before setting up a pair of companies in London that offered private investigations and "intelligence-led strategic communications." The rest of his back-ground, and the fact that virtually nothing about him existed on the internet, suggested that this might not be the full story.

Webb had grown up in Thailand, Ghana, Iran, and Washing-ton, all places where his father had nominally served as a British diplomat—in fact, he was an MI6 officer, who eventually rose to one of the seniormost roles in the agency. (A 2007 obituary in *The Tele-graph* praised the elder Webb's skill as "a developer of people" and noted his fondness for inviting Eastern Bloc embassy staff to his home for breakfasts of brandy and "Drambuie omelettes.") Others in London's investigative community, some of whom referred to Charles simply as "the Beard," assumed that he, too, had worked for the UK's security services at some point; if not, he certainly possessed the manner of someone who had. Why such an individual would be involved in the talks with Latchford, Gordon couldn't fathom, and it made him nervous.

As a result, Gordon was feeling a little apprehensive in early June 2018, when he landed in Abu Dhabi for an initial meeting with Webb and Copleston. His determination to confront Latchford had taken him into territory that no one before him had ever traversed. Gordon was at the beginning of what he hoped would be the largest effort to repatriate looted antiquities in history. He had the backing of the Cambodian government, and could draw on the support of his American legal partner and employees in Phnom Penh. But he had no qualifications in the field and even less actual power. Who was he to be leading such an ambitious campaign? On his journey to the shores of the Persian Gulf, he'd also contemplated a darker question. What if Latchford, a wealthy man whose business had brought him into at least indirect contact with the Khmer Rouge, had decided Gordon was too much trouble, and needed to disappear? He had just arrived in a Middle Eastern city where he hardly knew a soul, for an assignation with someone he was pretty sure was an ex-spy.

At 9:30 the next morning, Gordon waited at his hotel for Webb and Copleston to collect him. Organized around broad highways and irrigated golf courses, kept antiseptically clean by brigades of South Asian migrant workers, Abu Dhabi was about as different from Phnom Penh as a place could be. It was less a city than a series of colocated malls and condominium towers, separated by acres of blacktop that shimmered in the heat. At home, Gordon preferred to dress in jeans and T-shirts, and for reasons he couldn't recall, he had packed a pink tie and, ridiculously, a matching pink shirt. Compared with the Emirati men milling around the lobby in starched white summer robes, he stood out like a blaring siren.

In the moments before he was picked up, Gordon wondered if he should have told someone about his plans and arranged to check in later, to confirm that he was safe. But it was already too late: A large SUV was drawing up. Copleston, who had a pinched, narrow face and wore dark sunglasses, was behind the wheel. Webb was beside him in the passenger seat, his eyes scanning the area. Gordon waved hello and climbed into the back. He made some small talk, trying to quiet his nerves as they drove on. They soon neared a vast mosque of white marble, topped with minarets as high as thirty-story buildings. Copleston slowed down, circled a roundabout, and pulled into an arched gateway designed in faux-Venetian style. To Gordon's relief, it appeared that he wasn't being escorted on a one-way trip into the desert. Instead, he was being taken to the Ritz-Carlton.

Copleston and Webb had booked a meeting room inside, and as they took their places around a conference table, Gordon's stomach fully settled. He had given a great deal of thought to how he wanted the discussion to play out. It was critical to show his counterparts that whatever leverage they believed they had was illusory. In Gordon's view, the artworks that Latchford had collected, sold, and profited off were stolen, full stop, and he had no say in what happened to them now. It wasn't for him to stipulate the circumstances under which the pieces would be returned to the people of Cambodia. They were the rightful owners, and if it had ever appeared otherwise, it was only because Latchford had taken direct advantage of a genocide.

Soon after sitting down, Gordon delivered a line he'd been rehearsing. "I've been working with Lion for years," he said. "He was a

Khmer Rouge child soldier. He killed a lot of people. And he took a lot of statues." Gordon explained that Lion had been extremely specific about the works he'd taken, including masterpieces like Shiva and Skanda, which Latchford had put on the cover of his first book. Copleston seemed rattled. "Douglas just bought the antiquities in River City," he said, referring to a Bangkok shopping complex known for its galleries. "Nothing he was doing was illegal."

It was a weak rebuttal; everyone in the business knew that River City was a high-end tourist trap where visitors to Thailand picked up souvenir statues, many of them clumsy fakes. To Gordon, the idea that the world's leading dealer of Khmer artworks, a key supplier to the Met and similarly prestigious venues, had sourced his offerings there was laughable. Webb, who'd worked in Cambodia in the 1990s, had a better answer: "People make up stories in the village." In his assessment, Gordon was too gullible. No one could be sure that Lion wasn't just spinning tales, claiming to have taken every sculpture that someone showed him a picture of.

Gordon had to admit, if only to himself, that Webb had a point. He didn't have much corroboration for his source's testimony, not without archaeologists excavating at least some of the relevant sites. Still, he was confident that Lion was reliable. Gordon had confirmation from others, including a former senior Khmer Rouge official, that he was among the country's most successful looters. And his recollections were tremendously detailed. In some cases, Lion said he remembered the precise spot within a vast temple complex where he'd removed an object, as well as the tools he'd used to get it out. That he might have fabricated it all struck Gordon as implausible. Then there was the fact that Lion knew the ultimate buyer as "Sia Ford". It was highly unlikely that such information could have filtered down to a semiliterate Cambodian, living in a small wooden house near Koh Ker, unless Lion had done more or less what he claimed. No, Gordon insisted to his interlocutors. Lion was reliable.

Before Gordon's trip to Abu Dhabi, he had been contemplating an agreement along the lines he'd first laid out: If Latchford agreed to give up his collection and trove of records, the Cambodian government would be prepared to ask the US to spare him from prosecution. Now Gordon wasn't sure whether any deal was possible. If Latchford and his intermediaries were unwilling to admit that he'd been selling looted works for all these years, let alone that he'd known about their origins, it was hard to imagine him signing anything that Gordon would find satisfactory. They had to start with the truth, which Webb and Copleston didn't seem ready to concede.

Then they made a suggestion that took Gordon by surprise. Instead of having another formal meeting the next day, they could visit a recently opened museum. With a collection spanning from ancient Egypt to twentieth-century European abstractionists, the Louvre Abu Dhabi was the product of a bilateral deal between France and the United Arab Emirates, greased by a generous helping of oil money. It was among the latest expressions of a desire that appears to be universal among nations on the rise: to gather and possess the artistic treasures of other cultures, just as Napoleon had done for France, Queen Victoria's generals for Britain, and the benefactors of the Met for the US. The Emirati sheikhs' version was a hypermodern building on an artificial island, sheltered by a 180-meter-wide dome constructed from eight layers of stainless steel and aluminum.

The three men moved slowly through the exhibits. Each layer of the structure overhead was perforated in a distinct geometric pattern, admitting narrow shafts of sunlight that shifted almost imperceptibly as they walked. Compared with the cloistered atmosphere of a hotel meeting room, the environment was better suited to a wide-ranging discussion, on much friendlier terms. They stayed for hours, Gordon talking about his background, his love for Cambodia, his work tracking antiquities, and what he believed their return could mean for the country. Copleston said he wanted to learn more about its history, and Gordon gave him recommendations for books to read.

By the time they parted, Gordon's pessimism had lifted. It seemed like Webb and Copleston were beginning to understand what he did—the enormity of what had been done to Cambodia and, perhaps, the role Latchford had played in it. There remained major obstacles to an agreement, and in the end it was the man himself who had to accept it, not the figures around him with whom Gordon was building a rapport. But it looked like it might just be possible to pull off.

Gordon returned to Phnom Penh feeling energized, and ready to push forward with Latchford. He had no idea what was happening half a world away in New York, and how it would soon change the situation completely.

25

Jessica Feinstein turned to the man sitting in the witness box and asked a preliminary question: "Did you have a clear view from where you were of the chicken restaurant?" The SDNY prosecutor needed him to describe what he'd seen outside a fast-food joint called Kennedy Chicken, on the corner of White Plains Road and Saint Ouen Street in the North Bronx, one night in 2012.

"Yes."

"And then what happened?"

"I saw someone come down the hill, turn the corner, stand in front of the chicken spot, and start shooting into it."

"Did you recognize the shooter?"

"Looked like to be La Brim."

"How did you recognize the shooter as La Brim?"

"His size, his height, his body build, his complexion."

"Could you observe what happened?"

"I could see the glass was shattering, basically busting out the glass with the bullets."

"Were you able to observe what La Brim did after the firing stopped?

"I saw him going back around the corner, back up the hill. . . . About five minutes later, I saw Weezy come out the chicken spot, kind of limping like he was hit and trying to get a cab."

Feinstein was partway through the most complex legal proceeding of her young career: the 2019 trial of Latique Johnson, a.k.a. La Brim, and fellow members of the Blood Hound Brims, a gang that sold crack cocaine throughout New York City and acted against rivals with unflinching force. Johnson had been indicted on racketeering, attempted murder, assault, conspiracy, and firearms charges. The witness Feinstein was questioning was a self-described pimp who'd agreed to testify against Johnson in hopes of receiving a reduction in his own sentence for sex trafficking. Giving him a break was an unappealing prospect. At one point, Feinstein asked him to "describe generally for the jury how you ran your business," and how he treated the women in his employ. (It was better for a prosecutor to get such facts on the record than to wait for the defense to do it.) He responded: "I beat them. I threatened them. Deprived them of sleep." Yet without such deals, Feinstein knew, it would be far harder to put even worse criminals, like Johnson, into federal prison.

His trial would mark the end of a chapter for Feinstein, who was in her mid-thirties, with shoulder-length brown hair and a courtroom manner much more commanding than her modest stature would suggest. She had been working on violent crime since joining SDNY five years earlier. Starting out, Feinstein had wanted to prosecute murders, and she certainly got her wish—including a case in which two members of the Bloods stabbed and strangled to death a man who had threatened to betray them, then stuffed his dismembered body into a shopping cart. (Both pleaded guilty and received thirty-plus-year sentences.) Driven and methodical, she steadily advanced to more complex cases, building a reputation as one of the sharpest young attorneys at Saint Andrew's Plaza, a considerable feat in an office stocked with hard-charging graduates of top law schools.

Feinstein found the job at once absorbing and draining. Many of the defendants she encountered had been brutalized by violence as children, then come of age in neighborhoods where crime offered one of the only routes to money and status. As adults, they brutalized others in turn—at least until they got caught and, if their actions violated federal law, landed on Feinstein's docket. While she was confident that serious crimes warranted serious consequences, it was hard not to feel like she was part of a never-ending cycle. Taking a gangster off the streets might make a community safer for a time, but someone else would soon fill the empty space, bringing with them guns, drugs, and a willingness to do great harm.

Eager for a change, and a chance to feel like she was making a longer-term difference, Feinstein had asked to be transferred into a newly expanded division of SDNY, the Money Laundering and Transnational Criminal Enterprises Unit, which focused on white-collar financial crimes and asset forfeitures. Her request was granted, and after the conclusion of the Johnson trial—the gang leader and his codefendants were convicted on all counts—she joined the team full-time. Early in the transition, she walked into the office of her new boss, Alexander Wilson, for a meeting to discuss the files she would be taking on.

It had been some seven years since the start of the Duryodhana litigation against Sotheby's, and nearly as long since Wilson had become convinced that Douglas Latchford deserved to be criminally charged for his sales of looted antiquities. Though that effort was largely dormant, Wilson was still fascinated by the topic. Some years earlier, one of SDNY's paralegals had presented him with a poster at the office Christmas party. It featured Wilson dressed up in Indiana Jones–style khaki, standing in front of a vine-covered ruin under the tagline "New York Wilson and the Temple of Koh Ker." Wilson loved it, and he'd put it up on one wall of his cluttered workspace, where it still hung as he sat talking to Feinstein.

His new recruit wasn't familiar with the Latchford investigation, which had been "sitting too long," Wilson complained, entering a kind of stasis that could be fatal to a prosecution. Evidence could disappear while a case was idle, and priorities and personnel would inevitably change, making it ever harder to restart. Then there was the problem of Latchford's age. He was already eighty-seven; if the government was going to charge him while he was still alive and healthy enough to stand trial, it had to become an urgent priority. Wilson wasn't sure if such an indictment was even possible, and given his supervisory responsibilities, his schedule was too packed to find out. Feinstein, on the other hand, was coming to his unit with a relatively open calendar and an outstanding track record. "I wish we could get this guy," Wilson told her. "If you can do something with this, I'll be forever grateful to you."

Wilson's suggestion was motivated by more than respect for Feinstein's legal skills. In some regards, she fit the usual SDNY mold: Originally from the Bay Area, she had gone to Yale, then Stanford Law School, and came across as someone whom it was very hard to imagine ever getting a B. More unusually, she also had a master's degree in art history from Oxford. There, Feinstein had studied the history of collecting, and she'd written about the ways in which a love for objects can grow so intense that it tips into mania. In one paper, she discussed Henry James's novel *The Spoils of Poynton*, and what she described as its portrayal of "a fixated and demonic character who manipulates the lives of the people around her for the preservation of her collection." The book ends with that character losing her treasured objects to a fire, "the culmination," Feinstein wrote, "of her passionate and destructive collecting tendencies."

Feinstein had flirted with the idea of becoming an academic before deciding on the more practical path of law school. At Stanford, she'd taken a course called Art and the Law, and she thought she would find a legal job focused on issues related to the art world. She soon realized how few such roles actually existed, and so she pursued her second choice, criminal law. Feinstein clerked for a federal judge and then applied to join SDNY.

After her time prosecuting murderers and drug dealers, a chance to pursue an art-related case had finally arrived. When Wilson proposed that she take on the Latchford file, she didn't have to give it more than a second's thought.

A paralegal had been keeping watch over SDNY's Latchford material, which consisted of two boxes full of papers and an accompanying archive of digital files. Feinstein saw with dismay that the documents—emails, bank account statements, and various auction-house records obtained by the government—were a mess, left in no apparent order and with no indication that anyone had ever gone through all of them systematically. It was a bewildering tangle of information. *Who are these people?* Feinstein wondered as she tried to make sense of the characters involved. Worse, much of the evidence—particularly Latchford's correspondence with the New York dealer Nancy Wiener—included language that she found impenetrable. Feinstein's studies in art history had focused on nineteenth-century Europe. She had no idea what Latchford and Wiener were referring to when they spoke of the transcendent qualities of an "Angkor Borei Buddha" or a "Baphuon Shiva."

As a recent arrival to her unit, Feinstein's other commitments were limited, and in the spring and summer of 2019, she put in long hours to orient herself. The correspondence she had was incomplete, since it came from Wiener's computer and thus didn't include Latchford's exchanges with others. (His own email account was with a Thai provider, and SDNY had no access to it.) Feinstein's first priority was organizing the messages to and from Wiener chronologically, and then categorizing which of Latchford's sales pitches he appeared to have sent only to her, rather than to a broader distribution list. Then she could cross-reference the emails with Latchford's banking records.

In this way, she could narrow down which of his many proposals had led to actual transactions. Feinstein still felt uncertain of how much progress she was making. Because the case had lain dormant for so long, it was hard to know which of the files had been fully analyzed before her assignment. Some of the investigators and prosecutors involved had moved on to other jobs, while others didn't remember the details. *Is this a good email?* Feinstein sometimes asked herself—*good* in the sense of being useful for an eventual indictment. Or had someone already looked at it and decided, for reasons she wasn't aware of, that it was a dead end?

Gradually, Feinstein concluded that many of them were good emails, and the more familiar she became with the case, and with the market for Khmer artifacts, the more they made her skin crawl. There were other dealers, she had learned, but none whose impact was as profoundly damaging as Latchford's. The tone of his messages suggested that he had no qualms about ripping away other people's artistic heritage—nor, it seemed, any fear that documenting his actions could blow back on him. "Hold on to your hat," Latchford had said in a 2007 email to Wiener, boasting about a recently discovered Buddha. "It's still across the border, but wow." Later, he sent her a photograph of a bronze figure of Durga, a ferocious Hindu goddess, lying on its back and crusted with what looked to Feinstein like dirt.

He wanted as much as $36 million for it, an astronomical sum that may have been partly explained by where the piece originated. Unusually for Latchford, who followed up with an aerial image of the location, it wasn't in Cambodia or Thailand. Instead, he indicated that the Durga had come from a complex of Hindu temples in central Vietnam called My Son. Feinstein looked it up and was shocked to discover that My Son was listed by UNESCO as a World Heritage Site—a distinction reserved for places of "outstanding universal value to humanity," such as Westminster Abbey and the Taj Mahal.

Less disturbing, though potentially just as useful, were the provenance documents that Latchford had provided to Wiener and others. Again and again, when the history of an important, expensive piece needed to be substantiated, he produced a letter purportedly from the same individual, the British businessman Ian Donaldson. As far as Feinstein could determine, Donaldson was a real person. British records indicated that a man by that name, who lived at the same Hong Kong address as the one given in the provenance letters, had died in 2001. If the letters were accurate, Donaldson had either owned or seen an improbably large number of significant Khmer statues in the 1960s, just before the 1970 cutoff that made dealing in them legally complicated. *That's not how the art market works*, Feinstein thought. If an object had really spent decades in international circulation, Latchford wouldn't have had to rely on just one individual; plenty of other people would have been available.

It seemed far more likely that he had forged the Donaldson letters, which could qualify as straightforward fraud. Still, all of this wasn't necessarily enough. Before proceeding with an indictment, Feinstein wanted to accumulate an overwhelming volume of evidence—enough to intimidate Latchford into pleading guilty or, failing that, to virtually eliminate the possibility that he could be acquitted at trial. Documents, some of which were ambiguous or hard to understand, would take her only so far.

She needed a cooperating witness, ideally one who had intimate knowledge of how Latchford did business and could impart that information to a jury. The obvious candidate—perhaps the only one—was Wiener. And while SDNY had never come close to reaching a cooperation agreement with her, Feinstein wasn't ready to write Wiener off. In her guns-and-gangs work, she had successfully flipped far tougher witnesses, violent men operating within a culture where snitching was among the cardinal sins. Surely she could find a way to make a deal with an Upper East Side gallery owner.

As Jessica Feinstein continued to dig into the Douglas Latchford case in New York, Bradley Gordon, unaware of her work, thought he was finally getting somewhere. Since their initial meeting in Abu Dhabi, Gordon had conducted further discussions with the dealer's intermediaries about an accord that would see the return of most or all of his personal collection. The talks, which Gordon was juggling with the needs of his legal practice, had continued productively, even though there'd been no news from the US about his proposal to give Latchford some kind of immunity from prosecution. Of course, in Gordon's ideal world, there wouldn't be a negotiation at all. Instead, Latchford would be forced under penalty of law to return all that he'd taken. But Gordon could hardly kick down his door and retrieve Cambodia's looted property unilaterally. At this point, he had no alternative but to try to make a deal, and by the spring of 2019, he felt that he was closing in on one.

Still, his progress was agonizingly slow, partly because there were four people on the other side—Latchford; his daughter, Julia; her husband, Simon Copleston; and the consultant Charles Webb, who was formally advising Julia but not her father—all of whom had different opinions. The family was particularly reluctant to provide full access to Latchford's personal archives, in addition to repatriating the objects in his possession. For Gordon, this was nonnegotiable. Latchford was important not only because he had so much, but also because his emails, invoices, and photographs might contain crucial clues that could help Gordon track down thousands of works—and prove that they had been stolen. And he needed to see all the files, with no carveouts for documents that Latchford or those around him deemed too damaging.

There was also a larger question: Gordon still didn't know whether Latchford, at his core, really wanted to resolve the situation. The two men had never met in person, and what Gordon knew of his views was largely filtered through Copleston and Webb. Latchford's stance, as conveyed by them, appeared to change often. On one day, Gordon would be told that Latchford was determined to repair his relationship with Cambodia by giving up everything. Then, at the next update, he would hear that Latchford was willing to discuss handing over only a few pieces. Gordon couldn't figure out if the reversals were a negotiating tactic, or if they reflected the intransigence of a man who was being asked to give up his life's work—even if, in Gordon's view, that work was unquestionably malign. Either way, they were maddening.

The truth, unbeknownst to Gordon, was closer to the latter. Though hobbled by Parkinson's disease and heart problems, rarely leaving his apartment except for medical appointments, Latchford could still summon the same relentless determination that he'd used to operate his business for decades. His physical diminishment meant that many daily tasks were now impossible for him to perform without assistance. Visiting temples in Cambodia or flying to London to spend time at his second home in Mayfair was out of the question. But as long as Latchford could operate a laptop, he would continue to feed his obsession—and there was nothing Gordon could do to stop him.

In February 2019, he sent an email to one of his long-standing clients, the Bangkok tycoon Harald Link, to say that he'd been "shown a very rare early Cambodian bronze, which is known as a 'stargazer.'" Perhaps two thousand years old, the object was remarkable: an abstracted male figure with thin, elongated limbs, as though it had been created by a pre-Angkorian forebear to Alberto Giacometti. Latchford offered no information on its provenance, except to note that it was "reported to have come from Kampong Chhnang," in central Cambodia. He was soon at it again, recording the sale of three works to a Swiss collector for a total of more than $800,000. In addition to generating ongoing profits for Latchford, such transactions had the effect of further scattering Khmer pieces around the world, making Gordon's dream of tracking them down even harder to realize.

One core element of Latchford's business had changed, however: his relationship with Emma Bunker, who was now eighty-eight years old. Bunker had long been an eager collaborator in his sales, going so far as offering to supply him with letterhead from defunct American galleries—perfect for creating false paper trails stretching back to the 1960s. That she was a full and willing participant was obvious to law enforcement. She and Latchford both featured in the text of the State of New York's criminal complaint against the dealer Nancy Wiener, their identities thinly veiled as "Co-Conspirator No. 1" and "Co-Conspirator No. 2." Yet Bunker tried to retrospectively downplay her role, telling Latchford in an email that she was furious about being "subtly connected with a whole bloody mess with which I was never connected."

For almost two decades up to this point, Bunker had remained closer to Latchford than virtually anyone, but as his health declined and more old friends fell away, losing patience with his self-centered personality or simply struggling with medical problems themselves, he had grown paranoid. He was no longer sure he could trust even Bunker, whom he worried might be conspiring with those he considered his enemies: an amorphous group of US law-enforcement officials, activists, and academics that he believed had been targeting him ever since the surfacing of the Duryodhana statue at Sotheby's. In 2015, amid the pressure over that case, he had complained that Bunker was "highly dangerous" and "capable of saying anything." More recently, he'd begun recording their phone calls, presumably so she couldn't misrepresent what he'd said.

In fact, amid the wreckage of Latchford's other relationships, Bunker had stayed loyal—and silent, her only substantive interaction with the Department of Justice a single meeting with SDNY prosecutors in 2013. She remained committed and tenderly affectionate to her friend, particularly as both confronted the indignities of aging, and the terrible certainty of its conclusion. "Growing old is a real bore," she wrote to Latchford during a health crisis that had him hospitalized in Bangkok. "But it's part of the life cycle, so grin and relax. Our next life will be exciting, as we will again be young and handsome, as we once were in this world. Will we recognize each other in the next? I think so, so what do you think?"

It took until the summer of 2019 for a single, small crack to emerge in Bunker's fealty. Frail though still mentally sharp, she was visiting

Asia on what she must have known could be her last trip across the Pacific, and via a Cambodian cultural official they both knew, Gordon arranged to meet her in Phnom Penh. He found Bunker at the National Museum, where repatriated works like the Kneeling Attendants—the looted Koh Ker statues that Latchford had donated to the Met—were now on display, some thirty years after being spirited out of the country. Gordon was interested that day in another major Koh Ker piece: Skanda on a Peacock. It had featured in Bunker and Latchford's first book, *Adoration and Glory*, and ranked among the most significant Khmer works known to be in existence. And Lion, as Gordon continued to refer to the ex-looter Toek Tik, had admitted to stealing it in 1997.

The problem was that Gordon had no record of who'd bought it since, and therefore no way to use Lion's account to demand its return; in *Adoration and Glory*, its location had been listed as simply "Private collection, New York." Gordon had brought a copy of the book to his meeting with Bunker, and he flipped to the corresponding page. He wasn't sure if she would tell him what he wanted to know. It was exactly the kind of information that Latchford was trying to protect. But Bunker was willing to help. If anything, it seemed to Gordon that she was excited to be letting him in on a secret, like a character in a spy film. She said that Skanda on a Peacock had been purchased by a European mathematics professor with a name that sounded like "Mannucci." Gordon was thrilled. Since the earliest days of his work on looted antiquities, he'd come to crave moments like this, when the truth behind a mystery he'd been obsessing over was finally revealed. It was a rush that made all the frustrations worthwhile.

He realized after the meeting, however, that any elation was premature, because Bunker had either misremembered the buyer's identity, or spelled his name wrong. There was no trace of anyone with the description she'd provided. Gordon tried searching for some possible variations, none of which turned up anything promising. Bunker had mentioned offhand that the man had a son whose lover operated a business in Kuala Lumpur, selling teacups. So Gordon spent hours scouring the websites of Malaysian crockery shops, trying and failing to track down scraps of information. It was a ridiculously inefficient way of working. If he had access to Latchford's records, he could go so much faster.

His negotiations were still going in circles when, around this time, Gordon received a call from Thailand. He answered and heard Latchford's voice, gravelly with age, on the line. This was a surprise, but his mind instantly snapped into focus. Gordon knew that this might be his last chance to make his case to Latchford directly. Why he was calling, Gordon couldn't be sure; later he would wonder whether the dealer, after so much denial and deflection, finally wanted to unburden himself, with no one standing in between.

"I'm back from the dead," Latchford said with a laugh; he'd evidently just recovered from some medical issue. Gordon had to admit that he found him charming. As Latchford made cheerful small talk, it was easy to understand how he'd been such an effective salesman for so long. But Gordon soon moved the conversation toward what he'd wanted to say for the better part of a decade, ever since his first conversations with Lion. He needed to tell Latchford that there was only one path forward, only one outcome that he would accept. "Look, Douglas," Gordon said, "we are going to bring everything back. We need your collection to come home. And if you truly love the Cambodian people, this would be the right thing to do."

Latchford laughed again. It was hard to tell if he was revealing a meaningful change in his thinking, or somehow toying with Gordon. "Yes," he finally said. "I would like to give back to Cambodia."

While Gordon pushed for a breakthrough with Latchford before he died, Feinstein was trying to make progress of her own, calling Nancy Wiener back to SDNY's offices in Lower Manhattan for another interview. Accompanied by her lawyers, the dealer was clearly unhappy to be there. To her, Feinstein was just the latest in a series of investigators intent on asking her uncomfortable questions. As they proceeded, Feinstein saw that the fundamental problem remained the same as when Alexander Wilson first met with Wiener more than a year before. No matter how much she was pushed, she wouldn't acknowledge that she had knowingly sold stolen art.

If the government was going to rely on Wiener to testify against Latchford, this was still essential, and to Feinstein, it amounted to a statement of the obvious. For months, she had been looking at emails in which Latchford offered to Wiener pieces that were still encrusted with dirt. Why dance around such a glaring truth? But it appeared that Wiener had long ago put such knowledge into the back of her mind, giving it no further attention until she became a target of law enforcement. Frustrated, and painfully aware that more inconclusive conversations would burn time that she didn't have, Feinstein at one point pulled Wiener's attorneys out of the room. "Look, this isn't working," she complained. If their client wanted a deal to avoid federal prosecution, her attitude would have to change.

Feinstein wasn't ready to give up, though; while working violent crime, she'd learned that building a rapport with a source was almost always a complicated process. She soon brought Wiener back for another try. This time, she wanted to employ a method that she had honed earlier in her career. When interviewing a witness to, say, a murder in the Bronx, she would arrive with a stack of photographs of suspected gang associates. Turning them over one by one, she would repeat an identical series of questions intended to connect the dots of a criminal network:

"Who is this?"

"How do you know him?"

"Was he there that night?"

"Did he have a gun?"

"What was his role in the crew?"

Feinstein had resolved to do the same now, only with Khmer statues rather than members of the Bloods. She had prepared meticulously, building a list of suspicious works that she wanted to know more about. Sitting across from Wiener, she reached into her files and pulled out an image of one of them, a tenth-century bronze Buddha. "Was this piece yours?" she asked. Once Wiener confirmed that it was, Feinstein continued, asking how she'd obtained it, how much she'd paid, and how Latchford had been involved.

Then she came to the most important question: "What were the indicia that it was looted?" Feinstein figured that this might be a better strategy than trying to get Wiener to explain what she *knew* about the origin of a work. In the case of the Buddha, the answer was that it appeared to have been struck with a farming tool—probably during its violent removal from a temple—and that Latchford and Bunker had provided three separate provenance statements for it, containing different details each time. With those facts on the table, Feinstein could walk Wiener up to the logical conclusion: That any reasonable person, if presented with the same information, would have concluded that the Buddha's origins were illicit.

After repeating this process over multiple meetings, and with dozens of Khmer artifacts, Feinstein felt like she and Wiener were getting into a rhythm. There was no moment of epiphany, no flash of remorse when the dealer finally admitted what she'd done. But as Feinstein marched her through the same questions again and again, Wiener was increasingly willing to say that the works she'd handled bore clear signs of theft. And for Feinstein, that was good enough. By the autumn of 2019, she was confident that she had the material, and a sufficiently credible witness, to finally charge Latchford. Marshaling the case files that she'd spent much of the year studying, she sat down at her desk to work on a federal criminal indictment. At a minimum, the document had to establish Latchford's identity and state exactly which laws he was accused of breaking and why. But Feinstein wanted to go far beyond these basics, and offer a historical narrative that put his actions into context.

"From the mid-1960s until the early 1990s, Cambodia experienced continuous civil unrest and regular outbreaks of civil war," Feinstein explained. "During these times of extreme unrest, Cambodian archaeological sites . . . such as Angkor Wat and Koh Ker, suffered serious damage and widespread looting." She emphasized that the thefts, and the sales of stolen objects, had continued well into the twenty-first century, in violation of both Cambodian and US laws. Then Feinstein came to Latchford. "The defendant," she wrote, "engaged in a scheme to sell looted Cambodian antiquities on the international art market, including to dealers and buyers in the United States. As part of that scheme, in order to conceal that Latchford's antiquities were the product of looting . . . Latchford created and caused the creation of false provenance for the antiquities he was selling."

Feinstein went on for eight more pages, detailing much of what she knew about Latchford's biography, beginning with his role in the 1970s as a key supplier of looted works to the London auction house Spink's. She summarized his relationship with Bunker and quoted extensively from his offers of stolen pieces to Wiener. And she described how he used the identity of a "false collector"—the late Ian Donaldson—to fake the origins of artifacts. In sum, Feinstein wrote, Latchford had "continued to act as a conduit for recently looted Cambodian antiquities" throughout his long career. In the opinion of the DOJ, his actions involved wire fraud, smuggling, conspiracy, and customs violations—five felony counts, each carrying the potential of a lengthy prison term.

As she was putting her finishing touches on the indictment, Feinstein learned about Gordon's ongoing negotiations with Latchford. She decided that they were irrelevant to her. Any deal to repatriate Latchford's collection wouldn't change her assessment that he had committed federal crimes. The government was not in the business of declining to prosecute fraudsters just because they returned what they'd taken from their victims; a carjacker couldn't expect to dodge charges in exchange for driving the vehicle back and offering an apology. Stolen statues were no different. If anything, their restitution was less meaningful, since the damage that looters caused to archaeological sites, and to historical knowledge, could never be repaired. Regardless of what Gordon believed he was accomplishing, Feinstein was determined to move ahead.

She had a similar reaction to secondhand information that Latchford was in poor health, a line Feinstein had heard before. Plenty of defendants claimed, upon learning that prosecution was imminent, to be suffering from some debilitating medical problem. They often turned out to be perfectly fit to stand trial and to be jailed, if it came to that. In any case, Feinstein reasoned that her job was to follow the evidence wherever it led, and it had brought her to Latchford. Even if there was a good chance that, given his age, he would never see the inside of a courtroom, she had documented wrongdoing that might have never otherwise entered the legal record.

Feinstein's next step was to present her work to a grand jury, a panel of randomly selected citizens who review whether there is probable cause to charge a defendant. The group voted to proceed, and the indictment against Latchford was filed on October 17, 2019. It would remain sealed for the time being, in hopes that he might travel outside Thailand and be taken into custody. To that end, the court issued a one-page document bearing Feinstein's name.

"Authorized law enforcement officer," it read. "YOU ARE COM-MANDED to arrest and bring before a United States magistrate judge without unnecessary delay DOUGLAS LATCHFORD."

27

On December 3, 2019, two officers from the Thai Immigration Bureau, acting on a request from the US Department of Homeland Security, pulled up to Chidlom Place, Douglas Latchford's home for decades. Clad in ocher-red tiles that glinted in the tropical sunlight, the condominium tower he'd built in central Bangkok remained a prestigious address, shielded from the busy streets outside by a high wall that wrapped around its perimeter. The pair entered through the front gate, monitored by overhead security cameras. They passed the swimming pool, decorated with a marble pavilion housing a statue of a Hindu goddess, where Latchford had long spent a significant part of every day, receiving visits from art buyers and bodybuilders. Then they entered the porte cochere, framed on one side by an unusual water feature: a six-tiered fountain in black slate, shaped like a broad ziggurat. To those knowledgeable about Latchford's interests, its profile was familiar. It looked remarkably like the central pyramid of Koh Ker.

In the elevator, the immigration agents rode to the ninth floor, where banking records obtained by the US government indicated that Latchford resided. They knocked on the door of the unit, explaining that they were looking for him. But the dealer wasn't there, and they came away with the impression that he no longer lived in the building. For the moment, they reported to DHS, his whereabouts were a mystery.

After Jessica Feinstein's five-count indictment was filed in mid-October, SDNY had kept it under seal for several weeks, waiting to see if Latchford would travel to a country from which he might be extradited with a minimum of legal drama. When that didn't happen, Feinstein decided to go public with the charges. The accompanying press release said they would send "a clear message to the art market and to those who profit from the illegal trafficking of cultural treasures: the United States . . . will use every legal tool to stop the plundering of cultural heritage." The effectiveness of such a message relied on the certainty of arrest, and in official terms, Latchford was now "at large," with the American government bound to do everything in its power to capture him.

The actual logistics of doing so were a matter for frontline law enforcement and thus fell not to Feinstein but to J. P. Labbat, a DHS special agent she'd worked with to pull together the indictment. He was less accepting than Feinstein of the possibility that Latchford might never enter an American courtroom. Slim and fit, with his dark hair neatly trimmed, Labbat was a classic federal-agent type: Growing up in Bay Ridge, Brooklyn, his favorite TV show was *America's Most Wanted*. He was determined to get Latchford onto a plane to New York for arraignment, regardless of the defendant's advanced age, but as he dug into the problem, he realized that it might be more complicated than the average extradition.

When an American fugitive was located in Thailand, US law-enforcement agencies usually followed a standard process, first asking the State Department to cancel the individual's passport, the possession of which is viewed by the government as a privilege, not a right. Then they would inform the Thai government that the person no longer had a valid travel document, making their presence in the country illegal. The next step would typically be deportation to the US, without the complexities of a full-blown extradition. But Latchford was British, and as Labbat soon learned, he was a naturalized Thai citizen as well. It was thus impossible to have him deported; technically, the Immigration Bureau, whose agents had first attempted to find him, couldn't even handle his case. There was also another challenge to overcome.

In early January 2020, a little over a month after the SDNY indictment was unsealed, lawyers whom Latchford had hired in the US reached out to the government. They said that their eighty-eight-year-old client was severely ill, his condition so dire that they'd been unable to discuss the charges with him. According to the attorneys, he was in an intensive-care unit in Thailand, diagnosed with "end of life" organ failure. Labbat was extremely skeptical. "We feel that Latchford's attorney is exaggerating the facts," he said in an email to colleagues. Labbat wouldn't accept anything less than positive confirmation of his condition, which meant getting a direct look at Latchford as soon as possible.

For Labbat, who'd spent the vast majority of his career making arrests and executing warrants on American soil, operating at a remove from the action was frustrating. He still didn't know where Latchford was; DHS had been able to confirm that he'd recently been hospitalized, but he seemed to have been discharged. And with his Thai nationality established, the task of locating Latchford was now in the jurisdiction of the Royal Thai Police, who operated under much tighter legal constraints than the immigration authorities. A Thai officer explained that if they wanted to enter Chidlom Place for a more thorough check, they would need to obtain a search warrant first. Labbat was furious. "Unfortunately for us, it seems like we contacted the laziest and most inept police officer in Bangkok," he complained in a January 16 email. "To suggest that a search warrant is the only path to conducting an inquiry or a knock on the door for information is not acceptable. If that were the case, every bad guy in Bangkok would rent space at this condominium complex."

Labbat soon learned, however, that he was focusing on the wrong location, because Latchford wasn't at home after all. He was at Bumrungrad International Hospital, a state-of-the-art health-care complex favored by the Bangkok elite. Labbat called the US embassy and insisted that someone be dispatched to see him. Though Thailand was the first country outside China to report confirmed cases of the illness later known as COVID-19, serious restrictions on hospitals and other public facilities were still weeks away. Two American agents entered the building without incident and went upstairs, threading between smiling nurses in starched white uniforms and patients bearing bandages from the cosmetic surgeries that were among Bumrungrad's offerings. Finally, they reached the intensive-care unit, and came to a room with a sliding wood-trimmed glass door. There was one bed inside, surrounded by beeping monitors.

Latchford's once-powerful body had shriveled away, and his blue hospital gown hung loosely on his skeletal frame. His long arms, which he'd kept dense with muscle well into old age through regular squash games, lay limp and useless on the bedsheets, and thick tubing wrapped around his drawn, sunken face. He was almost entirely incapable of communicating; the best he could do was point nonsensically to words on a board. Disturbing him might create a scene that the agents' superiors wouldn't approve of, and after a short time observing Latchford, they left.

They sent word back to Labbat: His lawyers had been telling the truth. Latchford's health had collapsed in the autumn of 2019, when Feinstein was completing work on the indictment. He was so far gone he didn't even know that the moment he'd feared for almost a decade, since the Duryodhana case first put him on the radar of American prosecutors, had finally arrived. Even for an office as aggressive as SDNY, extraditing him across the Pacific was out of the question. In New York, Feinstein struggled with the news. The goal of any prosecution was obviously to put a defendant in a courtroom, so in that sense, Latchford had won. While the country whose heritage obsessed him was consumed by genocide and civil war, he'd lived a long and comfortable life. In that time, he had taken direct advantage of the violence unleashed by Pol Pot, profiting through sales to others and satisfying his own irrepressible desire to possess the finest artworks of ancient Cambodia, whatever the cost to its people.

Yet the consequences that Latchford had directly experienced were modest: a degree of social stigma following the Duryodhana revelations, and the loss of some, though by no means all, of his hard-won standing in the world of Asian art. These were manageable enough that he had continued to make deals until almost the moment that he went into intensive care. And when he finally faced real accountability—the kind delivered by agents with badges and guns—he was too old and too sick for it to matter. If Latchford had been born only five or ten years later, Feinstein thought, the result could have been so different.

Still, she was less disappointed than she might have been with a more conventional case. That Latchford would evade extradition was always a possibility. If not for her work, his actions might have remained forever lost to history, and they certainly never would have been enumerated in a federal indictment. The theft of Cambodia's archaeological glories was an unusual crime. To anyone who bothered to look into the matter, the evidence of its scale was obvious and shocking: broken pedestals, sheared-off bas-reliefs, decapitated statues. There was no mystery, in a general sense, as to where the supply chain that began with all this shattered stone ultimately led: to the museums and mansions of New York, London, and other Western cities. By investigating Latchford, Feinstein had revealed all the links in between, and found extensive violations of American law. Regardless of what happened to the dealer, that information was still useful to her.

One of the key responsibilities of SDNY's Money Laundering and Transnational Criminal Enterprises Unit was to handle asset forfeitures. Feinstein's job was not only to prosecute defendants, but also to seize property connected with criminal activity. And even though Latchford would soon be gone, the stolen artifacts that he'd bought and sold would endure. The challenge was to somehow find them, before they scattered further.

Bradley Gordon, too, was disappointed. Since almost the beginning of his own investigation, he'd considered Latchford a criminal, more culpable than any other individual for what Gordon had come to view as the largest art heist in history. Though he'd tried, for a time, to get the US government to treat Latchford leniently in exchange for returning artworks, he believed that the charges were richly deserved, and in a fairer universe, Latchford would have had to answer for them in an American court. Still, like Feinstein, Gordon was trying to take a wider view.

Negotiating with Latchford had been infuriating, with Gordon never sure if the dealer really intended to give up his statues and records—or if he was just stringing the process along, playing for time while he turned more of his collection into cash. But Latchford's position was no longer relevant. While he lay in the hospital, his daughter, Julia, applied to a Thai court to have him declared incapacitated. Julia's petition was granted in March 2020, leaving her as the decision-maker over his affairs.

Gordon hammered out a draft agreement between the government of Cambodia and the Latchford family, represented by Julia and her husband, Simon Copleston. It was a lawyerly contract of seventeen pages, but the most important clauses were right at the beginning. If the deal was executed, Julia would commit to repatriating all Khmer artifacts in her family's "possession, custody or control"—in other words, the entire collection that her father had spent a lifetime building. Just as important, she would also hand over "customer lists and locations of customers, supplier lists, pricing sheets, maintenance log[s], and other books, notes, journals, [and] records" pertaining to the many more works that Latchford had handled and sold. Though Julia still hadn't signed, Gordon believed that she eventually would. It was the only way she could ever be free of her father's misdeeds.

Nearly up to this point, Gordon had not had any contact with Feinstein. Half a world apart, they had been investigating the same subject independently, documenting events that both found outrageous. As a result, Feinstein had no awareness of the intensive research Gordon had been conducting into the history of looting in Cambodia, or of his plan for a global investigation to track down stolen pieces. Nor did she know how much he'd learned from Lion, who had apparently been involved in the thefts of many of the most significant works.

In early 2020, the two attorneys finally spoke. At first, Feinstein wasn't sure what to make of the man on the other end of the line, who'd evidently been spending much of his time analyzing Latchford's operation. But she did know that she wasn't done investigating it herself. In some ways, in fact, she was just getting started.

28

In the summer of 2020, Bradley Gordon sent Jessica Feinstein an intriguing piece of information. Over the past several months, he'd kept in touch with the New York prosecutor by phone and email, updating her on his talks with the Latchford family, as well as on what he was learning from Lion, whom he continued to interview even as the pandemic made in-person meetings challenging. It wasn't exactly a collaboration. Gordon had no formal relationship with SDNY, and he was providing far more to Feinstein than he was getting back. But their goals were aligned, and Gordon thought she might be able to help with a mystery that had been nagging him.

It had to do with the 2008 *Architectural Digest* story that he'd been sent by an estranged adviser to Douglas Latchford, the one featuring a palatial Florida home filled with Khmer artifacts. The identity of the owners—"a low-key couple based in New York," as the article described them—had eluded him for years. He'd originally zeroed in on the painting by the French cubist Fernand Léger that hung over a sitting area, thinking he might be able to track who'd bought it, but that lead went nowhere. Then Gordon spotted the same painting in an *AD* piece from 2019, this one devoted to "an airy, light-filled retreat" on Miami's Biscayne Bay. The second residence was radically different in style from the one featured eleven years before, yet it had evidently been commissioned by the same people. The write-up referred to their previous house, in Palm Beach, describing it as "a cluster of hip-roofed shadowy pavilions . . . that showcased their collections of contemporary art, Art Deco furniture, and museum-quality Southeast Asian sculptures." As if designed to taunt Gordon, a photo of the Miami villa included a large standing Khmer figure that had also appeared in the earlier article.

After cross-referencing the two stories with real-estate items in the South Florida press, Gordon eventually came up with a name: George Lindemann. Lindemann was a major art collector and an extremely successful dealmaker, having parlayed the sale of a family eye-care company into massive telecommunications and energy investments. While building a fortune that stood at more than $3 billion by the time of his death in 2018, he and his family had managed to largely avoid publicity, with one exception. In the early 1990s, one of his sons was caught up in a bizarre scandal: At elite American horse farms, once-prized animals were being killed for insurance money. As federal prosecutors unraveled what turned out to be a large-scale horse murder ring, they investigated George Lindemann Jr., an accomplished equestrian. He was accused of having a thoroughbred named Charisma electrocuted in order to collect $250,000, a pittance compared with his father's resources. George Jr. was convicted of three counts of wire fraud and sentenced to thirty-three months in prison for what the judge said were "despicable and reprehensible" acts. But none of this slowed down the elder Lindemann, who continued to build his empire and make major real-estate deals.

The Palm Beach *Daily News* had reported in 2008 on his sale of a twenty-seven-thousand-square-foot "Balinese-style" mansion for around $70 million, a description that matched the original *AD* spread, and Gordon had no doubt that George Sr. and his wife, Frayda, now a widow, were the mystery couple who had assembled a vast collection of looted Cambodian works. He showed the photos to Lion, who remembered stealing some of the pieces from Koh Ker. Specifically, Lion said he'd taken them in 1997, during the same raid in which he'd removed Skanda on a Peacock and Shiva and Skanda from a small temple called Prasat Krachap. How exactly they'd made their way from Prasat Krachap to the Lindemanns was unclear; Gordon wanted them back regardless.

He laid out this detective work in a pair of emails to Feinstein. "If you have more info, this would be very appreciated as these pieces also would be of great importance," he wrote. But the Lindemanns' name wasn't new to her. In fact, the family had been on SDNY's radar for some time. In the early days of his investigation into the Duryodhana at Sotheby's, Alexander Wilson, Feinstein's boss, had come across old auction paperwork suggesting that George Sr. might have bought one of the statues from the same grouping. But the documents weren't conclusive, and Feinstein had no idea that he and his wife had purchased so much more.

She found the magazine photos staggering. Acquiring and possessing stolen artworks was wrong, and likely illegal, no matter where they were kept. Yet Feinstein drew a distinction between private collections and museums. At least artifacts on display at places like the Met could be studied by scholars, appreciated by the public, and, in theory, seen by the citizens of their countries of origin, if they were ever able to make the trip to New York. The Lindemanns, by contrast, had not only purchased looted objects, thus contributing to the financial incentive for men like Lion to ransack Cambodia's temples amid the carnage of the civil war. They'd then hidden the results away, in their own kind of Aladdin's cave.

In Palm Beach, they had placed a monumental sculpture of the god Vishnu in a sitting room, and a life-size seated Koh Ker figure, identified with total ignorance by *AD* as a "Buddha," at the end of their dining table. (This was the piece that had once stood behind the Duryodhana.) They had also mounted a trio of severed stone heads—representations of Hindu *devas* and *asuras*, benevolent and malevolent deities, respectively—above a fireplace. The heads were from Angkor Thom, the twelfth-century temple complex considered by some experts to be the apotheosis of Khmer architecture. *It's like having gargoyles from Notre-Dame in your living room*, Feinstein thought.

J. P. Labbat, the DHS investigator who was working the Latchford case with Feinstein, began trying to gather more evidence, to bolster a case for seizing the works. Figuring that George Sr. might have passed them to his children, he sought information from George Jr.—who'd become a prominent investor and philanthropist—and his brother, Adam. That turned out to be a dead end; neither of George Sr.'s sons had the pieces from *AD*. DHS also reached out to Frayda, who still lived in the house featured in the magazine's second article. It was located on Star Island, an enclave of waterfront mansions ranked by Zillow as the most expensive neighborhood in America, with an average home price north of $23 million. She and her family soon made it clear, however, that they didn't think the Department of Justice had a right to know about any trove of Khmer artifacts that might be in their possession. The Lindemanns instructed a New York law firm to run interference, prompting months of legal back-and-forth. They had apparently decided to stonewall, betting that if they created enough headaches, the government would move on.

Feinstein followed the process with some frustration. She'd given birth to her second child in May 2020 and was spending part of her maternity leave in Maine, where she tried to keep the Cambodia investigation moving from her laptop while also caring for her newborn son. She and Labbat had a number of promising leads—and, she thought, a good chance of seizing a large number of stolen works from American collections. But if everyone fought as hard as the Lindemanns, it was going to be a long, difficult slog.

Through all of this, Latchford remained in intensive care at Bangkok's Bumrungrad hospital, barely conscious of his surroundings. Since confirming the severity of his condition in early 2020, Feinstein had given up on arresting him; even if he had been healthier, the COVID-19 situation would have made extradition extremely complicated. Confined to his bed, Latchford had no awareness of the lengths to which she, Gordon, and whole teams of lawyers and investigators were going to unravel his activities. Nor did he have any idea that—officially, at least—he remained a defendant in a US criminal prosecution.

In the meantime, his only child was trying to come to terms with his legacy. For much of her life, Julia Latchford hadn't known her father well. She'd been raised by her Thai mother, who'd left him in the early 1970s, when Julia was a toddler. Nonetheless, she was protective of Latchford, with whom she'd become closer as an adult. Some of the darkest insinuations about him, spread by American activists, struck Julia as absurd: that he was a gangster who paid off Thai generals in return for protection, or that the bodybuilders whose company he so enjoyed were in fact musclebound enforcers, deployed to protect him.

If his detractors were so wrong in those assumptions, she reasoned, there was no need to believe them when it came to anything else. In conversations with Julia and her husband, Latchford had emphatically and specifically denied almost every accusation of wrongdoing, and in the absence of strong contradictory evidence, they'd been prepared to believe him. Julia conceded that his obsession with Khmer antiquities might have led him to cut some corners on provenance, but he was hardly the only dealer who'd done so, and she didn't see how that made him a criminal mastermind.

Even with Latchford at death's door, however, the allegations against him weren't going away, and Julia had come to realize that they could affect her too. She was her father's principal heir, and their finances were entwined. In his early eighties, Latchford had set up a pair of trusts in the Channel Islands tax haven of Jersey. Through these vehicles, he ultimately intended to transfer to Julia his antiquities collection, as well as property and financial assets, including an investment portfolio worth more than $12 million. Then, in early 2020, Julia tried to move some of the funds—and found that she couldn't. She assumed they had been frozen at the request of the Department of Justice; in fact, Jersey regulators had acted on their own after Latchford's indictment. (Feinstein hadn't even known the money was there.) Either way, the action had the effect of focusing Julia's mind—as did a creeping sense, as she gained access to more of her incapacitated father's files, that he hadn't been telling her the truth. Charles Webb, the London consultant who was advising her, urged Julia to do something dramatic. The only way to find peace, Webb told her, was through a total surrender. The entire collection needed to go back to Cambodia, just as Gordon had proposed.

By the summer, there was nothing more to be done for Latchford at Bumrungrad, and Julia had him brought back to his condominium, where a team of nurses would care for him until the end. On August 2, 2020, a doctor who lived in the building came over to pronounce him dead; officially, the cause was organ failure brought on by Parkinson's disease. Latchford's body was loaded into a car and driven through central Bangkok, emptied by the pandemic of some of its notorious traffic. The city's skyscrapers and shopping malls, its moldering tenement blocks and canalside shanties, gave way to industrial sprawl and then to the hot, flat plains of central Thailand— lands once ruled by the ancient Khmer. Latchford's destination was a monastery in the north of the country. Though not formally religious, he said he believed in reincarnation and had asked to be cremated, a process that, in some Buddhist traditions, is said to free the spirit for whatever awaits.

The artworks that had determined the course of Latchford's life were as eternal as anything crafted by human hands. When he discovered them, they had already survived for a millennium or longer, silent witnesses to the rise and fall of kings, the arrival and retreat of new religions, and, ultimately, the ravaging of the nation that had created them, in the service of an ideology that would have been incomprehensible to their makers. To obtain them and hold on to them, to hoard them and profit from them, Latchford had stolen, lied, and cheated, ruining relationships and breaking laws. But even this intense connection was transient. Immortality was the preserve of gods in stone and bronze.

Six days after his death, monks in saffron-orange robes placed the coffin containing Latchford's body on an open pyre and lit its logs from below. They stood back as the flames began to lick at his remains, sending tendrils of smoke into the tropical sky. It didn't take long for him to be consumed.

———

Julia resolved to settle her father's affairs as quickly as possible, and in mid-September, she signed a formal agreement with the Cambodian government, represented by Gordon, in which she promised to return all of his Khmer works. Masterpieces such as Shiva and Skanda would be repatriated almost immediately; the rest would follow as Julia cleaned out Latchford's homes and storage facilities in Thailand and the UK. Gordon was as happy as he'd ever been in his life. Even if Latchford had escaped accountability, Gordon had taken a huge step toward righting his misdeeds, bringing back an unprecedented number of objects that belonged to no one but the Cambodian people. He was already talking to power brokers in Phnom Penh about how they could be put on public display—in an expanded and updated National Museum, or one day in a new institution, befitting the grandeur of the Khmer civilization.

Gordon was equally excited by another provision of the deal. As he'd hoped, Julia had agreed to turn over Latchford's personal records, memorializing his sales to museums and collectors around the world, and she had instructed Webb to help make sense of them. The archive wouldn't be enough to trace the whereabouts of all the pieces on Gordon's target list, now growing into the thousands, nor to prove that they had all been stolen. It was more likely to provide clues, which Gordon would have to follow with a great deal of investigation. But as he undertook that daunting work, he knew he would be able to rely on the best possible source—a living witness to many of the crimes he was trying to document, who wanted to tell Gordon all that he remembered.

29

Eight years after first meeting Lion at his home near Koh Ker, Gordon trusted him instinctively. In long, discursive interviews, the former looter had revealed so much about his life—about his time as a child soldier in the Khmer Rouge, and his participation in killings that became sickeningly familiar. He'd offered detailed accounts of his raids on temples, taking responsibility for actions that amounted to serious crimes under Cambodian law. And, eventually, he revealed something that he had held back in their early conversations: that his father and uncle were involved in the ransacking of Prasat Chen in the early 1970s. This was the origin of the Duryodhana, whose theft Gordon had first been hired to investigate.

There remained a cultural gulf between the two men. Lion had no formal education and had never traveled outside Southeast Asia; Gordon had a pair of Ivy League degrees and had lived for decades as an expatriate. His command of the Khmer language was limited, and they spoke mostly through translators. Yet as their relationship deepened and Gordon spent more time with Lion and his family, he came to think of him as a dear friend as much as a source. He felt a deep loyalty, an emotion he would later describe as a kind of love. Gordon was conscious, nonetheless, of a problem at the core of their relationship.

Lion's stories of his exploits as a looter were just that: stories, without definitive corroboration. It was no simple matter to verify the details of a temple raid in, say, 1993, when the civil war was at a boil and the reach of the government barely extended beyond Siem Reap. Gordon thought it was incredibly unlikely that Lion was making up his accounts. He had no motive to lie, and the details seemed far too specific to be the product of imagination. But it was certainly possible that he'd misremembered some of them. Could he really be sure, after twenty-five years or more, where and when he'd found a specific statue? It wasn't as though he had kept an inventory. If Gordon wanted to use Lion's testimony to bring artworks back to Cambodia—and, especially, if he wanted to convince Feinstein that Lion was solid enough to rely on in litigation—he needed more. Otherwise, it would be too easy for collectors and museums to dismiss him as a teller of tales, an uneducated villager whose claims deserved no consideration.

In October 2020, Lion finally got a chance to prove that what he'd told Gordon was accurate. Some of his most vivid memories centered on Prasat Krachap, where he said he'd removed Shiva and Skanda and Skanda on a Peacock in late 1997—the peak of his looting career, and less than a year before the death of Pol Pot. With Gordon's encouragement, Cambodia's Ministry of Culture and Fine Arts authorized an excavation. Lion joined an archaeological team at the site, showing them the spot where he remembered finding both statues: a small antechamber connected to the temple's central shrine.

Prasat Krachap had been studied much less intensively than better-known ruins closer to Angkor, and if Lion was right, he understood more about it than the archaeologists did. Its structures had been exposed to the encroaching jungle for ten centuries, and parts were half buried under mounds of compacted soil. The engineering genius of the ancient Khmer remained obvious nonetheless. The western gopura, or entrance pavilion, was still imposing, twice the height of a man and crowned by tall triangular pediments dusted with moss. Inside the temple compound, the filigreed columns at either end of the antechamber were intact; so were the walls, many of their bricks as squared off as they'd been the day they were laid, in the early tenth century.

The archaeological team's first priority was the central sanctuary, where they dug a trench three meters long by two and a half meters wide. Then, following Lion's guidance, they moved on to the antechamber, beginning to clear the sediment covering the floor. Regardless of its outward appearance, there was no way to be sure that the structure hadn't been undercut by erosion, and they proceeded gingerly, wary of doing anything that could destabilize it. Brushing away the earth, they began to reveal fragments of stone, each of which they measured and photographed. After analyzing the results, they made an astonishing discovery.

In Latchford's collection, Shiva and Skanda wasn't fully intact. Its childlike Skanda figure had lost part of its left arm, and Skanda's father, Shiva, was missing an ear, which had been replaced with modern restorations. And among the more than three thousand items recovered from the excavation, some so tiny that they were best described as shards, the archaeologists identified the originals—and also located a fragment that matched the base of Skanda on a Peacock. Elsewhere at Prasat Krachap, they had found pieces of an intricately carved roof pediment depicting the same image: Skanda, the Hindu god of war, seated atop the bird that was said to carry him into battle. The presence of the motif was unlikely to be a coincidence. Instead, it had probably been repeated within multiple artworks inside the temple—one of them the statue that Lion said he'd removed.

The dig had succeeded beyond Gordon's wildest imaginings. The temple was just one site, and the works Lion had taken there represented only a small fraction of his overall haul. Still, if his recollections of Prasat Krachap could be corroborated, then the same was surely true of other locations. After the archaeologists relayed their findings, Gordon was buzzing. He'd never doubted that Lion was the real deal, and now he could prove it.

Shiva and Skanda was already going back to Cambodia, thanks to Julia Latchford's repatriation deal with the government, but Skanda on a Peacock was a more complicated challenge. The year before the excavation, Emma Bunker had disclosed to Gordon the identity of the man who bought it—a mathematics professor with a name that sounded like "Mannucci." But Bunker had the wrong spelling, and Gordon struggled to locate anyone who was a plausible candidate. When he and Feinstein connected after Latchford's indictment, Gordon gave her what meager information he had. Feinstein agreed that recovering the sculpture was a priority, but she couldn't find the buyer, either. So she brought the question to Nancy Wiener. The Manhattan dealer, whose testimony had been crucial to charging Latchford, knew as much about the market for Asian antiquities as anyone in the US. Surely, Feinstein thought, she would have an idea of who Bunker was referring to.

Wiener quickly solved the problem. The person they were looking for was an Italian academic, Mario Mignucci. He had lived an unusual life. Mignucci had been a scholar not of mathematics but of ancient logic, who'd published well-regarded analyses of the works of Aristotle and Plato. And he'd evidently been interested enough in Khmer antiquities, and had the necessary cash, to buy Skanda on a Peacock from Latchford for $1.5 million. Mignucci had died in 2004, just under four years after making that purchase. Feinstein soon learned that he'd bequeathed the work to a relative and, incredibly, that it was now located in her jurisdiction. Specifically, it had been brought to Manhattan, where it sat in the living room of a Midtown apartment. She still found it shocking that anyone would keep such an artwork, with all its historical and spiritual importance to the people of its country of origin, hidden away in their home.

Feinstein wrote up a civil forfeiture complaint, which would allow the piece to be seized. The document was a milestone: For the first time, SDNY was explicitly relying on testimony from Lion, whom Feinstein called "Looter-1" and described as "a Cambodian national who was previously engaged in the theft and looting of antiquities." She summarized Lion's background, his rise as perhaps the most prolific temple robber of his time, and his activities at Prasat Krachap—strong evidence that Skanda on a Peacock met the legal definition of a stolen object. And she explained how it and other works taken by Lion had been sold to "a man whom Looter-1 knew as 'Sia Ford,' a foreign national with a large collection of Khmer antiquities in Bangkok." She continued: "The man known as 'Sia Ford' was Douglas Latchford." It was a summary of much of what Gordon had learned through years of investigation, distilled into twelve concise paragraphs.

Unlike Sotheby's, which had fought bitterly when SDNY tried to seize the Duryodhana, the inheritor of the Peacock wasn't interested in a courtroom battle, and agreed not to contest the forfeiture. In the summer of 2021, the Department of Homeland Security's J. P. Labbat went with a team of specialized movers to pick up the sculpture so it could be shipped to Cambodia. (As a matter of policy, DHS agents tried to avoid relocating heavy, priceless objects without expert assistance.) After the crew brought Skanda on a Peacock downstairs, Labbat couldn't resist taking a photo of it on the sidewalk, amid hot-dog carts and honking taxis, then sending the image to Feinstein. It wasn't the kind of scene that either of them had expected to encounter when they entered law enforcement.

Around the same time, Feinstein was chasing an even more tantalizing lead. From Wiener and other sources, she and Labbat had learned that one of Latchford's major customers was Jim Clark, the Silicon Valley billionaire. As a child of the Bay Area, she was familiar with his biography; Feinstein's older brother had worked for a time at Netscape, the early dot-com giant that Clark cofounded, and considered him a hero. And if he'd approached his purchases of Khmer antiquities with anything like the energy he brought to other extracurricular activities—the author Michael Lewis had built an entire book, *The New New Thing*, around Clark's obsessive quest to build a computer-controlled sailing yacht—his collection could be significant.

The problem was that for such a prominent businessman, Clark was very hard to track down, and Feinstein couldn't turn up any current contact information for him. Finally, Labbat located a company in Florida that Clark had used for some financial work. He contacted the firm and explained that the government intended to ask Clark for information about his collection. Clark agreed to comply, and his representatives soon sent over an extensive package of documents: purchase lists, bills of sale, and photographs from years of transactions.

Feinstein was sitting in her makeshift, pandemic-era home office—a desk in the hallway of her Brooklyn apartment—when she opened the email. She was stunned by what she saw. Clark had bought $35 million worth of works from Latchford, some of them clearly masterpieces. There was a massive Koh Ker sculpture of Ganesha, the Hindu elephant god, that weighed four thousand pounds; an eleventh-century statue of Vishnu, standing almost eight feet tall; and a pre-Angkorian Buddha with a sensuous, rippling cloak carved from flawless sandstone. The thirty-plus pieces were a mini-encyclopedia of the artistic accomplishments of the Khmer Empire, ranging across more than five centuries of history and representing an enormous variety of styles. After Latchford's own, it was perhaps the largest and most exquisite collection in private hands.

Feinstein kept clicking through the files, looking again and again at the statues and bronzes. Some of them seemed familiar, and it didn't take long for her to realize why. In Latchford's emails to Wiener, which Feinstein had reviewed exhaustively while preparing his indictment, he'd pitched some of the very same pieces. But in the photos that he'd attached, they were covered in dirt and debris—the obvious residue of recent looting. Now she was looking at them clean, lit, and in the possession of one of America's richest men. Feinstein forwarded the material to her boss, Alexander Wilson. "You're not going to believe this," she said.

After the successful dig at Prasat Krachap, Gordon began interviewing Lion even more intensely, certain that his memories could be used to guide more excavations, which in turn might yield more fragments that matched artifacts in Western collections. Gordon could then bring the findings to Feinstein. If she was satisfied, and especially if there was corroborating evidence from the Latchford correspondence and other records to which Gordon now had access, she could act to seize the pieces. They would have to work as quickly as they could. Latchford's files represented snapshots in time, and with each passing month, more of the works in them could be dispersed to new buyers. As word of Gordon and Feinstein's collaboration got out, collectors could go to ground, destroying records that might be needed in court. But between the Latchford documents, Lion's testimony, and the power of US law enforcement, it seemed as if there were no limits to how many stolen works they could recover.

To speed up the research, Gordon began spending much of his time in Siem Reap, closer to Lion's home. Balancing his antiquities work with client meetings and court hearings in Phnom Penh was already a challenge, and devoting so much of his attention to Lion wouldn't make it easier. But by this point, Gordon had little choice in the matter. He thought about his investigation day and night, peppering archaeologists and other experts with questions at all hours. To help him handle the volume of work, he assembled a team of young Cambodians, covering their costs out of his own pocket. Scouring Latchford's records, he developed an ever-lengthening list of all the institutions and collectors he intended to confront, and demand they repatriate the stolen treasures in their possession.

Each object was evidence of a historic crime, which Gordon felt a single-minded need to solve. It was an obsession that, in certain ways, mirrored the one of the man whose emails he was now reading. Both Gordon and Latchford had chosen to spend their lives in Southeast Asia, eschewing the more conventional paths available in their home countries; in time, both had grown entranced by the vibrancy of the region's cultures, and the deep history underpinning them. And just as it had for Latchford, a particular aspect of that history had become Gordon's central focus. The difference, of course, was that where Latchford had done his utmost to rip the sculptures of the ancient Khmer from their temples and scatter them around the world, Gordon was doing everything he could to gather them up. What Latchford had taken, Gordon was determined to bring back.

He reasoned that the most productive strategy for working with Lion would be to travel with him to the sites where he recalled stealing objects, allowing this to jog his memory. They visited more than twenty temples together, Gordon sometimes joining conference calls with corporate clients from the back of the car. Once they arrived, Lion would give firsthand demonstrations of what he recalled doing, supported by maps that he sketched out in pen. To explain the size and configuration of a statue that he'd removed, he might slap one of his arms or legs, comparing its dimensions with his own, or maneuver himself into the same pose as the piece. It was as though he were conjuring the memories from within his own body.

Though Gordon helped Lion out where he could—for example, by covering medical costs for his family—Lion's willingness to work so hard was obviously born of genuine passion. Gordon sometimes marveled at how much their first meeting, which began when he showed up at Lion's door unannounced in 2012, had shaped both of their lives. Lion knew more about the looting of Cambodia than Gordon thought possible, and he pledged to share all of it. "I'm going to transfer everything in my head to you," he told Gordon. "I'm going to tell you everything, every secret."

The more he did, and the more Gordon told him about the progress that was being made toward repatriations, the more invigorated he seemed to become. Lion was now over sixty, but he remained surprisingly strong, and after a long drive to a remote archaeological site, he would bound away from the car at a pace that Gordon, sweating through his usual uniform of jeans and a dark T-shirt, found impossible to match. Moments later, Lion would disappear beyond the tree line, leaving no word as to where he was going. When he eventually returned, he had refamiliarized himself with a place he hadn't seen in decades, and he would begin to guide his companions through. Lion had told Gordon about how he'd escaped from the Khmer Rouge as a young man, concealing himself in the jungle at a time when detection meant almost certain death. Seeing him melt into the foliage, it wasn't hard to imagine how he had survived.

This was how they proceeded until the spring of 2021, when Gordon noticed that Lion's stamina had begun to flag. He was suddenly sluggish, often needing to rest as they moved around a site. Travel was becoming difficult. Lion told Gordon that he was struggling with back pain, a dull, persistent ache that seemed to shift around his torso. Gordon arranged for him to see a doctor, who at first wasn't especially concerned. But the pain persisted, and Lion went back for some tests, which revealed what was wrong. He had pancreatic cancer.

30

Even when caught early—a rare occurrence, since the symptoms are initially subtle—pancreatic cancer has a long-term survival rate of less than 50 percent. Once it has spread to other parts of the body, as Lion's tumor had, the odds of beating it are remote. For Gordon, losing Lion was almost unimaginable. He wasn't just a crucial source for the investigation that had taken over much of Gordon's life. He had become more like family.

Gordon resolved to do everything in his power to keep Lion alive. If he was going to receive more than rudimentary care in a public hospital, Gordon would have to pay for it. His assignment for the Cambodian government remained pro bono, and he was committing his own money to what could be a very large, open-ended expense. Yet Lion was too important, and Gordon's affection for him too deep, to consider any alternative. Without aggressive treatment of a kind that Gordon wasn't even sure was available in Cambodia, he would be dead in a few months at most.

With help from a client, Gordon arranged for doctors in Singapore to evaluate Lion's medical file. If they believed they could help him, Gordon was prepared to make it happen, even as border restrictions, intended to slow the spread of COVID-19, made travel within Asia extremely challenging. After reviewing the scans, the doctors told Gordon that there would be no point in bringing Lion over. The cancer, which was rapidly enveloping the blood vessels and lymph nodes around his pancreas, was inoperable. Chemotherapy would only slow its progression. After that, the only thing to do would be to ease his pain.

Gordon certainly would have understood if Lion wanted to bring their collaboration to a close, and devote the last days of his life to his wife and eight children. But he told Gordon that he wanted to keep going. "I want the gods to come home now," he said. Gordon began interviewing him as many as five days a week. Instead of driving out to temples with him, Gordon projected satellite images onto the wall of the room where they met, trying to make it easier for him to describe each site. The specificity of his recollections remained remarkable. Lion could still look at photos of an artifact—in one of Douglas Latchford's books, for example—and say exactly where within a temple complex it came from. After the information he'd provided to guide the excavation of Prasat Krachap, Gordon had little doubt that he was right.

As his cancer advanced, and as chemotherapy left him nauseous and exhausted, their sessions became more and more difficult. Yet Lion remained determined to share everything he knew before it was too late. On a good day, he could spend an entire morning with Gordon and his researchers. On days when he was overcome with sickness, he would say, "I can give you an hour." Sometimes Lion lay on the floor as he spoke, because it was too painful to sit. To ensure that none of his recollections were lost, Gordon had his staff videotape their discussions, creating a record that archaeological specialists could review.

Later, Gordon brought Lion to Phnom Penh to witness some of what his testimony had made possible. The first works to be repatriated under the deal between Latchford's daughter, Julia, and the Cambodian government had begun to arrive. They included the pride of Latchford's collection, the father-and-son tableau of Shiva and Skanda. After decades in the dealer's private possession, it now sat on a low platform in the conservation workshop of Cambodia's National Museum, waiting to be put on display.

The severity of Lion's illness was evident as he stood before the sculpture. A royal-blue jacket hung loosely on his emaciated frame, and his exposed skin was taut and coppery, revealing a latticework of veins. Lion and Gordon both knew that he might never again be in the presence of the masterpiece he had last seen twenty-five years before, when he had used every ounce of his strength and ingenuity to dislodge and haul it away from Koh Ker. If there was anything he wanted to express to the gods, this was his chance.

Lion walked across the room and sat down on a wooden stool, his own body just inches from the Shiva figure. After pausing for a few moments, he extended his right arm and placed his fingers gently on the statue's forehead, feeling the cool stone.

As he continued his sessions with Lion, Bradley Gordon sent regular updates to Jessica Feinstein in New York. By the summer of 2021, she was back in her downtown office, with a busy docket of cases involving fraud, money laundering, and investment scams. The Latchford probe was just one of many assignments, but it continued to engross her despite the death of its initial target. Feinstein had wanted to work on art-related cases since law school, and this was one of the most complex investigations of the art market that SDNY had ever undertaken.

Her priority remained the tech billionaire Jim Clark. After his representatives had handed over documents that made clear how many pieces he'd bought from Latchford, Feinstein had tried to put together ironclad arguments for seizing them. The prospect of going up against Clark was at least somewhat daunting. He had vast financial resources, and he'd spent a great deal of money, some $35 million, on his Khmer collection. *This guy is going to come in here with an army of lawyers*, Feinstein thought. *He's going to fight us tooth and nail.* And apart from collaborating with DHS Special Agent J. P. Labbat, she was largely working alone. Though her superiors were pleased that she was so passionate about the Latchford file, their interest didn't translate into giving her a crack team of colleagues to help move it forward.

Clark was, however, open to a discussion, which put him in a different category than the family of George Lindemann Sr., whose collection Gordon had identified from photos in *Architectural Digest*. Whereas the Lindemanns were continuing to stonewall Feinstein's attempts to gather more information, Clark had provided detailed records to the government. He'd also agreed to sit down with Feinstein and Labbat in New York. In preparation for the meeting, Feinstein put together binders of evidence on the works he'd bought, collating what she and Labbat had been able to find out about their history, and drew up a list of talking points. She also read *The New New Thing*, Michael Lewis's 1999 biography of Clark, hoping to better understand his motivations.

Feinstein expected the discussion to be difficult. Clark was certain to arrive flanked by his attorneys, who would ensure that he conceded nothing. So she was surprised and a little puzzled to see the seventy-seven-year-old entrepreneur, who had thinning gray hair, a square jaw, and a sailor's tan, arrive alone at SDNY's offices. While he wasn't the target of a prosecution, knowingly possessing stolen property was still a crime. In Feinstein's experience, nearly everyone who showed up to discuss a matter proximate to the federal criminal code did so with their lawyers present—especially when they were as wealthy and sophisticated as Clark.

They took their places in a meeting room, where Feinstein and Labbat engaged in some small talk about the pandemic and Clark's recent investments. Then Clark, speaking with the slight drawl of his Texas childhood, began to summarize his thinking about the issue at hand. He explained that he didn't necessarily want a fight over his Khmer pieces. Instead, he said that he might be willing to hand them over voluntarily if Feinstein and Labbat made a convincing case that they were stolen. "I'm not just going to give these things back because you tell me to, but I'm also not going to throw good money after bad," Clark offered. "I'm not being difficult. I'm being fair."

Across the table, Feinstein was beginning to understand why he hadn't bothered to bring a lawyer. To Clark, they were primarily talking about a business matter, which he viewed in the dispassionate terms of risk and reward. If there was strong evidence that the works were looted, and especially if that evidence became public, then Clark's substantial investment would be worthless; it would be all but impossible to sell them, and anyone he bequeathed them to would be inheriting problems, not treasures. He also had to consider the reputational cost of a dispute with SDNY, which was certain to attract attention from the media. In such a scenario, the financially rational choice would be to cap his losses at the $35 million he'd paid and move on.

This was a logic that Feinstein could work with. The central message of *The New New Thing*, and of other material she'd read on Clark, was that he was either the smartest man in the Silicon Valley of the 1990s or had its biggest ego. Either way, Clark had a long track record of being savvier and more forward-thinking than those around him. When he took Netscape public in 1995—creating a frenzy among retail investors and firing the starting gun on the dot-com boom—news stories still included explanatory lines like "A browser is software that lets computer users get around the World Wide Web." Later, when the iPhone was still in its infancy, he'd bet heavily on Apple shares, correctly predicting that the company would hit a $1 trillion valuation.

And yet from the information she had compiled, Feinstein could see that Latchford had lied to Clark, and he'd fallen for it. To demonstrate, she opened her binders on the table and laid out some of the evidence for him. In 2007, when Latchford was pitching an ornate bronze boat prow dating to the twelfth century, Clark had specifically asked whether it was a recent find. Latchford had replied that it was "found sometime [*sic*] ago" and was "clean, no problem, you have my assurance." His concerns allayed, Clark bought the bronze and placed it in the home office of his Miami penthouse, overlooking South Beach. But three years before that exchange, Latchford had presented the very same object to someone else as a "New Find" and attached photos showing part of it covered in dirt. Feinstein had similar images of other works that Clark had purchased, taken from Latchford's emails to the New York dealer Nancy Wiener.

For another object, an unusual stone statue of the Buddhist deity Avalokiteshvara, Latchford had provided Clark with a letter from Ian Donaldson, the deceased Hong Kong businessman who popped up again and again in the paperwork for his sales. As in other statements purportedly from Donaldson, this one claimed that he'd bought the piece in the 1960s, which, if true, would make it legally unimpeachable. After her interviews with Wiener, Feinstein could say with confidence that such letters were forged. And in this case, Latchford's correspondence with others indicated that the statue's removal from Cambodia was much more recent—and that he somehow knew that when it was found, it was "broken at the neck, the ankles and at the elbows."

Feinstein didn't have much sympathy for anyone who'd hoarded Cambodia's stolen heritage, particularly at Clark's scale. Still, even if he could have asked more pointed questions, she didn't believe that he'd really known about the origins of what Latchford was selling. After all, the dealer had been broadly respected at the time Clark made his purchases in the mid-2000s, with wealthy clients all over the world. If she wanted Clark to cooperate, Feinstein figured that the best approach was to get him to accept that he'd been duped. "You're a victim here in some ways," she told him. Clark appeared pained by what he was hearing, less because of his feelings toward the objects and more because he'd made such a bad investment. In a moment of frustration, he looked at Feinstein and said, "I asked for provenance, and he told me the pieces were good."

The meeting ended cordially. To Feinstein, it felt like Clark was realizing that the wisest decision he could make, for his finances and his reputation, would be to accept her arguments and give up the stolen works. He agreed to look for any other records he might have, which would help Feinstein put together an eventual forfeiture complaint. Not long afterward, he invited Labbat to visit him in Florida and take an inventory. There, Labbat got a close look at one of the reasons why Clark could discuss the collection he'd amassed in such detached, bloodless terms.

He'd sold his Miami apartment—decorated in a "Thai" style, with purchases from Latchford on display in almost every room—for $21.5 million. There was evidently no place for most of the works in the other homes that Clark owned—in Florida, Manhattan, and Greenwich. As a result, the bulk of one of the most significant collections of Southeast Asian artifacts ever assembled by an individual, representing the finest artistic achievements of the ancient Khmer and carrying immense spiritual significance for the people of modern Cambodia, was now in a place where not even Clark could easily view it: a windowless storage facility in West Palm Beach, by a clutch of auto-repair shops and an overpass to I-95.

In what he feared could be his final weeks with Lion, Gordon was focused on Prasat Thom, a large temple adjacent to Koh Ker's central pyramid. Lion had said that in 1997, he and his crew discovered three nearly life-size stone statues at the site, standing in a row inside an imposing laterite sanctuary. The middle figure was a large male, a representation of the god Shiva, which Lion said had been taken by another looter he knew. The statues on either side were female; Lion claimed to have stolen those himself, carrying them out by oxcart. He sketched all three for Gordon, who sent the drawings to Éric Bourdonneau, the French archaeologist who'd been focused on Koh Ker for more than a decade.

Bourdonneau told Gordon that he recognized one of the female figures—and he was pretty sure he'd seen it before. Gordon, too, could go look at it anytime he wanted. All he needed to do was visit the Metropolitan Museum of Art, where it stood in Gallery 249, above the corner of Fifth Avenue and East Eighty-Fourth Street. According to its public-facing online catalog, the work Bourdonneau had in mind, known as Standing Female Deity, had come to the Met in 2003 from Nancy Wiener's late mother, Doris. About five feet tall, it was a remarkable representation of an idealized female form, with pouting lips, an hourglass figure, and high bare breasts. The minimal information that the museum provided about the piece's origins lined up with Lion's account. It had apparently only been in Doris's possession since 1998; no prior provenance was listed. Bourdonneau had been suspicious about it for years, partly because of that lack of information. On a visit to the Met in 2016, he had alarmed security guards by taking dozens of close-ups, which he subsequently used to create a three-dimensional digital model.

Though bringing back Latchford's personal holdings and pursuing other private buyers took up a great deal of his time, Gordon also viewed the Met as a priority. It had been so crucial to building Latchford's reputation as a dealer, and the Khmer collection it had assembled with his help was arguably the most important in the world—rivaled only by that of the Musée Guimet, France's national institution for Asian art. Further, its acquisitions were far more recent. The works held by the Guimet had largely left Cambodia before the end of colonial rule in 1953, and many had been taken from their original sites following official, documented excavations by the École Française d'Extrême-Orient, the same institution that now employed Bourdonneau. (Many other artifacts removed during

French expeditions were placed in the National Museum in Phnom Penh.) The Khmer assets of the Met, by contrast, had been assembled between the 1980s and early 2000s—the heyday of smash-and-grab looting, and some of the most lucrative years for Latchford's business.

With its long record of ignoring or slow-rolling repatriation demands, a confrontation with the Met would require solid proof that its works were stolen—ideally, eyewitness testimony corroborated by physical evidence. Lion was still willing to help Gordon assemble it. By early November 2021, his cancer had progressed to stage IV, with metastases throughout his body. His condition made him extremely vulnerable to COVID, which was spreading widely in Cambodia. He nonetheless agreed to join a team of government archaeologists who were conducting an excavation at Prasat Thom. Like at Prasat Krachap, where fragments matching Shiva and Skanda and Skanda on a Peacock had been unearthed a year earlier, the goal of the dig was to recover remnants of the statues that Lion had described.

The weather was sweltering, and Lion was obviously fatigued. Yet despite his illness, the man who'd astonished Gordon with his ability to disappear into the jungle was still surprisingly nimble. On the perimeter of the Prasat Thom sanctuary, where he remembered finding the three figures, he made his way through a rubble of weathered stone blocks, pausing to pick up anything that intrigued him. At one point, he took a trowel and began probing the debris. With his large eyes darting left and right, Lion pushed clumps of soil into his free hand, moving them to the side as he tried to reveal what lay underneath.

That he retained a core of unwavering energy was even more obvious inside the chamber. Despite a millennium of erosion, it was an imposing edifice, with two of its high walls still standing; restoration crews had wrapped portions of them in a web of thick ropes to prevent further collapse. Leaning for support on the roots of a tall tree that had grown inside the structure, Lion knew exactly where he was going—toward what appeared to be a rectangle of stone on the ground, a little less than three meters long. On the surface, only parts of its edges were visible. The rest was covered by sediment and displaced rocks. The archaeological team stood back to give him space.

After looking the area over, Lion reached down to grab a hoe and flipped it, so that the top of its metal handle was pointing down at his feet. Motioning for the others to watch, he dragged it around the perimeter of the rectangle with a loud scrape. "This is the support as I saw it," he said. Then, at the end farthest from the tree, he drew a rough circle in the dirt. Lion turned to stand inside the shape, hopping up and down for emphasis: "These are the legs."

The crew, a mix of professional archaeologists in government-issued uniforms and local laborers, some of them in flip-flops, began to clear the chamber, using brushes to expose the rest of the stone and filling plastic buckets with debris. Lion squatted down at the edge of the dig site to watch. Slowly, the nature of the object that he had traced became legible. The true floor of the sanctuary was buried a meter below where they were standing. The stone rectangle, one of the only features that could be discerned on the surface, was the top of a large pedestal, whose sides were soon exposed. It was certainly big enough to hold a trio of statues standing in a row, just as Lion had recalled.

From its central cavity and the surrounding area, the archaeologists recovered seven jagged chunks of stone, which they carried to a patch of flat ground a short distance away. Then they reassembled the pieces inside a wooden frame, filling in the gaps with jute sacks.

Arranged correctly, they fit together like a jigsaw puzzle. The pieces had obviously once been part of a single block, before being shattered. And along the top, there were the unmistakable remains of three sets of carved feet.

On his computer, Bourdonneau superimposed his model of the Met statue onto the newly discovered base. The result was a perfect match.

———

Weak and in near-constant pain, Lion knew that he was running out of time. Incredibly, he told Gordon, "I promise I'll work more on this. We're not done yet." Then, just a couple of weeks after the Prasat Thom dig, Lion was infected by the coronavirus. His cancer had weakened his immune system, and at sixty-two his age alone put him at higher risk of complications. He was soon admitted to a public hospital in Siem Reap, struggling to breathe as the virus ravaged his lungs.

His only hope for surviving a little longer was to be placed on a ventilator. They were in short supply. From Phnom Penh, Gordon frantically worked the phones, calling every Cambodian contact he could think of. He eventually found an available machine at a private facility, but as he finalized plans to move his friend there, he received a call from Lion's doctors. It was too late, they said. Lion was gone.

31

In early December 2021, Jessica Feinstein and J. P. Labbat headed uptown for another meeting with Jim Clark. Instead of bringing the entrepreneur back to SDNY's offices, they'd agreed to go to the Upper East Side, where Clark owned a neoclassical townhouse in the East 70s, just off Park Avenue—a Manhattan milieu very different from the day-to-day experience of two public servants. The years that Feinstein had spent prosecuting Bronx gang members felt far away indeed.

Over the previous several months, she and Labbat had made considerable progress with Clark. Labbat had visited him in Palm Beach and taken an inventory of the Khmer sculptures that he'd bought from Douglas Latchford, many of which had been languishing in storage since the sale of Clark's Miami penthouse. After Feinstein showed him extensive evidence that they had been looted, Clark seemed to be on the verge of accepting her arguments, reasoning that if she was right, there was no point spending money to fight her in court. That would allow the government to seize them without the drama of a legal dispute, and then to return them to Cambodia. Yet

Clark still hadn't signed off, and Feinstein worried that he was getting cold feet. She hoped that this discussion would end with a firm commitment.

The three gathered in Clark's living room, where Feinstein noticed a work on the wall by the Russian abstractionist Wassily Kandinsky, one of her favorite artists. Clark seemed nervous. He wanted to know more about SDNY's strategy for handling what was sure to be intense interest from the media. Feinstein told him that she was happy to keep their deal anonymous, with Clark's identity excluded from legal filings, though Labbat warned him that journalists would almost certainly figure it out. He also wondered if by giving up objects on which he'd spent over $30 million, he might be able to claim a loss on his taxes. Feinstein, who didn't know the answer, was bemused. Clark really was laser-focused on the bottom line, she thought, which was probably why he was a billionaire and she wasn't.

Feinstein went back over some of the same material she'd presented during their initial meeting at SDNY several months earlier, emphasizing that the Department of Justice didn't consider Clark a villain, and wouldn't present him that way to the outside world. She also reminded him of how important the works were to the people of Cambodia, who deserved to have them back. Wasn't that a better outcome than leaving them hidden away? As a prosecutor, Feinstein had been in many situations where the best strategy was confrontation. She'd concluded that this one called for a softer approach, at least for the moment.

By the end of the meeting, Clark was on board, and in early January, Labbat returned to Florida to execute the formal seizures. Accompanied by a crew of specialized movers, he arrived early in the morning at the West Palm Beach warehouse where Clark kept his

Khmer collection. Clark had signed a legal document called a notice of abandonment; from that moment forward, he had no say in what happened to the artifacts. It took several hours for Labbat to load them up for shipment to a government facility, taping an image of each one to the front of its wooden crate. Before they finished for the day, he and a colleague, both in DHS-branded polo shirts, posed for a photo in front of the two-ton statue of the elephant god Ganesha.

Feinstein filed the papers a week later. In keeping with the conventions of forfeiture law, the "defendants" were the objects themselves, and her complaint was formally titled *United States of America v. A Late 12th Century Bayon-Style Sandstone Sculpture Depicting Eight-Armed Avalokiteshvara*, followed by more than thirty other such descriptions. Clark was identified only as "an American collector," though he subsequently revealed his identity in media interviews. The filing explained how Latchford had "supplied the Collector with false provenance documents and false information about the origin" of some of the pieces, and had lied to US Customs and Border Protection about the nature of others. As a result of these and other violations of American law, they were "subject to forfeiture to the United States."

It amounted to one of the largest seizures of antiquities in American history—and, for Feinstein, a major milestone. Her goal of getting Latchford into a courtroom had been impossible to achieve, but she'd managed to recover virtually everything he'd sold to his biggest customer, putting others who'd done business with him on notice. With so much evidence about the nature of Latchford's operations now in the public record, it was becoming harder and harder for them to pretend that their collections of Khmer artifacts were anything other than the products of systematic theft. Indeed, at the rate it was progressing, Feinstein's work stood a chance of putting an end to the entire US market for such looted objects. No one wanted to spend millions on a statue just so it could be seized by the DOJ.

Momentum for even more returns was building. A few months earlier, Nancy Wiener had pleaded guilty to state charges of conspiracy and criminal possession of stolen property, stemming in part from her relationship with Latchford. Entering her plea in a Manhattan courtroom, the dealer admitted that in her business, "obfuscation and silence were accepted responses to questions" about artworks' origins, a situation that amounted to "a conspiracy of the willing." (Because of her cooperation with law enforcement, Wiener received no prison time.) Shortly after she appeared in court, the Denver Art Museum—with which Latchford's longtime collaborator, Emma Bunker, had a close relationship—voluntarily gave up four pieces it had acquired from him. Lion had told Bradley Gordon that he or his crews took all four, a fact that Feinstein cited in the forfeiture complaint. Yet despite these successes, one of Feinstein's primary targets remained difficult to chase down.

After the Florida billionaire George Lindemann Sr. died in 2018, the massive Khmer collection he'd accumulated passed to his widow, Frayda, and their daughter, Sloan Lindemann Barnett. The two women had been resisting Feinstein and Labbat's attempts to talk to them for nearly a year. As this continued, Feinstein and Labbat grew open to other options. Regardless of George Sr.'s death, the artifacts were still stolen property—indeed, Lion had claimed to have removed some of them too—and the knowing possession of stolen property was a federal crime. The problem would be proving the "knowing" part. If they were charged, Frayda and Sloan could plausibly claim to have no knowledge of how the works in their possession came to be outside Cambodia, even if the answer would seem obvious to anyone familiar with the nation's history.

Then, in August 2022, Feinstein and Labbat had a flash of good fortune, thanks to a story in *The Washington Post* that had been prompted, in turn, by yet another spread in *Architectural Digest*. The year before, *AD* had featured Sloan's San Francisco residence, a $33 million mansion high atop Pacific Heights that had "been described, with good reason, as the most beautiful house in America." What followed was, in most respects, a standard design-magazine article, drawing readers' attention to features such as "Maria Pergay coffee tables" and a living room "sheathed in neoclassical boiserie." On closer inspection, though, something about it was odd.

The caption for the opening spread, which showed a Spanish Revival–style indoor courtyard, referred to "Southeast Asian sculptures" on display, and so did the description of the living room. Yet no such sculptures were visible. In fact, the courtyard contained a number of empty black plinths that looked an awful lot like pedestals. The *Post* reporters, who'd previously covered the Latchford case, were suspicious, and they compared *AD*'s photos with those on the website of the house's architect, Peter Marino. A well-known designer of residences for the superrich, and of sumptuous flagship stores for retailers like Chanel and Louis Vuitton, Marino was also responsible for George Sr. and Frayda's homes in Florida.

Marino's online portfolio featured an image of the courtyard that was identical to the one published in *AD*, and credited to the same photographer, but in that photo, there were several Khmer stone heads on the black plinths. They appeared to be the same representations of benevolent *devas* and malign *asuras* that had been mounted above a fireplace in the elder Lindemanns' Palm Beach estate. Moreover, the *AD* photo betrayed signs of crude airbrushing: parts of the leaves on plants near the plinths were also missing. The conclusion, which a spokesperson for the magazine didn't deny, was obvious. The image had been doctored to remove the artifacts, presumably close enough to publication that no one caught the erroneous captions. And after the *Post* contacted Marino to ask about the discrepancy, the original was abruptly removed from his site.

To Labbat, the switch was clear evidence of mens rea, or "guilty mind," an indication that whoever had asked *AD* to alter the photos understood that the works were stolen. He and Feinstein were suddenly in a stronger position to pursue a potential criminal case, which everyone involved knew would be an extremely significant escalation. Fighting a civil forfeiture might be seen by a billionaire family as a cost of doing business. Facing a federal indictment, and the public attention it would surely bring, was another matter entirely. Not long after the *Post* story ran, and with other media outlets also beginning to scrutinize their purchases, Feinstein and Labbat got word that the Lindemanns were willing to come to the table.

The Ganesha was too heavy for the elevator. In early August 2022, Feinstein and her colleagues were making plans for a ceremony in which the US government would formally transfer the works it had seized—from Jim Clark's collection, from the Denver Art Museum, and elsewhere—to the government of Cambodia. Before the artifacts were crated up and flown to Phnom Penh, Feinstein wanted to show off a selection to the media and various dignitaries at a gathering in SDNY's second-floor library. Skanda on a Peacock was an obvious choice; it was among the most beautiful and unusual Khmer sculptures that anyone had ever seen. So was the pre-Angkorian Buddha, resplendent in a rippling stone cloak, that had once stood in the living room of Clark's Miami penthouse. But Feinstein was told that getting the Ganesha upstairs was impossible. She would have to settle for a printed image, mounted on a stand.

Ganesha or not, the event marked a new height for Feinstein's soaring career. Her Latchford investigation was yielding high-profile wins in both legal and PR terms. (Operating in the media capital of the world, her managers had a long-standing interest in positive headlines.) Feinstein was being promoted to cochief of SDNY's Money Laundering and Transnational Criminal Enterprises Unit, with responsibility for investigations into topics as diverse as Russian sanctions violations and cryptocurrency frauds. She would continue to pursue the Latchford case in what remained of her spare time. It was too absorbing, and Feinstein too invested in its progress, to give up.

US Attorney Damian Williams, SDNY's top lawyer, was the first to speak. "These statues and artifacts," he said, "are of extraordinary cultural value to the Cambodian people, and we are delighted to be sending them home." He continued, summarizing the scope of the evidence that Feinstein had compiled: "Organized looting networks, including looters affiliated with the Khmer Rouge, sent these statues to a well-known antiquities dealer, Douglas Latchford. Latchford then sold these priceless cultural artifacts to Western dealers, collectors, and institutions." Williams was followed by Cambodia's minister of culture and fine arts, Phoeurng Sackona, who had lost her entire immediate family to the Khmer Rouge. In a video message, she said that the works being returned were more than stone and bronze; they represented "the souls of Cambodia's ancestors, which have illegally departed from the motherland during a period of war."

Gordon was in New York for the ceremony, and both speakers made a point of thanking him and his team for their on-the-ground research. Seated in the audience, he felt a complicated mix of emotions. Lion, whom he missed intensely, had told Gordon about Skanda on a Peacock on the very first day they met, ten years earlier. It was astonishing to consider the sculpture's journey. A millennium ago, Khmer artisans, their names now lost to history, had carved it to honor the gods of a religion created in India, some two thousand miles across the Bay of Bengal. It rested undisturbed until Lion, his life upended by the actions of a genocidal totalitarian regime, ripped it from its temple in 1997. Propelled by the unstoppable force of twenty-first-century commerce, it was then transported across the Thai border and into the hands of Douglas Latchford, who sold it to an Italian academic. A relative of that buyer had brought it to New York and put it on display in a living room, where Feinstein eventually found it. And now, thanks to Lion's determination to make amends for the crimes of his past, it was sitting in front of Gordon in a different part of Manhattan, and it would soon be in Cambodia once again.

Gordon had set out to reclaim the stolen heritage of his adopted country, and to a remarkable extent, he'd succeeded. Without his involvement, making the same progress might have taken decades, if it ever happened at all. Still, he didn't find the moment entirely satisfying. Even as he took in the spectacular works that Feinstein had arrayed on either side of the podium, part of his mind kept returning to the other looted pieces that he knew Latchford had placed just a few miles uptown, in the galleries of the Met.

32

By the time of the repatriation ceremony in New York, Jessica Feinstein had been investigating the Met for the better part of a year.* The museum had first contacted her in the autumn of 2021, while she was still trying to recover artifacts from Jim Clark. With its huge Khmer collection and extensive dealings with Douglas Latchford, it was obvious to the Met's lawyers that Feinstein could eventually

---

* The Met declined to make any of its staff available for interviews for this book, or to provide substantive information beyond what was already in the public domain. In response to a fact-checking request before publication, a spokesperson sent the following statement:

> The Met is committed to the responsible collecting of art and the shared stewardship of the world's cultural heritage and goes to great lengths to ensure all objects entering the collection meet its strict standards. The Museum prioritizes continual research into the past ownership of works across our collections and has made significant investments in accelerating this effort—spearheaded by the largest provenance research team in the world—and has a long track record of working collaboratively when questions have arisen about an object's prior history. The Met also publishes all known ownership history for works on its website—one of the few institutions in the field to do so. The Museum is continuing to review its collection of Khmer art and remains committed to collaborating with Cambodia on constructive resolutions.

target the institution—not least because a work mentioned in Latchford's indictment, a seventh- or eighth-century statue of a Hindu deity known as Harihara, stood in its galleries. By reaching out to her, they hoped to get ahead of the problem, and to minimize the fallout. Thanks in part to Bradley Gordon, Feinstein already had a number of questions.

Drawing upon Lion's testimony and Latchford's own records, to which he'd been given access by Latchford's daughter, Julia, Gordon had compiled a detailed list of works in the Met that he believed to be looted. It had forty-five priority items, including what the museum referred to as a Standing Female Deity: the voluptuous figure that Lion had stolen from Koh Ker in 1997, leaving behind traces of its feet that would later be discovered by Cambodian archaeologists. In all, Lion claimed to be responsible for taking thirty-three of the pieces on Gordon's list. At least six had once been owned by Latchford; others had links to his closest partners, like the London dealer Spink & Son.

Gordon wanted any dealings with the Met to proceed from a different starting point than past efforts at repatriation. With the Kneeling Attendants, the Latchford-linked statues that the Met had agreed to give up in 2013, the Cambodian government first built a dossier of evidence, including photos of the figures' empty pedestals, showing that they'd been stolen from Koh Ker—which the museum ultimately accepted. (At the same time, it stressed that the return set no precedent for future cases.) Gordon now believed that the process should be precisely the opposite. Since becoming independent, Cambodia had virtually never given permission for artifacts to be exported, and a tiny share of those that were now housed overseas had been removed in documented, authorized excavations.

It therefore stood to reason that almost all of the Khmer works in New York had originally been looted. That was especially true if they came onto the market after the civil war intensified in 1970. If one accepted this premise, then Gordon felt it wasn't up to him to prove that a piece was dirty, though in many cases he could. It was up to the Met to prove it was clean or, if that was impossible, give it back without argument. Gordon suggested that this principle should apply not just to objects connected to Latchford and his collaborators but to the Met's entire Khmer collection, including some items listed as originating outside the boundaries of modern Cambodia.

Feinstein viewed that as unrealistic, and Gordon's insistence on it frustrated her. She didn't intend to clean out the Met's entire Southeast Asian wing, depriving its patrons of any opportunity to appreciate the masterpieces within. Instead, she went through his list and crossed off entries that had no possible connection to Latchford—for example, because they'd been acquired before he was active on the market. She sent the ones that remained to the Met's outside counsel, a former SDNY prosecutor named Anjan Sahni. While the museum listed basic provenance information in its online catalog, Feinstein wanted to see much more: internal correspondence, meeting minutes, invoices, and condition reports, any of which might reveal something about a piece's true origins.

The degree of disclosure she demanded was doubtlessly uncomfortable for the Met, a private institution that had long sought to keep its inner workings confidential, especially if they risked putting its staff or trustees in an unfavorable light. In 2005, when one journalist set out to write a comprehensive history of the museum, its head of external affairs told him, "The only kind of books we find even vaguely palatable are those we control." Director Philippe de Montebello added that "the museum has no secrets"—then refused to be interviewed or share any information beyond what was already in the public domain.

As Feinstein began probing its collection, the Met arguably remained the most powerful cultural institution in New York, and therefore in the United States. In its 2019 fiscal year, before COVID measures kept people at home, it had attracted more than seven million visitors—a level of patronage exceeded by only a few overseas venues—and brought in $370 million in operating revenue. For the city's most fortunate citizens, there was still no better way to make a mark than by supporting it. The Met's board of trustees included the likes of Blair Effron, the investment banker, and Anna Wintour, the longtime editor of *Vogue*, and in 2021, it announced its largest-ever capital gift—a $125 million donation from an asset-management billionaire.

The Met was nonetheless struggling to reconcile its mandate as a "universal museum" with persistent allegations that it served as a treasure house for the stolen history of other nations. And in an age of social media and instantaneous communication, skeletons had a way of tumbling out of its closets. Shortly after taking over in 2018, its new director, Max Hollein, received an embarrassing reminder of the damage that could result, courtesy of Kim Kardashian.

At that year's Met Gala, a celebrity-packed benefit for the museum's Costume Institute, the reality TV star had been photographed next to the gold-plated coffin of an ancient Egyptian priest. The image went viral, and among the millions who saw it was a member of the looting crew that had stolen the coffin around 2010, during the turbulence of the Arab Spring. To make it easier to transport, he'd dumped the mummy it contained into the Nile. The Met bought it for

$4 million in 2017, and the looter had never received his share. He complained about this injustice to a friend, who happened to be a source for the Manhattan District Attorney's Office.

The artifact was, at that very moment, the centerpiece of a major Met exhibition called *Nedjemankh and His Gilded Coffin*. After prosecutors presented the evidence, the museum was forced to close the show. It claimed to have been swindled, saying in a statement that "false ownership history, fraudulent statements, and fake documentation" had fooled its curators into thinking the coffin had been legally exported from Egypt in 1971. (The state attorney on the case was skeptical, telling an interviewer that with the same information, "my kids [would] know it's looted.") Announcing its immediate repatriation, Hollein said that the Met needed to "be a leader among our peers in the respect for cultural property and in the rigor and transparency of the policy and practices that we follow."

Gordon, who'd been researching deeply into the history of its Khmer collection, found declarations like that laughable. Latchford had been indicted not long after Hollein's statement. Almost two years later, the Met had never publicly addressed the role it played in legitimizing him as a dealer. With buyers in the US and beyond, Latchford had been able to demonstrate his bona fides by advertising how many of the works he'd sold, donated, or otherwise handled were on display there. Meanwhile, some of its most significant Khmer treasures, with little to no provenance, had been acquired during the most horrific years of the civil war, when violence in Cambodia was literally front-page news. It would have taken a stunning level of ignorance, or indifference, for the Met's staff not to have made the connection.

Gordon was particularly disturbed by what he'd learned about

Latchford's relationship with the man responsible for many of those acquisitions. The dealer's email archive contained extensive correspondence with Martin Lerner, the Met's longtime curator of South and Southeast Asian art. Over his thirty-one years in the role, Lerner had transformed a modest collection into one of the world's best. He and Latchford were close friends, and Latchford had donated the Kneeling Attendants in Lerner's honor. The fact that the statues came in parts—first the two heads, then the heavier torsos—and had no documented ownership before 1986 was no deterrent to placing them at the entrance to the galleries that Lerner oversaw. (Earlier in the 1980s, Lerner had publicly declared that "no reputable dealer, collector, or museum professional would go near a stolen object.") In 1998, another Latchford donation—a haunting bronze face that likewise lacked any prior provenance—was also listed as having been given "in honor of Martin Lerner."

Then, after retiring from the Met in 2003, Lerner had assisted Latchford as a paid consultant, offering glowing appraisals of pieces that the dealer sold to private buyers. A twelfth-century bronze Buddha seated on a serpent was "a most extraordinary sculpture both in terms of its quality and condition"; a kneeling female figure in the style of the Bayon period was likely "of extreme importance" and "clearly the product of a well-trained and highly talented artist." In at least one case, Lerner had helped Latchford shore up the provenance of a piece, providing a letter that opened with almost exactly the same phrasing that Latchford had requested: "I recall seeing this bronze Standing Four-armed Maitreya (87 cm), some time [*sic*] around 1968, at Spink and Son, London." Naturally, that put it outside Cambodia before the 1970 cutoff that made sales more complicated. Lerner's consulting work continued until 2019, long after accusations that

Latchford was involved in looting had made him radioactive to many academic experts. (Lerner did not respond to interview requests; in 2022 he said that "Knowing what I know now, I should probably not have worked so closely with Mr. Latchford.")

Gordon believed that, in its dealings with Cambodia, the Met had acted like a crew of pirates, with Lerner at the helm. He wanted to crank up the pressure. Feinstein was keeping him apprised of her exchanges with the museum, and in October 2021, Gordon leaked word of them to *The New York Times*. The resulting story read, in part: "Officials with the U.S. Attorney's Office, which has previously assisted Cambodia in recovering illicit antiquities, met with museum staff members last week to request they review the provenance of a number of [allegedly looted] items." Cambodia's culture minister, Phoeurng Sackona, told the paper, "These are not just some decorations for your homes. They are items that have a soul."

Sahni, the attorney representing the Met, was concerned; he had expected the discussions with Feinstein to be kept confidential. She, too, was annoyed with Gordon. Her goal was to get back as many stolen statues as she could, not to embarrass the museum. The best strategy, she had concluded, was to negotiate, and that would only be productive if the two sides felt like they could trust each other. After the leak, Feinstein decided that she could no longer share information about the Met with Gordon. "You serve a different master," she told him. It was a reminder that while the interests of Gordon's clients in the Cambodian government often overlapped with those of the Department of Justice, they weren't the same.

The museum soon complied with Feinstein's requests for documentation on works that might be connected to Latchford, and she began reviewing the archive of PDFs it provided. She found the task fascinating. As an art lover living in New York, Feinstein cherished the Met; now she was getting a rare glimpse into how it really operated. While working on the file, she went uptown to look more closely at its Khmer collection. She stood before the Standing Female Deity taken by Lion, admiring the graceful form of the goddess. In a case nearby was the bronze face that Latchford had given in honor of Lerner, its lips pursed in an enigmatic half smile. Another work on display, a tenth- or eleventh-century bronze called the Bodhisattva Avalokiteshvara Seated in Royal Ease, was featured in a photo on Latchford's computer, its theft so recent that deposits of soil were visible in the picture. According to Gordon's looter sources, it had been stolen from the vicinity of Kulen Mountain around 1990. Feinstein thought about how much was missing from the sparse, sanitized information cards that the curators had provided. The story of how each piece had made it to Manhattan was an epic all on its own. *I know where this came from*, she said to herself.

Some of the paperwork that the Met shared with Feinstein was startling—for example, condition reports noting that an object had arrived with dirt on its surface, or with damage that was obviously indicative of looting. What most surprised her, however, was the number of instances in which the documentation was minimal. Lerner had repeatedly gotten sign-off for acquisitions in which his own recollection of seeing an artifact somewhere constituted the main provenance. A few objects had come with bills of lading or statements to customs authorities purporting to explain why it would be legal to import them; others arrived with letters from Latchford that claimed to substantiate their history. By this point, Feinstein knew what those were worth.

And yet they were accepted. The Met had been willing, again and again, to augment its collection with works whose legitimacy rested on the slenderest wisps of evidence, and that came from a country convulsed by genocide, war, and starvation. There had been no grand conspiracy to falsify the origins of these pieces, no shadowy network duping one of the world's greatest cultural institutions. Such subterfuge would have been unnecessary, because it seemed that no one in a position of authority at the museum had really cared.

Until she boarded her flight to Cambodia in late 2022, the farthest that Feinstein had traveled for her government job was Florida. It would be her first visit to the country, and her first chance to actually see the ancient sites whose looting she was trying to document. Before leaving, she reviewed a remarkable historical text: In the 1930s, Feinstein's grandfather had toured Angkor while on a round-the-world trip, and had filmed parts of his visit with a hand-cranked camera. The tape included shots of him outside the temple of Angkor Thom, its approach lined with stone figures of *devas* and *asuras*. At that time, the statues were mostly intact. In the decades since, many had been stolen, their heads proving particularly popular among collectors—including George Lindemann Sr., who put some above his fireplace in Palm Beach.

As she experienced Angkor herself, taking in the staggering scale of its architecture and the enduring artistry of its bas-reliefs and carved lintels, Feinstein was amazed to see how Cambodians related to the temples and their remaining contents. To a Westerner, they were the awe-inspiring remnants of a distant, long-vanished civilization. But to that civilization's descendants, they were part of a living religious culture. Monks roamed the grounds of Angkor Wat and Angkor Thom, praying at sites they still considered to be suffused with the divine. Where statues were intact—or, sometimes, where only feet remained—ordinary people bowed and left offerings of coconuts, flowers, and cans of beer. All of this was true despite the fact that many of the temples were built as monuments to Hindu gods in a country that had become overwhelmingly Buddhist. Reverence for them was part of a set of syncretic beliefs, stretching back centuries, that had survived even the nihilism of the Khmer Rouge.

It was an example of the limitations of dealing with the world through PDF files and Zoom screens. From her desk in Manhattan, Feinstein never could have grasped in the same visceral way that she wasn't simply seizing objects of stone and bronze. She was doing much more: recovering works of art that at least some Cambodians believed to have souls, just as Phoeurng Sackona had said. Earlier in her career, when prosecuting drug dealers and gang leaders, she had worried that her successes were fleeting, making communities safer for only a short time. At Angkor, Feinstein could see that the impact of these cases was more durable. She really was helping to right a historic wrong, even if the other injustices of Cambodia's civil war, and the fathomless cost of Pol Pot's genocide, could never be redressed. To know that—to understand that her work was changing things for the better—was deeply moving.

Feinstein also went to Koh Ker, where she walked ruins that she'd been studying intensely for more than three years—and saw some of the shattered pedestals belonging to works stolen by Lion and his confederates. Back in Siem Reap, Gordon arranged for her and DHS Special Agent J. P. Labbat to interview a pair of ex-looters, additional sources to whom Lion had connected the lawyer before his death. Feinstein knew that the conversation would be challenging. It usually took multiple meetings to build up trust with a cooperating witness;

here she had only one shot. Even worse, as representatives of a foreign law-enforcement agency, the Americans needed to have a Cambodian police official in the room. Sensing that her witnesses were anxious, Feinstein asked him to stand as far back as possible and not interfere. She wanted to do the talking, albeit through a translator.

Feinstein had brought a binder containing images of items she wanted to know more about, including photos of the Lindemann collection from *Architectural Digest*. The looters didn't recognize many of the works—or, at most, said that they remembered taking similar artifacts, which wasn't much help. But when she got to a huge Koh Ker–style Shiva, photographed in the Lindemanns' sitting room, the men suddenly perked up. One of them recalled it distinctly. "That's from Prasat Thom," he said—the same location where Lion had found the Met's Standing Female Deity. Lion had said it was part of a triptych: a male flanked by two females. The only one that Gordon and Feinstein had located so far was the Met piece. Now this witness was identifying the missing male.

Feinstein was astonished; she'd just visited Prasat Thom and looked at the empty base, excavated on Lion's instructions the year before, that had once held the three figures. The match would have to be verified, ideally by taking detailed measurements of the Lindemann statue. Nonetheless, another piece of the historical puzzle she'd set out to solve was snapping into place. Feinstein soon returned to New York, determined to keep pushing forward—in pursuit of the Lindemann collection and, especially, of the Met. She now understood so much about how statues had traveled from ransacked Cambodian temples to Fifth Avenue—about the actions of the looters themselves, about Latchford's essential role as a middleman, and about the willing participation of the curator Martin Lerner. How could the Met refuse to give them back?

33

Compared with the gravity of confronting the Met, everything else Jessica Feinstein had done since Latchford's indictment was a warm-up. It was clear to her that New York's leading museum wasn't going to give up its treasures easily. Repatriating its Khmer works would set a precedent—not just for objects from Cambodia, but from the many other countries whose lost heritage adorned its galleries. If enough of those nations' demands were successful, the Met's very business model—indeed, its entire ethos of accumulating within its walls the finest artworks from around the world, without excessive regard for how they got there—could come under threat. The same was true for dozens of other American institutions, which had hardly been more scrupulous.

The Met therefore had an interest in admitting as little wrongdoing as possible, preferably none at all. Feinstein's task was to demonstrate just how much evidence she had, and to convince its lawyers of the folly of fighting her in court. After the Met provided her with provenance records on much of its Khmer collection, she began assembling a long document, collating what was known about the origins of each artifact. It combined the museum's own information with testimony that Bradley Gordon had obtained from Lion and the other looters in his network, as well as all the related records in SDNY's possession. She and J. P. Labbat believed that around forty works held by the Met could be linked to Douglas Latchford in some way, and ought to be part of a discussion about repatriation.

In November 2022, not long after their trip to Cambodia, Feinstein and Labbat arranged to meet with the Met's outside counsel, Anjan Sahni, and a member of its internal legal team. Feinstein had boiled her findings down into a presentation, focusing on what she called "big red flags"—for example, clear Latchford connections, solid information from looters, and inconsistent or incomplete documentation. She viewed the meeting, which would be held at Saint Andrew's Plaza, as an opportunity to share information, not to issue threats. Because the Met had reached out to her—even if it had waited until almost two years after Latchford's indictment to do so—Feinstein felt it was only fair to give Sahni a chance to absorb what she'd compiled and then propose a way forward for his client. And besides, in a discussion with a federal prosecutor, the legal threats were implied.

Feinstein also wanted to make clear that she had a different agenda than Gordon. "The Cambodian view is not our view," she told her visitors, who were keenly aware of Gordon's attempts to pile on public pressure. From Phnom Penh, he was continuing to call on the Met to make a positive case for the legitimacy of every one of its Khmer pieces or, if that was not possible, hand them over. As a prosecutor, Feinstein's mandate was to focus on the objects in the museum whose possession could be shown to violate American law. The fate of the Met's broader collection was an ethical question, not necessarily a legal one.

Feinstein went through her talking points, pausing to answer occasional questions from Sahni and the Met attorney accompanying him. Labbat backed her up, noting that, in some cases, the museum's own condition reports contained telltale clues of recent looting, recording, for example, the presence of residual soil on a sculpture when it arrived in New York. Much of the information they imparted was brand-new; by this point, Feinstein and Labbat knew more about many of the pieces' origins than the Met's curators did. Sahni seemed especially interested in what the government had learned from the Cambodians who claimed to have taken the objects—not just Lion, who'd died about a year before, but others from his network who were still alive and conceivably might be available to testify. To hear in court from a former child soldier telling a federal judge about all the statues in the Met that he remembered stealing in order to survive would be a remarkable spectacle.

As Feinstein and Labbat piled on their evidence, however, they noticed that their counterparts' reaction was muted. Labbat, in particular, had expected them to be shocked. They were being shown the proverbial smoking gun: solid evidence that many of the Khmer works on the Upper East Side had been stolen by men who were, at most, a degree or two removed from the Khmer Rouge. Only weeks before, in Siem Reap and at Koh Ker, Labbat and Feinstein had talked to some of the looters personally, and seen shattered pedestals that provided physical corroboration for their testimony. If that didn't jolt one's conscience, it wasn't clear what would. Still, Sahni and the Met lawyer were doing a good job of concealing any surprise they might have felt.

They departed, saying that they would consider the evidence and get back in touch. Soon, they communicated the Met's position. When it came to applying the National Stolen Property Act, the most obvious tool available to federal authorities for the forfeiture of antiquities, three criteria had to be met. The government of the source country had to have asserted ownership, through a law stating that artifacts were public property. The items in question had to have come from inside the country's modern borders. And they had to have left those borders after the passage of the ownership law. Anything taken before that time was beyond the reach of the NSPA, forcing prosecutors to rely on other, potentially less useful statutes.

The Met told Feinstein that it believed the relevant date for Cambodia was 1992, when a "Land Law," passed during the transition period before the arrival of UN peacekeepers, made clear that "historical patrimonies" belonged to the state. This was a far later cutoff than the Department of Justice had cited in the past, notably in its litigation with Sotheby's over the Duryodhana. One critical date that Feinstein's predecessors noted in arguments for that forfeiture was 1970, when the UNESCO cultural-heritage treaty was signed in Paris, and ratified soon afterward by Cambodia. But they argued that the timeline extended back much further, emphasizing that André Malraux, France's future minister of culture, had received a prison sentence for looting the temple of Banteay Srei in 1924—obvious evidence that it was a crime by that point. They also noted that a quarter century before, the governor of French Indochina had issued a decree for the protection of monuments. But these claims had never been tested in a federal court, since Sotheby's had settled the Duryodhana case before it went to trial.

The Met's alternative interpretation was remarkable in at least two respects. First, it insisted that a nation that had put the spires of Angkor Wat on its flag as soon as it became independent in 1953—and then kept them there through several regimes of wildly different ide-ological orientations—had waited almost four decades to unequivo-cally protect such sites by law. Claiming 1992 as the key date also left works that had been taken during the bloodiest phases of Cambodia's recent history as fair game. The cutoff excluded most of the civil war, from the rise of Pol Pot through the Khmer Rouge genocide and the bulk of the guerrilla conflict that followed. It also meant that as far as the Met was concerned, the majority of the pieces that Feinstein be-lieved to be problematic were perfectly legitimate, because they'd been outside Cambodia for long enough.

The museum's lawyers informed her that as a result, it would be willing to part with only a tiny number of artifacts in the collection: six, to be precise. To Feinstein, this was unacceptable. They were talk-ing about the mass looting of an entire ancient civilization, and the largest assembly of its stolen patrimony in the United States. Repatri-ating a mere half dozen objects fell short of the barest minimum. She wanted, nonetheless, to think coolly about her next moves before re-sponding. One option was to begin working on a forfeiture com-plaint, which could force the Met to defend its legal theories before a judge. But Feinstein had a feeling that instead of resorting to such an escalation, her best strategy might be to wait.

The museum's PR headaches over Cambodia were only getting worse, with news articles and podcasts continuing to highlight its dealings with Latchford. (Gordon, who had come to see media cover-age as a crucial tool, appeared in many of them.) Eventually, Feinstein figured, its lawyers and trustees would realize that they needed to make a much more significant offer to stem the bad press. In the meantime, she tried to find an expert on Cambodian legislative his-tory to assist the government. If she was going to take the Met to court, she would need a solid argument regarding when the country had declared its ownership of artifacts. There was an argument for trying to start the clock in the 1920s, with Malraux's conviction, but Feinstein was hesitant, fearing that Cambodia's early twentieth-century laws were too ambiguous.

She also had plenty of other work to keep her busy, some of it focused on Julia Latchford. Feinstein had never considered Julia to be an accomplice to her late father, and she wasn't a target for prosecution. Nevertheless, SDNY still had business with her. Julia had inherited most of Latchford's money, including what Feinstein believed to be the proceeds of illegal antiquity sales. As a result, her lawyers had been negotiating with the government on a settlement. Calculating what portion of Julia's assets could be ascribed to such transactions was complicated, not least because Latchford had spent a great deal of what he made. They'd eventually agreed on a number: $12 million, which would be transferred to the US government. (Julia would also be required to repatriate a stunning bronze, looted from a World Heritage Site in Vietnam, that Latchford had tried to sell for tens of millions of dollars.) In June 2023, Feinstein announced the deal, which stipulated that Julia denied "any fault, liability, or wrongdoing."

Feinstein kept Gordon out of the negotiations; she'd been less forthcoming with him ever since he had leaked to the press that SDNY was in conversation with the Met. When he heard the news of the settlement with Julia, he was livid. The Cambodian government wasn't a party to the agreement, and it included no provisions for how the funds would be used. If his clients believed that the money rightly belonged to them, Gordon would have to apply for its "remission" by the DOJ and hope for a favorable decision. That felt flagrantly unfair. Twelve million dollars amounted to about 0.0002 percent of the US federal budget—a number that made no difference in Washington. In Cambodia, by contrast, it would be enough to train and employ an entire cohort of archaeologists, or to radically upgrade conservation programs at sites like Koh Ker. "We are the victim here," Gordon wrote in an irate letter to Feinstein, "and everything the US government takes from the known wrongdoers, takes away from what Cambodia can obtain eventually."

Yet whatever their disagreements, Gordon knew that Feinstein, who could call on the vast resources of the US government, remained an essential partner. And he was encouraged by the knowledge that she was making progress on other fronts. For months, the prosecutor had been working to make a deal with the Lindemann family, whose collection of Khmer artifacts was among the most significant in private hands. Ever since learning of its scale, Feinstein had wanted to sit down with Frayda Lindemann and her daughter, Sloan Lindemann Barnett, and explain why it was so wrong to hoard Cambodia's looted heritage in their opulent homes. But their lawyers had refused to arrange the meeting, or to enter serious discussions on a settlement.

Then, after it became apparent that *Architectural Digest* photos of Sloan's San Francisco mansion had been doctored, the government had new leverage. That evidence made potential criminal charges more feasible, and along with mounting interest in their collection from the media, helped bring the Lindemanns to the table. The talks were still tense, and until almost their conclusion, Feinstein wasn't sure if she would be able to recover all the works on her list—or even if the family still had them. But in early September, they finally agreed to a deal.

The Lindemanns would hand over thirty-three objects, including the monumental statue of Shiva that had been taken from the same pedestal as the Standing Female Deity, stolen by Lion in 1997, which stood in the Met. Another of the pieces—a sculpture of Vishnu reclining on a coiled serpent, looted in 1995—was utterly different from other depictions of the god, and therefore of great interest to archaeologists. A faint inscription was just visible on its surface: a never-studied fragment that might add to the scant historical record of the ancient Khmer. In exchange for their renunciation of rights to the collection, SDNY pledged that it would "not criminally prosecute, nor bring any civil claim, against any member" of the Lindemann family arising from it. The office also said the agreement was "not to be construed as a legal or factual determination that the Lindemanns have violated any federal law."

Identifying the Lindemanns, compiling evidence on what they'd acquired, and getting them to negotiate had required enormous efforts on the part of both Gordon and Feinstein. In the wake of the agreement, it was possible to feel like a dam was breaking—and that the Met's section might be the next to go. But neither of them could be sure.

Even with nothing like Feinstein's power, Gordon was enough of a nuisance that he couldn't simply be ignored in New York, and the Met soon invited him for a discussion with some of its executives. It was late October 2023; around the Great Lawn of Central Park, just behind the museum, falling leaves carpeted the jogging paths in a riot of orange and yellow. Gordon entered from Fifth Avenue, passing knots of visitors heading into a major show of paintings by Manet and Degas. Beyond the soaring entrance hall were galleries that bore the names of some of America's wealthiest families: Lehman, Tisch,

Kravis, Rockefeller—donors whose largesse had allowed the Met to accumulate so much of the physical heritage of humanity.

Gordon knew that the next hour could be crucial in his quest to hold the museum to account. His meeting was with a large group, including one of its deputy directors, as well as John Guy, a British art historian who'd taken over as curator of South and Southeast Asian art, the job formerly held by Latchford's friend Martin Lerner. Also present would be the Met's general counsel, Sharon Cott. Gordon had spoken with Cott several weeks earlier, urging her to do something "bold and just" by offering a major return of Khmer artifacts. But he'd never been given such an opportunity to make his case to the Met's broader leadership. Never before had he been able to tell them about the magnitude of the tragedies that had afflicted Cambodia, and what it would mean to reclaim some of what was lost.

Despite the stakes, Gordon found that he wasn't nervous as he walked in. He had learned so much in his investigation, and he believed so deeply in what he was doing, that nerves were no longer part of the equation. He felt, instead, a kind of serene confidence, born of the years of work it had taken for him to get to this moment. Whatever was about to unfold, Gordon knew he could handle it. And he would be handling it while wearing jeans. He had made it this far largely without putting on a suit, and he wasn't about to change now.

He was soon shown to a blandly corporate conference room. Disappointingly, there was little to distinguish it from any other meeting space in the city: no works by Old Masters on the wall, no Egyptian amphorae on the table. After some pleasantries, Gordon began to speak, slouching slightly in his chair. "These are blood antiquities, and we have the evidence," he said firmly.

Gordon told the group about some of what he'd learned of Latchford's relationship with Lerner, who had turned a blind eye to the origins of so many of the dealer's works—and then, after retiring from his post, profited from helping Latchford sell more of them. He talked about Lion and his life: his conscription as a child soldier, his turn to looting as a means of survival, and his later determination to make a positive impact while he still could. Gordon wanted his hosts to know about the violence that Lion had experienced—the murders and massacres, the land-mine detonations and gunfights—and how essential he had been to Latchford's operation. At one point in the 1990s, Gordon recounted, word came to Lion and his team that Latchford wanted more bronzes in the style of Prakhon Chai—a hoard of Khmer artifacts discovered in eastern Thailand three decades earlier, which Latchford had helped sell at the time. (The Met had acquired a number of them.)

Eager to please his biggest customer, Lion recalled scouring the countryside for objects that met the criteria. "Do you actually believe that?" Guy asked. After spending hundreds of hours with Lion, Gordon certainly did. Yet even with all the other research he'd done, and the extensive archaeological findings that corroborated Lion's accounts, the people in possession of looted works were still reluctant to take his testimony seriously. It was like Gordon's first meeting with Latchford's intermediaries in Abu Dhabi, five years before, when he'd been told, dismissively, that "people make up stories in the village"—tales that deserved no serious consideration by well-credentialed lawyers and curators.

It might have been a fair comment then; now such skepticism just made him angry. How much more evidence did he have to uncover? Did Gordon need to fly some empty pedestals from Koh Ker to JFK and drop them off on the sidewalk, perhaps with instructions for matching their measurements to those of the statues inside? A couple of years earlier, Gordon could have brought Lion himself and dared Met officials to say to his face that they didn't think he was credible. That was no longer possible, but he had developed relationships with other ex-looters, hard men who'd endured—and perhaps inflicted— horrors that were impossible to imagine from inside the Met's walls. "I have former Khmer Rouge," Gordon told the group. "Do you want to meet them? I can bring them here."

Gordon felt the atmosphere in the room growing tense. He was confronting his interlocutors with the reality of where some of their treasures had come from, information that the museum had long sought to ignore. If the Met was the cultural equivalent of a Michelin-starred restaurant, Gordon was talking about conditions in one of the slaughterhouses that supplied it. Cott made clear, however, that such a dramatic gesture would be unnecessary. It seemed that the combination of Gordon's pressure, and Feinstein's ongoing work, had been having the effect he hoped for. (So had the risk of a potentially disastrous media cycle: with Gordon's encouragement, *60 Minutes* was working on a piece, helmed by anchor Anderson Cooper, that would highlight the Met's ties to Latchford.) The Met, Cott told him, intended to go further than it had previously contemplated and make a major return of works to Cambodia.

This was a breakthrough, though Gordon wasn't ready to believe that it would be enough. He didn't know which items would be included, nor when Cott proposed to send them back. And just as he'd insisted with the Latchford family, Gordon didn't want physical returns alone. After the meeting came to an end, he wrote a follow-up letter to Cott emphasizing that he wanted to see the paperwork for everything: "all provenance documents you have with respect to your entire Cambodian collection." He was certain that they would expose further complicity in looting.

Of course, Gordon had no ability to enforce such demands, and Feinstein, the person who did, hadn't had a substantive discussion with the Met since it offered to return a paltry half dozen Khmer pieces. She had yet to decide which Cambodian law she believed should be the basis of their negotiations—and of a forfeiture action, if she decided to initiate one. But with the ever-present possibility that its next contact with law enforcement might involve a team of DHS agents in raid jackets, the museum suddenly expanded its proposal. Later, Feinstein's colleague J. P. Labbat would compare it to the buyers of a house making an initial offer and then, after hearing nothing back, anxiously upping their bid. The Met said that it was now willing to transfer fourteen works to Cambodia, some of them among the highlights of its Southeast Asian collection. Six specifically listed Latchford in their published provenance, including the enigmatic bronze face that he'd donated "in honor of Martin Lerner."

Others, such as the Standing Female Deity, had come from his known associates, including the New York dealer Doris Wiener and Spink & Son in London. With three exceptions—a female figure that Latchford had sold through Spink's in 1983, a Buddha head that he had donated the same year, and a large statue of a male deity donated by a wealthy New York couple in 1987—all had entered the collection in 1992 or later. Just as it had insisted in discussions with SDNY, the Met continued to view the majority of its acquisitions from earlier in the civil war as legitimate. It planned, for example, to keep a figure of the deity Harihara that was specifically mentioned in the Latchford indictment. The museum had purchased that statue in 1977—the midpoint of Pol Pot's genocidal rule—from Spink's. It had no listed provenance before that year.

When Feinstein set out to recover works from the Met, she had a much larger number in mind. Formally, the decision on whether to accept the new proposal wasn't hers. Almost none of SDNY's attorneys stayed with the office for their entire careers, and she was no exception. Feinstein had left in late September 2023, about two months before the Met made its expanded offer. Unlike most of her colleagues, she was bound not for a white-shoe law firm but for a job as a federal prosecutor in Houston. She was nonetheless happy for her successor to take the win, and SDNY concluded its deal with the Met on December 15. As it had with the Lindemanns, the office pledged that in exchange for the return of the works, it would neither initiate a prosecution nor launch civil litigation.

The museum offered a public account of its actions that was, at the very least, generous regarding its own motives. It said in a statement that it had "proactively reached out" to the Department of Justice after Latchford's indictment, eliding the roughly twenty-two-month gap between those two events. Director Max Hollein added that it had been "diligently working with Cambodia and the US Attorney's Office for years to resolve questions regarding these works of art." The first part of his comment certainly wasn't how Gordon would have described the situation. The Met also said that the deal meant it was "effectively removing from its collection all Angkorian sculptures . . . known by the Museum to be associated with the dealer Douglas Latchford." Gordon wasn't so sure about that, either. Despite his years of intensive research, he still felt that he didn't know the full scope of Latchford's activities. He didn't trust the Met, and he didn't have access to its internal records. And then there were all the other looted Khmer pieces in its possession, ones that hadn't passed through Latchford's hands. After all, he was far from the only dealer trading in them.

More than a decade earlier, while escorting a group of Cambodian lawyers on a visit to the US, Gordon had brought them to the Met— and seen the shock on their faces as they walked among its sculptures. Even then, he knew what he had to do: "We'll get it back," he told them. Now, having done all he could to deliver on that promise, he again found it hard to be satisfied. There were too many stolen treasures still out in the world, waiting to be tracked down. In villages up and down Cambodia, there were more ex-looters waiting to be found. And in Latchford's vast digital archive—tens of thousands of emails, photographs, invoices, and other documents—there were more secrets waiting to be uncovered. Gordon certainly wasn't done with the Met, nor with other museums across the US, nor with a roster of private collectors that kept expanding as he dug further into Latchford's files.

It was the work of a lifetime, demanding every ounce of energy and perseverance that Gordon could give. And while he found it captivating, and knew how meaningful each success was to his Cambodian friends and colleagues, what made him determined to continue was different. It was his gratitude, and love, for the man who let Gordon into his house one day in 2012, and then began telling the story of his extraordinary life. To honor his memory, the only choice was to keep going. The gods were coming home, and Lion had sent them on their way.

Afterword

In late 2023, in the midst of my work on this book, I arranged to meet Bradley Gordon at the National Museum in Phnom Penh. Though it can hardly compare to the scale of the Met, it's an impressive place. Opened by the French colonial authorities in 1920, the building was designed as an homage to traditional Khmer architecture and set in gardens that provide a cool respite from the dust and traffic outside its perimeter. Abandoned during Pol Pot's rule, it reopened in 1979 with a skeleton staff of survivors and a tiny budget; for years, a colony of bats occupied the roof, dropping guano on visitors. After the end of the civil war, a new generation of curators, assisted by international experts, worked heroically to bring it up to international standards.

I'd been waiting only a few minutes when Gordon pulled up in a white SUV, wearing jeans and a dark T-shirt, as usual. It had been an intense year. In March, he'd sat in the audience as the government held a formal ceremony to welcome artworks being returned to Cambodia from the Latchford family, Jim Clark, and other private collectors who'd been convinced, or legally pressured, to repatriate their looted pieces. After speeches from Prime Minister Hun Sen and various dignitaries, the guests were permitted to approach the statues and view them up close. Inevitably, some took selfies with sculptures like Skanda on a Peacock. Others dropped to their knees and prayed, pressing their heads rhythmically to the stone. One middle-aged woman wept as she did so. Shortly afterward, Gordon and his law partner were granted Cambodian citizenship in recognition of their work. He was no longer an outsider; his adopted country had adopted him.

There had also been moments when the strain of what Gordon was trying to accomplish while also running a busy legal practice overwhelmed his usual good cheer. One of his collaborators told me he was suffering from something like "combat stress." Not long before our appointment at the museum, Gordon had visited River City, a Bangkok shopping complex that used to function as a supermarket for dubiously acquired antiquities. Nowadays, most of them are fake. Gordon still ended up in a shouting match with a gallery owner who he knew had some dealings with Latchford, telling the man he had one hour to pack up everything in his shop for shipment to Cambodia. Unsurprisingly, that demand was refused, and when Gordon returned the next day, the gallerist called security on him.

Meanwhile, his work was moving into a new phase. Clark and the Lindemann family, who possessed two of the largest Khmer collections in the US, had given up what Gordon wanted, and though he considered the Met to be unfinished business, its repatriation deal was significant. For the next round of targets, he would be working with different partners. Jessica Feinstein's new job as a prosecutor in Texas had taken her off the Latchford investigation; J. P. Labbat, meanwhile, had retired after thirty years of government service. Gordon had been passed to new contacts at SDNY and the Department of

Homeland Security, and he wouldn't know for some time whether they shared their predecessors' passion.

He had begun to think seriously about issues that went beyond repatriation, too. For instance, how would Cambodia ultimately care for, protect, and display the huge number of artifacts that were coming home? At the time of this writing, it stood at more than one thousand. The National Museum's galleries were already crammed, and its staff of curators and conservationists too small to cope with the influx. There would need to be a significant expansion or even a new institution—ideally, one integrated enough into the Cambodian system that the government would consider it a priority, but independent enough to attract funding from international donors. Figuring out how that would work might be a full-time job in itself.

Yet on this afternoon in late November, all of that was in the future. Instead, Gordon wanted to spend some time with the objects he'd been thinking about day and night for years. Smiling broadly, he led me through the entrance of the museum and toward the hall on the left, where some of them had recently been installed. Earlier in the day, the space had been busy with groups of tourists and eager Cambodian schoolchildren, learning about a heritage that had nearly been lost forever. Now it was quiet, the statues easily outnumbering the remaining visitors. Gordon offered casual commentary as we walked. "This is from Denver," he said of a standing figure of the Hindu sun god, Surya. Of a standing Buddha, he remarked, "This came from Jim Clark."

We paused at a section devoted to Prasat Chen, where the Sotheby's Duryodhana was stolen in 1972. After it and other pieces from the site were repatriated, curators had attempted to reassemble them in the museum as they once stood: in a tableau that also included the Kneeling Attendants given up by the Met. The heroic warrior figure of the Duryodhana was in the middle, facing the Bhima—its rival from the epic of the Mahabharata, returned by the Norton Simon Museum. Of the seven monumental pedestals surrounding the combatants, only one was still empty. Gordon was still working on tracking down the statue that it had been carved to support. "Ultimately, this will be completely full," he said. "I think we'll get there."

Shiva and Skanda and Skanda on a Peacock, both taken by Lion from the temple of Prasat Krachap, stood nearby. It was my second time seeing them, after the government's welcoming ceremony in March. They were still among the most powerful works of art I'd ever experienced. As a parent, I found the emotions on the face of the adult Shiva, his hands being clasped by Skanda, his tiny son, to be instantly recognizable across the centuries: pride, protectiveness, and, above all, love. Then, depicted as a full-grown warrior astride his mount, the Skanda of the other sculpture communicated a martial determination that made it easier to understand how the ancient Khmer, ranging from Angkor across mainland Southeast Asia, had been able to dominate so much of it, and for so long.

For Gordon, the two pieces had a significance greater than anything else in the museum—because of their artistry, and because of the life-altering journey he'd taken to get them back. He said that archaeologists had recently discovered another fragment from the base of Skanda on a Peacock at Prasat Krachap, providing even more proof that Lion's account of where he found them was accurate. "It's just an emotional moment," Gordon said softly. He remarked on the similarities between the two sculptures, in scale and detailing: "I just wonder, is there one master artist? They're both so perfect." Gordon still found it hard to fathom that they'd spent decades in private homes. "Can you imagine?" he asked me.

We were running out of time, and we began slowly making our way toward the exit. I got the sense that even though he lived in Phnom Penh and could return whenever he wanted, Gordon found it hard to leave. Just outside, under clouds that hinted at rain, we came face-to-face with a work I'd somehow missed earlier. Gordon pointed it out: a massive sculpture of the elephant god Ganesha, sitting cross-legged. This was the statue that Feinstein had learned was too heavy for SDNY's elevators when she wanted to display it at a press conference. It had also been too large for the National Museum's staff to bring inside. So it remained in the garden, protected by a canopy.

There was a small wooden table below its pedestal, with a ceramic pot that held tiny sticks of incense. On either side were two cups, each with a bottle of water for making offerings. I'd previously seen Cambodians perform such gestures of reverence toward Khmer Empire statues at temples, but never before on the streets of modern, fast-developing Phnom Penh. It was as though the object provided a portal to some place deep in collective memory.

I knew that the Ganesha had come back to Cambodia from Jim Clark, to whom Latchford had sold it in 2006—part of about $11 million in purchases made by the entrepreneur that year. And I was aware that before Latchford got it, it had been looted from Koh Ker, probably in the mid-1990s. What Gordon told me next, however, was new. He said that after Clark bought the two-ton statue, his interior decorator didn't think it fit with the design of his Miami apartment. Gordon shook his head in disbelief. "He never opened the crate."

Acknowledgments

This book began life as a feature for *Bloomberg Businessweek*, a publication that I am unbelievably lucky to call my professional home. Even luckier, I've been able to work for, and with, a succession of exceptional editors at Bloomberg: Jim Aley, Brian Bremner, John Fraher, Reto Gregori, Heather Harris, Jeremy Keehn, Madeleine Lim, David Merritt, John Micklethwait, Emma O'Brien, Kristin Powers, Jacqueline Simmons, Brad Stone, and Joel Weber, among others. A special thanks also goes to Randy Shapiro, who has kept me out of trouble (and out of court) with exceptional grace and good humor for more than a decade.

For working to bring the project from article to proposal to manuscript, I owe a great debt to the brilliant Ethan Bassoff, agent extraordinaire, and his colleagues at WME, who assiduously fought my corner. There was never any question that, like my last book, I wanted to publish this one with Portfolio, and specifically with Noah Schwartzberg. Noah was a staunch supporter from day one, and his suggestions improved the manuscript immeasurably. He and the rest of the Portfolio crew—Adrian Zackheim, Niki Papadopoulos, Amanda Lang, Brian Borchard, Yuki Hirose, Alena Perszyk, Lucile Culver, Katherine Jimenez, Kirstin Berndt, Daniel Marx, and Lauren

Morgan Whitticom—are, for my money, the best in the business. The same is true of the team at Penguin Life in London, led by Celia Buzuk and Matt James.

I was supported during the writing of this book by New America, and specifically by the Jonathan Logan Family Foundation Fellowship. To join the New America community, which includes dozens of writers and thinkers I admire, was an honor and a thrill—augmented by the hard work of Awista Ayub and Sarah Baline in Washington, DC, and the humbling talent of the other members of my fellowship class.

As I learned very quickly, writing without a coauthor means spending an enormous amount of time inside one's own head. To get out of it, and to help transform my piles of prose into something that—hopefully—a few people will want to read, I turned to the extraordinary Joel Lovell, whose editorial judgment I trust absolutely. I also relied on one of the best writers I've ever met, Kit Chellel, who read chapters before I let any other soul see them and provided sage, constructive notes. A big thanks also goes to friends Stephanie Baker, Mike Bird, James Crabtree, Katie Engelhart, Zeke Faux, Shibani Mahtani, Alexandra Stevenson, and Nick Summers, who never failed to answer my frantic WhatsApp messages seeking advice.

I am far from the first journalist to find Douglas Latchford's story irresistible. Making sense of it would have been much harder without the outstanding work of Tom Mashberg and Graham Bowley of *The New York Times*, who dug into this saga long before I had even heard of it. The same is true of Jason Felch of *Chasing Aphrodite*, a vast resource for anyone interested in the looting of Cambodia, and in issues of stolen artifacts more broadly. My friends Tom Wright and Timothy McLaughlin, the masterminds behind the *Dynamite Doug* podcast, provided essential assistance with hunting down key sources and documents. I am also grateful for the expertise of Angela Chiu, Thomas Cristofoletti, Tess Davis, Ashley Thompson, and Nadim Roberts.

Assembling the material in these pages required significant volumes of reporting in several countries, and in languages I can't begin to understand. For this, I received substantial help from Ryan Mingcharoen in Bangkok and Danielle Keeton-Olsen in Phnom Penh. Once the manuscript was complete, I turned to Gabriel Baumgaertner, who fact-checked it with sometimes maddening scrupulousness; any errors that remain are, of course, my own. Anisa Said and Addison Mitchell organized the endnotes, while Jane Yeomans helped track down photos and secure rights, both processes sparing me considerable existential angst. Daniel Lagin produced a beautiful and informative map, while Ilsa Brink spruced up my website. Jenelyn Dato-on ensured that I had the time, space, and environment needed to work productively, often anticipating my needs before I knew I had them. Stephen A. Murphy of SOAS University of London and Martin Polkinghorne of Flinders University were kind enough to review portions of the manuscript, catching errors of fact and interpretation large and small.

Many of the sources I spoke to in my reporting asked to remain anonymous, and I can express my gratitude to them only as a general category. Among those I can name, thanks to Kong Vireak, Chea Socheat, Long Dany and the Documentation Center of Cambodia, Lois de Menil, Josh Kurlantzick, Sebastian Strangio, Christophe Pottier, Étienne Clément, Bill and Kathy Heinecke, Simon Warrack, Éric Bourdonneau, the late Damian Evans, Joyce Clark, and Anne Lemaistre. One person, however, is in a category all his own: Bradley Gordon. I first met Brad in the lobby of a Phnom Penh hotel in early 2022. By the end of that initial conversation, I was convinced that the magazine story I was working on needed to be a book—and, in a way, a book about Brad and his life-changing relationship with the man he knew as Lion. That it now exists is, in considerable part, the result of Brad's willingness to share so much about himself, and about the passion that keeps him going.

The first people I told about this idea were members of my family, for whom no mere words on a page are adequate thanks. My parents, Debra and Barry Campbell, were crucial sounding boards throughout the process, and they were among the first to read chapters as I got them down, suggesting countless improvements. My wife and best friend, Lauren Myers-Cavanagh, was an unwavering source of editorial, practical, and moral support—most of all when reminding me that despite whatever crisis I imagined myself to be experiencing, everything would turn out OK. For a further reminder, I needed only to spend time with our children, Theo and Bea, dynamos of energy and curiosity who make all other pursuits feel insignificant.

Image Credits

Insert page

1 (*top*) Paul Brown/Shutterstock

1 (*bottom*) Photograph by Thomas Cristofoletti for Edenbridge Asia

2 (*top*) Courtesy of the Government of Cambodia

2 (*middle*) Courtesy of the Government of Cambodia

2 (*bottom*) John Duricka/AP Photo

3 (*top*) Hemis/Alamy

3 (*bottom*) Photograph © EAST24 Co., Ltd. www.thaibody.com

4 (*top*) Courtesy of the Government of Cambodia

4 (*bottom*) Sovannara/Xinhua/Alamy Live News

5 (*top*) Photograph by Thomas Cristofoletti for Edenbridge Asia

5 (*bottom*) © Scott Frances/OTTO

6 (*top*) Photograph by Thomas Cristofoletti for Edenbridge Asia

6 (*bottom*) Photograph by Thomas Cristofoletti for Edenbridge Asia

7 (*top*) Andrew Kelly/Reuters

7 (*bottom*) Andrew Kelly/Reuters

8 (*top*) Used by permission

8 (*bottom*) Photograph by Thomas Cristofoletti for Edenbridge Asia

Notes

FOREWORD

xi **As an adolescent:** Tom Mashberg, "He Sold Away His People's Heritage. He's in the Jungle to Get It Back," *New York Times*, November 21, 2021, nytimes.com/2021/11/21/arts/design/toek-tik-cambodian-artifacts.html; and Simon Mackenzie and Tess Davis, "Temple Looting in Cambodia: Anatomy of a Statue Trafficking Network," *British Journal of Criminology* 54, no. 5 (September 2014): 731.

xi **two million people dead:** Ewa Tabeau and They Kheam, *Khmer Rouge Victims in Cambodia, April 1975—January 1979: A Critical Assessment of Major Estimates*, E3/2413, September 30, 2009, gsp.yale.edu/sites/default/files/files/Demographic%20Expert%20Report%2C%202009%2C%20E3_2413_EN.PDF.

xii **"some three pounds":** Michael D. Coe and Damian Evans, *Angkor and the Khmer Civilization* (Thames & Hudson, 2003), 136.

xii **with tusks sheathed in gold:** Ian Mabbett and David Chandler, *The Khmers* (Blackwell, 1995), 211.

xii **they left buildings:** Mabbett and Chandler, *Khmers*, 2.

xiii **The artifacts were three:** Cambodian Department of Antiquities, *The Return of Our Ancestors' Souls* (Ministry of Culture and Fine Arts of Cambodia, 2024), 70–77.

xiii–xiv **The male figure:** Judith Thurman, "Striking a New Note in Palm Beach," *Architectural Digest*, January 2008.

xiv **By 1998, it was in:** Standing Female Deity, 10th century, stone, 61 ½ × 10 ¼ × 20 ½ in. (156.2 × 26 × 52.1 cm), Metropolitan Museum of Art, New York, object no. 2003.605, archived January 14, 2022, at web.archive.org/web/20220114102412/https://www.metmuseum.org/art/collection/search/72387.

ONE

1 **On a humid evening:** Alan Parkhouse, "A Rare Find," *Bangkok Post*, December 9, 2010, ki-media.blogspot.com/2010/09/rare-find-rare-khmer-artefacts-to

.html; Douglas Latchford, "Gold of the Gods," interview by Louise Nicholson, *Apollo*, November 2008, 32; and "A Man of Ancient Torsos and Modern Muscles," *Phnom Penh Post*, January 11, 2008, phnompenhpost.com/national/man -ancient-torsos-and-modern-muscles.

2 **Just twenty-four years old:** Tom Mashberg, "Douglas A. J. Latchford, Khmer Antiquities Expert, Dies at 88," *New York Times,* August 27, 2020, nytimes .com/2020/08/27/arts/douglas-aj-latchford-khmer-antiquities-expert-dies -at-88.html.

2 **The host of the dinner:** Latchford, "Gold of the Gods," 32; Parkhouse, "Rare Find."

2 **It was located in the:** David Lyman, "Yesteryear—Bangkok in 1956: What Was It Like When AmCham Thailand Was Founded?," presentation to AmCham Thailand, April 26, 2006, 5, tilleke.com/wp-content/uploads/2011/05/AMCHAM -50th-Anniv-DL-Speech-26-Apr-06_0_0.pdf.

3 **In addition to the challenges:** Lyman, "Yesteryear," 8–9.

4 **For not much more:** Lyman, "Yesteryear," 6.

5 **The US plowed tens:** Joshua Kurlantzick, *The Ideal Man: The Tragedy of Jim Thompson and the American Way of War* (John Wiley & Sons, 2011), 100, 138, Kindle.

5 **Soon there were enough:** "A Short History of Mandarin Oriental, Bangkok," Mandarin Oriental Bangkok, archived March 31, 2022, at web.archive.org /web/20220331003148/http://photos.mandarinoriental.com/is/content/Man darinOriental/bangkok-140-short-history.

5 **In less prestigious quarters:** See, for example, Tim Elliott, "Heart of the Slums," *Sydney Morning Herald*, December 21, 2013, smh.com.au/national /heart-of-the-slums-20131216-2zfwe.html.

5 **Beyond the royals:** Carol Hollinger, *Mai Pen Rai Means Never Mind* (Asia Books, 1998), 60–61.

5 **His route to Bangkok:** "Business Abroad: The Silk King," *Time*, April 21, 1958, archived February 29, 2024, at web.archive.org/web/20240229114750 /https://content.time.com/time/subscriber/article/0,33009,810324,00.html.

6 **As a graduate:** Kurlantzick, *Ideal Man*, 27; and Michael Warner, *The Office of Strategic Services: America's First Intelligence Agency* (Central Intelligence Agency, 2000), cia.gov/resources/csi/static/Office-of-Strategic-Services.pdf.

6 **He served heroically:** Kurlantzick, *Ideal Man*, 31.

6 **Though Thompson had:** Kurlantzick, *Ideal Man*, 91.

6 **Thompson built a profitable:** Kurlantzick, *Ideal Man*, 93.

6 **He abhorred being:** Kurlantzick, *Ideal Man*, 3, 132–35.

6 **Rather than live in:** "The House That Was the Talk of the Town," Jim Thompson House, archived November 9, 2017, web.archive.org/web/20171109193841 /http://www.jimthompsonhouse.com/museum/index.asp.

6 **Once Thompson's guests:** Kurlantzick, *Ideal Man*, 132–35.

6 **There he would tell:** Kurlantzick, *Ideal Man*, 134.

6 **While the talk was often:** Kurlantzick, *Ideal Man*, 122.

7 **Like Latchford, Thompson felt:** "Foundation," Jim Thompson House, archived September 29, 2022, at web.archive.org/web/20220929045156/https://jimthompsonhouse.org/foundation.

7 **At one end of his:** Jim Thompson to Lisa Lyons, letter, 22 February 1961; and Jim Thompson to Lisa Lyons, letter, 19 March 1962, reproduced at 594–97 and 626–31 in Llewellyn M. Toulmin, "The Disappearance of Jim Thompson, the "Silk King of Thailand—A Search and Rescue Analysis" (self-published, May 2015); archival correspondence provided by University of Pennsylvania Museum of Archaeology and Anthropology; https://www.academia.edu/414 77816/The_Disappearance_of_Jim_Thompson_the_Silk_King_of_Thailand _A_Search_and_Rescue_Analysis_Report.

7 **Thompson and Latchford were:** Parkhouse, "Rare Find."

7 **One of the most enthusiastic:** Eric Pace, "Doris Duke, 80, Heiress Whose Great Wealth Couldn't Buy Happiness, Is Dead," *New York Times*, October 29, 1993, nytimes.com/1993/10/29/obituaries/doris-duke-80-heiress-whose-great -wealth-couldn-t-buy-happiness-is-dead.html.

7 **After a visit to Bangkok:** Michelle Falkenstein, "A Trove of Treasures in a Barn," *New York Times*, October 19, 2003, nytimes.com/2003/10/19/nyregion /a-trove-of-treasures-in-a-barn.html.

7 **John D. Rockefeller III was:** "John D. Rockefeller, 3rd, 1906–1978," Rockefeller Archive Center, archived February 12, 2025, at web.archive.org/web/2025 0212215529/https://rockarch.org/resources/about-the-rockefellers/john-d -rockefeller-3rd; and Jim Thompson to Lisa Lyons, letter, 9 June 1957, at 496– 500 in Toulmin, "The Disappearance of Jim Thompson."

7 **In what was still:** Jim Thompson to Elinor Douglas, letter, 23 November 1959, at 580–82 in in Toulmin, "The Disappearance of Jim Thompson.

8 **"in we went":** Thompson to Douglas, 23 November 1959, at 580–82 in in Toulmin, "The Disappearance of Jim Thompson.

9 **At their greatest extent:** David Chandler, *A History of Cambodia*, 3rd ed. (Silkworm Books, 2003), 61.

TWO

10 **Latchford had vistas like:** Alan Parkhouse, "A Rare Find," *Bangkok Post*, December 9, 2010, ki-media.blogspot.com/2010/09/rare-find-rare-khmer-artefacts -to.html.

11 **Almost all foreign visitors:** Anabel I. Janssen, "Jungle Trip to See the Ruins of Angkor Wat," *New York Times*, May 5, 1957, timesmachine.nytimes.com /timesmachine/1957/05/05/90800931.html.

11 **At its height:** Damian Evans et al., "A Comprehensive Archaeological Map of the World's Largest Preindustrial Settlement Complex at Angkor, Cambodia," *PNAS* 104, no. 36 (September 2007): 14277, pnas.org/doi/epdf/10.1073/pnas

.0702525104; Sarah Klassen et al., "Diachronic Modeling of the Population Within the Medieval Greater Angkor Region Settlement Complex," *Science Advances* 7, no. 19 (May 2021): science.org/doi/10.1126/sciadv.abf8441.

11 **No other buildings:** John Sanday, "The Triumphs and Perils of Khmer Architecture: A Structural Analysis of the Monuments of Angkor," in *Sculpture of Angkor and Ancient Cambodia: Millennium of Glory*, ed. Helen Ibbitson Jessup and Thierry Zéphir (Thames & Hudson, 1997), 85.

12 **The ancient Khmer wrote:** Michael D. Coe and Damian Evans, *Angkor and the Khmer Civilization* (Thames & Hudson, 2003), 189–90.

12 **The most ubiquitous were about:** Coe and Evans, *Angkor and the Khmer Civilization*, 39.

12 **Then there were the works:** Coe and Evans, *Angkor and the Khmer Civilization*, 131.

12 **Finally, historians could consult:** David Chandler, *A History of Cambodia*, 3rd ed. (Silkworm Books, 2003), 71–76.

12 **Much of what he learned:** Coe and Evans, *Angkor and the Khmer Civilization*, 131.

12 **The start of the Khmer:** Coe and Evans, *Angkor and the Khmer Civilization*, 97–99.

13 **The majority of Angkorian:** Coe and Evans, *Angkor and the Khmer Civilization*, 39.

13 **Part of the power:** Chandler, *History of Cambodia*, 56.

13 **There was neither hereditary nobility:** Coe and Evans, *Angkor and the Khmer Civilization*, 133.

13 **No system of succession applied:** Ian Mabbett and David Chandler, *The Khmers* (Blackwell, 1995), 161.

13 **In Zhou's telling:** Coe and Evans, *Angkor and the Khmer Civilization*, 139.

13 **When it was time:** Mabbett and Chandler, *Khmers*, 211.

13 **"The ministers and princes":** G. Coedes, *The Indianized States of Southeast Asia*, ed. Walter F. Vella, trans. Susan Brown Cowing (East-West Center Press, 1968), 216.

14 **The resulting flood:** Brian Eyler and Regan Kwan, "Mekong Floodpulse," Stimson, February 16, 2024, stimson.org/2024/mekong-floodpulse.

14 **the crop that gave:** Elizabeth Becker, *When the War Was Over: Cambodia and the Khmer Rouge Revolution*, rev. ed. (PublicAffairs, 1998), 31.

14 **The wealth of Khmer society:** Mabbett and Chandler, *Khmers*, 174.

14 **"kneel down, join their hands":** Chandler, *History of Cambodia*, 73.

14 **Slave labor was crucial:** Helen Ibbitson Jessup, "Temple-Mountains and the *Devarāja* Cult," in Jessup and Zéphir, *Sculpture of Angkor and Ancient Cambodia*, 101–15.

14 **For the tenth-century monarch:** "Koh Ker: Archaeological Site of Ancient Lingapura or Chok Gargyar," World Heritage List, UNESCO World Heritage

Convention, archived April 1, 2025, at web.archive.org/web/20250401105623 /https://whc.unesco.org/en/list/1667.

14 **The god's potency was:** Madeleine Giteau, *Khmer Sculpture and the Angkor Civilization*, trans. Diana Imber (Thames & Hudson, 1965), 19.

15 **Millions of tons of sandstone:** Sanday, "Triumphs and Perils," 86–87.

15 **In addition to slaves:** Coe and Evans, *Angkor and the Khmer Civilization*, 134.

15 **Some also probably bore:** See, for example, "Head from an Image of Vishnu or a Deified King," Minneapolis Institute of Art, accessed June 13, 2025, collections.artsmia.org/art/1752/head-from-an-image-of-vishnu-or-a-deified-king -khmer-artist.

15 **Not a single one:** Coe and Evans, *Angkor and the Khmer Civilization*, 158.

15 **Aside from the fact:** Thierry Zéphir, "Introduction to Khmer Sculpture: General Remarks," in Jessup and Zéphir, *Sculpture of Angkor and Ancient Cambodia*, 132; Christian Fischer et al., "From Quarries to Temples: Stone Procurement, Materiality, and Spirituality in the Angkorian World," in *The Angkorian World*, ed. Mitch Hendrickson et al. (Routledge, 2023), 370.

16 **But scholars have never:** Damian Evans et al., "Perspectives on the 'Collapse' of Angkor and the Khmer Empire," in Hendrickson et al., *Angkorian World*, 543–50.

16 **the region's principal port:** Coe and Evans, *Angkor and the Khmer Civilization*, 208.

16 **In 1860, a French explorer:** Henri Mouhot, *Travels in the Central Parts of Indo-China (Siam), Cambodia, and Laos, During the Years 1858, 1859, and 1860* (John Murray, 1864), 1:279–300.

16 **"It is grander":** Mouhot, *Travels*, 1:279–300.

17 **Mouhot hadn't discovered:** Charles Higham, *The Civilization of Angkor* (University of California Press, 2001), 1.

17 **Condescendingly, he speculated that:** Mouhot, *Travels*, 2:23.

17 **He saw only one way:** Mouhot, *Travels*, 2:20.

17 **But two years later:** Chandler, *History of Cambodia*, 141.

17 **Gradually, it became something:** André Malraux, *The Way of the Kings*, trans. Howard Curtis (Hesperus Press, 2005), 42–46.

18 **The French claimed to be:** Thomas Clayton, "Restriction or Resistance?: French Colonial Educational Development in Cambodia," *Education Policy Analysis Archives* 3, no. 19 (December 1995): 6–7, digitalcommons.usf.edu/cgi /viewcontent.cgi?article=1296&context=usf_EPAA.

18 **In addition to soldiers:** École Française d'Extrême Orient, *Conservation in Angkor, 1907–1972*, report submitted to the International Round Table on the Preservation of the Angkor Monuments, June 1990, 4.

18 **Poverty was the rule:** Chandler, *History of Cambodia*, 153.

18 **The French government:** Philip Short, *Pol Pot: Anatomy of a Nightmare* (Henry Holt and Company, 2004), 28–29.

19 **he had six wives:** Martin Woollacott, "King Norodom Sihanouk Obituary," *Guardian*, October 15, 2012, theguardian.com/world/2012/oct/15/king-norodom-sihanouk.

19 **He spoke flawless French:** Norodom Sihanouk, "Sihanouk: The Man We May Have to Settle for in Cambodia," interview by Oriana Fallaci, *New York Times Magazine*, August 12, 1973, timesmachine.nytimes.com/timesmachine/1973/08/12/90464640.html.

19 **On one occasion, he insisted:** William Shawcross, *Sideshow: Kissinger, Nixon and the Destruction of Cambodia* (Simon & Schuster, 1979), 50.

19 **He became enraged:** "Cambodia Isn't 'Tiny' or 'Small' or 'Petite,' Sihanouk Declares," *New York Times*, December 19, 1965, timesmachine.nytimes.com/timesmachine/1965/12/19/96724915.html.

19 **As one journalist wistfully recalled:** Becker, *When the War Was Over*, xv.

20 **Sihanouk was a near-absolute:** Mabbett and Chandler, *Khmers*, 258.

20 **If they were unlucky enough:** Chandler, *History of Cambodia*, 197–200.

20 **One opposition leader who:** Shawcross, *Sideshow*, 239.

20 **Raised in relative privilege:** Short, *Pol Pot*, 50.

20 **There he was admitted:** Short, *Pol Pot*, 63–64.

20 **After returning to Phnom Penh:** Short, *Pol Pot*, 120, 146.

THREE

22 **His brother, Trevor:** "Around Town," *Bangkok Post*, March 7, 1964.

22 **With a seventh-floor office:** Douglas Latchford to Samuel Eilenberg, letter, 12 March 1963.

23 **Its government had granted:** Abel Brodeur et al., "War, Migration and the Origins of the Thai Sex Industry," Center for Economic Performance Discussion Paper No. 1489 (July 2017), 7–8, eprints.lse.ac.uk/86581/1/dp1489.pdf.

24 **From a clandestine facility:** Tim Weiner, *Legacy of Ashes: The History of the CIA* (Anchor Books, 2008), 291–92.

25 **Its air-conditioning filters were:** "Patpong's Favourite Son: Tim Young," *Big Chilli*, September 9, 2013, thebigchilli.com/feature-stories/patpongs-favourite-son-tim-young.

25 **In early October 1965:** Peter A. Jackson, "An American Death in Bangkok: The Murder of Darrell Berrigan and the Hybrid Origins of *Gay* Identity in 1960s Thailand," *GLQ: A Journal of Lesbian and Gay Studies* 5, no. 3 (1999): 361–411, muse.jhu.edu/article/12116.

25 **A twenty-two-year-old:** "Thai Said to Admit Slaying American," *New York Times*, October 14, 1965, timesmachine.nytimes.com/timesmachine/1965/10/14/94989298.html.

26 **Those who traded:** "Memorandum: James Harrison Wilson Thompson Kidnap[p]ing—Malaysia," United States Embassy Manila, 25 April 1967, at 425–28 in Toulmin, "The Disappearance of Jim Thompson."

26 **He was also selling them:** Latchford to Eilenberg, 12 March 1963.

26 **In one letter, Thompson:** Jim Thompson to Lisa Lyons, letter, 16 August 1966, at 655-656 in Toulmin, "The Disappearance of Jim Thompson." 6.

26 **Several years earlier:** Karl E. Meyer, *The Plundered Past* (Atheneum, 1973), 4.

27 **According to one estimate:** Meyer, *Plundered Past*, 5.

27 **American museums, attentive to:** Neil Brodie and Jenny Doole, "The Asian Art Affair: US Art Museum Collections of Asian Art and Archaeology," in *Material Engagements: Studies in Honour of Colin Renfrew*, ed. Neil Brodie and Catherine Hills (McDonald Institute for Architectural Research, 2004), 94–100.

27 **Prasat Hin Khao Plai:** Emma Bunker, "The Prakhon Chai Story: Facts and Fiction," *Arts of Asia* 32, no. 2 (March–April 2022): 106–10.

28 **Word of the discovery:** Tanongsak Hanwong et al., "The Prakhon Chai Hoard Debunked: Unravelling Six Decades of Myth, Misdirection, and Misidentification," *International Journal of Cultural Property* 31, no. 2 (May 2024): 196–201.

28 **The total may have been:** Hanwong et al., "Prakhon Chai Hoard Debunked," 177–78.

28 **examples had been acquired:** Hanwong et al., "Prakhon Chai Hoard Debunked," 179–83.

29 **Thompson appeared exhausted:** Joshua Kurlantzick, *The Ideal Man: The Tragedy of Jim Thompson and the American Way of War* (John Wiley & Sons, 2011), 149.

29 **He was also deeply angered:** Kurlantzick, *Ideal Man*, 179–80.

29 **Thompson and Mangskau were staying:** "Memorandum: James Harrison Wilson Thompson" at 425–28 in Toulmin, "The Disappearance of Jim Thompson," and Kurlantzick, *Ideal Man*, 183–84.

30 **flew in to assist in the hunt:** "Clues Are Sought on Lost American," *New York Times*, April 29, 1967, timesmachine.nytimes.com/timesmachine/1967/04/29/83118420.html.

30 **An American diplomat in the region:** "Memorandum: James Harrison Wilson Thompson," at 425–428 in Toulmin, "The Disappearance of Jim Thompson."

FOUR

31 **Thomas Hoving was finishing:** Bernard Weinraub, "Out of the Cloisters—a Happening Called Hoving," *New York Times Magazine*, July 10, 1966, timesmachine.nytimes.com/timesmachine/1966/07/10/82481537.html.

31 **It belonged to the executive:** Thomas Hoving, *Making the Mummies Dance* (Simon & Schuster, 1993), 20–25.

31 **"Brace yourself, Tom":** Hoving, *Mummies*, 22.

32 **After cultivating a source:** "Captain James J. Rorimer (US Army)," Monuments Men and Women Foundation, accessed August 25, 2025, monumentsmenandwomenfnd.org/monuments-men-and-women/james-rorimer.

32 **The Met's president tasked:** Hoving, *Mummies*, 26–27.

32 **Tall and patrician:** Weinraub, "Happening Called Hoving."

32 **"my sister and I":** Hoving, *Mummies*, 86.

32 **He practiced it during:** Hoving, *Mummies*, 22.

32 **Hoving maintained a rebellious streak:** Weinraub, "Happening Called Hoving."

33 **As he completed his PhD:** Richard F. Shepard, "Museum May Name Hoving as Director," *New York Times*, December 16, 1966, timesmachine.nytimes.com /timesmachine/1966/12/16/96979160.html.

33 **Hoving was soon hired as:** Hoving, *Mummies*, 24.

33 **In late 1965:** Weinraub, "Happening Called Hoving."

33 **It didn't hurt that:** Hoving, *Mummies*, 17.

33 **which sits on city land:** Michael Gross, *Rogues' Gallery: The Secret Story of the Lust, Lies, Greed, and Betrayals That Made the Metropolitan Museum of Art* (Broadway Books, 2009), 9.

33 **Hoving hired a young staff:** Ada Louise Huxtable, "New Era for Parks," *New York Times*, February 10, 1966, timesmachine.nytimes.com/timesmachine/1966 /02/10/121501024.html.

33 **There were jazz concerts:** Ralph Blumenthal, "Hoving Bowing Out as City's Parks Chief Today," *New York Times*, March 16, 1967, timesmachine.nytimes .com/timesmachine/1967/03/16/83032972.html.

33 **A joke at the time:** Randy Kennedy, "Thomas Hoving, Remaker of the Met, Dies at 78," *New York Times*, December 10, 2009, nytimes.com/2009/12/11/arts /design/11hoving.html.

34 **He also had all:** Hoving, *Mummies*, 22–23.

34 **On March 17:** Hoving, *Mummies*, 54.

34 **He was just thirty-six:** Milton Esterow, "Hoving Is Named Museum Director," *New York Times*, December 21, 1966, timesmachine.nytimes.com/times machine/1966/12/21/90245818.html.

34 **As a Piedmontese soldier:** Gross, *Rogues' Gallery*, 30–33.

34 **He followed none:** Toby Wilkinson, *A World Beneath the Sands: The Golden Age of Egyptology* (W. W. Norton & Company, 2020), 167–72.

35 **One of his signal finds:** "Luigi Palma di Cesnola," British Museum, accessed June 29, 2025, britishmuseum.org/collection/term/BIOG61173.

35 **established in 1870:** Gross, *Rogues' Gallery*, 33–34.

35 **rented premises in Midtown:** Gross, *Rogues' Gallery*, 41–42.

35 **without a director on staff:** Gross, *Rogues' Gallery*, 45.

35 **Eventually, the group:** Karl E. Meyer, "Met Goes to the Closet, Gets Out Its Skeletons and Tells the Stories," *New York Times*, April 15, 2000, nytimes .com/2000/04/15/arts/met-goes-to-the-closet-gets-out-its-skeletons-and-tells -the-stories.html.

36 **In 1880, at a ceremony:** Gross, *Rogues' Gallery*, 49–50.

36 **a few months after he:** Gross, *Rogues' Gallery*, 50.

36 **passage of the War Revenue:** Margot L. Crandall-Hollick, *The Charitable Deduction for Individuals: A Brief Legislative History*, CRS Report No. R46178 (Congressional Research Service, 2020), crsreports.congress.gov/product/pdf /R/R46178/3.

37 **Other sellers came into their:** See, for example, Lynn H. Nicholas, *The Rape of Europa: The Fate of Europe's Treasures in the Third Reich and the Second World War* (Vintage Books, 1995), 429, 439.

37 **As a medieval curator:** Hoving, *Mummies*, 24.

38 **"My collecting style":** Hoving, *Mummies*, 24.

38 **Hoving's triumphs included:** Relief with the Annunciation, ca. 1180–1200, Carrara marble inlaid with serpentine (verde di Prato), 26 ½ × 24 × 4 ¾ in. (67.3 × 61 × 12.1 cm), Metropolitan Museum of Art, New York, object no. 601.40, archived May 30, 2023, at web.archive.org/web/20230530203152/https://www .metmuseum.org/art/collection/search/471848.

38 **Hoving located the relief:** Grace Glueck, "Hoving Cites Secret Deals for the Met," *New York Times*, September 28, 1981, timesmachine.nytimes.com/times machine/1981/09/28/029590.html.

38 **"the smartly dressed":** Glueck, "Hoving Cites Secret Deals for the Met."

38 **"Two weeks after":** Glueck, "Hoving Cites Secrets Deal for the Met."

38 **Later, once the norms:** Sharon Waxman, *Loot: The Battle over the Stolen Treasures of the Ancient World* (Henry Holt and Company, 2008), 194–95.

38 **That was why so many:** Karl E. Meyer, *The Plundered Past* (Atheneum, 1973), 240–53.

39 **In the late 1960s:** Jason Felch and Ralph Frammolino, *Chasing Aphrodite: The Hunt for Looted Antiquities at the World's Richest Museum* (Houghton Mifflin Harcourt, 2011), 102.

39 **Under Mexican law:** Meyer, *Plundered Past*, 42.

40 **In a 1968 letter:** Norodom Sihanouk, "Letter of Samdech Head of State to Spink and Son Ltd.," *Kambuja*, November 15, 1968, 46.

40 **It's sometimes said that looting:** Felch and Frammolino, *Chasing Aphrodite*, 2.

40 **As Meyer wrote:** Meyer, *Plundered Past*, xv.

40 **With something like that:** Alper Tasdelen, "Cambodia's Struggle to Protect Its Movable Cultural Property and Thailand," in *Cultural Property and Contested Ownership: The Trafficking of Artefacts and the Quest for Restitution*, ed. Brigitta Hauser-Schäublin and Lyndel V. Prott (Routledge, 2017), 46; and "Revised Draft Resolution Submitted by the Delegations of Mexico and Peru," 11th General Conference of UNESCO, Paris, France, December 1, 1960, unesdoc .unesco.org/ark:/48223/pf0000250014.

40 **Newly decolonized countries:** Patty Gerstenblith, "Implementation of the 1970 UNESCO Convention by the United States and Other Market Nations," in *The Routledge Companion to Cultural Property*, ed. Jane Anderson and Haidy Geismar (Routledge, 2017), 71.

41 **Like all American museum:** Hoving, *Mummies*, 217.

41 **Hoving believed that everything:** Hoving, *Mummies*, 44–45.

42 ***The Village Voice* wrote:** As cited in Gross, *Rogues' Gallery*, 335.

42 **Hoving came up with:** Hoving, *Mummies*, 55–63.

42 **The heavily marketed:** "The Met Welcomes 1,000,000th Visitor to the Costume Institute's *Heavenly Bodies* Exhibition," Metropolitan Museum of Art, August 23, 2018, metmuseum.org/press-releases/heavenly-bodies-millionth-visitor-2018 -news.

42 **As he wrote later:** Hoving, *Mummies*, 102.

42 **Hoving was vague about:** Meyer, *Plundered Past*, 305.

42 **media reports appeared:** Gross, *Rogues' Gallery*, 360.

42 **"the krater was definitely":** Harry Stathos, "Italy Asks FBI to Probe Vase," *Daily News* (New York), February 27, 1973, 5.

43 **more than thirty years:** Hoving, *Mummies*, 315.

43 **tomb robbers working near Rome:** Felch and Frammolino, *Chasing Aphrodite*, 211; and Elisabetta Povoledo, "Ancient Vase Comes Home to a Hero's Welcome," *New York Times*, January 19, 2008, nytimes.com/2008/01/19/arts /design/19bowl.html.

43 **But as Hoving would lament:** Hoving, *Mummies*, 155.

43 **Its holdings were so scant:** Tom Mashberg and Graham Bowley, "Cambodia Says It's Found Its Lost Artifacts: In Gallery 249 at the Met," *New York Times*, August 18, 2022, nytimes.com/2022/08/18/arts/design/met-artifacts-cambodia .html.

43 **He also needed art:** Hoving, *Mummies*, 371–72.

FIVE

44 **The guerrillas began:** Philip Short, *Pol Pot: Anatomy of a Nightmare* (Henry Holt and Company, 2004), 174.

44 **All that the insurgents:** Short, *Pol Pot*, 174.

44 **Since leaving Phnom Penh:** Short, *Pol Pot*, 147.

44 **He'd lived for a time:** Short, *Pol Pot*, 145.

44 **he traveled on foot:** Short, *Pol Pot*, 156–59.

44 **He was still developing his:** Matthew Galway, "From Revolutionary Culture to Original Culture and Back: 'On New Democracy' and the Kampucheanization of Marxism-Leninism, 1940–1965," *Cross-Currents: East Asian History and Culture Review* 6, no. 2 (November 2017): 655–56.

45 **Sar was intensely secretive:** Fox Butterfield, "Leading Cambodian in a Visit to Peking," *New York Times*, September 29, 1977, nytimes.com/1977/09/29/ar chives/leading-cambodian-in-a-visit-to-peking-trip-by-pol-pot-sheds-some .html.

45 **But it was clear to:** William Shawcross, *Sideshow: Kissinger, Nixon and the Destruction of Cambodia* (Simon & Schuster, 1979), 245.

45   **He responded with ferocious:** Short, *Pol Pot*, 176.

45   **"I do not care if":** Elizabeth Becker, *When the War Was Over: Cambodia and the Khmer Rouge Revolution*, rev. ed. (PublicAffairs, 1998), 110.

46   **And during the tumultuous:** Alan Parkhouse, "A Rare Find," *Bangkok Post*, December 9, 2010, ki-media.blogspot.com/2010/09/rare-find-rare-khmer-artefacts-to.html.

46   **Shortly before this trip:** Shawcross, *Sideshow*, 68.

47   **On March 16:** "Memorandum from the President's Assistant for National Security Affairs (Kissinger) to President Nixon," 16 March 1969, Office of the Historian, US Department of State, archived August 18, 2024, at web.archive.org/web/20240818090616/https://history.state.gov/historicaldocuments/frus1969-76v06/d40.

47   **To get such a deal:** David Kraslow and Stuart H. Loory, "The Search for Peace: How a Secret Channel Started Hanoi Talking," *Boston Globe*, April 4, 1968, 15.

47   **Nixon and Kissinger had:** Shawcross, *Sideshow*, 236.

48   **a "Bamboo Pentagon":** "Memorandum from the President's Assistant for National Security Affairs (Kissinger) to President Nixon," 19 February 1969, Office of the Historian, US Department of State, archived August 18, 2024, at web.archive.org/web/20240818123923/https://history.state.gov/historicaldocuments/frus1969-76v06/d22.

48   **"seize on this":** "Memorandum from the President's Assistant for National Security Affairs (Kissinger) to President Nixon," 16 March 1969.

48   **Cambodia was neutral:** Becker, *When the War Was Over*, 10.

48   **To minimize the risks:** Shawcross, *Sideshow*, 29; and Stanley Karnow, *Vietnam: A History* (Penguin Books, 1997), 606–7.

48   **The first missions, by B-52:** Shawcross, *Sideshow*, 23–35.

48   **In the narrowest terms:** "Sihanouk Says He'll Renew Relations with U.S.," *New York Times*, June 11, 1969, timesmachine.nytimes.com/timesmachine/1969/06/11/78383941.html.

49   **Word of the Breakfast strikes:** Shawcross, *Sideshow*, 33–35.

49   **Each was assigned:** Shawcross, *Sideshow*, 23.

49   **None of the boxes:** "Excerpts from Interview with Nixon About Domestic Effects of Indochina War," *New York Times*, May 20, 1977, nytimes.com/1977/05/20/archives/excerpts-from-interview-with-nixon-about-domestic-effects-of.html.

49   **Most, if not all, were:** Taylor Owen and Ben Kiernan, "Bombs over Cambodia," *Walrus*, October 2006, 62–69.

49   **This brought their estimated:** Short, *Pol Pot*, 185.

49   **ultimately into more regular:** Tad Szulc, "Chinese Said to Aid Revival of Cambodian Red Group," *New York Times*, May 9, 1970, nytimes.com/1970/05/09/archives/chinese-said-to-aid-revival-of-cambodian-red-group.html; and Owen and Kiernan, "Bombs," 67.

49   **As chaos and violence:** David Chandler, *A History of Cambodia*, 3rd ed. (Silkworm Books, 2003), 204.

50 **In January 1970:** Henry Kamm, "Sihanouk Reported Out in a Coup by His Premier; Cambodia Airports Shut," *New York Times*, March, 19, 1970, timesmachine.nytimes.com/timesmachine/1970/03/19/76717958.html.

50 **Within hours, the Cambodian:** "Memorandum from the President's Assistant for National Security Affairs (Kissinger) to President Nixon," 19 March 1970, Office of the Historian, US Department of State, archived June 16, 2024, at web.archive.org/web/20240616052001/https://history.state.gov/historicaldoc uments/frus1969-76v06/d205.

50 **Just after they seized power:** Richard Halloran, "U.S. Says Cambodia Coup Won't Affect Recognition," *New York Times*, March 20, 1970, nytimes.com /1970/03/20/archives/us-says-cambodia-coup-wont-affect-recognition.html.

50 **"get the CIA jerks":** "Transcript of Telephone Conversation Between President Nixon and His Assistant for National Security Affairs (Kissinger)," 17 April 1970, Office of the Historian, US Department of State, archived September 7, 2024, at web.archive.org/web/20240907172559/https://history.state.gov/his toricaldocuments/frus1969-76v06/d237.

50 **in his unmistakable:** "Underground Fight Urged by Sihanouk Against New Rulers," *New York Times*, March 25, 1970, timesmachine.nytimes.com/times machine/1970/03/25/76721722.html; and Shawcross, *Sideshow*, 125–26.

51 **It would be supported:** Short, *Pol Pot*, 202.

SIX

52 **Douglas Latchford rang in:** Vippy Rangsit, "Look," *Bangkok Post*, January 4, 1970, 22.

52 **For friends who were:** Rangsit, "Look," 22.

52 **His bride, Phuangpaka Tarmallpark:** "Female Overseas Student Files for Divorce from Her Cruel Farang Husband Who Abandons His Wife for Homosexual Relations," *Thairath*, September 14, 1973; and "Female Overseas Student Files for Divorce from Her Farang Husband Who Likes Flirting with Men," *Ban Muang*, September 15, 1973.

53 **Latchford's view was almost:** Douglas Latchford, "Gold of the Gods," interview by Louise Nicholson, *Apollo*, November 2008, 34.

54 **By 1974, he had realized:** Douglas Latchford to Adrian Maynard, letter, 7 November 1974.

54 **Latchford had recently donated:** Lintel, 10th century, carved sandstone, 23 × 52 × 4.33 in. (58.42 × 132.08 × 11 cm), British Museum, London, object no. 1971,0924.1, britishmuseum.org/collection/object/A_1971-0924-1; Lintel, 11th century, relief-carved sandstone, 26 ½ × 68 in. (67.31 × 172.72 cm), British Museum, London, object no. 1971,0924.2," britishmuseum.org/collection /object/A_1971-0924-2; and Boundary Stone, 8th–9th century, sandstone, 3 ½ ft. high, British Museum, London, object no. 1970,0310.1," britishmuseum.org /collection/object/A_1970-0310-1.

54 **One of the visitors:** Douglas Latchford to Sherman Lee, letter, 29 March 1972.

55 **Lee responded graciously:** Sherman Lee to Douglas Latchford, letter, 5 April 1972; and Douglas Latchford to Sherman Lee, letter, 8 May 1972.

55 **Before Lee could reply:** Douglas Latchford to Sherman Lee, letter, 24 May 1972.

55 **At 9:00 p.m. on April:** "President Richard Nixon Address to the Nation on the Situation in Southeast Asia, April 30, 1970," posted October 27, 2017, by Richard Nixon Presidential Library, YouTube, 22 min., 8 sec., youtube.com/watch?v=IkcqpGo97NI.

56 **At the time, however:** "Kennedy Describes Action in Cambodia as 'Madness,'" *New York Times*, May 2, 1970, nytimes.com/1970/05/02/archives/kennedy-describes-action-in-cambodia-as-madness.html.

56 **In the meantime, Nixon's:** François Bizot, *The Gate* (Vintage Books, 2004), 14.

56 **The Grand Hotel was now:** Bizot, *Gate*, 14; Gloria Emerson, "Prestige Termed Reds' Aim in Angkor Area," *New York Times*, June 12, 1970, nytimes.com/1970/06/12/archives/prestige-termed-reds-aim-in-angkor-area.html; Sydney H. Schanberg, "Temple Ruins at Angkor Reported in Foe's Hands," *New York Times*, June 12, 1970, nytimes.com/1970/06/12/archives/temple-ruins-at-angkor-reported-in-foes-hands-cambodia-says-angkor.html; and Henry Kamm, "Siemreap, Near Angkor Temples, Has Become a Besieged Camp," *New York Times*, July 16, 1970, nytimes.com/1970/07/16/archives/siemreap-near-angkor-temples-has-become-a-besieged-camp.html.

57 **Nol was erratic:** William Shawcross, *Sideshow: Kissinger, Nixon and the Destruction of Cambodia* (Simon & Schuster, 1979), 187.

57 **He had a long-standing:** Elizabeth Becker, *When the War Was Over: Cambodia and the Khmer Rouge Revolution*, rev. ed. (PublicAffairs, 1998), 123–24; Iver Peterson, "Amulets Are a Vital Part of a Cambodian Soldier's Equipment," *New York Times*, September 9, 1970, timesmachine.nytimes.com/timesmachine/1970/09/09/86396519.pdf.

57 **His commanders included characters:** Philip Short, *Pol Pot: Anatomy of a Nightmare* (Henry Holt and Company, 2004), 219; and Jon Swain, *River of Time* (Vintage, 1998), 26.

57 **In Phnom Penh, almost:** Haing Ngor with Roger Warner, *Survival in the Killing Fields* (Robinson, 2003), 73. Originally published in 1987 as *A Cambodian Odyssey*.

57 **By mid-1972, the Khmer:** Short, *Pol Pot*, 228.

57 **supplied from China via:** Short, *Pol Pot*, 202.

57 **Steadily, they supplanted:** Shawcross, *Sideshow*, 261; and Becker, *When the War Was Over*, 133.

57 **The man born:** Short, *Pol Pot*, 212.

57 **As fighting reached the:** "Plea Made for Safety of Temples at Angkor," *New York Times*, June 12, 1970, nytimes.com/1970/06/12/archives/plea-made-for-safety-of-temples-at-angkor.html.

58 **In Siem Reap, French:** International Council of Museums, *Cent objets disparus: Pillage à Angkor* (ICOM-EFEO, 1993), 20; and Bizot, *Gate*, 20.

58 **More than four thousand:** Carol Vogel, "Tracing Path of Artworks Smuggled Out of Asia," *New York Times*, April 23, 1997, nytimes.com/1997/04/23/arts /tracing-path-of-artworks-smuggled-out-of-asia.html; and ICOM, *Cent objets disparus*, 20.

58 **for the most part:** World Monuments Fund, "Excerpts from the Draft Report on 'The Conservation and Preservation of the Angkor Sanctuary, Cambodia,'" presented at the International Round Table of Experts on the Preservation of the Angkor Monuments, Bangkok, June 5–8, 1990, 3, unesdoc.unesco.org/ark: /48223/pf0000086373.

59 **In 1973, less than:** "Female Overseas Student," *Thairath*; and "Female Overseas Student," *Ban Muang*.

60 **Since long before Latchford:** Decl. of Matthew Rendall at 9, United States of America v. A 10th Century Cambodian Sandstone Sculpture, Currently Located at Sotheby's in New York, New York, No. 12 Civ. 2600 (GBD) (S.D.N.Y. August 20, 2012).

61 **In May 1974:** Adrian Maynard to Douglas Latchford, letter, 23 May 1974.

61 **Soon, Latchford and one:** Adrian Maynard to Douglas Latchford, letter, 31 October 1974.

61 **Based on the style:** Isidor Kahane to Adrian Maynard, letter, 20 November 1974.

61 **Compared with the more:** Helen Ibbitson Jessup and Thierry Zéphir, eds., *Sculpture of Angkor and Ancient Cambodia: Millennium of Glory* (Thames & Hudson, 1997), 189–90.

62 **The head and then:** Verified Am. Compl. at 8, April 9, 2013, *A 10th Century Cambodian Sandstone Sculpture.*

62 **To have any hope:** Maynard to Latchford, 31 October 1974.

62 **Shortly afterward, one of:** Kahane to Maynard, 20 November 1974.

SEVEN

63 **A little before dawn:** Sydney H. Schanberg, "Bomb Error Leaves Havoc in Neak Luong," *New York Times*, August 9, 1973, nytimes.com/1973/08/09/ archives/bomb-error-leaves-havoc-in-neakluong-us-bomb-error-leaves-havocl.html; and David Binder, "Crewman's Slip Cited in Bombing Error Fatal to 137," *New York Times*, August 24, 1973, nytimes.com/1973/08/24/archives /crewmans-slip-cited-in-bombing-error-fatal-to-137-beacon-wrongly.html.

63 **On August 6, 1973 airstrikes in Cambodia:** William Shawcross, *Sideshow: Kissinger, Nixon and the Destruction of Cambodia* (Simon & Schuster, 1979), 271.

64 **Civilians died by the:** Taylor Owen and Ben Kiernan, "Bombs over Cambodia," *Walrus*, October 2006, 67.

64 **None of this deterred:** Shawcross, *Sideshow*, 271.

64   **American planes had hit:** Holly High et al., "Electronic Records of the Air War over Southeast Asia: A Database Analysis," *Journal of Vietnamese Studies* 8, no. 4 (Fall 2013): 104–8.

64   **At first, it was possible:** Short, *Sideshow*, 229–30.

65   **Khmer Rouge members avoided:** François Bizot, *The Gate* (Vintage Books, 2004), 33–37; and Elizabeth Becker, *When the War Was Over: Cambodia and the Khmer Rouge Revolution*, rev. ed. (PublicAffairs, 1998), 141.

65   **To be deemed an opponent:** Rebecca Ratcliffe, "'I Lost Them All': A Family's Sole Survivor Recalls Their Slow Death Under Cambodia's Khmer Rouge," *Guardian*, September 22, 2022, theguardian.com/global-development/2022 /sep/22/seang-m-seng-cambodia-khmer-rouge-starvation.

65   **For Pol Pot, the goal:** Matthew Galway, "From Revolutionary Culture to Original Culture and Back: 'On New Democracy' and the Kampucheanization of Marxism-Leninism, 1940–1965," *Cross-Currents: East Asian History and Culture Review* 6, no. 2 (November 2017): 658–60.

65   **both radical and austere:** Kenneth M. Quinn, "The Khmer Krahom Program to Create a Communist Society in Southern Cambodia," airgram from US Consulate, Can Tho, to US Department of State, 20 February 1974, 17–33.

65   **Those who protested might:** Quinn, "Khmer Krahom Program," 19.

65   **The Khmer Rouge then set:** Quinn, "Khmer Krahom Program," 17–18.

66   **his fighters cut off:** Sydney H. Schanberg, "Big Convoy Poised for Cambodia Trip," *New York Times*, January 20, 1975, nytimes.com/1975/01/20/archives /big-convoy-poised-for-cambodia-trip-30-vessels-wait-at-border-to.html.

66   **Soon even those river:** Sydney H. Schanberg, "Battle for Mekong River Critical for Phnom Penh," *New York Times*, February 10, 2975, timesmachine .nytimes.com/timesmachine/1975/02/10/80126912.html.

66   **Swollen by refugees:** Shawcross, *Sideshow*, 183.

66   **But at the right price:** Jon Swain, *River of Time* (Vintage, 1998), 16, 24.

67   **In a final transmission:** Shawcross, *Sideshow*, 362–63.

67   **Cambodians with money or foreign:** Sydney H. Schanberg, "Cambodians Seek to Brace Morale," *New York Times*, March 11, 1975, nytimes.com/1975 /03/11/archives/cambodians-seek-to-brace-morale-capital-is-shaken-by-more -shelling.html.

67   **Of those left behind:** François Ponchaud, *Cambodge, année zéro* (Kailash, 2012), 16.

67   **Elements of the remnant population:** Philip Short, *Pol Pot: Anatomy of a Nightmare* (Henry Holt and Company, 2004), 264; Swain, *River*, 112.

67   **The government radio station:** Swain, *River*, 132.

67   **In simple black uniforms:** Ponchaud, *Cambodge*, 15.

68   **the fighters began to remove:** Bizot, *Gate*, 145.

68   **In March 1975:** John Canaday, "Some Great Asian Bronzes," *New York Times*, March 16, 1975, https://timesmachine.nytimes.com/timesmachine/1975/03/16 /317532832.pdf.

68 **Lerner devoted almost two:** Martin Lerner, *Bronze Sculptures from Asia* (Metropolitan Museum of Art, 1975), 28–29.

68 **The Met had purchased:** Kneeling Female, 11th century, bronze inlaid with silver and traces of gold, 17 × 7 ¾ in. (43.2 × 19.7 cm), Metropolitan Museum of Art, New York, object no. 1972.147, archived March 7, 2023, at web.archive.org /web/20230307094808/https://www.metmuseum.org/art/collection/search/ 39096. For decades the Met listed the figure as originating in Cambodia, but in 2023, the museum said that the statute had in fact come from Thailand. It was repatriated to the country in 2024. The Cambodian government has objected to this attribution.

69 **Spink's executives successfully imported:** Decl. of Brian Doctor QC at 2, United States of America v. A 10th Century Cambodian Sandstone Sculpture, Currently Located at Sotheby's in New York, New York, No. 12 Civ. 2600 (GBD) (S.D.N.Y. June 5, 2012).

69 **They photographed the statue:** "An Exceptionally Fine Sandstone Torso of a Yaksha," *Octagon*, Autumn 1975, 22.

69 **A Spink's receipt recorded:** Decl. of Peter G. Neiman in Supp. of Claimants' Mot. to Dismiss at Ex. 7, June 5, 2012, *A 10th Century Cambodian Sandstone Sculpture.*

EIGHT

70 **Within hours of taking:** Haing Ngor with Roger Warner, *Survival in the Killing Fields* (Robinson, 2003), 86–89.

70 **The command even applied:** François Ponchaud, *Cambodge, année zéro* (Kailash, 2012), 16–17; and Jon Swain, *River of Time* (Vintage, 1998), 146–47.

70 **Some Khmer Rouge said:** Philip Short, *Pol Pot: Anatomy of a Nightmare* (Henry Holt and Company, 2004), 271.

70 **When they were asked:** Haing Ngor with Warner, *Survival*, 102–3.

70 **Heedless, the columns kept:** Haing Ngor with Warner, *Survival*, 98–99.

71 **"Resolutely maintain high":** Haing Ngor with Warner, *Survival*, 98–99.

71 **For a time, merchants:** Haing Ngor with Warner, *Survival*, 106, 110.

71 **But before long:** François Bizot, *The Gate* (Vintage Books, 2004), 182; and Ponchaud, *Cambodge*, 40.

71 **The only way to buy:** Haing Ngor with Warner, *Survival*, 120.

71 **In pursuit of total:** Elizabeth Becker, *When the War Was Over: Cambodia and the Khmer Rouge Revolution*, rev. ed. (PublicAffairs, 1998), 166.

71 **The foreigners who remained:** Swain, *River*, 147–70.

71 **Cambodians who'd also:** See, for example, David A. Andelman, "Urban Exodus Complete, Cambodia Refugees Say," *New York Times*, June 13, 1975, nytimes.com/1975/06/13/archives/urban-exodus-complete-cambodia -refugees-say-recent-cambodian.html.

72 **Those who revealed:** Becker, *When the War Was Over*, 162.

72 **Even the staff of the:** *Safeguarding and Development of Angkor* (UNESCO, 1993), 11, unesdoc.unesco.org/ark:/48223/pf0000097228.

72 **After days of marching:** Dany Long, "PA Field Trip Report: Koh Ker Village, Srayang Commune, Koulen District, Preah Vihear Province (12–18 May 2013)," 2, Documentation Center of Cambodia Archives.

72 **As they entered the:** Dany Long, "Field Trip Report," 10.

72 **"Cadres," as Khmer Rouge:** Dany Long, "Field Trip Report," 2–6.

72 **The community punctuated:** Sok Vannak, "Interview with Proem Chin, Male, Age 68," 2013, p. 4, Documentation Center of Cambodia Archives.

72 **But the Khmer Rouge had:** Dany Long, "Field Trip Report," 6, 22–24.

72 **Looting largely ceased:** Douglas Latchford, "Gold of the Gods," interview by Louise Nicholson, *Apollo*, November 2008, 34.

72 **Angka's authority over Koh Ker:** Dany Long, "Field Trip Report," 6–12.

73 **The experience of a boy:** Dany Long, "Field Trip Report," 15.

73 **The rations were far:** Sok Vannak, "Interview with Lim Sotr, Male, Age 51," 2013, p. 11, Documentation Center of Cambodia Archives.

73 **Care was sometimes provided:** Laurence Picq, *Beyond the Horizon: Five Years with the Khmer Rouge,* trans. Patricia Norland (St. Martin's Press, 1989), 114.

73 **In nearly empty Phnom Penh:** Short, *Pol Pot*, 346.

73 **Soon, Lim Sotr could:** Sok Vannak, "Interview with Lim Sotr," 11–16.

73 **Most terrifying of all:** Picq, *Beyond the Horizon*, 97–98.

74 **Around 1977, a local:** Dany Long, "Interview with Niem Thang, Male, Age 54," 2013, 7–10, Documentation Center of Cambodia Archives.

74 **was under house arrest:** Becker, *When the War Was Over*, 206–8.

74 **In 1976, the Khmer Rouge:** William Shawcross, *The Quality of Mercy: Cambodia, Holocaust and Modern Conscience* (Simon & Schuster, 1984), 23.

74 **"There is absolutely no":** "DK Constitution," Documentation Center of Cambodia, archived June 15, 2023, at web.archive.org/web/20230615215246 /https://d.dccam.org/Archives/Documents/DK_Policy/DK_Policy_DK _Constitution.htm.

74 **the government formally abolished:** Short, *Pol Pot*, 7; and Sheridan T. Prasso, "The Riel Value of Money: How the World's Only Attempt to Abolish Money Has Hindered Cambodia's Economic Development," AsiaPacific Issues, Analysis from the East-West Center No. 49, January 2001, files.ethz.ch/isn/28638/ api049.pdf.

74 **In the summation:** Short, *Pol Pot*, 291.

75 **It wasn't lost on some:** Becker, *When the War Was Over*, 187–88.

75 **Much of his six-hour:** *Long Live the 17th Anniversary of the Communist Party of Kampuchea: Speech by Pol Pot, Secretary of the Central Committee of the Kampuchean Communist Party, Delivered on September 29, 1977,* trans. Group of Kampuchean Residents in America (Liberator Press, 1977), cambodiatokampu chea.wordpress.com/wp-content/uploads/2018/02/1977-17-cpk_anniversry.pdf.

75 **They also appeared on:** Short, *Pol Pot*, 301.

75 **Toek Tik was eleven:** Tom Mashberg, "He Sold Away His People's Heritage. He's in the Jungle to Get It Back," *New York Times*, November 21, 2021, nytimes.com /2021/11/21/arts/design/toek-tik-cambodian-artifacts.html; and Simon Mackenzie and Tess Davis, "Temple Looting in Cambodia: Anatomy of a Statue Trafficking Network," *British Journal of Criminology* 54, no. 5 (September 2014): 731.

76 **The length of his service:** See, for example, Bizot, *Gate*, 71; and Becker, *When the War Was Over*, 203.

76 **The people of every commune:** Haing Ngor with Warner, *Survival*, 231–34.

76 **When a citizen was:** Teeda Butt Mam, "Worms from Our Skin," in *Children of Cambodia's Killing Fields*, comp. Dith Pran, ed. Kim DePaul (Silkworm Books, 1997), 11–18.

76 **oversaw the fetid Khmer Rouge prisons:** Haing Ngor with Warner, *Survival*, 257, 323–33.

77 **A short distance away was:** "Phnom Kulen: Archeological Site / Ancient Site of Mahendraparvata," World Heritage Tentative List, UNESCO World Heritage Convention, archived October 13, 2024, at web.archive.org/web/2024 1013064220/https://whc.unesco.org/en/tentativelists/6460.

NINE

78 **In fleeing from the Khmer:** Tom Mashberg, "He Sold Away His People's Heritage. He's in the Jungle to Get It Back," *New York Times*, November 21, 2021, nytimes.com/2021/11/21/arts/design/toek-tik-cambodian-artifacts.html; and Simon Mackenzie and Tess Davis, "Temple Looting in Cambodia: Anatomy of a Statue Trafficking Network," *British Journal of Criminology* 54, no. 5 (September 2014): 731.

78 **Clear streams meandered:** William Dalrymple, *The Golden Road: How Ancient India Transformed the World* (Bloomsbury, 2024), 199–202.

78 **He studied the animals:** Mashberg, "He Sold Away His People's Heritage."

78 **In AD 802:** Dalrymple, *Golden Road*, 199–202; and "Phnom Kulen: Archeological Site / Ancient Site of Mahendraparvata," World Heritage Tentative List, UNESCO World Heritage Convention, archived October 13, 2024, at web .archive.org/web/20241013064220/https://whc.unesco.org/en/tentativelists /6460.

79 **At another site:** "Angkor Archeological Park: Kbal Spean," Apsara Authority, archived August 14, 2024, web.archive.org/web/20240814104030/https://ap saraauthority.gov.kh/2021/08/05/kbal-spean.

79 **In early 1978:** Philip Short, *Pol Pot: Anatomy of a Nightmare* (Henry Holt and Company, 2004), 382–83.

79 **Instead, Pol Pot instructed:** Short, *Pol Pot*, 382.

80 **As the international press:** "Rights Abuses Cited," *Newsday*, April 22, 1978, 8.

80 **As relations between the two:** David Chandler, *A History of Cambodia*, 3rd ed. (Silkworm Books, 2003), 220–25.

80   **Before 1975, Cambodian:** William Shawcross, *Sideshow: Kissinger, Nixon and the Destruction of Cambodia* (Simon & Schuster, 1979), 387–90.

80   **Fourteen divisions of:** Elizabeth Becker, *When the War Was Over: Cambodia and the Khmer Rouge Revolution*, rev. ed. (PublicAffairs, 1998), 432–33.

80   **By early January:** Short, *Pol Pot*, 400.

81   **Soon, great numbers:** Haing Ngor with Roger Warner, *Survival in the Killing Fields* (Robinson, 2003), 388.

81   **A small international:** William Shawcross, *The Quality of Mercy: Cambodia, Holocaust and Modern Conscience* (Simon & Schuster, 1984), 112–20.

82   **One witness later:** Sebastian Strangio, *Hun Sen's Cambodia* (Yale University Press, 2014), 155.

82   **Some estimates put:** See, for example, Ben Kiernan, "The Demography of Genocide in Southeast Asia: The Death Tolls in Cambodia, 1975–79, and East Timor, 1975–80," *Critical Asian Studies* 35, no. 4 (2003): 586–87; and Damien de Walque, "Selective Mortality During the Khmer Rouge Period in Cambodia," *Population and Development Review* 31, no. 2 (June 2005): 352.

82   **The oft-repeated claim:** Becker, *When the War Was Over*, 162–63.

82   **A startlingly low proportion:** Henry Kamm, "Cambodian Refugees Depict Growing Fear and Hunger," *New York Times*, May 13, 1978, nytimes.com/1978 /05/13/archives/cambodian-refugees-depict-growing-fear-and-hunger-only -implicit.html.

82   **There was almost no:** Seth Mydans, "The World: The Khmer Rouge Legacy; In the Killing Fields, Even the Future Died," *New York Times*, January 10, 1999, nytimes.com/1999/01/10/weekinreview/the-world-the-khmer-rouge-legacy -in-the-killing-fields-even-the-future-died.html.

82   **Despite Pol Pot's:** Masha Lafont, *Pillaging Cambodia: The Illicit Traffic in Khmer Art* (McFarland & Company, 2004), 30.

82   **It was said:** Shawcross, *Quality of Mercy*, 38; Haing Ngor with Warner, *Survival*, 389.

82   **It was into this shattered:** Mashberg, "He Sold Away His People's Heritage." See also Mackenzie and Davis, "Temple Looting in Cambodia," 731–32.

TEN

86   **No Western expert:** *Safeguarding and Development of Angkor* (UNESCO, 1993), 11–12, unesdoc.unesco.org/ark:/48223/pf0000097228.

86   **With the end:** Dany Long, "PA Field Trip Report: Koh Ker Village, Srayang Commune, Koulen District, Preah Vihear Province (12–18 May 2013)," pp. 2–18, Documentation Center of Cambodia Archives.

87   **In 1982, the UN:** UNGAOR, 37th Sess., 42nd Plen. Mtg., UN Doc. A/37/ PV.42 (25 October 1982), digitallibrary.un.org/record/38945; UNGAOR, 37th Sess., 43rd Plen. Mtg., UN Doc. A/37/PV.43 (25 October 1982), digitallibrary .un.org/record/38946; UNGAOR, 37th Sess., 44th Plen. Mtg., UN Doc. A/37

/PV.44 (26 October 1982), digitallibrary.un.org/record/38952; UNGAOR, 37th Sess., 45th Plen. Mtg., UN Doc. A/37/PV.45 (26 October 1982), digitallibrary .un.org/record/38947; and Bernard D. Nossiter, "Iran Challenges Israel's Right to Seat at U.N.," *New York Times*, October 26, 1982, nytimes.com/1982/10/26 /world/iran-challenges-israel-s-right-to-seat-at-un.html.

87 **The flag of Pol Pot's:** Jonathan Power, "World May Turn Against Khmer Butchers," *Plain Dealer*, September 15, 1987, 19.

87 **It was joined:** Steven R. Ratner, "The Cambodia Settlement Agreements," *American Journal of International Law* 87, no. 1 (January 1993): 1–41, doi.org /10.2307/2203851.

88 **They wouldn't stand:** Philip Short, *Pol Pot: Anatomy of a Nightmare* (Henry Holt and Company, 2004), 421.

88 **Amid the fighting:** Simon Mackenzie and Tess Davis, "Temple Looting in Cambodia: Anatomy of a Statue Trafficking Network," *British Journal of Criminology* 54, no. 5 (September 2014): 731–32.

88 **The looters struck:** Henry Kamm, "Looting and Graffiti Eat Away at the Treasure of Angkor," *New York Times*, April 15, 1980, timesmachine.nytimes .com/timesmachine/1980/04/15/140233532.pdf; and Colin Campbell, "Gunshots Still Punctuate Angkor's Fragile Glories," *New York Times*, April 29, 1983, ny times.com/1983/04/29/world/gunshots-still-punctuate-angkor-s-fragile -glories.html.

88 **In 1986, a group:** Chea Socheat, "Enquête de terrain sur la disparition de sculptures dans les temples de Koh Ker" (Musée National du Cambodge; École Française d'Extrême-Orient, April 2012), 2–3; Éric Bourdonneau with Phin Samnang, "The Duel Between Bhima and Duryodhana and the Sculpted Group of the Western Gopura I of Prasat Chen at Koh Ker" (École Française d'Extrême-Orient, July 2012), 25.

88 **More than one thousand:** Éric Bourdonneau, "Sculpted Groups of the Eastern Gopura I in Prasat Chen (Koh Ker, Cambodia) and Khmer Art Collections of American Museums" (École Française d'Extrême-Orient; APSARA Authority, September 2014), 3.

89 **Like much of rural Cambodia:** David Wigg, "Cambodia Landmine Campaign by Hanoi," *Daily Telegraph*, November 30, 1985, 7; Barbara Crossette, "Cambodians Say Vietnam Appears to Dig In," *New York Times*, January 6, 1985, nytimes.com/1985/01/06/world/cambodians-say-vietnam-appears-to-dig-in .html.

89 **After more turns of:** Bourdonneau with Phin Samnang, "Duel Between Bhima and Duryodhana," 8–12.

89 **One of the men digging:** Chea Socheat, "Enquête de terrain," 2–3.

90 **A number of Koh Ker's:** Tess Davis and Simon Mackenzie, "Crime and Conflict: Temple Looting in Cambodia," in *Cultural Property Crime: An Overview and Analysis of the Contemporary Perspective and Trends*, ed. Joris D. Kila and Mark Balcells (Brill, 2015), 300–303. See also Dany Long, "Field Trip

Report"; and Keiko Miura, "Destruction and Plunder of Cambodian Cultural Heritage and Their Consequences," in *Cultural Property and Contested Ownership: The Trafficking of Artefacts and the Quest for Restitution*, ed. Brigitta Hauser-Schäublin and Lyndel V. Prott (Routledge, 2017), 29.

90 **Even by the standards:** William Shawcross, *The Quality of Mercy: Cambodia, Holocaust and Modern Conscience* (Simon & Schuster, 1984), 26; and Short, *Pol Pot*, 259.

90 **In the 1980s, living:** Davis and Mackenzie, "Crime and Conflict," 303.

91 **working at the well-regarded:** Allan Schwartzman, "The Metropolitan Plays Its Asia Card," *Los Angeles Times*, April 13, 1994, latimes.com/archives/la-xpm-1994-04-13-ca-45295-story.html.

91 **Under the Met's:** Thomas Hoving, *Making the Mummies Dance* (Simon & Schuster, 1993), 155, 371; and Thomas Hoving, *The Chase, The Capture: Collecting at the Metropolitan* (Metropolitan Museum of Art, 1975), 9.

91 **Lerner worried at first:** Philippe de Montebello, ed., *Notable Acquisitions, 1982–1983* (Metropolitan Museum of Art, 1983), 3.

91 **His successor was more:** Michael Gross, *Rogues' Gallery*, 416.

91 **He scored a coup:** Grace Glueck, "Art: Met Displays Gains in South Asia Collection," *New York Times*, December 17, 1982, nytimes.com/1982/12/17/arts/art-met-displays-gains-in-south-asia-collection.html.

91 **The following year, Lerner's department:** De Montebello, *Notable Acquisitions*, 78–79.

92 **the headline read:** Irvin Molotsky, "Bill to Curtail Stolen-Art Trade Is Near Passage," *New York Times*, December 20, 1982, nytimes.com/1982/12/20/arts/bill-to-curtail-stolen-art-trade-is-near-passage.html.

92 **In a letter to the:** Martin Lerner, "Unesco Pact Doesn't Concern 'Stolen Art,'" letter to the editor, *New York Times*, January 5, 1983, nytimes.com/1983/01/05/opinion/l-unesco-pact-doesn-t-concern-stolen-art-141758.html.

93 **For example, the Met:** Standing Female Deity, Probably Uma, ca. mid-11th century, stone, 29 ¾ × 9 × 4 ¼ in. (75.6 × 22.9 × 10.8 cm), Metropolitan Museum of Art, New York, object no. 1983.14, archived March 8, 2024, web.archive.org/web/20240308024636/https://www.metmuseum.org/art/collection/search/38300.

93 **Just months later:** Head of a Buddha, ca. 920–50, stone, 7 ¼ × 4 ⅝ × 4 ⅜ in. (18.3 × 11.7 × 11.1 cm), Metropolitan Museum of Art, New York, object no. 1983.551, archived March 8, 2024, at web.archive.org/web/20240308024546/https://www.metmuseum.org/art/collection/search/38447.

93 **In late July 1986:** Douglas Latchford to Nathan Halpern, letter, 28 July 1986.

ELEVEN

96 **Spink's remained his main pipeline:** Douglas Latchford to Anthony Gardner, letter, 7 July 1989.

97 **As he put together:** Katya Kazakina, "What Will Become of a Tycoon's Art Gems?," *New York Times*, December 20, 2020, nytimes.com/2020/12/20/arts /design/solow-art-museum-auction.html.

97 **In November 1989 alone:** Peter Watson, *Sotheby's: The Inside Story* (Random House, 1997), 116.

97 **more than $40 million:** Chris Romoser, "SOLD: Picasso's Au Lapin Agile Fetches $40.7 Million," *Palm Beach Daily News*, November 17, 1989, 1.

97 **Though some warned:** Watson, *Sotheby's*, 99–100.

97 **The following year, Taubman:** Michael Gross, *Rogues' Gallery: The Secret Story of the Lust, Lies, Greed, and Betrayals That Made the Metropolitan Museum of Art* (Broadway Books, 2009), 435.

97 **Kravis was one:** Gross, *Rogues' Gallery*, 457–58.

98 **In 1988, Sotheby's:** Tess Davis, "Supply and Demand: Exposing the Illicit Trade in Cambodian Antiquities Through a Study of Sotheby's Auction House," *Crime, Law and Social Change* 56, no. 2 (September 2011): 161–64.

98 **In one of its first:** Geraldine Norman, "Five-Headed Khmer Figure Sold for Record £319,000," *Independent*, November 15, 1988, 3; and Bust of Five-Headed Shiva, ca. mid-10th century, stone, 31 ½ in. (80 cm) high, Metropolitan Museum of Art, New York, object no. 1993.387.1, archived May 21, 2024, at web.archive.org/web/20240521133837/https://www.metmuseum.org/art/col lection/search/38620.

98 **At the Musée Guimet:** Simon de Bruxelles and Philippe Flandrin, "Row over Sotheby's Sale of Stolen Khmer Statues," *Observer*, November 27, 1988, 8.

99 **"had we received":** Bruxelles and Flandrin, "Row over Sotheby's Sale."

99 **But unlike the parts:** Holland Cotter, "A Watershed Event at the Met," *New York Times*, April 10, 1994, nytimes.com/1994/04/10/arts/art-view-a-watershed -event-at-the-met.html.

100 **So Lerner began planning:** *Annual Report of the Trustees of the Metropolitan Museum of Art*, 1988–1989 (Metropolitan Museum of Art, 1989), 17.

100 **Two heads from Koh Ker statues:** "Metropolitan Museum of Art to Return Two Khmer Sculptures to Cambodia," Metropolitan Museum of Art, archived March 18, 2025, at web.archive.org/web/20250318235005/https://www.met-museum.org/press-releases/cambodian-returns-2013-news.

100 **As preparations advanced:** Two Kneeling Attendants, 10th century, stone, head (1987.410) attached to body (1992.390.1): 46 ¼ × 26 × 27 ½ in. (117.5 × 66 × 69.9 cm), head (1989.100) attached to body (1992.390.2): 48 ¼ × 23 ½ × 31 in. (122.6 × 59.7 × 78.7 cm), Metropolitan Museum of Art, New York, archived May 13, 2025, web.archive.org/web/20250513045238/https://www.metmuseum .org/art/collection/search/904942.

100 **Restored, they looked:** Éric Bourdonneau, "Statues et linteaux du style de Koh Ker au Metropolitan Museum of Art de New York" (École Française d'Extrême-Orient, March 2013), 2–12; Éric Bourdonneau with Phin Samnang,

"The Duel Between Bhima and Duryodhana and the Sculpted Group of the Western Gopura I of Prasat Chen at Koh Ker" (École Française d'Extrême-Orient, July 2012), 25; and Chea Socheat, "Enquête de terrain sur la disparition de sculptures dans les temples de Koh Ker" (Musée National du Cambodge; École Française d'Extrême-Orient, April 2012), 2–3.

100 **Cambodia's civil war continued:** Steven Erlanger, "Loss of Border Battle to Khmer Rouge Signals Trouble for Cambodian Army," *New York Times*, August 20, 1989, nytimes.com/1989/08/20/world/loss-of-border-battle-to-khmer-rouge-signals-trouble-for-cambodian-army.html.

100 **In the largest settlement:** Ashley Thompson, "Oh Cambodia! Poems from the Border," *New Literary History* 24, no. 3 (Summer 1993): 533.

101 **To discourage the notion:** Barbara Crossette, "Trapped at Thai Camps, Cambodians Despair," *New York Times*, September 21, 1987, nytimes.com/1987/09/21/world/trapped-at-thai-camps-cambodians-despair.html.

101 **The Soviet Union no:** Steven Erlanger, "With Vietnamese Out, Cambodia Faces Bitter Fight," *New York Times*, September 27, 1989, nytimes.com/1989/09/27/world/with-vietnamese-out-cambodia-faces-bitter-fight.html.

101 **But there was no way:** Clifford Krauss, "U.S. Weighs a Shift on Cambodia Policy," *New York Times*, July 8, 1990, nytimes.com/1990/07/08/world/us-weighs-a-shift-on-cambodia-policy.html.

101 **China, which had generously:** Clifford Krauss, "U.S. Says China Backs Halt in Weapons to Khmer Rouge," *New York Times*, July 21, 1990, nytimes.com/1990/07/21/world/us-says-china-backs-halt-in-weapons-to-khmer-rouge.html.

TWELVE

103 **More than a decade after:** David Chandler, *A History of Cambodia*, 3rd ed. (Silkworm Books, 2003), 235–37.

103 **Every month, hundreds:** Eric Stover, *Land Mines in Cambodia: The Coward's War* (Human Rights Watch; Physicians for Human Rights, 1991), 59, phr.org/our-work/resources/cowards-war.

103 **As a result of Pol:** Stover, *Land Mines in Cambodia*, 62–63.

103 **Virtually no Westerners:** *Safeguarding and Development of Angkor* (UNESCO, 1993), 11–12, unesdoc.unesco.org/ark:/48223/pf0000097228.

104 **In faculty lounges:** World Monuments Fund, "Excerpts from the Draft Report on 'The Conservation and Preservation of the Angkor Sanctuary, Cambodia,'" presented at the International Round Table of Experts on the Preservation of the Angkor Monuments, Bangkok, June 5–8, 1990, 3, unesdoc.unesco.org/ark:/48223/pf0000086373.

104 **The new teams encountered:** See, for example, Joel R. Charny and Anne E. Goldfeld, "Cambodia: Don't Look Away," *New York Times*, May 10, 1990, nytimes.com/1990/05/10/opinion/cambodia-don-t-look-away.html; Steven Erlanger,

"No Haven from Agony for Cambodians," *New York Times*, May 2, 1991, ny times.com/1991/05/02/world/cambodia-s-voiceless-a-special-report-no-haven -from-agony-for-cambodians.html; and Philip Shenon, "Cambodian Refugees Face Minefields on Their Return," *New York Times*, November 10, 1991, ny times.com/1991/11/10/world/cambodian-refugees-face-minefields-on-their -return.html.

105 **Remarkably, more than twenty:** World Monuments Fund, "'Conservation and Preservation of the Angkor Sanctuary,'" 3–8.

106 **"More damage was apparent":** World Monuments Fund, "'Conservation and Preservation of the Angkor Sanctuary,'" 8.

106 **In October 1991:** Gareth Evans, "Cambodia: The Peace Process—and After," presentation to the Cambodia Roundtable, Monash University, November 2, 2012, archived July 15, 2024, at web.archive.org/web/20240715012712/https:// www.gevans.org/speeches/speech498.html.

106 **the following year, UNTAC:** Elizabeth Becker, *When the War Was Over: Cambodia and the Khmer Rouge Revolution*, rev. ed. (PublicAffairs, 1998), 512.

106 **The Khmer Rouge still:** Philip Short, *Pol Pot: Anatomy of a Nightmare* (Henry Holt and Company, 2004), 418–31.

107 **In fact, in the run-up:** Steven Erlanger, "Khmer Rouge Get More China Arms," *New York Times*, January 1, 1991, nytimes.com/1991/01/01/world/khmer -rouge-get-more-china-arms.html.

107 **They soon reneged:** Becker, *When the War Was Over*, 513.

107 **An incident in May 1992:** Sebastian Strangio, *Hun Sen's Cambodia* (Yale University Press, 2014), 53–54.

107 **one night in February:** Charles P. Wallace, "Soldiers Storm Cambodian City Mitterrand Is Scheduled to Visit," *Los Angeles Times*, February 11, 1993, A6.

107 **"commando units of unknown origin":** *Safeguarding and Development of Angkor*, 29.

108 **The gunmen removed:** Philip Shenon, "11 Valuable Historic Statues Fall to Thieves in Cambodia," *New York Times*, February 13, 1993, nytimes.com /1993/02/13/world/11-valuable-historic-statues-fall-to-thieves-in-cambodia .html.

108 **Just two months later:** "Cambodia Temples Plagued by Organized Art Thefts," *Miami Herald*, May 23, 1993, 6A.

108 **UN officials tried:** *Safeguarding and Development of Angkor*, 29.

108 **One of its first acts:** Decl. of Matthew Rendall at 26, United States of America v. A 10th Century Cambodian Sandstone Sculpture, Currently Located at Sotheby's in New York, New York, No. 12 Civ. 2600 (GBD) (S.D.N.Y. August 20, 2012).

108 **One such site:** "The Archeological Complex of Banteay Chhmar," World Heritage Tentative List, UNESCO World Heritage Convention, archived July 18, 2024, at web.archive.org/web/20240718232049/https://whc.unesco.org/en/ten tativelists/6456.

109 **an opposition leader named:** Christophe Pottier, "Rapport sur le temple de Banteay Chmar LL 816 (Cambodge)" (École Française d'Extrême-Orient, September 1992), shs.hal.science/halshs-01976139v1.

109 **"We can only be":** Pottier, "Rapport sur le temple de Banteay Chmar," pt. 4.3.

110 **After seven years of preparation:** Allan Schwartzman, "The Metropolitan Plays Its Asia Card," *Los Angeles Times*, April 13, 1994, latimes.com/archives /la-xpm-1994-04-13-ca-45295-story.html.

111 **Chest-beating claims like:** Thomas Hoving, *Making the Mummies Dance* (Simon & Schuster, 1993), 102.

111 **A leading critic hailed:** Holland Cotter, "A Watershed Event at the Met," *New York Times*, April 10, 1994, nytimes.com/1994/04/10/arts/art-view-a-watershed -event-at-the-met.html.

111 **The Met, for its part:** Schwartzman, "Metropolitan Plays Its Asia Card."

111 **The two kneeling:** Tom Mashberg and Ralph Blumenthal, "The Met Will Return a Pair of Statues to Cambodia," *New York Times*, May 3, 2013, nytimes .com/2013/05/04/arts/design/the-met-to-return-statues-to-cambodia.html.

THIRTEEN

113 **Toek Tik had worked:** Tom Mashberg, "He Sold Away His People's Heritage. He's in the Jungle to Get It Back," *New York Times*, November 21, 2021, ny times.com/2021/11/21/arts/design/toek-tik-cambodian-artifacts.html; and Simon Mackenzie and Tess Davis, "Temple Looting in Cambodia: Anatomy of a Statue Trafficking Network," *British Journal of Criminology* 54, no. 5 (September 2014): 731–33.

113 **Virtually everyone in rural areas:** "Landmine Monitor—Cambodia Country Report," Landmine & Cluster Munition Monitor, archived March 22, 2023, at web.archive.org/web/20230322064557/http://archives.the-monitor.org/index .php/publications/display?url=lm/1999/english/cambodia.html.

114 **One of Toek Tik's uncles:** Mackenzie and Davis, "Temple Looting in Cambodia," 732.

115 **Unlike many who lived:** Tom Mashberg, "Cambodia Says Looter Helping It Reclaim Stolen Artifacts Has Died," *New York Times*, December 5, 2021, ny times.com/2021/12/05/arts/design/cambodian-effort-to-find-artifacts-wont -end-with-informants-death.html.

115 **UNTAC, the largely impotent:** David Chandler, *A History of Cambodia*, 3rd ed. (Silkworm Books, 2003), 239–40.

115 **When neither of the:** Sebastian Strangio, *Hun Sen's Cambodia* (Yale University Press, 2014), 58–59.

116 **time of the election:** Philip Short, *Pol Pot: Anatomy of a Nightmare* (Henry Holt and Company, 2004), 431.

116 **by 1996, when one:** Chandler, *History of Cambodia*, 242.

116 **Khmer Rouge ambushes:** Philip Sherwell, "Mine-Clearance Expert Is Taken at Gunpoint," *Daily Telegraph*, March 27, 1996, 10.

116 **Pol Pot was still:** Strangio, *Hun Sen's Cambodia*, 76.

116 **The decrease in violence:** Mashberg, "He Sold Away His People's Heritage"; and Mackenzie and Davis, "Temple Looting in Cambodia," 731–33.

116 **The government had little:** Seth Mydans, "Treasures Trickle Back to a Plundered Cambodia," *New York Times*, December 20, 1996, nytimes.com/1996/12/20/world/treasures-trickle-back-to-a-plundered-cambodia.html.

117 **His teams brought:** Mackenzie and Davis, "Temple Looting in Cambodia," 733–34; and Compl. for Forfeiture at 6, United States of America v. A 10th Century Cambodian Sandstone Sculpture Depicting Skanda on a Peacock, No. 21 Civ. 6065 (S.D.N.Y. July 15, 2021).

117 **At each step:** See, for example, Compl. for Forfeiture at 8, *A 10th Century Cambodian Sandstone Sculpture Depicting Skanda on a Peacock*.

117 **Toek Tik and those who worked:** Mackenzie and Davis, "Temple Looting in Cambodia," 733–34; and Compl. for Forfeiture at 5–8, *A 10th Century Cambodian Sandstone Sculpture Depicting Skanda on a Peacock*.

120 **One of the missing:** Claude Jacques and Sébastien Cavalier, *Rapport de mission au temple de Banteay Chmar, 15–18 janvier 1999* (UNESCO, 1999), 3–4.

120 **The temple was so remote:** Seth Mydans, "Raiders of Lost Art Loot Temples in Cambodia," *New York Times*, April 1, 1999, nytimes.com/1999/04/01/world/raiders-of-lost-art-loot-temples-in-cambodia.html.

121 **In 1997, isolated and:** Chandler, *History of Cambodia*, 242.

121 **Soon, another member:** Short, *Pol Pot*, 440–41.

122 **"Crush, crush, crush":** Strangio, *Hun Sen's Cambodia*, 80; and Dale Keiger, "In Search of Brother Number One," *Johns Hopkins Magazine*, November 1997, pages.jh.edu/jhumag/1197web/brother.html.

122 **"Look at me":** Nate Thayer, "Day of Reckoning," *Far Eastern Economic Review*, October 30, 1997, bannedthought.net/Cambodia/PolPot/NateThayerInterviewWithPolPot-971030.pdf.

122 **Barely anyone came:** Seth Mydans, "At Cremation of Pol Pot, No Tears Shed," *New York Times*, April 19, 1998, nytimes.com/1998/04/19/world/at-cremation-of-pol-pot-no-tears-shed.html.

122 **Through interviews with local:** "The Raiders of Banteay Chmar," *Phnom Penh Post*, archived September 16, 2013, at web.archive.org/web/20130916025638/https://www.phnompenhpost.com/national/raiders-banteay-chmar; and Masha Lafont, *Pillaging Cambodia: The Illicit Traffic in Khmer Art* (McFarland & Company, 2004), 52–55.

123 **Opposition figures began:** Strangio, *Hun Sen's Cambodia*, 81–83.

123 **"Saddam Hun Sen":** William Branigin and R. Jeffrey Smith, "Saddam Hun Sen?," *Washington Post*, July 20, 1997, washingtonpost.com/archive/opinions/1997/07/20/saddam-hun-sen/d50fbf7d-d8d9-4342-85fd-6191a59ff798.

123 **A former Khmer Rouge:** See, for example, Seth Mydans, "Under Prodding, 2 Apologize for Cambodian Anguish," *New York Times*, December 30, 1998, nytimes.com/1998/12/30/world/under-prodding-2-apologize-for-cambodian -anguish.html.

123 **The only direct:** Lafont, *Pillaging Cambodia*, 55–56; and "Raiders of Banteay Chmar," *Phnom Penh Post*.

124 **The area around Koh:** Dany Long, "PA Field Trip Report: Koh Ker Village, Srayang Commune, Koulen District, Preah Vihear Province (12–18 May 2013)," pp. 17–18, Documentation Center of Cambodia Archives.

124 **Like Angkor, Koh Ker:** Ministry of Culture and Fine Arts of Cambodia, "Koh Ker: Nomination Dossier," submission to the UNESCO World Heritage List, January 2021, iii–ix.

124 **The worst looting:** Éric Bourdonneau with Phin Samnang, "The Duel Between Bhima and Duryodhana and the Sculpted Group of the Western Gopura I of Prasat Chen at Koh Ker" (École Française d'Extrême-Orient, July 2012), 25.

125 **There, in a towering:** Cambodian Department of Antiquities, *The Return of Our Ancestors' Souls* (Ministry of Culture and Fine Arts of Cambodia, 2024), 70–77.

125 **After Toek Tik pulled:** Standing Female Deity, 10th century, stone, 61 ½ × 10 ¼ × 20 ½ in. (156.2 × 26 × 52.1 cm), Metropolitan Museum of Art, New York, object no. 2003.605, archived January 14, 2022, at web.archive.org/web /20220114102412/https://www.metmuseum.org/art/collection/search/72387.

125 **The sun was low:** Compl. for Forfeiture at 6, *A 10th Century Cambodian Sandstone Sculpture Depicting Skanda on a Peacock*.

125 **On surviving pillars:** *Prasat Krachap–Koh Ker: Epigraphic Survey No. 1* (Hungarian Southeast Asian Research Institute, 2020), 9.

125 **They began to dig:** See, for example, Cambodian Department of Antiquities, *Return of Our Ancestors' Souls*, 50; and Compl. for Forfeiture at 6, *A 10th Century Cambodian Sandstone Sculpture Depicting Skanda on a Peacock*.

125 **about three and a half:** Emma C. Bunker and Douglas Latchford, *Adoration and Glory: The Golden Age of Khmer Art* (Art Media Resources, 2004), 142–43.

126 **As they dug:** Bunker and Latchford, *Adoration and Glory*, 146–48.

126 **After handing the works:** Compl. for Forfeiture at 6, *A 10th Century Cambodian Sandstone Sculpture Depicting Skanda on a Peacock*.

126 **The two sculptures, which:** Compl. for Forfeiture at 8, *A 10th Century Cambodian Sandstone Sculpture Depicting Skanda on a Peacock*.

FOURTEEN

129 **At one edition of:** "Latchford Classic (2006)," ThaiBody, accessed December 5, 2024, www.thaibody.com/post/2006/11/11/646eze14.html.

130 **Latchford and Charoenrith stepped:** Emma C. Bunker and Douglas A. J. Latchford, "Jayavarman IV's Grandiose Capital at Koh Ker and the Recovery of an Important Lost Sculpture," *Arts of Asia*, May/June 2003, 77–85.

130 **A substantial number:** "Koh Ker Social Development and Tourism Project: Final Report," Heritage Watch, January 2009, 3.

131 **The obvious highlight:** Ministry of Culture and Fine Arts of Cambodia, "Koh Ker: Nomination Dossier," submission to the UNESCO World Heritage List, January 2021, 26, 32 .

131 **Latchford declined to scale:** Ministry of Culture and Fine Arts of Cambodia, "Koh Ker: Nomination Dossier," 67, 91.

132 **She'd married as well:** Virginia Culver, "Sugar Exec Let Others Get In on His Sweet Life," *Denver Post*, June 6, 2005, denverpost.com/2005/06/06/sugar-exec -let-others-get-in-on-his-sweet-life.

133 **The authors provided:** Emma C. Bunker and Douglas Latchford, *Adoration and Glory: The Golden Age of Khmer Art* (Art Media Resources, 2004), 142.

133 **The same went for:** Bunker and Latchford, *Adoration and Glory*, 146.

133 **which they called Uma:** Bunker and Latchford, *Adoration and Glory*, 156.

133 **They tried to justify:** Bunker and Latchford, *Adoration and Glory*, xviii.

133 **The institution lacked:** Bunker and Latchford, *Adoration and Glory*, xv; and "A Man of Ancient Torsos and Modern Muscles," *Phnom Penh Post*, January 11, 2008, phnompenhpost.com/national/man-ancient-torsos-and-modern -muscles.

134 **In an article on:** Michelle Vachon, "In Pursuit of Provenance," *Cambodia Daily*, May 29, 2004, web.archive.org/web/20240221040804/https://english .cambodiadaily.com/news/in-pursuit-of-provenance-906.

135 **Clark had more or less:** See, for example, Michael Lewis, *The New New Thing: A Silicon Valley Story* (W. W. Norton & Company, 2014), 165–70.

135 **In particular, he had:** "Private Properties," *Wall Street Journal*, updated October 21, 2011, https://www.wsj.com/articles/SB1000142405297020448530457664 1340686831376; and Julie Zeveloff and Meredith Galante, "House of the Day: Billionaire Netscape Founder Jim Clark's Miami Penthouse Is for Sale at $27 Million," *Business Insider*, December 1, 2011, businessinsider.com/jim-clark -netscape-miami-for-sale-2011-11.

135 **After the mass looting in 1998:** Compl. for Forfeiture at 4–5, United States of America v. A Late 12th Century Khmer Sandstone Sculpture Depicting Standing Prajnaparamita, No. 21 Civ. 9217 (S.D.N.Y. November 8, 2021).

136 **His looting days:** Tom Mashberg, "He Sold Away His People's Heritage. He's in the Jungle to Get It Back," *New York Times*, November 21, 2021, nytimes .com/2021/11/21/arts/design/toek-tik-cambodian-artifacts.html.

136 **He sold his first:** Compl. for Forfeiture at 12, United States of America v. A Late 12th Century Bayon-Style Sandstone Sculpture Depicting Eight-Armed Avalokiteshvara, No. 22 Civ. 229 (S.D.N.Y. January 11, 2022).

137 **Soon he was offering:** Compl. for Forfeiture at 13–15, *A Late 12th Century Bayon-Style Sandstone Sculpture.*

137 **They'd reassembled it:** Bertrand Porte, "Curieuses sculptures khmères," *Arts Asiatiques* 59, no. 1 (2004): 176–77.

137 **Later evidence suggests:** Chea Socheat, "Enquête de terrain sur la disparition de sculptures dans les temples de Koh Ker" (Musée National du Cambodge; École Française d'Extrême-Orient, April 2012), 2.

137 **Latchford's solution was:** Compl. for Forfeiture at 14–15, *A Late 12th Century Bayon-Style Sandstone Sculpture.*

138 **To sidestep the import:** Compl. for Forfeiture at 14–17, *A Late 12th Century Bayon-Style Sandstone Sculpture.*

138 **In April of that year:** Civil Compl. for Forfeiture at 6, United States of America v. Any and All Funds Up to and Including the Sum of $12 Million Contained in Rathbones Investment Management Portfolio 702461, Containing Accounts 5870246110, 5870246120, 5870246121, and 5870246180, No. 23 Civ. 5286 (S.D.N.Y. June 22, 2023).

FIFTEEN

139 **In the second half:** Sharon Waxman, *Loot: The Battle over the Stolen Treasures of the Ancient World* (Henry Holt and Company, 2008), 151; Jason Felch and Ralph Frammolino, *Chasing Aphrodite: The Hunt for Looted Antiquities at the World's Richest Museum* (Houghton Mifflin Harcourt, 2011), 102; Roger Atwood, *Stealing History: Tomb Raiders, Smugglers, and the Looting of the Ancient World* (St. Martin's Press, 2004), 158, Kindle.

139 **In 1998, the Clinton:** Office of the Special Envoy for Holocaust Issues, "Washington Conference Principles on Nazi-Confiscated Art," US Department of State, accessed October 11, 2024, state.gov/washington-conference-principles -on-nazi-confiscated-art.

140 **In the US, this was:** Catherine Hickley, "Nations Agree to Refine Pact That Guides the Return of Nazi-Looted Art," *New York Times*, March 5, 2024, nytimes.com/2024/03/05/arts/nations-agree-to-refine-pact-that-guides-the -return-of-nazi-looted-art.html.

140 **Manhattan District Attorney Robert:** Judith H. Dobrzynski, "District Attorney Enters Dispute over Artworks," *New York Times*, January 8, 1998, nytimes .com/1998/01/08/nyregion/district-attorney-enters-dispute-over-artworks.html.

140 **Just hours later, his federal:** Judith H. Dobrzynski, "Strategy in Schiele Art Case Questioned," *New York Times*, October 12, 1999, nytimes.com/1999/10 /12/arts/strategy-in-schiele-art-case-questioned.html.

141 **First passed in 1934:** Stephen K. Urice, "Between Rocks and Hard Places: Unprovenanced Antiquities and the National Stolen Property Act," *New Mexico Law Review* 40, no. 1 (2010): 133.

NOTES

141 **Beginning in the 1970s:** Urice, "Between Rocks and Hard Places," 131.

142 **They also drew on another:** Greg Donahue, "Crime of the Centuries," *New York*, February 15, 2023, nymag.com/intelligencer/article/michael-steinhardt-antiquities-stolen-artifacts.html.

142 **Schultz was convicted in:** Celestine Bohlen, "Antiquities Dealer Is Sentenced to Prison," *New York Times*, June 12, 2002, nytimes.com/2002/06/12/arts/antiquities-dealer-is-sentenced-to-prison.html.

142 **The conviction held up:** "Antiquities Dealer Frederick Schultz Case," Archaeological Institute of America, June 25, 2003, archaeological.org/antiquities-dealer-frederick-schultz-case.

142 **The same year that Schultz:** Felch and Frammolino, *Chasing Aphrodite*, 227, 259.

142 **"If you were a collecting":** Waxman, *Loot*, 194–95.

143 **Under pressure from Italy:** Randy Kennedy, "Thomas Hoving, Remaker of the Met, Dies at 78," *New York Times*, December 10, 2009, nytimes.com/2009/12/11/arts/design/11hoving.html.

143 **As Hoving knew but strenuously:** Atwood, *Stealing History*, 148.

143 **His successor, the aristocratic:** "Statement by the Metropolitan Museum of Art on Its Agreement with Italian Ministry of Culture," Metropolitan Museum of Art, February 20, 2006, metmuseum.org/press/news/2006/statement-by-the-metropolitan-museum-of-art-on-its-agreement-with-italian-ministry-of-culture.

143 **The governments and advocates:** See, for example, Waxman, *Loot*, 372–75.

144 **Just after the announcement:** "Museums and Cultural Property," C-SPAN, April 17, 2006, c-span.org/video/?192075-1/museums-cultural-property.

145 **Hun Sen and other senior:** *Hostile Takeover: The Corporate Empire of Cambodia's Ruling Family* (Global Witness, 2016), gw.hacdn.io/media/documents/Hostile_Takeover_Cambodia_report_July_16.pdf.

145 **His government had dragged:** Sebastian Strangio, *Hun Sen's Cambodia* (Yale University Press, 2014), 254–56.

146 **The court would ultimately:** Seth Mydans, "16 Years, 3 Convictions: The Khmer Rouge Trials Come to an End," *New York Times*, September 22, 2022, nytimes.com/2022/09/22/world/asia/cambodia-khmer-rouge-tribunal.html.

146 **summing up his philosophy:** Seth Mydans, "Under Prodding, 2 Apologize for Cambodian Anguish," *New York Times*, December 30, 1998, nytimes.com/1998/12/30/world/under-prodding-2-apologize-for-cambodian-anguish.html.

146 **To tap the new:** Sealed Indictment at 9–13, United States of America v. Douglas Latchford, No. 19 Crim. 748 (S.D.N.Y. October 17, 2019).

147 **Soon, Latchford-sourced objects:** Julie Zeveloff and Meredith Galante, "House of the Day: Billionaire Netscape Founder Jim Clark's Miami Penthouse Is for Sale at $27 Million," *Business Insider*, December 1, 2011, businessinsider.com/jim-clark-netscape-miami-for-sale-2011-11; and Rachel Quigley, "The 'Mack

Daddy' Penthouse: World's Most Expensive Beach Apartment Sells for $21.5M," *Daily Mail*, December 10, 2011, dailymail.co.uk/news/article-2072331 /Worlds-expensive-beach-penthouse-sold-21-5m.html.

147 **In one of the bedrooms:** Compl. for Forfeiture at 4 and Ex. E, United States of America v. A Late 12th Century Bayon-Style Sandstone Sculpture Depicting Eight-Armed Avalokiteshvara, No. 22 Civ. 229 (S.D.N.Y. January 11, 2022).

147 **In the airy kitchen:** Compl. for Forfeiture at 7 and Ex. Z, *A Late 12th Century Bayon-Style Sandstone Sculpture.*

147 **In the dining room:** Compl. for Forfeiture at 4 and Ex. B, *A Late 12th Century Bayon-Style Sandstone Sculpture.*

147 **And under the twenty-foot:** Compl. for Forfeiture at 4 and Ex. D, *A Late 12th Century Bayon-Style Sandstone Sculpture.*

147 **All told, between 2003:** Tom Mashberg, "Netscape Founder Gives Up $35 Million in Art Said to Be Stolen," *New York Times*, January 12, 2022, nytimes .com/2022/01/12/arts/design/james-clark-cambodian-antiquities.html.

148 **It was a twelfth-century:** Compl. for Forfeiture at 16 and Ex. DD, *A Late 12th Century Bayon-Style Sandstone Sculpture.*

SIXTEEN

149 **Latchford had chosen:** "Gold and Bodybuilders," *ThaiBody*, December 18, 2007, thaibody.com/photos/?sel=ab&sid=306&s=697f31b39c120bea0d95112b654 84d3f.

149 **This one, *Khmer Gold*:** Emma C. Bunker and Douglas A. J. Latchford, *Khmer Gold: Gifts for the Gods* (Art Media Resources, 2008), abebooks.com/97815888 60972/Khmer-Gold-Emma-Bunker-Douglas-1588860973/plp.

149 **The ancient Khmer were believed:** Emma C. Bunker and Douglas Latchford, *Adoration and Glory: The Golden Age of Khmer Art* (Art Media Resources, 2004), 435–36; and Helen Ibbitson Jessup and Thierry Zéphir, eds., *Sculpture of Angkor and Ancient Cambodia: Millennium of Glory* (Thames & Hudson, 1997), 194.

150 **Thanks to his financial support:** Alan Parkhouse, "A Rare Find," *Bangkok Post*, December 9, 2010, ki-media.blogspot.com/2010/09/rare-find-rare-khmer -artefacts-to.html.

150 **Less than a year after:** Douglas Latchford, "Gold of the Gods," interview by Louise Nicholson, *Apollo*, November 2008, 32–36.

151 **Though Bunker had no:** Compl. for Forfeiture at 14, United States of America v. A Late 12th Century Bayon-Style Sandstone Sculpture Depicting Eight-Armed Avalokiteshvara, No. 22 Civ. 229 (S.D.N.Y. January 11, 2022).

151 **Her husband of nearly:** Virginia Culver, "Sugar Exec Let Others Get In on His Sweet Life," *Denver Post*, June 6, 2005, denverpost.com/2005/06/06/sugar-exec -let-others-get-in-on-his-sweet-life.

152 **"Oh dear," Latchford wrote:** Douglas Latchford to Emma Bunker et al., email, 6 December 2007 (emphasis in the original).

152 **Bunker replied with her:** Emma Bunker to Douglas Latchford, email, 6 December 2007 (emphasis in the original).

152 **Latchford appeared to genuinely:** Emma C. Bunker and Douglas A. J. Latchford, *Khmer Bronzes: New Interpretations of the Past* (Art Media Resources, 2011), amazon.com/Khmer-Bronzes-New-Interpretations-Past/dp/1588861112.

152 **She was uninvolved in:** "ADORATION—The Siamese Male Physique," Newswit, February 21, 2025, newswit.com/en/j05a7uk020fqwb4r1sgawt7s8chm7vha.

153 **The gold standard was:** Patty Gerstenblith, "The Meaning of 1970 for the Acquisition of Archaeological Objects," *Journal of Field Archaeology* 38, no. 4 (November 2013): 364–65.

153 **That's what he'd done:** Compl. for Forfeiture at 12, *A Late 12th Century Bayon-Style Sandstone Sculpture*.

153 **"Went through all":** Emma Bunker to Douglas Latchford, email, 28 June 2009.

154 **Though it was now:** "Koh Ker Social Development and Tourism Project: Final Report," Heritage Watch, January 2009, 3.

155 **About a third of:** Bunker and Latchford, *Adoration and Glory*, 149–51.

156 **He decided to produce:** Simon Warrack, "Report Concerning the Statuary of Prasat Chen in Koh Ker" (German Apsara Conservation Project, May 2007).

156 **The Norton Simon had:** Tom Mashberg and Ralph Blumenthal, "Christie's to Return Cambodian Statue," *New York Times*, May 6, 2014, nytimes.com/2014/05/07/arts/design/christies-to-return-cambodian-statue.html.

157 **At the time, only:** Decl. of Matthew Rendall at 37, United States of America v. A 10th Century Cambodian Sandstone Sculpture, Currently Located at Sotheby's in New York, New York, No. 12 Civ. 2600 (GBD) (S.D.N.Y. August 20, 2012).

157 **Rather than serving as:** Éric Bourdonneau, "Koh Ker: Prasat Chen and Its Sculptures," *World Heritage Review* 68 (2013): 95–96, unesdoc.unesco.org/ark:/48223/pf0000221079.

158 **Bourdonneau's hypothesis was:** Éric Bourdonneau, "Sculpted Groups of the Eastern Gopura I in Prasat Chen (Koh Ker, Cambodia) and Khmer Art Collections of American Museums" (École Française d'Extrême-Orient; APSARA Authority, September 2014), 18–19; and Éric Bourdonneau with Phin Samnang, "The Duel Between Bhima and Duryodhana and the Sculpted Group of the Western Gopura I of Prasat Chen at Koh Ker" (École Française d'Extrême-Orient, July 2012), 4–6.

158 **In the 1950s, French:** Eric Bourdonneau, "Sculpted Groups of the Eastern Gopura," 5–6.

SEVENTEEN

160 **The five-foot-tall statue:** Verified Compl. at 9–10, United States of America v. A 10th Century Cambodian Sandstone Sculpture, Currently Located at Sotheby's in New York, New York, No. 12 Civ. 2600 (GBD) (S.D.N.Y. April 4, 2012).

161 **In the spring of 2010:** Decl. of Peter G. Neiman in Supp. of Claimants' Mot. to Dismiss at Ex. 1, June 5, 2012, *A 10th Century Cambodian Sandstone Sculpture.*

161 **According to a study:** Tess Davis, "Supply and Demand: Exposing the Illicit Trade in Cambodian Antiquities Through a Study of Sotheby's Auction House," *Crime, Law and Social Change* 56, no. 2 (September 2011): 166–67.

162 **In May 2010:** Decl. of Peter G. Neiman in Opp'n to Plaintiff's Mot. for Leave to Amend at Ex. 2, December 3, 2012, *A 10th Century Cambodian Sandstone Sculpture.*

162 **Ghosh-Mazumdar asked:** Decl. of Peter G. Neiman in Opp'n to Plaintiff's Mot. for Leave to Amend at Ex. 2, *A 10th Century Cambodian Sandstone Sculpture* (emphasis in the original).

162 **"I had the sculpture":** Decl. of Peter G. Neiman in Opp'n to Plaintiff's Mot. for Leave to Amend at Ex. 3, *A 10th Century Cambodian Sandstone Sculpture* (emphasis in the original).

162 **"to sign to say":** Decl. of Peter G. Neiman in Opp'n to Plaintiff's Mot. for Leave to Amend at Ex. 2, *A 10th Century Cambodian Sandstone Sculpture.*

162 **His business and writing partner:** Decl. of Peter G. Neiman in Opp'n to Plaintiff's Mot. for Leave to Amend at Ex. 1, *pt. 2, A 10th Century Cambodian Sandstone Sculpture.*

163 **Latchford had then collaborated:** Verified Am. Compl. at 7–9, April 9, 2013, *A 10th Century Cambodian Sandstone Sculpture.*

163 **Another aspect of marketing:** Decl. of Peter G. Neiman in Supp. of Claimants' Mot. to Dismiss at Ex. 1, *A 10th Century Cambodian Sandstone Sculpture.*

163 **Given the resemblance:** Douglas Latchford to Anthony Gardner, letter, 7 July 1989.

164 **"I think things could":** Emma Bunker to Douglas Latchford, email, 1 June 2010, 5:10 p.m.

164 **Later in the morning:** Decl. of Peter G. Neiman in Opp'n to Plaintiff's Mot. for Leave to Amend at Ex. 3, *A 10th Century Cambodian Sandstone Sculpture.*

164 **An hour after that:** Emma Bunker to Douglas Latchford, email, 1 June 2010, 8:25 p.m.

164 **"We all need to stick":** Emma Bunker to Douglas Latchford, email, 2 June 2010, 10:30 a.m.

164 **Then, a few weeks:** Decl. of Peter G. Neiman in Supp. of Claimants' Mot. to Dismiss at Ex. 1, *A 10th Century Cambodian Sandstone Sculpture.*

165 **Bunker also urged:** Decl. of Peter G. Neiman in Supp. of Claimants' Mot. to Dismiss at Ex. 2, *A 10th Century Cambodian Sandstone Sculpture.*

165 **But after consulting:** Decl. of Peter G. Neiman in Supp. of Claimants' Mot. to Dismiss at Ex. 3, *A 10th Century Cambodian Sandstone Sculpture.*

165 **The official didn't reply:** Verified Am. Compl. at 20, *A 10th Century Cambodian Sandstone Sculpture.*

165 **She and her team:** Sotheby's, *Indian and Southeast Asian Works of Art* (Sotheby's, 2011).

EIGHTEEN

169 **He worked through:** Éric Bourdonneau, *Un trésor du patrimoine cambodgien en vente à Sotheby's* (École Française d'Extrême-Orient, 2011).

170 **On March 21:** Decl. of Peter G. Neiman in Supp. of Claimants' Mot. for Judgment on the Pleadings and for a Stay of Discovery at Ex. 1, United States of America v. A 10th Century Cambodian Sandstone Sculpture, Currently Located at Sotheby's in New York, New York, No. 12 Civ. 2600 (GBD) (S.D.N.Y. September 9, 2013).

171 **On March 22:** Decl. of Peter G. Neiman in Supp. of Claimants' Mot. for Judgment on the Pleadings and for a Stay of Discovery at Ex. 2, *A 10th Century Cambodian Sandstone Sculpture.*

173 **"I am unable to do":** Decl. of Peter G. Neiman in Supp. of Claimants' Mot. for Judgment on the Pleadings and for a Stay of Discovery at Ex. 2, *A 10th Century Cambodian Sandstone Sculpture.*

173 **After deliberating over:** Decl. of Peter G. Neiman in Supp. of Claimants' Mot. to Dismiss at Ex. 7, *A 10th Century Cambodian Sandstone Sculpture.*

173 **The Duryodhana auction:** Sotheby's, *Indian and Southeast Asian Works of Art* (Sotheby's, 2011).

174 **About a week later:** Decl. of Peter G. Neiman in Supp. of Claimants' Mot. for Judgment on the Pleadings and for a Stay of Discovery at Ex. 4, *A 10th Century Cambodian Sandstone Sculpture.*

175 **He'd been digging deeper:** Decl. of Peter G. Neiman in Supp. of Claimants' Mot. for Judgment on the Pleadings and for a Stay of Discovery at Ex. 5, *A 10th Century Cambodian Sandstone Sculpture.*

NINETEEN

177 **No one working there:** Verified Compl. at 2–6, United States of America v. A 10th Century Cambodian Sandstone Sculpture, Currently Located at Sotheby's in New York, New York, No. 12 Civ. 2600 (GBD) (S.D.N.Y. April 4, 2012).

177 **drawn on work by:** Tess Davis, "Returning Duryodhana," *Bostonia*, Summer 2014, bu.edu/bostonia/summer14/cambodia/; Tom Mashberg and Ralph Blumenthal, "Mythic Warrior Is Captive in Global Art Conflict," *New York Times,* February 28, 2012, https://www.nytimes.com/2012/02/29/arts/design/sothebys-caught-in-dispute-over-prized-cambodian-statue.html.

178 **Malraux had been convicted:** Verified Am. Compl. at 27, April 9, 2013, *A 10th Century Cambodian Sandstone Sculpture*; and André Malraux, *The Way of the Kings*, trans. Howard Curtis, Modern Voices (Hesperus Press, 2005), xii.

178 **In their initial complaint:** Verified Compl. at 6–7, *A 10th Century Cambodian Sandstone.*

179 **The company said in a:** Ralph Blumenthal and Tom Mashberg, "Officials Are Set to Seize Antiquity," *New York Times*, April 4, 2012, nytimes.com/2012/04/05/arts/design/ancient-cambodian-statue-is-seized-from-sothebys.html.

179 **The first hearing in:** Transcript of hearing, April 11, 2012, *A 10th Century Cambodian Sandstone Sculpture.*

182 **Every part of this:** Isidor Kahane to Adrian Maynard, letter, 20 November 1974.

182 **Then, after it was sold:** Adrian Maynard to Douglas Latchford, letter, December 16, 1975.

182 **He stated explicitly that:** Douglas Latchford to Nathan Halpern, letter, 28 July 1986.

183 **At a hearing in September:** Transcript of hearing, September 27, 2012, *A 10th Century Cambodian Sandstone Sculpture.*

184 **Since identifying the statues:** Éric Bourdonneau with Phin Samnang, "The Duel Between Bhima and Duryodhana and the Sculpted Group of the Western Gopura I of Prasat Chen at Koh Ker" (École Française d'Extrême-Orient, July 2012), 5–25.

187 **After its initial reluctance:** Tom Mashberg and Ralph Blumenthal, "Cambodia Says It Seeks Return of Met Statues," *New York Times*, June 1, 2012, nytimes .com/2012/06/02/arts/design/cambodia-to-ask-met-to-return-10th-century -statues.html.

TWENTY

189 **"American and European galleries":** Mark V. Vlasic and Tess Davis, "Should Cambodian "Blood Antiquities" Be Returned?," CNN, June 7, 2012, edition .cnn.com/2012/06/07/opinion/vlasic-davis-cambodia-art/index.html.

191 **When a stock exchange:** Abheek Bhattacharya, "The Cambodian Wild West," *Wall Street Journal*, May 10, 2012, wsj.com/articles/SB10001424052702304203604577395600458028114.

192 **Many were former Khmer Rouge:** "Koh Ker Social Development and Tourism Project: Final Report," Heritage Watch, January 2009, 5.

194 **In November 2012:** Decl. of Alexander J. Wilson in Supp. of the Government's Mot. for Leave to File an Am. Compl. at 1–2, United States of America v. A 10th Century Cambodian Sandstone Sculpture, Currently Located at Sotheby's in New York, New York, No. 12 Civ. 2600 (GBD) (S.D.N.Y. November 9, 2012).

194 **But the draft complaint:** Decl. of Alexander J. Wilson in Supp. of the Government's Mot. for Leave to File an Am. Compl. at 13–28, *A 10th Century Cambodian Sandstone Sculpture.*

195 **In the same Sotheby's:** Statement of Special Agent Brenton Easter at 3, People of the State of New York v. Nancy Wiener, No. SCI 5191-2016 (N.Y. Crim. Ct. December 21, 2016); and Transcript of proceedings at 10, September 30, 2021, *Nancy Wiener.*

195 **Wiener had also provided:** Transcript of proceedings at 13–14, *Nancy Wiener.*

195 **paid him $500,000:** Transcript of proceedings at 11–12, *Nancy Wiener.*

195 **For the third:** Transcript of proceedings at 11, *Nancy Wiener.*

196 **In 2011, the National:** Anne Davies, "Returning the Gods," National Gallery of Australia, February 13, 2024, nga.gov.au/stories-ideas/returning-the-gods.

196 **After a launch party:** "Gold and Bodybuilders," *ThaiBody*, December 18, 2007, thaibody.com/photos/?sel=ab&sid=306&s=697f31b39c120bea0d95112b65 484d3f.

196 **There, in a ceremony:** Sarah Macklin, "Ancient Bronze Back in Kingdom," *Phnom Penh Post*, July 11, 2011, phnompenhpost.com/lifestyle/ancient-bronze -back-kingdom.

196 **He'd also assembled:** Christopher Shay, "Foreign Dealers, Collectors Return Angkorian Antiquities," *Phnom Penh Post*, June 15, 2009, phnompenhpost .com/national/foreign-dealers-collectors-return-angkorian-antiquities.

197 **Amid all these successes:** Tom Mashberg, "Claims of Looting Shadow Expert in Khmer Art," *New York Times*, December 12, 2012, nytimes.com/2012/12 /13/arts/design/us-links-collector-to-statue-in-khmer-looting-case.html.

198 **On one expedition:** Tess Davis and Simon Mackenzie, "Crime and Conflict: Temple Looting in Cambodia," in *Cultural Property Crime: An Overview and Analysis of the Contemporary Perspective and Trends*, ed. Joris D. Kila and Mark Balcells (Brill, 2015), 300–302.

TWENTY-ONE

204 **Paul then turned to:** Decl. of Peter G. Neiman in Supp. of Claimants' Mot. to Dismiss at 6, United States of America v. A 10th Century Cambodian Sand-stone Sculpture, Currently Located at Sotheby's in New York, New York, No. 12 Civ. 2600 (GBD) (S.D.N.Y. June 5, 2012).

205 **Two months earlier:** Verified Am. Compl. at 18, April 9, 2013, *A 10th Century Cambodian Sandstone Sculpture*.

205 **Over the previous year:** Éric Bourdonneau, "Statues et linteaux du style de Koh Ker au Metropolitan Museum of Art de New York" (École Française d'Extrême-Orient, March 2013), 1–6.

206 **The Met seemed to have:** See, for example, Michael Gross, *Rogues' Gallery: The Secret Story of the Lust, Lies, Greed, and Betrayals That Made the Metro-politan Museum of Art* (Broadway Books, 2009) , 443–45.

206 **In May 2013:** "Metropolitan Museum of Art to Return Two Khmer Sculptures to Cambodia," Metropolitan Museum of Art, archived March 18, 2025, at web .archive.org/web/20250318235005/https://www.metmuseum.org/press -releases/cambodian-returns-2013-news.

206 **"establishes no precedent":** Denise Hruby, "More Artifacts May Be Returned to Cambodia," *Cambodia Daily*, May 7, 2013, english.cambodiadaily.com/2013 /05/07/more-artifacts-may-be-returned-to-cambodia.

206 **In separate comments:** Tom Mashberg and Ralph Blumenthal, "The Met Will Return a Pair of Statues to Cambodia," *New York Times*, May 3, 2013, nytimes

.com/2013/05/04/arts/design/the-met-to-return-statues-to-cambodia
.html.

207 **On September 12:** Transcript of hearing, September 12, 2013, *A 10th Century Cambodian Sandstone Sculpture.*

207 **Lawyers for the auction house:** Mem. of Law in Supp. of Claimants' Mot. for Judgment on the Pleadings and for a Stay of Discovery at 3–8, September 9, 2013, *A 10th Century Cambodian Sandstone Sculpture.*

207 **The lawyers argued:** Mem. of Law in Supp. of Claimants' Mot. for Judgment on the Pleadings and for a Stay of Discovery at 25–28, September 9, 2013, *A 10th Century Cambodian Sandstone Sculpture.*

207 **In his response, Wilson:** Letter Response to Mot. Addressed to Judge George B. Daniels from Alexander Wilson at 4–5, September 11, 2013, *A 10th Century Cambodian Sandstone Sculpture.*

208 **The move was "just improper":** Transcript of hearing at 4–7, *A 10th Century Cambodian Sandstone Sculpture.*

208 **"The motion to stay":** Transcript of hearing at 33, *A 10th Century Cambodian Sandstone Sculpture.*

209 **After Wilson's earlier statements:** Stipulation and Order of Settlement at 2–4, December 13, 2013, *A 10th Century Cambodian Sandstone Sculpture.*

210 **In May 2014, Christie's said:** Tom Mashberg and Ralph Blumenthal, "Christie's to Return Cambodian Statue," *New York Times,* May 6, 2014, nytimes.com/2014/05/07/arts/design/christies-to-return-cambodian-statue.html.

210 **At almost the same:** Mike Boehm, "Norton Simon's 'Temple Wrestler' Statue Heading Home to Cambodia," *Los Angeles Times*, May 21, 2014, latimes.com/entertainment/arts/la-et-cm-norton-simon-statue-20140521-story.html.

213 **"Admittedly these things were moonlighted":** Tom Mashberg, "With a Gift of Art, a Daughter Honors, if Not Absolves, Her Father," *New York Times*, January 29, 2021, nytimes.com/2021/01/29/arts/design/cambodia-artifacts-douglas-latchford.html.

213 **For all their crimes:** Éric Bourdonneau, "En attendant Hiraṇyakaśipu, recoller les morceaux et s'interroger à nouveau: Qui tient le burin des pilleurs?," in *Liber Amicorum: Mélanges réunis en hommage à Ang Chouléan*, ed. Grégory Mikaélian et al. (Association Péninsule; Association des Amis de Yosothor, 2020), 180.

214 **"Hi Jim," he wrote:** Douglas Latchford to Jim Clark, email, 30 October 2014.

214 **Clark had since:** Tom Mashberg, "Netscape Founder Gives Up $35 Million in Art Said to Be Stolen," *The New York Times*, January 12, 2022, nytimes.com/2022/01/12/arts/design/james-clark-cambodian-antiquities.html.

214 **"possibly the most important":** Douglas Latchford to Jim Clark, email, 31 October 2014.

214 **In his reply, Clark expressed:** Jim Clark to Douglas Latchford, email, 31 October 2014.

215 **Latchford assured his client:** Latchford to Clark, 31 October 2014.

TWENTY-TWO

216 **Brenton Easter knew that:** Tom Mashberg, "Another Gallery Is Raided in Antiquities Case," *New York Times*, March 18, 2016, nytimes.com/2016/03/19/arts/design/another-gallery-is-raided-in-antiquities-case.html.

216 **Over the past several years:** "Ancient Antiquities and Saddam Hussein–Era Objects Returned to Iraq," US Immigration and Customs Enforcement, March 16, 2015, archived at ice.gov/news/releases/ancient-antiquities-and-saddam-hussein-era-objects-returned-iraq.

216 **finely painted sarcophagus:** "ICE Returns Ancient Artifacts to Egypt at National Geographic Society," US Immigration and Customs Enforcement, April 22, 2015, archived at ice.gov/news/releases/ice-returns-ancient-artifacts-egypt-national-geographic-society.

216 **pair of skeletons:** Ralph Blumenthal, "Dinosaur Skeleton to Be Returned to Mongolia," *New York Times*, May 5, 2013, nytimes.com/2013/05/06/arts/design/dinosaur-skeleton-to-be-returned-to-mongolians.html.

217 **Its eponymous owner:** "DORIS WIENER Obituary," Legacy, April 10, 2011, legacy.com/us/obituaries/nytimes/name/doris-wiener-obituary?id=26822785.

217 **With the Latchford file:** David Klein, "India Sentences Notorious Antiquities Trafficker from Manhattan," OCCRP, November 7, 2022, occrp.org/en/news/india-sentences-notorious-antiquities-trafficker-from-manhattan.

218 **In 2005, the piece:** Compl. for Forfeiture at 13–14, United States of America v. A Late 12th Century Bayon-Style Sandstone Sculpture Depicting Eight-Armed Avalokiteshvara, No. 22 Civ. 229 (S.D.N.Y. January 11, 2022).

218 **The following year, under:** Compl. for Forfeiture at 15–16, *A Late 12th Century Bayon-Style Sandstone Sculpture*; and Sealed Indictment at 19, United States of America v. Douglas Latchford, No. 19 Crim. 748 (S.D.N.Y. October 17, 2019).

218 **"recently found around the":** Sealed Indictment at 9, *Douglas Latchford*.

218 **"56 cm Angkor Borei":** Compl. for Forfeiture at 17, *A Late 12th Century Bayon-Style Sandstone Sculpture*.

219 **In 2007, she'd been:** Statement of Special Agent Brenton Easter at 5, People of the State of New York v. Nancy Wiener, No. SCI 5191-2016 (N.Y. Crim. Ct. December 21, 2016). See also Transcript of proceedings at 12–13, September 30, 2021, *Nancy Wiener*.

219 **"I herewith declare":** Certificate of Ownership from Ian Donaldson, 15 October 1985, as cited in Jason Felch, "The End of the Beginning: NGA Returns Kushan Buddha and Two Kapoor Objects," *Chasing Aphrodite*, September 18, 2016, chasingaphrodite.com/tag/kushan-buddha.

219 **Nonetheless, when it came:** Statement of Special Agent Brenton Easter at 5, *Nancy Wiener*; and Transcript of proceedings at 12, *Nancy Wiener*.

220 **The number of annual visitors:** Chea Vannak, "Angkor Tickets Valued at $60 Million in 2014," *Khmer Times*, January 20, 2015, khmertimeskh.com/53955/angkor-tickets-valued-at-60-million-in-2014.

220 **The most recent was:** Ray Mark Rinaldi, "Denver Art Museum Returns Looted Sculpture to Cambodia," *Denver Post*, June 8, 2016, denverpost.com /2016/02/29/denver-art-museum-returns-looted-sculpture-to-cambodia.

223 **the situation was worse:** Douglas Latchford to Harald Link, email, 24 December 2015.

223 **"I have this problem developing":** Latchford to Link, 24 December 2015.

223 **Not long after that correspondence:** Douglas Latchford to Harald Link, email, 15 February 2016.

224 **Of one stone statue:** Douglas Latchford to Harald Link, email, 2 May 2016.

224 **In May 2016, Link bought:** Douglas Latchford to Harald Link, email, 4 May 2016.

224 **Latchford would later:** Douglas Latchford to Harald Link, email, 26 November 2016; and Douglas Latchford to Harald Link, email, 7 December 2016.

224 **received an email:** Emma Bunker to Douglas Latchford, email, 17 January 2016.

225 **On the morning of:** Notice of Appearance at 4–5, April 3, 2018, *Nancy Wiener*; and Tom Mashberg, "Prominent Antiquities Dealer Accused of Selling Stolen Artifacts," *New York Times*, December 21, 2016, nytimes.com/2016/12 /21/arts/design/prominent-antiquities-dealer-accused-of-selling-stolen -artifacts.html.

TWENTY-THREE

229 **as "just excavated":** Compl. for Forfeiture at 17, United States of America v. A Late 12th Century Bayon-Style Sandstone Sculpture Depicting Eight-Armed Avalokiteshvara, No. 22 Civ. 229 (S.D.N.Y. January 11, 2022).

229 **"fresh out of the ground":** Compl. for Forfeiture at 15–16, *A Late 12th Century Bayon-Style Sandstone Sculpture*.

229 **and "recently found":** Sealed Indictment at 9, United States of America v. Douglas Latchford, No. 19 Crim. 748 (S.D.N.Y. October 17, 2019).

230 **he'd attached photographs:** Sealed Indictment at 9, *Douglas Latchford*; and Compl. for Forfeiture at 13–15, *A Late 12th Century Bayon-Style Sandstone Sculpture*.

235 **In May 2018:** Minister Phoeurng Sackona to Bradley Gordon and Steve Heimberg, "Re: Appointment by the Ministry of Culture and Fine Arts of the Kingdom of Cambodia with Respect to Khmer Antiquities," letter, May 2018.

TWENTY-FOUR

237 **"I have been giving it":** Douglas Latchford to Simon Copleston, email, 10 May 2018.

237 **Bunker, with whom Latchford:** Emma Bunker to Douglas Latchford, email, 29 June 2018.

237 **Latchford had various:** Bradley James Gordon et al. to U.S. Ambassador William A. Heidt, "Memorandum: Return of Khmer Cultural Properties," 15 May 2018.

238 **"A rare and perhaps":** Gordon et al. to Heidt, "Memorandum: Return of Khmer Cultural Properties."

239 **"I ran the name":** [Redacted] to [Redacted], "RE: Stolen Khmer Art in Bangkok," email, 10 May 2018.

239 **In the years since:** Charles Edel, "Cambodia's Troubling Tilt Toward China," *Foreign Affairs*, August 17, 2018, foreignaffairs.com/articles/china/2018-08-17/cambodias-troubling-tilt-toward-china.

239 **Chinese money had poured:** Anna Fifield, "This Cambodian City Is Turning into a Chinese Enclave, and Not Everyone Is Happy," *Washington Post*, March 29, 2018, washingtonpost.com/world/asia_pacific/this-cambodian-city-is-turning-into-a-chinese-enclave-and-not-everyone-is-happy/2018/03/28/6c8963b0-2d8e-11e8-911f-ca7f68bff0fc_story.html.

240 **Soon after receiving Gordon's:** US Ambassador William A. Heidt, "Cambodia Seeks Global Solution to Douglas Latchford Antiquities Smuggling Ring," cable, May 2018.

242 **But he did know that:** Compl. for Forfeiture at 6, United States of America v. A 10th Century Cambodian Sandstone Sculpture Depicting Skanda on a Peacock, No. 21 Civ. 6065 (S.D.N.Y. July 15, 2021).

243 **worked for a security firm:** Hanuman Partners, accessed October 26, 2025, hanuman-global.com; and Sanzaru Communications, accessed October 26, 2025, sanzaru-communications.com.

243 **A 2007 obituary in:** "George Webb Obituary," *Daily Telegraph*, December 15, 2007.

247 **With a collection spanning:** Alan Riding, "Price of a Good Name? For Louvre: $520 Million," *New York Times*, March 6, 2007, nytimes.com/2007/03/06/world/europe/06cnd-louvre.html.

TWENTY-FIVE

249 **Jessica Feinstein turned to:** Transcript of March 5, 2019, trial proceedings at 7–10, United States of America v. Johnson, No. 16 Cr. 281 (S.D.N.Y. April 4, 2019).

250 **Feinstein was partway through:** "Thirteen Members and Associates of the Blood Hound Brims Gang Charged in Federal Court with Racketeering, Narcotics and Firearms Offenses," US Department of Justice, January 4, 2017, justice.gov/usao-sdny/pr/thirteen-members-and-associates-blood-hound-brims-gang-charged-federal-court.

250 **At one point, Feinstein asked:** Transcript of trial proceedings at 13–14, *Johnson*.

250 **Starting out, Feinstein had:** "Two Bloods Gang Members Sentenced to 30 and 35 Years in Prison for 2010 Strangling Murder and Dismemberment in the

Bronx," US Department of Justice, July 8, 2022, justice.gov/usao-sdny/pr/two
-bloods-gang-members-sentenced-30-and-35-years-prison-2010-strangling
-murder-and.

251 **Her request was granted:** "Leaders of the 'Blood Hound Brims' Gang Convicted in Federal Court of Racketeering, Narcotics, and Firearms Offenses," US Department of Justice, March 28, 2019, justice.gov/usao-sdny/pr/leaders -blood-hound-brims-gang-convicted-federal-court-racketeering-narcotics -and.

255 **"It's still across the border":** Compl. for Forfeiture at 17, United States of America v. A Late 12th Century Bayon-Style Sandstone Sculpture Depicting Eight-Armed Avalokiteshvara, No. 22 Civ. 229 (S.D.N.Y. January 11, 2022).

255 **Later, he sent her:** Civil Compl. for Forfeiture at 8–10, United States of America v. Any and All Funds Up to and Including the Sum of $12 Million Contained in Rathbones Investment Management Portfolio 702461, Containing Accounts 5870246110, 5870246120, 5870246121, and 5870246180, No. 23 Civ. 5286 (S.D.N.Y. June 22, 2023).

255 **He wanted as much:** Douglas Latchford to Titus Kendall, email, 6 July 2011.

TWENTY-SIX

259 **In February 2019, he sent:** Douglas Latchford to Harald Link, email, 5 February 2019.

259 **Bunker had long been:** Emma Bunker to Douglas Latchford, email, 28 June 2009.

259 **She and Latchford both:** Statement of Special Agent Brenton Easter at 2–4, People of the State of New York v. Nancy Wiener, No. SCI 5191-2016 (N.Y. Crim. Ct. December 21, 2016).

259 **Yet Bunker tried to:** Emma Bunker to Douglas Latchford, email, 29 June 2018.

260 **In 2015, amid the pressure:** Douglas Latchford to Nancy Wiener, email, 5 October 2015.

260 **"Growing old is a real":** Emma Bunker to Douglas Latchford, email, 31 March 2019.

261 **It had featured:** Emma C. Bunker and Douglas Latchford, *Adoration and Glory: The Golden Age of Khmer Art* (Art Media Resources, 2004), 146–47.

264 **In the case of the:** Sealed Indictment at 12, United States of America v. Douglas Latchford, No. 19 Crim. 748 (S.D.N.Y. October 17, 2019).

264 **provided three separate provenance:** Transcript of proceedings at 11, September 30, 2021, *Nancy Wiener.*

265 **"From the mid-1960s":** Sealed Indictment at 2–5, *Douglas Latchford.*

265 **Then Feinstein came to Latchford:** Sealed Indictment at 5–6, *Douglas Latchford.*

266 **In sum, Feinstein wrote:** Sealed Indictment at 9, *Douglas Latchford.*

TWENTY-SEVEN

269 **The accompanying press release:** "Antiquities Dealer Charged with Trafficking in Looted Cambodian Artifacts," US Department of Justice, November 27, 2019, ustice.gov/usao-sdny/pr/antiquities-dealer-charged-trafficking-looted-cambodian-artifacts.

270 **"We feel that Latchford's attorney":** J. P. Labbat to [Redacted], "RE: New York Times," email, 10 January 2020.

TWENTY-EIGHT

276 **It had to do with:** Judith Thurman, "Striking a New Note in Palm Beach," *Architectural Digest*, January 2008.

276 **Then Gordon spotted:** Michael Boodro, "AD100 Architect Peter Marino Designs an Art-Filled Home for Contemporary Luxury in Miami's Biscayne Bay," *Architectural Digest*, January 19, 2019, architecturaldigest.com/story/ad100-architect-peter-marino-designs-an-art-filled-home-for-contemporary-luxury-in-miamis-biscayne-bay.

277 **While building a fortune:** "George Lindemann & Family," *Forbes*, accessed October 27, 2025, forbes.com/profile/george-lindemann.

277 **As federal prosecutors unraveled:** Carrie Teegardin and Martha Woodham, "Rider Facing Biggest Obstacle: Federal Charges in Horse's Death," *Atlanta Constitution*, September 6, 1995.

277 **George Jr. was convicted:** "3-Year Term in '90 Killing of Prize Horse," *New York Times*, January 19, 1996, nytimes.com/1996/01/19/us/3-year-term-in-90-killing-of-prize-horse.html.

278 **The Palm Beach *Daily News*:** Robert Janjigian, "Lindemanns Sell Blossom Way Home Sell Blossom Way Home," *Palm Beach Daily News*, April 8, 2008, corcoran.com/nyc/press-mention/display/6811.

278 **"If you have more":** J. P. Labbat to Jessica Feinstein, email, 9 July 2020.

279 **In Palm Beach, they had:** Thurman, "Striking a New Note in Palm Beach."

279 **The heads were from:** "U.S. Attorney Announces Return of Significant Collection of Antiquities to Cambodia," US Department of Justice, September 12, 2023, justice.gov/usao-sdny/pr/us-attorney-announces-return-significant-collection-antiquities-cambodia.

279 **It was located on Star:** Alexandre Tanzi et al., "America's Priciest Neighborhoods Are Changing as the Ultra-Rich Move to Florida," *Bloomberg*, February 14, 2023, bloomberg.com/news/articles/2023-02-14/the-most-expensive-neighborhoods-in-the-us-from-florida-to-new-york.

281 **In his early eighties:** David Conn and Malia Politzer, "Offshore Loot: How Notorious Dealer Used Trusts to Hoard Khmer Treasures," *Guardian*, October 5, 2021, eguardian.com/news/2021/oct/05/offshore-trusts-used-pass-on-looted-khmer-treasures-leak-shows-douglas-latchford.

281 **Through these vehicles:** *Civil* Compl. for Forfeiture at 2–7, United States of America v. Any and All Funds Up to and Including the Sum of $12 Million Contained in Rathbones Investment Management Portfolio 702461, Containing Accounts 5870246110, 5870246120, 5870246121, and 5870246180, No. 23 Civ. 5286 (S.D.N.Y. June 22, 2023).

282 **On August 2, 2020:** Tom Mashberg, "Douglas A. J. Latchford, Khmer Antiquities Expert, Dies at 88," *New York Times,* August 27, 2020, nytimes.com/2020/08/27/arts/douglas-aj-latchford-khmer-antiquities-expert-dies-at-88\.html.

283 **Julia resolved to settle:** Ministry of Culture and Fine Arts, Kingdom of Cambodia, "The Return of Khmer Cultural Objects to the Kingdom of Cambodia," press release, January 29, 2021; and Tom Mashberg, "With a Gift of Art, a Daughter Honors, if Not Absolves, Her Father," *New York Times,* January 29, 2021, nytimes.com/2021/01/29/arts/design/cambodia-artifacts-douglas-latchford.html.

TWENTY-NINE

285 **Lion had no formal:** Simon Mackenzie and Tess Davis, "Temple Looting in Cambodia: Anatomy of a Statue Trafficking Network," *British Journal of Criminology* 54, no. 5 (September 2014): 732, jstor.org/stable/43819219.

286 **In October 2020:** Compl. for Forfeiture at 6–7, United States of America v. A 10th Century Cambodian Sandstone Sculpture Depicting Skanda on a Peacock, No. 21 Civ. 6065 (S.D.N.Y. July 15, 2021).

287 **The archaeological team's first priority:** "Archaeological Excavation at Prasat Krachap," National Authority for Preah Vihear, October 26, 2023, napv.gov.kh/activities/significant_achievements/excavation-work/Archaeological-excavation-at-Prasat-Krachab.html?lang=kh.

287 **Elsewhere at Prasat Krachap:** Compl. for Forfeiture at 7, *A 10th Century Cambodian Sandstone Sculpture Depicting Skanda on a Peacock.*

289 **Mignucci had been a scholar:** Paolo Fait, "Mario Mignucci, *Ancient Logic, Language, and Metaphysics: Selected Essays,*" *Ancient Philosophy Today* 3, no. 1 (April 2021): 126–32, doi.org/10.3366/anph.2021.0046.

289 **And he'd evidently been interested:** Compl. for Forfeiture at 8–9, *A 10th Century Cambodian Sandstone Sculpture Depicting Skanda on a Peacock.*

289 **Mignucci had died:** "Our History: Ancient Philosophy in the University of London," L-CAP, accessed October 27, 20205, lcap.ics.sas.ac.uk/our-history.

289 **The document was a milestone:** Compl. for Forfeiture at 5–9, *A 10th Century Cambodian Sandstone Sculpture Depicting Skanda on a Peacock.*

290 **And if he'd approached:** Michael Lewis, *The New New Thing: A Silicon Valley Story* (W. W. Norton & Company, 2014), 30–31.

291 **Clark had bought:** Tom Mashberg, "Netscape Founder Gives up $35 Million in Art Said to Be Stolen," *New York Times,* January 12, 2022, nytimes.com/2022/01/12/arts/design/james-clark-cambodian-antiquities.html.

291 **There was a massive:** Compl. for Forfeiture at 4–9, United States of America v. A Late 12th Century Bayon-Style Sandstone Sculpture Depicting Eight-Armed Avalokiteshvara, No. 22 Civ. 229 (S.D.N.Y. January 11, 2022).

294 **"I'm going to transfer everything":** Anderson Cooper, "How Cambodian Artifacts Stolen from Temples Ended Up in American Museums, Private Collections," CBS News, December 17, 2023, cbsnews.com/news/stolen-cambodian-artifacts-american-museums-private-collections-60-minutes-transcript.

THIRTY

296 **"I want the gods":** Tom Mashberg, "Cambodia Says the Met Museum Has Dozens of Its Looted Antiquities," *New York Times*, October 24, 2021, nytimes.com/2021/10/24/arts/cambodia-met-museum-looted-antiquities.html.

300 **When he took Netscape:** Julie Pitta, "Investors Get Caught Up in the Netscape," *Los Angeles Times*, August 10, 1995.

300 **"A browser is software":** Bloomberg News, "Netscape to Sell Internet Browsers," *New York Times*, June 5, 1995, nytimes.com/1995/06/05/business/netscape-to-sell-internet-browsers.html.

300 **Later, when the iPhone:** Ryan Mac, "Jim Clark: The Comeback Billionaire Who Bet on Apple," *Forbes*, March 8, 2012, forbes.com/sites/ryanmac/2012/03/08/jim-clark-the-comeback-billionaire-who-bet-on-apple.

300 **In 2007, when Latchford:** Compl. for Forfeiture at 16, United States of America v. A Late 12th Century Bayon-Style Sandstone Sculpture Depicting Eight-Armed Avalokiteshvara, No. 22 Civ. 229 (S.D.N.Y. January 11, 2022).

301 **For another object:** Compl. for Forfeiture at 12–13, *A Late 12th Century Bayon-Style Sandstone Sculpture*.

302 **He'd sold his Miami apartment:** Laura Yarborough, "The World's Most Expensive Beach Apartment Sold for $21.5 Million Dollars," *Haute Living*, December 12, 2011, hauteliving.com/2011/12/the-world%E2%80%99s-most-expensive-beach-apartment-sold-for-21-5-million-dollars.

302 **There was evidently no place:** Jennifer Gould, "'Comeback Billionaire' Jim Clark Buys Bunny Mellon Mansion for $37M," *New York Post*, January 28, 2015, nypost.com/2015/01/28/comeback-billionaire-jim-clark-buys-bunny-mellon-mansion-for-37m.

302 **The middle figure:** Cambodian Department of Antiquities, *The Return of Our Ancestors' Souls* (Ministry of Culture and Fine Arts of Cambodia, 2024), 70–76.

303 **All he needed to do:** Standing Female Deity, 10th century, stone, 61 ½ × 10 ¼ × 20 ½ in. (156.2 × 26 × 52.1 cm), Metropolitan Museum of Art, New York, object no. 2003.605, archived January 14, 2022, at web.archive.org/web/20220114102412/https://www.metmuseum.org/art/collection/search/72387.

304 **The Khmer assets:** Neil Brodie and Jenny Doole, "The Asian Art Affair: US Art Museum Collections of Asian Art and Archaeology," in *Material Engagements:*

Studies in Honour of Colin Renfrew, ed. Neil Brodie and Catherine Hills (McDonald Institute for Architectural Research, 2004), 85.

304 **By early November 2021:** Tom Mashberg, "He Sold Away His People's Heritage. He's in the Jungle to Get It Back," *New York Times*, November 21, 2021, nytimes.com/2021/11/21/arts/design/toek-tik-cambodian-artifacts.html.

305 **The stone rectangle:** Cambodian Department of Antiquities, *Return of Our Ancestors' Souls*, 71–73.

306 **His cancer had weakened:** Tom Mashberg, "Cambodia Says Looter Helping It Reclaim Stolen Artifacts Has Died," *New York Times*, December 5, 2021, nytimes.com/2021/12/05/arts/design/cambodian-effort-to-find-artifacts -wont-end-with-informants-death.html.

THIRTY-ONE

307 **Instead of bringing:** Jennifer Gould, "'Comeback Billionaire' Jim Clark Buys Bunny Mellon Mansion for $37M," *New York Post*, January 28, 2015, nypost .com/2015/01/28/comeback-billionaire-jim-clark-buys-bunny-mellon -mansion-for-37m.

309 **Feinstein filed the papers:** Compl. for Forfeiture at 1–9, United States of America v. A Late 12th Century Bayon-Style Sandstone Sculpture Depicting Eight-Armed Avalokiteshvara, No. 22 Civ. 229 (S.D.N.Y. January 11, 2022).

309 **Clark was identified:** See, for example, Spencer Woodman and Peter Whoriskey, "Tech Billionaire Surrenders Cambodian Relics Sold by Indicted Art Dealer," *Washington Post*, January 13, 2022, washingtonpost.com/business /2022/01/13/james-clark-netscape-latchford-pandora-papers.

309 **The filing explained how:** Compl. for Forfeiture at 11–12, *A Late 12th Century Bayon-Style Sandstone Sculpture*.

310 **A few months earlier, Nancy:** Transcript of proceedings at 16–20, People of the State of New York v. Nancy Wiener, No. SCI 5191-2016 (N.Y. Crim. Ct. September 30, 2021).

310 **Shortly after she appeared:** Compl. for Forfeiture at 1–6, United States of America v. A Late 12th Century Khmer Sandstone Sculpture Depicting Standing Prajnaparamita, No. 21 Civ. 9217 (S.D.N.Y. November 8, 2021).

311 **Then, in August 2022:** Peter Whoriskey et al., "A Luxury Magazine Photo Hid Relics Cambodia Says Could Be Stolen," *Washington Post*, August 15, 2022, washingtonpost.com/business/2022/08/15/lindemann-cambodian-investigation -architectural-digest.

311 **by yet another spread:** Mitchell Owens, "Bay Watch," *Architectural Digest*, January 2021.

311 **The year before, *AD* had:** Aidin Vaziri, "Laurene Powell Jobs Sets San Francisco Real Estate Record with $70 Million Home," *San Francisco Chronicle*, July 12, 2024, sfchronicle.com/realestate/article/laurene-powell-jobs-home-1957 0275.php.

311 **Marino's online portfolio:** "San Francisco Residence," Peter Marino Architect, archived January 24, 2022, at web.archive.org/web/20220124180112/https://www.petermarinoarchitect.com/interior-design/work/san-francisco-residence.

313 **"These statues and artifacts":** "U.S. Attorney Announces Return of 30 Looted Antiquities to Kingdom of Cambodia," posted August 9, 2022, by USAO Southern District of New York, YouTube, 29 min., 40 sec., youtu.be/yRcsR6-cEHQ?si=v5Gd4QT8z3OAf7eW.

314 **"the souls of Cambodia's ancestors":** "U.S. Attorney Announces Return of 30 Looted Antiquities to Kingdom of Cambodia."

THIRTY-TWO

315 **Given the institution's huge:** Sealed Indictment at 7, *United States of America v. Douglas Latchford*, No. 19 Crim. 748 (S.D.N.Y. October 17, 2019).

316 **It had forty-five priority:** Tom Mashberg, "Cambodia Says the Met Museum Has Dozens of Its Looted Antiquities," *New York Times*, October 24, 2021, nytimes.com/2021/10/24/arts/cambodia-met-museum-looted-antiquities.html.

317 **In 2005, when one journalist:** Michael Gross, *Rogues' Gallery: The Secret Story of the Lust, Lies, Greed, and Betrayals That Made the Metropolitan Museum of Art* (Broadway Books, 2009), 1–3, 490–91.

318 **In its 2019 fiscal:** Metropolitan Museum of Art, *Annual Report for the Year 2018–2019* (Metropolitan Museum of Art, 2019), 6, 45.

318 **The Met's board of trustees:** Metropolitan Museum of Art, "The Metropolitan Museum of Art Announces Landmark Gift of $125 Million from Oscar Tang and Agnes Hsu-Tang," press release, January 1, 2021, metmuseum.org/press-releases/the-met-announces-landmark-gift-2021-news.

318 **At that year's Met Gala:** Stephen J. Dubner, host, *Freakonomics Radio*, podcast, episode 541, "The Case of the $4 Million Gold Coffin," produced by Morgan Levey, May 3, 2023, freakonomics.com/podcast/the-case-of-the-4-million-gold-coffin.

319 **It claimed to have been:** Metropolitan Museum of Art, "The Metropolitan Museum of Art Returns Coffin to Egypt," press release, February 15, 2019, metmuseum.org/press/news/2019/metropolitan-museum-of-art-returns-coffin-to-egypt.

320 **He and Latchford were close:** Two Kneeling Attendants, 10th century, stone, head (1987.410) attached to body (1992.390.1): 46 ¼ × 26 × 27 ½ in. (117.5 × 66 × 69.9 cm), head (1989.100) attached to body (1992.390.2): 48 ¼ × 23 ½ × 31 in. (122.6 × 59.7 × 78.7 cm), Metropolitan Museum of Art, New York, archived May 13, 2025, web.archive.org/web/20250513045238/https://www.metmuseum.org/art/collection/search/904942.

320 **Earlier in the 1980s:** Martin Lerner, "Unesco Pact Doesn't Concern 'Stolen Art,'" letter to the editor, *New York Times*, January 10, 1982.

320 **In 1998, another Latchford:** Face from a Male Deity, Probably Shiva, ca. 930–60, bronze with silver inlay, 8 × 3 ½ × 3 ⅜ × 4 ⅜ in. (20.3 × 8.9 × 8.6 × 11.1 cm), Metropolitan Museum of Art, New York, metmuseum.org/art/collection/search/39996.

320 **Then, after retiring from:** Tom Mashberg and Graham Bowley, "Cambodia Says It's Found Its Lost Artifacts: in Gallery 249 at the Met," *New York Times*, August 18, 2022, nytimes.com/2022/08/18/arts/design/met-artifacts-cambodia.html.

320 **A twelfth-century bronze Buddha:** Martin Lerner to Douglas Latchford, email, 27 February 2016.

320 **clearly the product of:** Douglas Latchford to Harald Link, email, 29 June 2019.

320 **In at least one case:** Mashberg and Bowley, "Cambodia Says It's Found Its Lost Artifacts."

321 **The resulting story read:** Mashberg, "Cambodia Says the Met Museum Has Dozens of Its Looted Antiquities."

322 **Another work on display:** The Bodhisattva Avalokiteshvara Seated in Royal Ease, late 10th–early 11th century, copper alloy and silver inlay, 22 ¾ × 18 × 12 in. (57.8 × 45.7 × 30.5 cm), Metropolitan Museum of Art, New York, metmuseum.org/art/collection/search/39184.

322 **its theft so recent:** Anderson Cooper, "How Cambodian Artifacts Stolen from Temples Ended Up in American Museums, Private Collections," *CBS News*, December 17, 2023, cbsnews.com/news/stolen-cambodian-artifacts-american-museums-private-collections-60-minutes-transcript.

THIRTY-THREE

328 **When it came to applying:** Stephen K. Urice, "Between Rocks and Hard Places: Unprovenanced Antiquities and the National Stolen Property Act," *New Mexico Law Review* 40, no. 1 (2010): 123–61.

329 **The Met told Feinstein:** Decl. of Brian Doctor QC at 25, United States of America v. A 10th Century Cambodian Sandstone Sculpture, Currently Located at Sotheby's in New York, New York, No. 12 Civ. 2600 (GBD) (S.D.N.Y. June 5, 2012).

329 **One critical date that:** Verified Am. Compl. at 24–27, April 9, 2013, *A 10th Century Cambodian Sandstone Sculpture*.

329 **But they argued that:** André Malraux, *The Way of the Kings* (Modern Voices, 2005), xii.

331 **They'd eventually agreed on:** Stipulation and Order of Settlement at 1–3, United States of America v. Any and All Funds Up to and Including the Sum of $12 Million Contained in Rathbones Investment Management Portfolio 702461, Containing Accounts 5870246110, 5870246120, 5870246121, and 5870246180, No. 23 Civ. 5286 (S.D.N.Y. June 28, 2023).

331 **Julia would also be:** Civil Compl. for Forfeiture at 8, June 22, 2023, *Any and All Funds.*

332 **"We are the victim":** Bradley Gordon to Jessica Feinstein, letter, 23 June 2023.

332 **But in early September:** United States Attorney Damian Williams to Mark P. Ressler and Joshua E. Hollander, letter, 7 September 2023, US Department of Justice, Southern District of New York; and "U.S. Attorney Announces Return of Significant Collection of Antiquities to Cambodia," US Department of Justice, September 12, 2023, justice.gov/usao-sdny/pr/us-attorney-announces-return-significant-collection-antiquities-cambodia.

333 **Another of the pieces:** Cambodian Department of Antiquities, *The Return of Our Ancestors' Souls* (Ministry of Culture and Fine Arts of Cambodia, 2024), 54–57.

335 **The Met had acquired:** Tanongsak Hanwong et al., "The Prakhon Chai Hoard Debunked: Unravelling Six Decades of Myth, Misdirection, and Misidentification," *International Journal of Cultural Property* 31, no. 2 (May 2024): 177–201.

337 **"all provenance documents":** Bradley Gordon to Sharon Cott, letter, 10 November 2023.

337 **The Met said that:** Letter to Anjan Sahni and Claire Guehenno, 15 December 2023, US Department of Justice, Southern District of New York; and "U.S. Attorney Announces Return of Collection of Antiquities from the Metropolitan Museum of Art to Cambodia," US Department of Justice, December 15, 2023, justice.gov/usao-sdny/pr/us-attorney-announces-return-collection-antiquities-metropolitan-museum-art-cambodia.

337 **With three exceptions:** Standing Female Deity, Probably Uma, ca. mid-11th century, stone, 29 ¾ × 9 × 4 ¼ in. (75.6 × 22.9 × 10.8 cm), Metropolitan Museum of Art, New York, object no. 1983.14, archived March 8, 2024, web.archive.org/web/20240308024636/https://www.metmuseum.org/art/collection/search/38300.

337 **a Buddha head that he:** Head of a Buddha, ca. 920–50, stone, 7 ¼ × 4 ⅝ × 4 ⅜ in. (18.3 × 11.7 × 11.1 cm), Metropolitan Museum of Art, New York, object no. 1983.551, archived March 8, 2024, at web.archive.org/web/20240308024546/https://www.metmuseum.org/art/collection/search/38447.

337 **and a large statue of:** Male Deity, Probably Shiva, mid-11th century, sandstone, 46 ¾ × 17 ¾ × 6 ¾ in. (118.7 × 45.1 × 17.1 cm), Metropolitan Museum of Art, New York, metmuseum.org/art/collection/search/38301.

338 **The museum had purchased that:** Harihara, late 7th–early 8th century, sandstone, 35 ½ × 13 ⅜ × 6 in. (90.2 × 34 × 15.2 cm), Metropolitan Museum of Art, New York, object no. 1977.241, metmuseum.org/art/collection/search/38162.

338 **She was nonetheless happy:** Letter to Anjan Sahni and Claire Guehenno, 15 December 2023.

338 **The museum offered a public:** Metropolitan Museum of Art, "The Metropolitan Museum of Art Announces the Return of 16 Khmer Sculptures to Cambodia and

Thailand," press release, December 15, 2023, metmuseum.org/press-releases
/return-of-khmer-works-2023-news.

AFTERWORD

340 **Opened by the French:** Christophe Pottier, "Présentation: À propos du temple de Banteay Chmar," *Aséanie* 13 (2004): 133, persee.fr/doc/asean_0859-9009 _2004_num_13_1_1815.

340 **Abandoned during Pol Pot's:** Helen Ibbitson Jessup and Thierry Zéphir, eds., *Sculpture of Angkor and Ancient Cambodia: Millennium of Glory* (Thames & Hudson, 1997), xxvi.

342 **At the time of this:** Niem Chheng, "Over 1,000 Precious Cultural Treasures Returned to Cambodia Since 1996," *Phnom Penh Post*, August 22, 2024, phnom penhpost.com/national/over-1-000-precious-cultural-treasures-returned -to-cambodia-since-1996.

344 **I knew that the Ganesha:** Compl. for Forfeiture at 13–14, United States of America v. A Late 12th Century Bayon-Style Sandstone Sculpture Depicting Eight-Armed Avalokiteshvara, No. 22 Civ. 229 (S.D.N.Y. January 11, 2022).

344 **part of about $11 million:** Civil Compl. for Forfeiture at 6, United States of America v. Any and All Funds Up to and Including the Sum of $12 Million Contained in Rathbones Investment Management Portfolio 702461, Containing Accounts 5870246110, 5870246120, 5870246121, and 5870246180, No. 23 Civ. 5286 (S.D.N.Y. June 22, 2023).

344 **And I was aware:** Chea Socheat, "Enquête de terrain sur la disparition de sculptures dans les temples de Koh Ker" (Musée National du Cambodge; École Française d'Extrême-Orient, April 2012), 2.

Index

INDEX